MOHAMMED

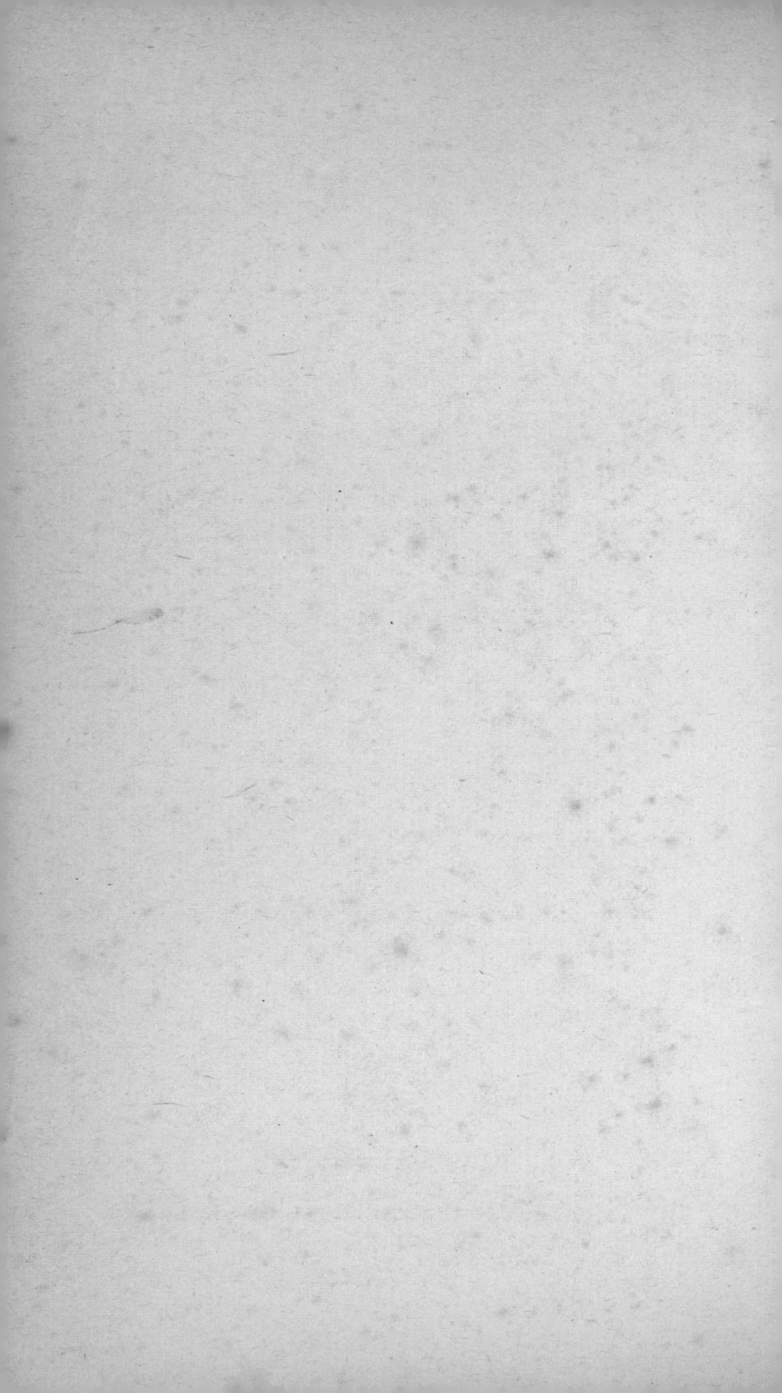

MAXIME RODINSON

MOHAMMED

Translated by Anne Carter

VINTAGE BOOKS

A DIVISION OF RANDOM HOUSE, NEW YORK

VINTAGE BOOKS EDITION,
August 1974

 Published in the United States by Random House, Inc., New York. Originally published in the United States by Pantheon Books, a division of Random House, Inc., in 1971; and in France as *Mahomet* by Club français du livre second edition (revised) published by Éditions du Seuil, 1968. This translation first published in Great Britain by Allen Lane The Penguin Press, London.

Acknowledgement is gratefully extended to Harcourt Brace Jovanovich, Inc., for permission to quote from *Anabasis* by St. John Perse, translated by T. S. Eliot, 1970.

Library of Congress Cataloging in Publication Data

Rodinson, Maxime.
Mohammed.
Bibliography: p.
1. Muhammad, The prophet.
[BP75.13.R613 1974] 297'.63 [B] 73–14953
ISBN 0–394–71677–9

Manufactured in the United States of America

Contents

And not that a man be not sad, but arising before day and biding circumspectly in the communion of an old tree, leaning his chin on the last fading star, he beholds at the end of the fasting sky great things and pure that unfold to delight.

St-John Perse, *Anabasis*,
translated by T. S. Eliot

Foreword

A BOOK such as this demands some justification. A great many lives of Islam's Prophet have been written, a number of them quite recently. Many of them are competent, some absolutely excellent. Why, then, should I tell the story over again?

Certainly I have no new facts to relate; it would be hard indeed to find any, since no new source has been discovered, nor is likely to be. The major sources have long been done very well, and one can, at best, only improve on a few details.

Yet, on the basis of the same facts, every generation writes history afresh; its own dominant concerns give it its own kind of understanding of past events, and of the human encounters and interplays of power that they represent. The beginnings of Islam have been seen in a new light since the work of Caetani, Becker and Lammens. Nowadays we have begun to consider the social evolution of Arabia at the period, a point of view which earlier generations did not really take into account. In this perspective W. Montgomery Watt has produced a remarkable work for which I have made clear my admiration. Though my biography is conceived in a similar way, there is however a slight change: events of recent years, and certain circumstances in my own life, have combined to lead me to reflect on the invariables of ideologies, and of movements based on ideologies. My attention was quite naturally drawn to those invariables as they were manifested in the events I relate. Then, too, I have followed with close attention the controversies now taking place about the interpretation of a man's life through the experiences of his youth and his personal circumstances among his relatives and early acquaintances, an interpretation which some people try to reconcile with the Marxist theory of the social causality of the lives of individuals. I have tried to show how, in the case of the Prophet, these two series of causes – those related to the person, the family and the early milieu, as well as those issuing from the society at large – converged, thus making it possible for us to understand his story. I hope that this attempt has a certain methodological value.

In brief, I have tried both to narrate and to interpret. From the latter point of view, I have tried not so much to suggest any new explanations as to try to make the partial explanations suggested in the past tally with one another, seeing the place to be accorded to each, determining the area in which each may be considered valid and the amount of truth in each; and thus discovering how they fit together and produce a coherent total picture. What this really involves is starting with a concrete example and going on from that to reflect on problems which people often try to resolve in the over-rarefied air of pure concepts. This approach, it seems to me, can be nothing but helpful.

But I have also aimed to produce a book that is readable; mainly narrative, that is to say. It is a risky proceeding; a biography of Mohammed limited only to absolutely unquestioned facts could amount to no more than a few dry pages. Yet it is possible to present a probable, and now and then a highly probable, picture of what that life must have been like; to do so, one must use some information from sources of whose veracity we have little proof.

I refer constantly to such sources. Though I believe I have kept fully up to date on the work of all my predecessors in this field, I have not merely made my own compilation of the information to be found in their books. I have constantly referred to all the major sources. I have always had on my desk Ibn Is'ḥāq, Ṭabarī, Wāqidī and Ibn Sa'd, and have often immersed myself in the ocean of 'tradition'. Any specialist who reads this book will recognize the fact.

But though these are the sources, it must be admitted that

they are far from being certain historical fact. The oldest texts we have concerning the life of the Prophet go back to about 125 years after his death, slightly less than the time that has now elapsed since the death of Napoleon. They of course quote older sources (mostly oral ones), and claim that these go back to actual eye-witnesses of the events they recount. But it has been shown (especially by Golziher and Schacht) that one can in fact have little confidence in such 'traditions'. As the Muslim authors themselves realized, a great deal was forged, or at least re-written to suit the interests of a particular party, cause, family, or theory. How can one distinguish what is basically authentic from what is not, the true from the false? There is no absolutely sure criterion. Those who forged the traditions certainly had a true literary gift; they gave their fictions that vivid, easy, familiar quality that makes them so delightful to read – those animated dialogues, those details that seem as though they must have been experienced, those turns of phrase in reported speech, those moments of humour, all seem more redolent of literary talent than of historical authenticity. All these writings are liberally sprinkled with archaic words, either taken from dictionaries, or discovered in the course of real anthropological fieldwork in the desert during the eighth and ninth centuries. There is nothing of which we can say for certain that it incontestably dates back to the time of the Prophet.

Must one then give up in despair? Must one abandon all thought of a biography, and even, as one Soviet author has done, speak of a 'myth' of Mohammed? I do not think so. We still have the text of the Koran. It is very hard to use, being generally extremely enigmatic, and requiring lengthy labours to get it into chronological order (which remains uncertain); but it does provide a firm basis of undoubted authenticity. We also have certain facts upon which all the traditions are agreed. The first Arab compilers differ (slightly) as to the names of those who took part in the battle of Badr, as well as the circumstances, the preparations and the consequences of the fighting. They conflict with one another on all these points, each reflecting the party-struggles of his own day. But such disputes can only take place because everyone agrees that the battle *did* in fact take place, on its date (at least approximately) and with its result. We must therefore consider it as a proven fact, and endeavour to see how to place it in the total chain of cause and effect. As we try to do so, we may be led to refer to this or that piece of tradition which seems to fit in with the picture of events as we see it. It must be clearly said that when such 'evidence' is used to illustrate our account it remains subject to doubt. I have often used phrases like 'seemingly', 'it was said', 'as was recounted later', and the like. I should perhaps have used them even more often; yet what I have in fact done is to follow the example of the Arab chroniclers, who would quote a long list of contradictory traditions, concluding prudently: 'But God knows more than we do.'

I would ask readers whose background is Muslim not to rush to condemn my ignorance or ill-will if they find that I contest or ignore data which they consider well attested and historically acceptable. Just as with Roman history or biblical history, the scientific attitude begins with the decision to accept as fact only something declared as such by a source that has been proved reliable, and to treat everything else with the appropriate caution. This has led us to take as legendary, embroidered, or at best doubtful a number of the events which historians of the pre-critical era believed to be firmly established. To do so is not a by-product of our colonialism or Europe-centredness. European scholars began by approaching their own history in this way; and the need for such a critical attitude has long been recognized by historians of other civilizations (the Muslim above all), even though they may not always yet have worked out an absolutely reliable method of applying it. There may be people who have felt a certain malign satisfaction in thus destroying some of the vainglorious legends of non-European peoples; but such a deplorable psychological approach cannot destroy the principle that a scientific study demands a critical attitude towards source material. I have never rejected – explicitly or implicitly – any accepted version of the facts without compelling reasons. European critics may have been wrong on some points; but their Oriental contradictors have to criticize them in the same way, first studying them closely, and only rejecting their theories after careful analysis.

One last warning – and one last vindication. I am concerned with a religious founder, a man who, during most of his life at least, was profoundly and sincerely religious, with a keen sense of the direct presence of the divine. It may be objected that I, as an atheist, cannot possibly understand such a man. That may be so; after all, what actually constitutes understanding? However, I am convinced that, provided he takes enough trouble, and totally excludes any contempt, pharisaism or sense of superiority, an atheist can in fact understand a religious outlook – certainly as well as an art critic can understand a painter, an adult a child, a man of robust health an invalid (and vice versa) or a scholarly recluse a businessman. Certainly a religious man would understand my subject differently, but better? I am not so sure.

Founders of ideologies have given men reasons for living, and personal or social tasks to fulfil. When the ideologies are religious they have declared (and generally believed) that their message came from beyond our world, and that what they themselves represented was something more than merely human. The atheist can only say that this extra-human origin remains unproved. But that gives him no reason for denigrating the message itself; indeed he may even place a higher value on it, as being an admirable effort to surpass the human condition. Ultimately he may even be forced to admit that it may be rooted in functions of the human mind that we do not yet understand. I believe that he can sometimes capture the original excitement of it, and feel more at one with it than many of its conformist believers for whom that message has developed into something taken for granted; consoling, perhaps, or justificatory, but doing no more than cheaply enabling them to lead an unadventurous life with a clear conscience. To repeat the admirable words of Epicurus to Menoeceus: The impious man is not the man who rejects the gods of the multitude, but the man who adheres to the conception that the multitude has of the gods.*

One critic, who has had a certain influence on the fate of this book, objects that I display here too calm an attitude towards mystery. I remain calm, though I do not reject mystery. What we know is quite disturbing enough to make us require more proof than we yet have, before we declare that what we do *not* know is any more so.

A few more practical comments now. One problem when it comes to books and things Arabic, is the question of Arabic words and names. It is a problem that I cannot wholly solve. At the end of the book (p. 329) readers will find an explanatory table (besides an index, p. 347) giving information about words and names that occur frequently, with references to the pages where they are explicitly dealt with. As for the pronunciation, the attentive reader may find the following suggestions at least of some help.

There can be no real hope of achieving correct Arab pronunciation of the words, but I have tried to give as close as possible a guide to it. Long vowels are shown thus: ā, ī, ū. They are pronounced as in, respectively, 'can't', 'meet', and 'soon'. Of the short vowels, a is pronounced as in 'must', i as in 'fin', u as in 'took'; however they frequently vary. The diphthong ay is pronounced approximately as in 'time'; the diphthong aw approximately as in 'town'. Of the consonants for which we do not have a simple English equivalent, dh is pronounced as in 'the' (as contrasted with th, as in 'thin'); kh as in Scottish 'loch'; gh as the northern French r – rough and guttural. Q is like k, only pronounced further back in the throat. R is rolled. Semitic languages are distinguished from European in having emphatic consonants: in Arabic there is an emphatic d, s, t and (approximately) z. (These are represented by having a dot beneath them, thus: ḍ, ṣ, ṭ, ẓ.) In each case the consonant is pronounced, quite strongly, in the front of the mouth. Ḥ,

* Epicurus, *Ethica*, ed. C. Diano, Florence, Sansoni, 1946, p. 7. Karl Marx was particularly fond of this sentence; see the preface to his doctorate thesis (*Differenz der demokritischen und epikureischen Naturphilosophie*, 1841).

although signified in the same way, is not strictly an emphatic letter; it is a slightly aspirated h, midway between h and kh. Two consonants can only be represented by symbols, not by roman letters: a symbol facing to the left, ʾ, represents a glottal stop, such as one hears before each word in the emphatic phrase 'utterly original'; one facing to the right, ʿ, represents a sound 'rather like the noise you make at the beginning of saying "Aaah" when told to do so by the doctor' (Marcel Cohen). An apostrophe, ', between consonants indicates that they are pronounced separately.

The reader, however, should not be surprised to find the names I refer to here written differently – but equally correctly – in other books.

Proper names pose further problems. Arabs used to have various kinds of names, and might at one time use one, at another time, another. Every person had his proper name (Muḥammad, ʿAbdallāh, ʿAlī), and to identify him one would add his father's name preceded by '*ibn*' – son of – for a man, or '*bint*' – daughter of – for a woman. Thus Muḥammad ibn ʿAbdallāh, ʿUmar ibn al-Khaṭṭāb; Muḥammad's daughter would be Fāṭima bint Muḥammad. Then there might be added the tribal name or more generally the name of origin (at-Tamīmi, a man of the tribe of Tamīm), or a nickname, or the *kunya* – the name of the (generally eldest) son preceded by *Abū* (father of) or *Umm* (mother of): Umm Misṭaḥ is the mother of Misṭaḥ. As I have said, any one of these names can be used from time to time, and I have tried to vary them only in a reasonable way.

Tribal names in the plural are preceded by *Banū*, 'sons of'. Thus the tribe that dominates Mecca are the Banū Quraysh, or simply the Quraysh, or, with a Latin suffix, the Qurayshites.

Amid all these variations one may or may not find the article *al-* (which can also take the forms *ar-*, *az-*, etc.): thus *Ḥārith* or *al-Ḥārith*, or even at times the *a* is omitted, leaving us with *Banū l-Ḥārith*.

I have tried – without great conviction – to correct some of the false usages we have fallen into: thus I say 'Muḥammad' and not Mahomet, or Mohammed – the form of his name with which English-speaking people are most familiar.

All texts have been freshly translated but not without reference to existing translations. Thus, with the Koran, I have always studied the original, but have often used the fine translation into French by R. Blachère (in English the reliable translation by Richard Bell), though at times changing details to suit my own stylistic tendencies.

Foreword to the Second French Edition

I HAVE thoroughly revised the text of the first edition, though by no means re-written it. I have been influenced by a number of thoughtful observations made to me (especially by my mentors and friends Marcel Cohen, Gustav von Grunebaum, G. Levi della Vida and Louis Massignon), by the new works that have come to my attention, and by my own reading and thinking during the past six years. I have made a great many minor additions and corrections. I have, more importantly, added several pages on the literary character of the Muhammadan message, and have tried to define more clearly the central intuition which moulds the whole of the message. Though my book has, in the second French edition, been put into a series entitled 'Politics', paradoxically this edition lays more stress on aspects outside the strictly political–social framework. And rightly so. For though no human phenomenon can be understood without reference to that framework, neither can any such phenomenon be said to belong totally within it. Muḥammad was a religious genius, a great political thinker – and a man like you or me. He was not these things on three separate levels; they are three aspects of a total personality, and can only be seen in distinction by a careful analysis. Everything he did or said involved something of all these aspects of the man. Those whose main interest is in the religious man and his message have a lot to gain from understanding the non-religious motivations and repercussions of his actions. Those who see him primarily as a historical force should think carefully about the importance of the ideology which made him that kind of force; and indeed of that ideology itself. This does not mean to say that the political dynamism should be submerged in a hundred and one anthropological factors of every conceivable kind, as some have maintained. What is central to that dynamism is based on a definite series of specific factors, and these must not be overlooked. It is only by being inserted into the context of those factors that all the other phenomena can secure a strictly historical importance. Under certain conditions at least, this can be achieved, and it is vital that it should be. It is not belittling Muḥammad to see him as a political figure – but to see him as no more than that would be a mutilation. And anyone who thus mutilates Muḥammad is in fact mutilating himself in the domain of understanding. It would be he who was the *abtar* (Koran cviii; see below, p. 54).

Foreword to the English Edition

I HAVE seized the opportunity of the preparation of the English edition of this book to revise it a little. In a very few places I have inserted a phrase or two: for example on page 34, where, to a reference to events current in France in the sixth century, I have added a sentence on what was happening concurrently in Britain. I have modified a few passages, and made small additions where new research has made it desirable, or where my own reflections have led me to do so. I have corrected certain errors of detail that I have discovered or that have been pointed out to me; for example the reference, on page 13, to the camel's hardiness; for that I have to thank my friend Colonel Bernard Vernier, a man with a wide knowledge of that animal. I have checked again the translations from Arabic, Greek, Latin and so forth with their originals, and in doing so have discovered some minor inaccuracies that have now been put right. Above all I have profited greatly from the recent edition of the Arabic text of Wāqidī by Marsden Jones; when I was preparing the French editions I was only able to use the very unsatisfactory, antiquated text edited by Kremer, and the partial German translation of Wellhausen. I have now and then drawn the attention of Mr Christopher Walker, who has been in charge of the preparation of the English edition, to alternative translations of certain passages, and asked him to choose the one closest to the idea that I wished to express. My thanks to him, as well as to Miss Anne Carter, for the trouble they have taken in this task.

The British editor was keen to have references added to the text, which the French editions lacked. These have now been added, but have all – except for two or three essential ones – been banished to the back of the book, so as not to crowd the page with specialist notes and so put off the general reader. On the majority of points the curious reader will, without difficulty, find additional material in the works cited in the bibliography, notably in the excellent books of W. Montgomery Watt. It has consequently been enough for me to give references to the passages by other authors that I have quoted in my text, and to several assertions that might appear strange to some readers. As regards the passages from Ibn Hishām's biography of the Prophet, I have simply given the page-reference of Wüstenfeld's edition of the Arabic text. This reference appears in the margin of Guillaume's English translation.

The editor has also asked for a precise transcription of Arabic names – a procedure which was considered unnecessary for the French edition. This has the advantage of enabling the Arabic-speaker or arabist to grasp at once the exact original form of the name. It has the disadvantage of slightly puzzling the European reader. I hope that none will see in it any trace of tiresome pedantry. If Arabic names are of no interest to him, I hope that he will find in my book enough historical and sociological information – and even, perhaps, some pleasant reading – to interest him sufficiently to surmount a possible slight irritation.

One point of detail: the country which we now call Ethiopia I have sometimes called by this name and sometimes Abyssinia; the same applies to its inhabitants. The word 'Abyssinia' corresponds better to one of the terms used during this epoch, especially by foreigners; but it was not the official name, and 'Ethiopia', one of the names by which it was known in Greek, was definitely beginning to be used more widely by the indigenous people of the country themselves, whereas the term corresponding to 'Abyssinia', which was used especially by the Arabs, was loaded with certain pejorative overtones, which it has kept in the eyes of the modern Ethiopians. It seemed best to me to use the two terms concurrently.

I have added some English items to my final bibliography and brought it somewhat up to date.

I

Introducing a World

THIRTEEN hundred years had elapsed since the supposed year of Rome's foundation; rather more than five hundred since the birth of Christ; and something over two hundred since Constantine's transformation of Byzantium into Constantinople.

Christianity was triumphant. The Emperor of the Second Rome ruled on the shores of the Bosphorus and the Golden Horn as the first servant of Christ the King, the rightful master of the universe. Everywhere, churches were being raised to sing the praises of the God in Three Persons and celebrate the sacrament of the Eucharist. Missionaries carried the Gospel into ever more distant lands, from the misty northern forests and plains to the shores of the warm seas, the lands of fabulous wealth from which the way led on to India and China. True, there were some rebellious barbarians in the west; but these – Franks, Burgundians and Goths, divided and squabbling amongst themselves – were savages, admiring Roman greatness but incapable of creating a stable state of their own, and were being brought back, little by little, into the fold of the empire. Rome had certainly suffered at the hands of the barbarians and lost much of her ancient splendour; but Byzantium stood firm, dazzling in her magnificence, the centre of the world, unvanquished and, it seemed, invincible.

During this period an Egyptian merchant by the name of Cosmas, who travelled widely and who became a monk in his old age, wrote these stirring lines:

The Empire of the Romans thus participates in the dignity of the Kingdom of the Lord Christ, seeing that it transcends, as far as can be in this state of existence, every other power, and will remain unconquered until the final consummation; for he says that it 'shall not be destroyed for ever' [Daniel ii, 44] . . . For I assert with confidence, that though, by way of chastisement for our sins, hostile barbarians rise up for a short while against the Roman dominion, yet that by the valour of him who governs us, the empire will continue to be invincible, provided it does not restrict but widens the influence of Christianity. I say so because this imperial family believed in Christ before the others; and this empire is the servant of the dispensation established by Christ, on which account he, who is the Lord of all, preserves it unconquered till the final consummation . . .[1]*

Universal empire and universal religion went hand in hand. Cosmas again:

And so likewise among the Bactrians, and Huns and Persians and the rest of the Indians, Persarmenians and Medes and Elamites and throughout the whole land of Persia there is no limit to the number of churches with bishops, and very large communities of Christian people; as well as many martyrs and monks also living as hermits. So too in Ethiopia and Axôm, and in all the country about it; among the people of Happy Arabia who are now called Homerites, through all Arabia and Palestine, Phoenicia, and all Syria and Antioch as far as Mesopotamia; among the Nubians and the Garamantes, in Egypt, Libya, Pentapolis, Africa and Mauretania as far as southern Gadeira [Cadiz], there are everywhere churches of the Christians, and bishops, martyrs, monks and recluses, where the Gospel of Christ is proclaimed. So likewise again in Cilicia, Asia, Cappadocia, Lazica and Pontus, and in the northern countries occupied by the Scythians, Hyrcanians, Heruli, Bulgarians, Greeks and Illyrians, Dalmatians, Goths, Spaniards, Romans, Franks and other nations, as far as Gadeira on the ocean towards the northern parts, there are believers and preachers of the Gospel confessing the Resurrection from the Dead. And so we see the prophecies being fulfilled over the whole world.[2]

Let us put ourselves in the place of the inhabitants of these

* References will be found at the end of the book, p. 315.

northern and western regions so familiar to us today. There were many in those days who journeyed eastwards to the lands from which their faith had sprung. One such was the Spanish nun whose example is quoted by a Galician monk, Valerius, writing in the seventh century.

In the days when the beneficent Catholic faith was in its infancy and the glorious light of our holy Church shone out at last belatedly on these far western shores, the blessed nun Aetheria, burning with the flame of the desire for the grace of God, with all her might and main, with a brave heart, aided by the power and majesty of God, undertook to travel all across the world. And so, proceeding for some time with the Lord's guidance, she came to the longed-for holy places of the Nativity, the Passion and the Resurrection of Our Lord, as well as to divers towns and provinces where lie the bodies of countless martyred saints, and there devoted herself to prayer and moral improvement. And the more she learned of holy dogma, the more the unquenchable flame of holy longing burned in her heart.[3]

Aetheria made her journey somewhere about the year A.D. 400. Suppose we follow in her footsteps and set sail from the coast of Spain. We may perhaps dispense with the sight of Rome, now falling into ruin, its population depleted, its buildings ravaged by fire, its water supplies cut off. But curiosity, sanctioned by pious duty, urges us to visit the capital of Constantinople, the Second Rome. The City, as it was known at that time, was full of famous churches, the finest and most renowned being Santa Sophia, then in all its brand new splendour. At its inauguration on 25 December 537 Justinian exclaimed: 'I have surpassed thee, Solomon.' Constantinople was packed with famous monasteries and precious relics that made it a goal for pilgrims. Visitors marvelled at the

broad avenues running the length and breadth of the city, the great squares, each with a lofty column in the centre, lined with sumptuous palaces. Public monuments of classical design were still to be seen, with elegant houses built in the Syrian fashion. The streets and porticoes were adorned with antique statuary and the whole was altogether wonderful. . . . The splendour of the imperial palaces, of the great sacred palace . . . remarkable for the variety of the buildings, the beauty of the gardens in which they were set and the mosaics or paintings which adorned the apartments. All these things made Constantinople the cynosure of every eye, dreamed of the world over as a city of marvels glimpsed through a dazzle of gold.[4]

Beyond, one came, like Aetheria, to the Holy Land itself. Valerius goes on to describe her

seeking everywhere for all that comes into the books of the Old and New Testament, visiting all the places in the different parts of the world where miracles occurred, provinces, cities, mountains and desert places she had seen mentioned in the books, journeying for many years in her anxiety to go everywhere until, travelling throughout with God's help, she came at last to the countries of the East.[5]

The Byzantine East was rich in monuments and splendid churches, in prosperous cities swarming with people, huge monasteries and all kinds of relics of the biblical era and the beginnings of Christianity. Antioch, Alexandria and Jerusalem were very large and beautiful cities. Justinian had many great and splendid buildings erected, not only there but in other, less important cities listed by Procopius in his treatise on the subject. By way of example the rhetor Chorikios of Gaza describes with pride the beautiful churches of his native city.[6]

Aetheria travelled as far east as Charra, the ancient Harran where Abraham had dwelled. With her usual tireless curiosity about biblical relics, she asked the bishop of the city for the whereabouts of Ur, the town in which the Patriarch was born; but here she came up against a major difficulty. 'The place for which you ask, my daughter, is ten days' march from here, in Persia. . . . Nowadays all that region is occupied by the Persians and the Romans no longer have access to it.'[7]

This was the beginning of another empire. The Persian Empire of the Sassanids was the second greatest power in the world and ruled all the lands between the Euphrates and the

Indus. Its capital was a group of seven cities on the river Tigris, not far from ancient Babylon and modern Baghdad. The Syriac name for these towns was Maḥūzē or Medhināthā, in Arabic al-Madā'in, which means simply 'the towns'. The chief of these was Ctesiphon. The remains of the royal palace, called in Persian the Tāq-e-Kesrā, the arch of Khusrō, can still be seen on its site. The audience chamber, 90 ft wide, 140 ft long and 120 ft high, was roofed by a vast, elliptical vault. Here, the king of kings showed himself to his people. On audience days

> the crowd surged around the huge opening which formed the doorway to the *apadāna* and the great chamber was soon filled with people. The floor was covered with soft carpets and the walls also partly lined with carpets or, where they were left bare, with mosaic pictures. . . . The throne was set at the far end, behind a curtain, surrounded by high officials and other dignitaries, each standing at the correct distance from the curtain prescribed for him by etiquette. There was probably a barrier to divide the courtiers and great men from the crowd. Suddenly the curtain was drawn aside and the king of kings appeared, seated on his throne on a gold-brocaded cushion, dressed in magnificent gold-embroidered robes. The crown, covered with gold and silver, studded with pearls and encrusted with rubies and emeralds, was suspended above his head by a gold chain fixed to the ceiling, but so fine that it could only be seen from very close beside the throne. From a distance it looked as though the crown was resting on his head, although in fact it weighed over two hundred pounds and was far too heavy for any human head to bear its weight. The spectacle of all this pomp, seen through the dim light filtering in from the hundred and fifty openings, from five to seven inches from the roof, wrought such an impression on one beholding the sight for the first time as to make him fall involuntarily to his knees.[8]

The treasure of the Sassanid kings was vast and Arab authors have left lists and awed descriptions of it that have been further enhanced by tradition. They speak of a chess set with the pieces made of rubies and emeralds, a game of tric-trac in coral and turquoises. Their throne, writes Tha'ālibī, was made of ivory and teak with panels and arm-rests of gold and silver. The length of it was 180 cubits, the breadth 130 cubits and the height 15 cubits. On the steps were seats of blackwood and ebony framed in gold. This throne was surmounted by a baldaquin of gold and lapis lazuli on which were depicted the sky and the stars, the signs of the zodiac and the seven climes together with the kings in their various occupations, feasting, or in battle or the chase. There was also a device for showing the hours of the day. The throne itself was all covered over with four carpets of gold brocade adorned with pearls and rubies, each one related to a particular season of the year.[9]

In fact, this throne may well have been a gigantic, magnificently ornamental clock.

The army was very powerful. The principal shock troops, the cavalry, were recruited from the nobility. These horsemen were clad in close-fitting armour and formed, in the mass, something like a solid wall of metal gleaming in the sun. Behind the cavalry came the elephants, striking terror into the enemy with their trumpeting, their smell and terrible appearance; and after them the footsoldiers, a rabble of peasants conscripted for military service and of little practical value. A great deal more useful were the auxiliary forces made up of mercenaries and of mounted warriors from the Persians' warlike subject peoples.

This army, which was reorganized in the sixth century on strict disciplinary lines, had seen active service on all the borders of the empire, from Turkestan to India and the Caucasus, but most of all against the Roman Empire. In 531 a strong ruler came to the Persian throne. This was Khusrō (Chosroes), also called Anōsharwān, 'the immortal-souled'. Vigorously he re-established the social order which his father, moved by the sufferings of his people and seduced by the ideas of the communist reformer Mazdak, had done a good deal to upset. He reorganized the army and the financial system, and next invaded Roman Syria, captured Antioch and razed it to the ground. A fifty-year peace was concluded in 561, but it lasted barely ten years.

The two great empires fought each other bitterly for

supremacy. But they also stood for two quite different concepts of the world, two conflicting religions. Christianity ruled in Byzantium. The official religion of Iran was Mazdaism, a religion founded by Zarathustra and based on the cosmic opposition of the principles of Good and Evil. Man must range himself on the side of the Good by his good thoughts, good words and good deeds. But other religions were tolerated and even given honour and protection. The Mazdeans did not proselytize and their ephemeral persecutions of other faiths had other than religious causes. The motive, more often than not, was political. The followers of these religions often fought among themselves to the point of mutual slaughter or denounced one another to the government which, not unreasonably, feared Christian collusion with the Byzantine enemy. But in the fifth century, after Constantinople had denounced the Nestorian heresy for its insistence on the dual nature of Christ, the Nestorians fled to Iran. As fierce opponents of Byzantium they were given a warm welcome, prospered and gradually acquired great influence there and made Persia the starting point for evangelization in Asia.

Cosmas, who must have had at least a sneaking sympathy for the Nestorians, understandably presents the 'Empire of the Magi' as

> ranking next to that of the Romans, because the Magi, in virtue of their having come to offer homage and adoration to the Lord Christ, obtained a certain distinction. For it was in the Roman dominions that the preaching of Christianity first became current in the days of the Apostles, and it was immediately afterwards extended to Persia by the apostle Thaddaeus.[10]

The Jews, also, were generally well received, and protected from persecution by Christians. It was in the academies, bursting with intellectual activity, which existed in the swarming Jewish communities of Sassanid Mesopotamia, that the massive Babylonian Talmud was first set down in writing. Both the Katholikos, the grand metropolitan of the Christian Church in Iran, and the *Resh-galūthā*, or Exilarch, who was the head of the

Jewish community, were men of considerable importance possessed of great powers over their respective flocks. They ranked among the high councillors of the empire. In spite of some friction and brief outbreaks of persecution due, more often than not, to excessive proselytizing zeal or to the religious authorities meddling in high politics, Nestorians and Jews in Persia were comparatively well off. Those everywhere else in the world looked to it as a haven of safety.

In the eyes of a large portion of the world's population, the Byzantine Roman Empire and Sassanid Persian Empire constituted together the whole of the civilized universe, the 'two eyes to which divinity confided the task of illuminating the world' as one Persian emperor wrote to the ruler of Byzantium. He went on to add that 'by these two great empires, turbulent and warlike nations are controlled and the lives of men in general set in order and governed'.[11]

People were, of course, vaguely aware of the existence somewhere beyond of powerful empires enjoying a brilliant civilization and amazing wealth: T'ang China, the kingdoms of India, Burma, Indonesia, the Empire of the Khmers, Japan; but all these belonged to the realm of the fabulous dream countries of whose customs, institutions and history nothing concrete was known. Merchants like Cosmas had certainly ventured as far as Ceylon and even India (hence his surname *Indicopleustes*, 'he who has voyaged to the Indies') and had gleaned some information about the world beyond. But it was like another planet, already half way to the earthly paradise which lay beyond the eastern ocean, a planet with which from time to time some daring astronaut made remote contact.

Thence, too, came precious merchandise, especially silk, and spices, carried chiefly by the barbarian peoples, the Turks to the north, the Arabs in the south, who inhabited the vast intermediate zone between the two worlds and virtually monopolized all traffic between them. To reach their domain was in a sense like coming to the end of the world.

Let us suppose our imaginary traveller to have gone in this direction following in the footsteps of real pilgrims like the nun Aetheria. After Syria and Palestine she was guided to a place where 'the mountains between which we advanced drew apart, forming an immense valley as far as the eye could see, utterly flat and extremely beautiful; at the end of the valley rose God's holy mountain, Sinai'.[12] This mountain, which, on a closer approach, was seen to divide into several peaks, the pilgrims undertook to climb. It was not easy.

> The ascent of these mountains is an extremely arduous business, for one does not climb them gradually by going round about, in a spiral, as they say, but straight up, like a wall, and one has to go straight down these mountains one after the other until one comes to the foot of the middle one which is, properly speaking, Sinai. And so, by the will of Christ our Lord, aided by the prayers of the saints that were with us, I went forward with great pains because I was obliged to make the ascent on foot (since it was quite impossible to do it mounted). And yet I did not feel any pain and the reason for this was because I saw that desire I had coming true according to God's will.[13]

At the top the pilgrims found 'a church, not very big but of great beauty' and the monks showed them the view.

> We saw below us the mountains we had climbed first with such difficulty. Compared to the central mountain on which we stood, they looked like little hills. . . . Egypt, Palestine, the Red Sea, the Parthenian Sea which goes to Alexandria and finally the land of the Saracens stretching as far as the eye could see. All this we saw at our feet, from that place. One would scarcely believe it . . .[14]

The land of the Saracens . . . a barbaric and alarming people. The monks must have had some dealings with them. A hundred years after Aetheria, the tiny church had been abandoned, apparently haunted. 'It is impossible for a man', wrote Procopius, 'to pass the night on the mountain peak since the roar of thunder and certain other portents are heard constantly all through the night, striking with panic even the strongest and most resolute of men.' Some distance below, Justinian had built a fine church to the Mother of God, as well as a strong fortress held by a large garrison, 'so that wild Saracens might not be able to take advantage of the district being uninhabited and use the place as a base for invading, with all possible secrecy, the districts towards Palestine'.[15] Who were they, the men who lived in this desert land on the edge of the civilized world, and were so greatly feared?

2

Introducing a Land

THE people known at this period in Greek as 'Sarakenoi', 'Saraceni' in Latin, from which we get our modern English word 'Saracens', had previously been called 'Scenite Arabs', the Arabs who dwell in tents (from the Greek *skēnē*, a tent). They called themselves simply Arabs. They had lived in that arid land since time immemorial and none could recall that any people had been there before them.

The land is vast, very nearly as big as one third of Europe, but very sparsely populated. The low rainfall has made a great deal of it a desert. In some parts there may be no rain for ten years at a time. Huge areas are covered with dunes rising to heights of six hundred feet or more and several miles in length. One of these regions, the Rab' al-Khālī, is the size of France; another, the great Nafūd, farther north covers over 40,000 square miles. Elsewhere we find extensive lava fields, the legacy of volcanic activity at some time in the more or less distant past.

The river beds, or *wādīs*, bear witness to an era of greater humidity, but in historical times at least they have been dry for the most part, only dotted with occasional scattered pools. Now and then, without warning, a sudden downpour transforms them briefly into raging torrents. These 'floods', as the Arabs call them, wreak appalling havoc. But the water remains, sinking deep into the earth. Men dig deep wells in the ground to look for it; one is said to reach up to six hundred feet in depth. The Arabs have brought well-sinking to a fine art and can apparently sense a patch of wet sand well below the surface. Sometimes the water gushes out in a spring. Then an oasis appears, its green vegetation stark against the surrounding desert. And in other places, especially the *tihāmas*, the coastal plains where the rains are more frequent, the *wādī* lower parts retain enough water to make some agriculture possible. Even in the desert, a sudden downpour can bring about a burgeoning of wild flowers and grasses within a matter of hours.

The way of life was dictated by the land. Since most of the peninsula was desert, the natural way of life was nomadic and pastoral. During the second millennium before the Christian era, the inhabitants of these regions domesticated the camel, a creature ideally suited to the desert. From then on, small groups of nomads (*badw* in Arabic, hence our word 'Beduin') followed the camels which were their livelihood. Sprenger has described the Arab as a parasite on the camel. With the coming of the 'spring' rains, all converged on the areas made green by the waters, driving their camels before them. These were the days of ease and plenty when men gorged themselves against the lean times to come, scattering in small groups to make the most of the manna from heaven. Then the drought returned and human life concentrated around the permanent water holes where trees, shrubs and bushes survived.

A few cereals were grown elsewhere but in the oases a small, sedentary population cultivated the date palm, the tree of trees, of which not only the fruit, but every single part was utilized in some way. 'The mother and the aunt of the Arabs' it was called and for the mass of the poor Beduin it provided (with camel's milk) their staple diet.

All these elements of the population had to exist in some degree of symbiosis. The farmers who cultivated the date palms and the scattered fields of fruit and vegetables, Beduin camel-herds of the desert, peasants and townsfolk of the neighbouring regions all needed one another. Their swift mounts gave the camelherds a military advantage which led in practice to their domination of the settled peoples, especially in the oases, isolated in the midst of a sea of desert which was the realm of the nomad. In this situation, the cultivators generally bought protection from the herdsmen in service or in kind. In parts of

Arabia today, this is still referred to with wry humour as the brotherhood tax, the *khuwwa*.

Trade was another form of peaceful communication between these different peoples. The camel made it possible to traverse vast distances. It can carry loads of up to four hundredweight, cover sixty miles in a day, and is capable of travelling twenty days without water in temperatures reaching 120° F and more if a little green fodder is given to it; otherwise it can still go for some five days before it dies. The caravans provided a link between the civilized parts of South Arabia and the Fertile Crescent, carrying, as well as their own produce, goods in transit from India, East Africa and the Far East on the one hand, and from all over the Mediterranean world on the other. Unless some more powerful nation provided the caravan with a military escort, the Beduin took toll of all that passed through territories under their control. Relations on a more restricted scale existed, naturally, between the nomads and the settled peoples, even if only to permit the interchange of the dates and camel's milk which made up their diets. A number of markets and fairs grew up and some became permanent fixtures by a spring or a religious sanctuary. In this way scattered townships spread over the deserts, besides those which grew up naturally at the oases. These were collections of traders, craftsmen and, where terrain allowed, peasants; as well as some chieftains from the nomadic tribes who, surrounded by a more or less numerous following, ruled their wandering tribesmen from this seat of comparative luxury.

It was in these towns and in the oases and the cultivated lands that the social structures governing the life of the desert were maintained. The basic units were small groups, their numbers dictated by the necessities of life, which might be called clans or sub-tribes. A tribe was made up of clans which, rightly or wrongly, acknowledged some kind of kinship. Each tribe had its eponymous ancestor. The ideologists and politicians of the desert worked out genealogies in which the ties of kinship attributed to these ancestors reflected the various relations between the groups which bore their names.

These relations might be peaceful, but, given the appalling poverty against which Arab communities had often to contend, there was a strong temptation to lay forcible hands on the (often very relative) wealth of those who were somewhat more fortunate. What ensued was a *ghazū*, a *ghazwa* (razzia, or raid), the rules of which were laid down by tradition. Wherever possible, goods were seized without loss of life. This was because manslaughter carried severe penalties according to the unwritten law of the desert.

In practice the free Arabs were bound by no written code of law, and no state existed to enforce its statutes with the backing of a police force. The only protection for any man's life was the certainty, established by custom, that it would be dearly bought. Blood for blood and a life for a life. Undying shame attached to the man whom tradition designated as the avenger if he allowed a murderer to live. The vendetta, *tha'r* in Arabic, is one of the pillars of Beduin society.

This society was based in principle upon equality. Each member of the tribe was the equal of any other. Each group did in fact elect itself a leader, or *sayyid*, but his authority depended strictly on his personal prestige. He had to be constantly on the alert to maintain this. It was vital to his position. Consequently, he had to show many qualities – to retain his followers by his kindness and generosity, to display moderation in all circumstances, to fall in with the unspoken will of those he meant to govern and yet assert his own valour and authority. At a general meeting of the clan, the veto of a single man was enough to upset a major decision. Strictly speaking, however, all were not equal. Some clans had grown rich by plunder, trade or by preying on the settled tribes or even on other nomads. From time to time individuals belonging to a particular clan even built up private fortunes. There were, therefore, rich and poor; although a period of drought, or the misfortunes of war, would be enough to reduce all to equal wretchedness once more. Some used their ephemeral wealth to keep slaves – foreigners bought or taken captive in the course of a raid, or debtors unable to pay. But the conditions of a nomadic life did not lend themselves to the maintenance of slavery as an institution (with its constant watch on the captives' movements) as it was among the settled peoples; and the result was that slaves were often given their freedom. The freed slaves (*mawlā*) remained the dependants of their former master. A number of tribes or clans – such as, for example, tribes of smiths – were looked down on by the rest as inferior; these were perhaps the remnants of a people of different origin.

Ammianus Marcellinus said of the Saracens in the fourth century that

> Their life is always on the move, and they have mercenary wives, hired under a temporary contract. But in order that there may be some semblance of matrimony, the future wife, by way of dower, offers her husband a spear and a tent, with the right to leave him after a stipulated time, if she so elects: and it is unbelievable with what ardour both sexes give themselves up to passion.[1]

This description is undoubtedly an exaggeration. Altogether the wife does seem to have played, on the whole, a less subordinate role among the nomads than was the case with sedentary peoples, or than that which occurred after Islam.

In this crude and unstable society there was little room for the arts, with one exception: that of words. The Arabs admired men of eloquence – men who were able to produce a quick answer to an awkward question and who could get their advice adopted in argument in the council of the tribe or clan. Arab sages were highly thought of; but poetry was valued still more. The poet was a person of importance, and feared, because he was thought to be possessed by a spirit, as everywhere he sang of his loves and griefs, his joys and sorrows and of the savage beauty of his harsh land. There was already an entire art of poetry; poetical art forms included, for instance, the obligatory lament over the abandoned camp-site left by the beloved and her people. But the poet's chief use was as a propagandist; he was the journalist of the desert. Oratorical contests were held – often at the big fairs – at which each contestant boasted of his own tribe and mocked and reviled those of his opponents. Attack and counter-attack had to be in the same metre and with the same rhyme. Satire, degenerating rapidly into common insult, and panegyric or poetic self-glorification, with its tendency to turn into downright boastfulness and rodomontade, were among the most popular poetic forms.

The Beduin do not seem to have had much time for religion. They were realists, without a great deal of imagination. They believed the land was peopled by spirits, the jinns, who were often invisible but appeared also in animal form. The dead were thought to live on in a dim and ghostly state. Offerings were made to them and *stelae* and cairns of stones erected on their graves. Certain trees and stones (especially meteorites and those shaped to resemble human forms) housed spirits and divinities. Divinities dwelt in the sky and some were actually stars. Some were thought to be ancient sages made divine. The list of these divine beings, and above all the importance with which each was regarded, varied from one tribe to the next; but the chief of them were to be found all over the peninsula. This was especially true of Allah, 'the God, the Divinity', the personification of the divine world in its highest form, creator of the universe and keeper of sworn oaths. In the Hejaz three goddesses had pride of place as the 'daughters of Allah'. The first of these was Allāt, mentioned by Herodotus under the name of Alilat. Her name means simply 'the goddess', and she may have stood for one aspect of Venus, the morning star, although hellenized Arabs identified her with Athene. Next came 'Uzzā, 'the all-powerful', whom other sources identify with Venus. The third was Manāt, the goddess of fate, who held the shears which cut the thread of life and who was worshipped in a shrine on the sea-shore. The great god of Mecca was Hubal, an idol made of red cornelian.

Certain places where divine presence manifested itself became sacred. Bounds were set, and inside these no living creature could be killed. As a result they became places of asylum, where those pursued by an avenger could take refuge. They were tended by priestly families. Homage was paid to the divinity with offerings and the sacrifice of animals and perhaps, occasionally, of human beings. Certain sanctuaries were the object of pilgrimage (*ḥajj*) at which a variety of rituals were performed, consisting notably of ceremonial processions around the sacred object. Certain prohibitions had to be observed during these rites, such as in many cases abstention from sexual relations. The blood taboo was particularly widespread. Boys were ceremoniously circumcised. The Arabs practised divination from the flight of birds, or from the direction taken by animals. They sought oracles from the gods by shooting arrows. The truth could be discovered by means of ordeals. Magic was common. People feared the evil eye and protected themselves with amulets.

The members of these scattered, wandering tribes – half-starved and extremely anarchic – were in fact striving to conform to a moral ideal of their own, in the formation of which religion played no part. The ideal man possessed in the highest degree the quality known as *murūwa*, which can be literally translated as 'virility'. This comprised courage, endurance, loyalty to the group and to one's social obligations, generosity and hospitality. The feeling which drove a man to conform to this ideal was one of honour (*'irḍ*). Infringements of the moral code of the desert rendered him liable to insult, and hence to loss of honour. It has been amply demonstrated that among the Arabs the sense of honour took over many of the ordinary functions of religion. None of these ideals, none of the forces which ordered the life of society or the individual had any supernatural basis. What they all came down to was man. Man was the ultimate measure of things. But man in this context meant social man – man as a member of his clan and his tribe. That is why W. Montgomery Watt calls this concept 'tribal humanism', and the term seems to fit. The only limit to man's activities and potential was that represented by the intervention of blind fate (*dahr*). It was true that this was pitiless;

man's fate was a tragic one, and there was no escape from a fundamentally pessimistic view of life except in making haste to enjoy the fierce but fleeting pleasures it had to offer. Even so, human activity did make it possible to improve somewhat on the concessions of fate. The Beduin might be superstitious, but he was a realist; and the hard life of the desert disposed him less to meditation on the infinite (as had been gratuitously assumed at one time), than to a precise estimate of his own strength and weakness.

Authors bent on systematically running down the Arabs (paradoxically enough, a fairly popular sport with arabists) have described this society as barbaric. Arabs have taken offence at this and pointed to the ordered structure of its social life and the interest of its intellectual output. Clearly all depends on what you mean by 'barbaric'. The Arabs certainly did not live in a state of total anarchy for the very good reason that no such conditions have ever existed anywhere. But it must be admitted that the unwritten rules they followed were very often broken and that in the sphere of material culture their level was very low. Poetry is no more an index of cultural development, in the sense used by ethnologists, than are the plastic arts. Naturally, this low level in the scale of civilizations implies no congenital, inherited inferiority. It comes from the social conditions of the time set against a framework of the very unfavourable natural conditions in the Arabian peninsula. Hunger is never a good counsellor and the Arabs were often hungry. Hence the picturesque and savage excesses which appear, on certain occasions, among some of their tribes. In the fourth century Ammianus Marcellinus, an honest soldier of Syrian origin, was horrified by this people, of whom he said, 'I would not wish to have them either as friends or enemies.' He tells a typical story about them. In A.D. 378 a strong force of Goths, swelled by contingents of Alans and Huns, was marching on Constantinople after defeating the Roman army before Adrianople. The chief Roman generals and the Emperor Valens himself had fallen. The situation was critical in the extreme. It was then that a troop of Saracens in the service of the empire attacked the Western barbarians. The battle was indecisive. 'But', says Ammianus,

the oriental troop had the advantage from a strange event, never witnessed before. For one of their number, a man with long hair and naked except for a loin cloth, uttering hoarse and dismal cries, with drawn dagger rushed into the thick of the Gothic army, and after killing a man, applied his lips to his throat and sucked the blood that poured out. The Barbarians, terrified by this strange and monstrous sight, after that did not show their usual self-confidence when they attempted any action, but advanced with hesitating steps.[2]

Beyond the lands of the Saracens, in the south of what we now call Arabia, one came to a country which, while geographically a part of the same peninsula, was in many respects quite different. This, properly speaking, was what the ancients meant by 'Arabia the Blessed', although their geographical theories led them to include in it a good deal of the desert peninsula. But they spoke of the inhabitants of the south of the country in a tone quite different from the wretched Saracens. Ammianus again described the region in these terms:

The Parthians [Persians] are neighbours to the east and south [these were the geographical beliefs of the time] of the fortunate Arabs [*Arabes beati*], so called because they are rich in fruits of the field, as well as in cattle, dates and many varieties of perfumes. A great part of their country borders to the right on the Red Sea, while on the left they are bounded by the Persian Sea; and the people know how to avail themselves of all the advantages of both elements. On that coast there are both many anchorages and numerous safe harbours, trading cities in an uninterrupted line, uncommonly splendid and richly adorned royal palaces, natural hot springs of most health-giving water and an evident multitude of rivers and streams. Lastly, the climate there is so healthful that, to men of good judgement, they evidently lack nothing for supreme happiness. There are a great many towns, both inland and on the coast, with fruitful plains and valleys.[3]

The fact is that the land was completely different. The

mountains of South Arabia lie in the path of the monsoons from the Indian Ocean. A regular rainfall meant that these regions could be properly irrigated. Since very early times, the water had been canalized by an efficient irrigation system which, together with an arrangement of terraced fields, allowed agriculture to prosper. As well as the corn, fruit, vegetables and vines which provided food for the population, the coast of South Arabia which faced the Indian Ocean also bore myrrh- and incense-bearing trees. These, with the other perfumes and aromatics she produced, were a source of considerable wealth. The Mediterranean world consumed vast quantities of these products, chiefly for religious purposes but also for personal adornment, *cuisine* and other manifestations of luxurious living. In addition, South Arabia had long been a trans-shipment stage for produce coming from India on the one hand and from East Africa on the other.

In such markets as the great port of Muza, for example, one might find, as well as pearls from the Persian Gulf, ivory, silk, cotton, textiles and rice, pepper from India, slaves, monkeys, ivory, gold and ostrich plumes from East Africa, not to mention the local and Mediterranean products for which these were traded. This merchandise was sent on its way north by caravan. The South Arabians were busy traders; inscriptions carved by them have been found in Egypt, at Delos and in Mesopotamia.

Ever since a date on which scholars are still unable to agree but probably after the eighth century B.C., the South Arabians, who did not call themselves Arabs and spoke a language related to though not identical with Arabic, had arrived at a settled and even urbanized stage of civilization based on this agriculture and trade. They had formed states, called Saba, Maʿīn, Qatabān, the Ḥaḍramawt and Awsān. Each of these was controlled by one dominant and privileged tribe. For a time, at least, these were constitutional monarchies with kings and deliberative assemblies. Decisions would be taken, for example, 'by the king of Maʿīn and by Maʿīn'. All these states endlessly quarrelled and made alliances amongst themselves, the details of which we know very little. At all events, the growth of the Mediterranean civilizations had the corresponding effect of increasing the wealth of their South Arabian suppliers. In about A.D. 100 Artemidorus of Ephesus spoke in glowing terms of the luxury of the Sabaeans, their rich furnishings, gold and silver vessels, houses with gates, walls and roofs adorned with gold, silver, ivory and precious stones. Excavations have only recently become possible to attempt to verify and extend this information.

The Americans have begun to excavate Timnaʿ, the capital of the kingdom of Qatabān; a city, according to Pliny, boasting sixty-five temples. The southern gate of the city was flanked by a pair of massive towers built of blocks of undressed stone, some of which measured as much as 8 ft by 2 ft. Inside the gate was a square with stone benches where perhaps the husband of the virtuous woman 'known in the gates . . . sitteth among the elders of the land'.

A little farther on, the excavators unearthed two houses; the front of one was decorated with two bronze statues, distinctively Hellenistic in style, representing a pair of symmetrical lionesses, each bearing a chubby smiling infant. The group was apparently cast in bronze from an Alexandrian plaster representation of the Dioscuri. The Americans have also excavated the ancient Sabaean city of Mārib, or rather the great temple which was probably its chief monument and whose remains had been viewed by earlier travellers. The name of this temple, erected to the great Sabaean god Almaqah, was Awwām. It comprises a huge, oval precinct which was probably some 30 ft high, approximately 300 ft long and 250 ft broad, with an ornate portico and adjoining buildings culminating in a row of eight columns. Inside, the portico is decorated in part with false windows of imitation stone lattice-work.

These discoveries have confirmed what was already known: that the South Arabians were skilled architects. Their construction of monumental palaces is still echoed today in the tall, many-storeyed Yemeni houses. They constructed impressive water-works. The most celebrated of these in the

North Arabian tradition was actually in the neighbourhood of Mārib; its imposing remains can be seen today in the shape of three great dams with chunks of wall up to fifty feet high still standing.

The 'fortunate Arabs', then, enjoyed a highly developed civilization. This is further reflected in their visual art, in which, alongside objects of clumsy workmanship, we find statues on stylized lines showing great mastery and original inspiration. A great many works were inspired, as we have seen, by Roman and Hellenistic art, when not actually copied or even imported. Indian influences can also be detected in some pieces. Luxury objects, some of them in alabaster, are often elegant and exquisite. The elegance and perfect regularity of its characters makes South Arabian writing a work of art in itself. The characters are generally rather square, later becoming more curved, flexible and adorned with somewhat decadent flourishes. The people of South Arabia wrote a great deal. Thousands of inscriptions have come to light, the majority dealing with legal, administrative or religious matters. It is certain, too, that there existed a written literature inscribed on parchment or papyrus; but unfortunately nothing of this has survived.

Yet another contrast with the lands of the Saracens was in the existence of a widespread religious belief. There were many rich temples, which were served by a priesthood which played an important role in society. Worship took the form of offerings of perfumes and animal sacrifices, of prayers and pilgrimages, in the course of which sexual relations were unlawful. Any infringement of one of the numerous prescriptions concerning purity and impurity had to be paid for by a fine and a public confession, which was inscribed in bronze tablets and set up in the temple. The dead were buried with vessels and household objects. *Stelae* or monuments carried stylized representations of the deceased. Libations may have been made to them.

The South Arabians worshipped a great many gods and goddesses. Most important was 'Athtar, the god who personified the planet Venus (Astarte and Ishtar, the corresponding

Semitic deities in the north, were goddesses) and the lunar gods Almaqah in Saba, Wadd (which probably means 'love') in Ma'īn, 'Amm (father-in-law) in Qatabān and Sīn in the Ḥaḍramawt. The sun was personified by a goddess of the same name called Shams. The gods were known by different names at the different sanctuaries where they were worshipped. The various epithets attributed to them also served to differentiate the manifold aspects of the same divinity, each of which probably had its own devotees.

The settled, civilized people of South Arabia, living a life of wealth and luxury in organized states of great complexity with in all probability a well-established bureaucracy, presented a strong contrast to the Arabs or Saracens, who were a collection of wandering tribes with crude and occasionally savage customs, owning practically no material possessions, famished and free. They were employed by the South Arabians as mercenaries in their auxiliary forces. Each state had its own Beduin. Even so, from very early times they may have acknowledged a distant kinship as they did later on. Some northern tribes claimed, rightly or wrongly, to have come originally from the cultivated regions of the south.

After the triumph of Islam under Saracen leadership the South Arabians were rapidly assimilated, and the inhabitants of the peninsula as a whole embarked on the conquest of the world. But the memory of their brilliant civilization did not fade all at once. The Yemenis in the Muslim ranks stuck together in fierce opposition to the northern Arabs. Knowledge of the old tongue and the old writing persisted in some places for several centuries. Pre-Islamic luxury was celebrated by nostalgic verses on the theme of 'Where are the snows of yesteryear?' Men told of the splendours of the old royal palaces and a cycle of legends grew up around the glory of the kings of old, in which the historical facts were handed down with much exaggeration and distortion on the way. So it was that one king, Shammar, who was actually a conqueror on an Arabian scale, was credited with incursions as far as China; witness the name of the city of Samarkand which he was supposed to have founded. Until a comparatively recent date, intellectuals and local rulers of the Yemen fostered a kind of South Arabian nationalism, which approached blasphemy when it came to verses playing down the importance of the Prophet, a North Arabian, and his message. But to return to the days before the coming of this prophet.

The Arabs liked to present Arabia, the cradle of their religion and of their empire, as a world virtually in isolation, the firm, pure seed set in the rotten earth, which was to grow into the spreading tree of the Muslim world. Nothing could be further from the truth. Arabia was certainly not easy of access from the outside world, but it was criss-crossed by caravan routes; merchants ventured to travel there, and occasionally others too. Several times armies penetrated deep into the Arabian interior, in spite of the hardships and sufferings they endured. The Babylonian king, Nabonidus, in the sixth century B.C. reached Medina (Yatribu) and established himself for some years at Tayma in the Hejaz. The Seleucid king Antiochus III subjugated Gerrha in the region of Baḥrain. Pliny mentions the extinct Greek colonies of Arethusa, Larissa and Chalcis which seem to have been somewhere near the southern end of the peninsula. In the year 25–24 B.C. the Roman prefect of Egypt, Aelius Gallus, acting on the orders of Augustus, penetrated into the Yemen.

A great many Arabs also travelled in the contrary direction. They were to be found in Athens; their pressure on Egypt and the lands of the Fertile Crescent saw them settled there in considerable numbers from very early times, adopting the language and customs of the country. Xenophon, in 401 B.C., already referred to the north of Mesopotamia as Arabia, and the part of Egypt between the Nile and the Red Sea had long been so called. The Arabs of the Nabataean kingdom south of the Dead Sea (which became the Roman province of Arabia in A.D. 106) spoke Greek and a dialect of Aramaic, as also did the Arab dynasties of Chalcis in Coele Syria, Emesa (Ḥomṣ), Edessa and Palmyra. Elagabalus, the Roman emperor (218–222) who started out as high priest of Ḥomṣ, was an Arab; so too were his successor, Philip the Arabian (244–249), who celebrated the thousandth birthday of Rome, and Zenobia of Palmyra who took the title of Augusta in 270.

All these Arabs from the fringes of the desert were more or less deeply imbued with Aramaic or Hellenic culture. Later on they became Christians and produced bishops and priests. A certain Gessios from the city of Gea in Arabia Petraea was a famous doctor under the Emperor Zeno (474–491).

There were a number of studies of Arabia. A scholar named Uranius, writing perhaps in the first century B.C., produced an *Arabica* running into at least five volumes. At some indeterminate date another 'arabist' by the name of Glaucus produced an Arabian archaeology in four books. In the second century A.D. the great geographer Ptolemy of Alexandria had at his disposal sufficient information from all sources to draw a map of Arabia in which the co-ordinates were comparatively accurate.

Arabia was certainly open to foreign influences, especially Hellenistic ones. That this was so with the civilized states of South Arabia, among whom the owl coinage of Athens was in use, is beyond doubt. And a statuette discovered recently in Oman is of pure Indian workmanship. But these influences also extended into central Arabia. Continuous contact existed, even if only at second hand, between the assimilated Arabs of the periphery and the civilized Arabs of the south; and through them the ideas, customs and material possessions of the outside world filtered through, undergoing a certain amount of selection, adaptation and transformation on the way. Our most eloquent evidence of this is probably in the Arabic language, which even before Islam had assimilated Greek, Latin and other foreign words, for the most part through the channel of Aramaic, and which had become so thoroughly absorbed as to be indistinguishable from the old roots of the language.

The sixth century was a time of great upheavals in the middle east. As we have seen the two great empires, Byzantine and Sassanid, were at loggerheads. They were disputing economic mastery of the world and what would guarantee it, control of the routes by which the products of China and the Far East – above all silk – were brought to the west. Moreover, the Byzantines had not lost hope of consolidating their supremacy by reconquering Mesopotamia, which had once belonged to Rome in the time of Trajan, and Armenia. The Persians, on the other hand, in their most optimistic moods, aimed at rebuilding the empire of Darius by winning back Syria and Egypt from the Romans. From 502 to 505 there had been war under the reforming King of kings Kawādh. He resumed it in 527 over the Caucasus, and it was continued by his son Khusrō, who offered to make an eternal treaty of peace with Justinian in 532. But war broke out again in 540 and Antioch fell to Khusrō. After counter-attacks by Belisarius an armistice was signed in 545. This was renewed at intervals until a fifty-year peace was concluded in 562. However, war broke out once again in 572 for reasons which will be seen.

Lying partly in between the two empires was the Syrian desert, the home of Saracen nomads. Both sides endeavoured to gain their support. The hungry tribes of Arabia had long cast envious eyes on the fertile lands of Syria and Mesopotamia. A good many infiltrated peaceably and settled there. But, if the states ruling their cultivated lands ever became at all weakened, they became more aggressive and even went so far as to seize political power. This was probably the pattern for a good many movements of population from very early times. After a few generations the Arabs who had originally migrated into these northern lands became culturally assimilated into the settled populations and adopted their religion and customs and their common language, Aramaic. By the sixth century conditions were somewhat different. For perhaps a century or two, for reasons which are not altogether clear to us, the Arab tribes of the desert seem to have been infiltrating into the cultivated zones which bordered their domains – Syria–Palestine and Mesopotamia in the north, Saba and the Ḥaḍramawt in the south – in organized groups, in an increasingly massive and coherent fashion. The two great empires duly noted this phenomenon and determined to make use of it and direct it so as to guarantee themselves a permanent pool of Saracen auxiliaries for their armies. The Sassanids were the first to make the chiefs of one desert family, the Banū Lakhm, of the tribe of Tanūkh, kings of a vassal state. Their forebears seem to have been on good terms with the Romans, and we have an inscription from the tomb of one of them erected close by a Roman post on the Syrian border. It is the oldest inscription in the Arabic language, dated A.D. 328; in it, the man is described as 'king of all the Arabs'. However, the descendants of this Imru' l-Qays went into the service of the Persians and dwelt in the city of Ḥīra, not far from the Persian capital. They gave protection to Arab poets and a ready welcome to Nestorian Christians. Ḥīra was the seat of a bishopric. The castles which these kings built are famous in Arabic legend.

The kings played a substantial role in Persian politics. The Persian Emperor, Yazdgard, bestowed on one of them, Mundhir, the honorary titles of Rāmauzuh-Yazdgard, 'He who increases the joy of Yazdgard', and of Māhisht, 'the Greatest', as well as giving him custody of his son Vahrām, with whom he was on bad terms. On the mysterious death of Yazdgard in 421 it was Mundhir, at the head of the Arab and Persian troops whom he commanded, who installed his own protégé by force, while the nobles who had probably killed Yazdgard were still hesitating between the dead ruler's three sons.

In the service of the Sassanids, the Lakhmids of Ḥīra waged almost continual war against the Romans. In about 500, the Byzantine emperors chose another Arab family called Ghassān, nomads from the east of what is now the kingdom of Jordan, to combat them. In 529 Justinian bestowed on their chief, al-Ḥārith ibn Jabala (known in Greek as Arethas), the titles of phylarch and patrician. The Ghassānids adopted Monophysite Christianity, a creed popular in Syria and Egypt, which recognized only one nature in the person of Christ. They had no fixed capital. At one time their centre was at Jābiya in the Jawlān Heights (ancient Gaulanitid, south of the present Jebel Druze) and another time, for a moment, at Jilliq near Damascus. The struggles of al-Ḥārith and his son Mundhir (Alamundaros to Byzantine writers) against the Lakhmids were famous and full of great deeds. Mundhir's Monophysite faith earned him the distrust of the Emperor Justin. The phylarch was something of a theologian, and he took part in Monophysite councils. Some have suggested that he might have aimed at setting up a Monophysite state in Syria. Justin made an attempt to have him killed, whereupon the phylarch withdrew his allegiance from Byzantium for three years, leaving the Lakhmids to ravage Syrian territory undisturbed. Constantinople was obliged to come to terms with the rebellious Arab leader, and a peace was concluded on the tomb of St Sergius at Sergiopolis (Ruṣāfa in the Syrian desert), a saint especially venerated by the Arabs. Mundhir took Ḥīra and sacked and burned it, sparing only the churches. In 580, after Justin's death, the Emperor Tiberius conferred on him a royal crown (*tāgā*) in place of the diadem (*klīlā*), with the title of Supreme Phylarch of all the Arabs. But he remained under suspicion on account of his beliefs. His behaviour in the war against the Persians appeared to confirm these suspicions. He was seized unawares and taken to Constantinople where the new emperor, Maurice, condemned him to death. The penalty was commuted to one of exile in Sicily; but the phylarch's son, Nu'mān, avenged him by leading the Arabs in ravaging the whole of Syria. He was summoned to Constantinople, where the basileus promised to liberate his father if he defeated the Persians. But he refused to communicate with the Catholics, and on his way home was arrested and sent to join his father in Sicily. The Ghassānid kingdom was then divided among fifteen princes, most of whom went over to the Persians.

Christianity, both Nestorian and Monophysite, had clearly made some headway among the Arabs. In the south it had gone much further. South Arabia even had its churches and bishoprics. The great church of Najrān in the Yemen was a monument to rouse the admiration of the desert Arabs. There were Zoroastrians round about the shores of the Persian Gulf, where Persian influence and possibly even domination had extended. Judaism was widespread in the oases of the Hejaz, where the Jews had greatly increased the area of land under cultivation and made numerous palm plantations. Above all, it was in South Arabia that the important families had become converted. A Jewish poet, or more probably an Arab convert to Judaism, Samaw'al (Samuel) ibn 'Adiya, became a byword for loyalty among the desert Arabs. Besieged in his castle near Taymā' by the king of Ḥīra, Mundhir, he was called upon to deliver up goods left in his keeping by the king of Kinda, the great poet Imru' l-Qays, who was then at the court of Byzantium. The Lakhmid general captured the son of Samaw'al and threatened to kill him unless the father did as he asked. Samaw'al remained true to his promise and saw his son put to death before his eyes.

The Byzantines were endeavouring to extend their influence, in particular through the spread of Christianity, and they had a valuable ally in the region of the Red Sea. This was Abyssinia or Ethiopia, which at that time had its capital at Axūm. The Ethiopian nation, founded long before by South Arabians who had crossed the sea and colonized the indigenous populations who spoke Cushitic languages, had become very powerful. Adulis, its great port on the Red Sea, was not far from present-day Massawa in Eritrea. Egyptian and Byzantine merchants generally went no further and met there with traders from India, Africa or South Arabia. The emperors of Ethiopia (who were then known as *nagāshī*, a word derived from the same root as the modern one, negus) had been converted to Christianity in the first half of the fourth century. They also had possessions in South Arabia, into which Christianity had penetrated at about the same time. The Arian Emperor Constantius (351–361) sent a missionary of 'Indian' origin named Theophilus to spread Arianism, the doctrine which held the divine nature of Christ to be less than that of God the Father. Theophilus seems to have had some temporary success in South Arabia, but he apparently failed to spread his doctrine into neighbouring Ethiopia.

Towards the middle of the fifth century, South Arabia was unified and apparently powerful under its conquering king Abkarib As'ad, who drove north and north-eastwards to a distance of more than six hundred miles from Mārib. He bore the title of 'King of Saba, of Dhū Raydān, the Ḥaḍramawt and Yamanat and of their Arabs of the highlands and the coastal plain.' These Arabs were the Beduin, either vassals or mercenaries in his pay. Like Persia and Byzantium, he had his tributary princes among the nomads – the kings of Kinda who raided northwards and at one time came close to Ḥīra, and whose famous ruler, the poet Imru' l-Qays, has been mentioned earlier. Arab tradition has it that Abkarib As'ad became a convert to Judaism along with his people. Recent arguments put forward by J. Ryckmans lend strong support to this version.[4] It is from this moment that monotheistic inscriptions, probably of Jewish origin, begin to appear. In 1969 a bilingual inscription, in Sabaean and Hebrew, was discovered. Christianity also took root and must have offered some opposition; but the rulers seem in general to have professed the Jewish faith or to have followed at least some kind of judaizing creed.

Certainly, the year 510 or thereabouts – the chronology for this period is vague and open to a good deal of argument – marked a turning point for Judaism. A prince of the Jewish faith, Yūsuf As'ar, known to Arab tradition by the name of Dhū Nuwās, the man with the hanging locks, came to power in South Arabia. An inscription discovered recently adds to his name the appellation Yath'ar, the avenger, which sounds like a declaration. Arab tradition describes him as a good-looking young man who seized power by eluding the homosexual advances of his predecessor, killing him and so releasing the youths of the Yemen from their erotic servitude. He immediately set about persecuting the Christian Monophysites and getting on good terms with Persia.

He represented a religious, political and economic threat to Byzantium. Contemporary writers show a keen awareness of the practical issues at stake. Procopius explains that it was a matter of preventing the far-eastern trade routes from falling into the hands of enemies, who, once they had taken them, would exact payment in good Roman gold for these rare and precious wares. And Cosmas follows up the mystical reflections quoted earlier by adding, like a good businessman:

> And there is yet another sign of the power which God has accorded to the Romans, I refer to the fact that it is with their coinage that all the nations carry on trade from one extremity of the earth to the other. This money is regarded with admiration by all men to whatever kingdom they belong since there is no other country in which the like of it exists.[5]

In about 512, therefore, an expedition from Byzantium's ally Axūm crossed the Red Sea to go to the aid of the Christians. Possibly some of them who lived near the coast may have been under Ethiopian rule. Probably there were even genuine Ethiopian colonies, left over from earlier occupations. The war was a long and indecisive one. The bulk of the Ethiopian army, believing victory assured, or possibly recalled by other events, sailed for home, leaving garrisons behind it. Dhū Nuwās succeeded by a ruse in cutting off and massacring the Ethiopians. He set fire to the great church of the capital, Ẓafār, where two hundred and eighty Ethiopians had taken refuge, and attacked the coastal region of al-Ashʿar; his general, Sharaḥīl Dhū Yaz'an, burned the church belonging to the port of Mukhā. Finally the king initiated a wholesale persecution of Christians in Najrān, the bastion of Monophysite Christianity in South Arabia. According to one source he burned alive, without trial, 427 ecclesiastics, monks and nuns, killed 4,252 Christians and enslaved 1,297 children and young people below the age of fifteen. It may be to the massacres of Dhū Nuwās that a rather enigmatic passage of the Koran alludes. Certainly, these events, exaggerated, no doubt, for propaganda purposes, made a strong impression in Arabia. The Jewish king sent word to Ḥīra, urging the Lakhmid ruler Mundhir III to deal in the same way with the Christians in his domains as a reprisal for the persecution suffered by Jews in the Byzantine Empire. He may have addressed a similar request to the Persian King of kings. The Nestorian Christians, let it be said, seem to have supported him.

Byzantium urged Axūm to seek revenge. Cosmas, who was in Adulis about this time, witnessed the preparations for the expedition. The *nagāshī* assembled sixty vessels, a good many of them Byzantine, built another ten on Indian lines, and, in 525 (apparently), the Abyssinians crossed the sea and succeeded in making a landing – in spite of the mysterious chain, which later tradition somewhat imaginatively claimed to have barred the entire strait of Bab el-Mandeb! Contemporary inscriptions certainly mention a chain which Dhū Nuwās either had made or repaired. It may simply have been used to block the narrow entrance to a harbour. The invaders utterly defeated Dhū Nuwās. The Arabs said later that, in despair at the defeat of his army, the handsome Jewish king rode his horse into the sea until he disappeared beneath the waves.

After a period of pillage and general indiscriminate slaughter, in the course of which the South Arabians suffered without distinction of religion or sect, the Ethiopian troops, who were probably little more than savages, evacuated the country, leaving it in the hands of a native, Sumyafaʿ, whom Procopius calls Esimiphaios. He was probably a former Jewish convert who had reverted to Christianity and the Abyssinian cause. Inscriptions discovered recently give us a glimpse of all kinds of changes and counter-changes. In 530 or thereabouts the Ethiopian soldiers who had remained in Arabia, in conjunction possibly with the lower levels of the South Arabian population, rose against Sumyafaʿ and replaced him with Abraha, who had once been the slave of a Byzantine merchant of Adulis. The Ethiopian negus sent two unsuccessful expeditions to put down the revolt. Abraha stayed where he was, resisting all Justinian's attempts to use him against Persia and preserving a strictly neutral stance in the conflict of great powers, while waiting to see which way the wind would blow. He repaired the great dam of Mārib and put down a revolt perhaps led by the son of

Sumyafaʿ. Inevitably his neutrality made him a ruler very much courted. He received embassies from Ethiopia, Byzantium, Persia, Ḥīra and from the Ghassānid phylarch al-Ḥārith ibn Jabala. He defeated the Saracen tribe of Maʿadd. Towards the end of his reign he drew closer to Ethiopia, and it may have been during this period that he led the expedition northwards to the gates of Mecca with which he is credited in Arab tradition. Later accounts have it that his army, which, to the amazement of the people, included one or more elephants, was forced to fall back after being attacked by birds which cast down stones from the sky. There is an allusion in the Koran to this story about the 'elephant people'.

Abraha's successors pursued what was probably a still more actively anti-Persian policy. Byzantium meanwhile was busy trying to gain control of the overland silk route in the north and getting a firm grip on territories from which to recruit mercenaries. The Turks were the rising power in central Asia. Khusrō Anōsharwān had made an alliance with them and together they had destroyed the empire of the Hephtalites, which ruled over Turkestan, eastern Persia and Afghanistan. The allies had then divided the defeated empire between themselves. In 567 and 568 there was an exchange of ambassadors between the Byzantine Emperor Justin and Istemi, the *qaghan* (khan) of the western Turks, who aimed to sell silk directly to the Byzantines without reference to his old ally, Persia. Khusrō had refused to come to any arrangement on this point. The alliance between the Turks and Byzantium was concluded. In 572 Justin declared war on Persia.

The pro-Persian party in South Arabia, led by old supporters of Dhū Nuwās, was pressing Khusrō to act, to break the Byzantine grip on the region. In addition, the pro-Persian Arabs were launching scattered attacks on the South Arabian kingdom. The King of kings was threatened with encirclement by Byzantium. Shortly before 600 – the exact date is not known, but has long been put at 570 – he made up his mind to send a fleet to the Yemen under the command of one Wahriz. The Persians seem to have had an easy victory. The southern sea was no longer under Byzantine control, even if the overland northern route remained in dispute.

571 is the date traditionally assigned to the birth of the Prophet Muḥammad. This is by no means certain; but the date is anyway important from the point of view of international politics. It is worth mentioning one or two other things which were happening at the same time. The Byzantine Empire, although it was still fighting back vigorously in the east, was suffering serious set-backs in the west. Since 568 the Lombard invasion of Italy had been sweeping forward irresistibly. The Visigoths were attacking Byzantine possessions in Spain. Cordoba was captured for the first time in 572 and lost for good in 584. Fully occupied with affairs in the east, Byzantium reacted only diplomatically, by trying to set the Franks against the Lombards. But Gaul was divided among the grandsons of Clovis. This was the period of strife between Chilperic and Sigebert and their wives, Fredegund and Brunhilde; their brother, Gontran, was ruling peacefully in Burgundy. Celtic Britain was at this time in the process of being finally conquered by heathen Angles, Saxons and Jutes.

The duel of empires, which was echoed in the party strife especially noticeable in South Arabia, could not fail to have major repercussions in the world of the nomadic Saracens.

The conquest of South Arabia by the Ethiopians and later by the Persians reflected a decline in power which had begun long before. The Ptolemies had already tried to by-pass South Arabia by extending the operations of their own royal fleet in the Red Sea and trying to grow balsam in Egypt. Around the beginning of the Christian era, a Greek named Hippalos had discovered the laws of the monsoon, enabling Greek ships to make the voyage from Egypt to India and back in one hop. The overland route from India to the Mediterranean world by way of Palmyra and then by Edessa and Antioch, presented, whenever peace rendered it practicable, a serious rival to the sea route of the south. Internal wars between the South Arabian princes and foreign wars which affected the country – all of which were operations aimed at safeguarding this route – were an inevitable drain on its wealth and strength. Foreign conquest was probably fatal to this trade. The larger nations grew noticeably weaker and there was a corresponding increase in the numbers of petty feudal lords. As in the north, the desert Beduin seem to have infiltrated in an increasingly massive and thoroughgoing fashion. Later Arabic legend remarks this decline and attributes it to a technical accident: the breaching of the great Mārib dam. It is not at all unlikely that the big dams which controlled the irrigation of a wide area may have suffered severe damage; but, if they were not repaired (or if the work was inadequate – for, as we have seen, Abraha could still boast about his restoration of the Mārib dam), this was because the country's resources would no longer allow it.

All this gave an added importance to the Beduin. They were now in a position to charge more dearly for their services as guides or middlemen in overland traffic, which was still considerable on the western land route. Expeditions were sent against them, but these, although spectacular, were only temporary in their effect; the Beduin were still able to bargain their aid to the great powers in conflict and reap substantial rewards.

The old Beduin tribes were no sooner settled than men emerged to make a business of organizing caravans and dealing in the transport of valuable goods. They formed themselves into companies to finance caravans. The profits were large, amounting to as much as fifty or one hundred per cent. The towns which became the centres of their operations grew and prospered, foremost among them Mecca, halfway between South Arabia and Byzantine Palestine. The same conditions brought economic expansion to the whole of western Arabia. The town of Ṭā'if, south of Mecca, a hillside resort for the Meccans, did a roaring trade in its fruit, vegetables and wines. Throughout the Wādī l-Qurā ('the *wādī* of the towns' – this was the name of an almost continuous line of oases in the northern Hejaz) and south as far as Medina, Jewish settlements created a flourishing agricultural life.

A mercantile economy was growing up in the chinks of the nomadic world. As well as barter, money transactions using dinars (gold deniers) and dirhams (silver drachmae) were becoming commonplace. The Beduin borrowed from the rich merchants of the towns, got into debt and were sold into slavery or at any rate reduced to a dependent status. The disintegration of tribal society had begun. Large and prosperous markets grew up, like the one at 'Ukāẓ, attracting foreigners as well as Arabs from every tribe. The tribal limits had been overstepped.

Inevitably, along with this economic and social transformation, there came intellectual and moral changes. Shrewd men were seen to prosper. The traditional virtues of the sons of the desert were no longer the sure road to success. Greed, and an eye to the main chance, were much more useful. The rich became proud and overbearing, glorying in their success as a personal thing – no longer a matter for the whole tribe. The ties of blood grew weaker, giving way to others based on common interest.

At this point a new set of values began to transcend the old tribal humanism. The poor, the young and the honest were suffering from upstart arrogance. There was a vague feeling that the old tribal principles, which might have been invoked to prevent it, were somehow out of date. People began to turn to the universalist religions, religions of the individual which were concerned not with the ethnic group but with the individual salvation of each human being in his incomparable oneness. Judaism and Christianity were known, as we have seen, often in somewhat odd forms; but these were foreign faiths associated with the powers that were fighting for control of the Arab peninsula. They had all the prestige of foreignness – there was their undeniable superiority to the tribal religion and their links with mighty civilizations – but adopting them meant taking sides politically, something distinctly mortifying to Arab pride. Some hunted obscurely for something fresh, inspired by the foreign ideas to cast doubt on the powers of the countless tribal idols and to fear only Allah, who was so close to the supreme God of the Christians and the Jews.

At the same time, the Saracen lands were suffering from a sense of political inferiority. As mercenaries and auxiliaries, the Arabs were the mainstay of the great empires, who purchased their support, feared their revolts and played off the tribes against one another. Why not use their importance to their own advantage? To do that, a powerful state would be needed to unite all Arabia. It would then be in a position to safeguard its newly acquired wealth and commerce and to direct the avidity of the poorer Beduin outwards, instead of allowing it to prey on Arabia's own commercial interests. This was what the South Arabian kingdoms, with their colonizing attitude to the nomads and, for all their distant kinship, their lack of contact with the Beduin, had ultimately failed to achieve.

An Arab state, framed according to Arab ideals, tailored to the new conditions and yet still sufficiently close to the Beduin life that it had to incorporate, and able to take its place on an equal footing with the great empires – this was the great need of the times. The way was open for the man of genius who could respond to it better than any other. That man was about to be born.

3

Birth of a Prophet

NO ONE knows exactly when Muḥammad, who was to become the Prophet of Allah, was born. It was believed to have been during the reign of Khusrō Anōsharwān, that is before 579, which seems probable. It was said to have been in the Year of the Elephant – the year, that is, in which the birds of the air routed the army of Abraha before Mecca – but that is certainly untrue. The precise date, arrived at by means of some highly dubious calculations, varies between 567 and 573. The most commonly accepted year is 571.

Muḥammad, or Mahomet as we sometimes call him, was born in Mecca of a father called ʻAbdallāh and a mother whose name was Āmina. He belonged on his father's side to the clan of Hāshim of the tribe of Quraysh. These traditional statements, while not wholly incontestable, may reasonably be regarded as sure.

Mecca lies in a gorge in a range of mountains running parallel to the coast. The mountains are black and yellow, 'unbelievably bare, rocky crags with no scrap of soil, sharp, jagged, broken edges, sheer from top to bottom'.[1] The valley, which runs in a north-easterly direction, has been carved out by a wādī which, in particularly violent rainstorms, still overflows from time to time, flooding the city and its shrine so that the pilgrims have to swim their way out – as happened for instance in 1950. In this arid but well-placed valley, some fifty miles from the sea, is the famous well of Zamzam. The place may have been a sanctuary of long standing. The geographer Ptolemy, in the second century, described the region as the site of a place he called Makoraba. This could well be a transliteration of the word written in South Arabian characters (which omit the vowel sounds) as *mkrb*, in Ethiopic *mekwerāb*, meaning 'sanctuary', from which perhaps, by abbreviation, we get the historical name of the city.

At some date – not known to us – Mecca became a trading centre, probably as a result of its admirable situation at the junction of a road going from north to south, from Palestine to the Yemen, with others from east to west, connecting the Red Sea coast and the route to Ethiopia with the Persian Gulf. The sanctuary ensured that the merchants would not be molested. It was held initially by the tribe of Jurhum and afterwards passed into the hands of the Khuzā'a. Towards the end of the fifth century, perhaps, a strong man by the name of Quṣayy succeeded either by force or trickery in gaining control of the temple. He belonged to the tribe of Quraysh, an assemblage of several clans which, through him, supplanted the Khuzā'a. There may be some foundation of truth in the story that Qusayy had travelled in Syria, and had brought back from there the cult of the goddesses al-'Uzzā and Manāt, and had combined it with that of Hubal, the idol of the Khuzā'a. It has been suggested that he may actually have been a Nabataean.

In this way, Quraysh (the name means 'shark' and may have been derived from an ancient tribal emblem) acquired an ascendancy which was to grow unceasingly; and the history of the ensuing five hundred years may be seen in the light of the expansion of this one tribe to the dimensions of a world power. Quraysh was in fact composed of a number of individual clans. They were known as the Quraysh aẓ-Ẓawāhir, the 'outer Quraysh', who dwelt on the periphery, and the Quraysh al-Baṭā'iḥ, who settled in the valley bottom, immediately around the well of Zamzam and the curious shrine which stood beside it. This was like a small house, in the shape of a square box, called the Ka'ba, which means the cube. The object of especial veneration was a black stone, of meteoric origin, which may have been the cornerstone. Stones of this kind were worshipped by Arabs in most parts and by the Semitic races generally. When the young Syrian Arab Elagabalus, High Priest of the Black Stone of Emesa, was

Emperor of Rome in 219, he had the holy thing transported solemnly to Rome and built a temple for it, much to the horror of the old Romans. The Kaʿba at Mecca, which may have initially been a shrine of Hubal alone, housed several idols; a number of others, too, were gathered in the vicinity.

Later tradition tells how the four chief sons of ʿAbd Manāf, one of Quṣayy's sons, divided among themselves the areas where trade could be developed. One went to the Yemen, another to Persia, the third to Ethiopia and the fourth to Byzantine Syria. The tale is probably only legend, but it does reflect the truth. The Banū Quraysh did everything possible to foster the commercial development of their city. As we have seen, they were assisted by outside events. By about the end of the sixth century, their efforts had been rewarded by something like a position of commercial supremacy. Their caravans travelled far and wide to the cardinal points of international trade, represented by the four areas mentioned earlier. The chief merchants of Mecca had grown very rich. Mecca itself had become a meeting-place for merchants of all nations, and a fairly large number of craftsmen were to be found there. The holy place was attracting a growing number of pilgrims, who performed complicated rituals around the Kaʿba and the other small shrines round about. Judicious marriage alliances assured Quraysh of the support of the neighbouring nomadic tribes. There can be no doubt that money and, where necessary, arms provided an added incentive for friendship. Quraysh also had a part to play in international politics. What little we know points to a basic policy of neutrality, tempered by a slight leaning towards the Christian powers, Byzantium and Ethiopia. Abraha marched against the Meccans, however, and his object may have been to break their commercial hold which was damaging South Arabia. During the period 580–590 the Quraysh were at war with the tribe of the Hawāzin; a dependant of the Quraysh on one occasion killed a chieftain of the Hawāzin, who was leading a caravan for Nuʿmān, the pro-Persian king of Ḥīra.

Inevitably, the Qurayshite clans were struggling for

supremacy amongst themselves. The principal ones to come to the fore were the clans of Hāshim and ʿAbd Shams, both of whom were sons of ʿAbd Manāf. Hāshim's son, ʿAbd al-Muṭṭalib, seems to have had the upper hand at one time, at approximately the date of Muḥammad's birth; but Hāshim lost it before long to the family of Umayya, the son of ʿAbd Shams.

In general the Qurayshites were wise enough not to allow their internal squabbles to disrupt their unity in the face of the outside world. Decisions concerning them all were taken by a kind of senate, the *mala'*, an assembly of the chiefs and notables of the principal clans. But this can have been no more than a device aimed at producing agreement by discussion. There was no means of making one clan bow to the decisions of the rest except by persuasion, or compulsion of a more or less pacific nature.

ʿAbd al-Muṭṭalib may have owed his position to the fact that he was at the head of one of the coalitions formed by the Meccan clans in their struggle for power. Two of these groups were in a state of constant rivalry, while a third remained neutral. ʿAbd al-Muṭṭalib traded with Syria and the Yemen and had obtained certain profitable privileges at the shrine of Mecca. It was he who supplied the pilgrims with food and water. He is said to have entered into negotiations with Abraha when the army with its elephants appeared outside Mecca. There may be some reference here to an attempt on the part of one group of clans to win support from outside. He had a number of wives from different tribes who gave him ten sons, Muḥammad's father and uncles, as well as six daughters. Some of these we shall meet again.

One of these children was ʿAbdallāh, his son by Fāṭima bint ʿAmr of the Qurayshite clan of the Banū Makhzūm. We are told that ʿAbdallāh was a handsome fellow. His father, no doubt seeking an alliance with the clan of the Banū Zuhra, asked for the young Āmina bint Wahb as a bride for his son, and at the same time for her cousin, Hāla bint Wuhayb, of the same tribe, for himself.

In accordance with the Arab custom, Āmina seems to have remained with her own people and been visited there by ʿAbdallāh. Muḥammad was the first and only child of this marriage. While it can obviously have no historical value, it may perhaps be of interest here to cite one of the stories which circulated about Muḥammad's conception. This is in striking contrast to the Christian concern at making the birth of Christ as nearly as possible unconnected with any sexual relations whatever.

ʿAbdallāh went to the house of another wife he had besides Āmina bint Wahb. He had been working in the clay on some land he possessed, and he still had some splashes of clay left on him. He made some advances to her, but she put him off on account of the clay that was on him. He left her and washed himself, and cleaned off the clay. Then he went out again, to go to Āmina. He again passed by the other woman, who called to him; but he put her off and went to Āmina. He went in to her and possessed her. She then conceived Muḥammad, may God's blessing and peace be upon him. Then he went back to the other woman and asked her if she were willing; she said: 'No. When you passed by me there was a white light between your eyes. I called to you and you rejected me. You went to Āmina and she has taken away the light.'[2]

Another version of the story makes this woman not another of ʿAbdallāh's wives but a sister of the *ḥanīf* Waraqa ibn Nawfal,* or another woman who, like Waraqa, was versed in the scriptures. Seeing the light of prophecy upon ʿAbdallāh, she offered him a hundred camels to gain his favours. He refused her and, when he came away from Āmina, the light had gone.[3]

ʿAbdallāh died, either during his wife's pregnancy or shortly after her delivery, while on a business trip to Medina on his way home from Gaza. He left his wife very little, only one slave, five camels and a few sheep. Āmina cared for her son;

* A *ḥanif* was a man of monotheist tendency, who sought the One God, but was not willing to be enrolled in the ranks of Christianity or Judaism. See below, pp. 64-5.

but before long, when the child was only six years old, she too was dead.

Nothing is known for certain about Muḥammad's childhood. The void has gradually become filled with legends which grow ever more beautiful and edifying with the passage of time. Even the earliest and most moderate accounts must be treated with great caution. When Islam became the religion of a powerful state, precepts were needed to regulate social life. Divergent opinions and interests naturally existed. Political parties also grew up, centred round the Prophet's family and Companions. In addition, a great many people – impelled by curiosity, piety or even historical interest – demanded information about Muḥammad's life. Men began to appear who were professional repositories of traditions; they would spread a tale to satisfy this curiosity or that piety, or to provide a ruling as occasion demanded; for the Prophet's deeds had an exemplary value. When he acted in a particular way, it was to show his followers that this was the way all men should act, whether in serious matters such as the finer points of laws of succession (the principles of which were laid down by God himself in the Koran), or on the smallest details of everyday behaviour, like proper table manners. Like our modern historians, the keepers of tradition were expected to quote their sources; but these were oral ones. Such a story came from such a one who in turn had it from another, and so on all the way back to one of the Prophet's contemporaries who had seen him do it or heard him say it. It was of course a simple matter to make up false traditions (the Arabic word is *ḥadīth*, meaning 'narratives') to support one's own party or opinion. The great Arab historians and jurists knew this perfectly well. They tried to do away with the false traditions – those, for example, where the chain of authorities cited was manifestly impossible – but they made no claims to any degree of certainty. Instead, they were content to repeat contradictory traditions on the same subject, one after the other, quoting their sources for each. It was up to the reader to decide which one he liked to believe. 'But God knows best,' they would often add.

The oldest collections of historical traditions available to us date from about 125 years after the Prophet's lifetime. Much imagination may have gone to work in the meantime. And yet many facts can be established, as the parties who differ most widely are agreed on the main events of the Prophet's life, the names of his Companions and his wives, their kinship and genealogy, as well as on a great many other things, even down to details which are far from remarkable which nobody would have deemed worth inventing. But there are many points on which we are very far from certain; in particular, it is clear that little was known about the early years of Muḥammad's life, and that much has been made up about it. I shall occasionally quote some of these tales, whose only virtue from an historical point of view is that they create a picture of a world not unlike that in which the young Muḥammad must have grown up, besides giving us some idea of the way in which later Muslims pictured the life of their prophet.

According to the Qurayshites' custom, the young Muḥammad had a nurse from a nomadic clan. In this way, it was thought, the children of Quraysh would be filled with the pure air of the desert and grow strong. It was also a way of maintaining contact with the nomads – no small consideration, when we remember that foster-brotherhood was regarded as a powerful bond between two men. Muḥammad's nurse was a woman called Ḥalīma, of the clan of the Banū Sa'd, a branch of the great tribe of Hawāzin. She may have been the one mentioned in a traditional story, which I will quote here simply as a typical example of the amazing liveliness of these tales, which is however no guarantee of authenticity. It is recorded in the history of the Prophet and his Companions set down in writing by Ibn Sa'd at the beginning of the second century of the hegira (the ninth century A.D.).

We have it from 'Abdallāh ibn Numayr al-Hamdāni who had it from Yaḥyā ibn Sa'īd al-Anṣāri, that Muḥammad ibn al-Munkadir used to tell how a woman knocked on the door of the Prophet whose nurse she had been. When she went in he cried out, 'Mother, Mother!' and, fetching his cloak, spread it before her, and she sat on it.[4]

There is another tale about how the nurse came to choose the child.

Ten women of the Banū Sa'd came to Mecca to look for infants to nurse. All found them, except for Ḥalīma bint 'Abdallāh, who had with her her husband al-Ḥārith ibn 'Abd al-'Uzzā who was called Abū Dhu'ayb and their child 'Abdallāh ibn al-Ḥārith whom she was suckling and [their daughters] Anīsa and Judāma, she of the beauty spot who [later] carried Muḥammad with her mother and bore him on her hip. The Envoy of Allah was shown to her, but she said: 'An orphan! And with no money! And what can his mother do?' And the women departed and left her behind. Then Ḥalīma said to her husband: 'What do you think? My companions have gone and there is no boy left in Mecca to nurse except this orphan. Shall we take him? I should not like to return home with nothing.' Her husband said to her: 'Take him! Perhaps Allah will make him a blessing to us.' So she returned to the mother and took the child and set him on her lap and gave him her breast until milk trickled down from it. And the Envoy of Allah drank until he was satisfied. And his [foster]-brother also drank. Now this brother was not asleep because he was hungry [because his mother had little milk before this]. And the mother [Āmina] said: 'Nurse, question me about your [foster]-son, because he will be great.' And she told her what she had seen and what had been said at the time of his birth. . . . Ḥalīma was happy and rejoiced at all she heard. Then she departed to her own place with the babe. They saddled their she-ass, and Ḥalīma mounted, holding the Envoy of Allah before her. Al-Ḥārith rode on their aged camel. They caught up with their companions at Wādī Sirar. . . . 'Ḥalīma,' they said, 'what have you done?' And she answered: 'By God, I have taken the fairest babe that ever I saw, and he with the greatest *baraka* [a "blessed virtue", a mysterious, wonder-working force coming from God].' The women said, 'Is not that the child of 'Abd al-Muṭṭalib?' She answered, 'Yes.' 'Before we left that place,' Ḥalīma added, 'I saw envy in [the faces of] several of our women.'

It is to these years spent in the desert that a marvellous experience, assigned by other authors to different points in the Prophet's life, has been said to relate. Two angels came and, opening his breast, drew out the heart which they cleaned scrupulously before returning it to its place. Then they weighed him, putting in the other side of the scales first one man, then ten, then a hundred and then a thousand. Then one said to the other: 'Let be. Even if you were to set his whole community (*umma*) in the scale, he would still outweigh it.'[5]

Āmina died on the way home from a journey to Medina with her slave Umm Ayman and young Muḥammad. The boy was six years old. His grandfather, the venerable 'Abd al-Muṭṭalib, who was then eighty years old, took him to live with him. But he died two years later. Muḥammad was then taken in by one of his uncles, 'Abd Manāf, who is more generally known later by his *kunya*, or second name, Abū Ṭālib. (An Arab's second or more familiar name means 'father of', and generally referred to his eldest son.) In fact the meaning of his first name was idolatrous, signifying 'servant of the goddess Manāf'. He was a merchant in comfortable circumstances, the son of the same mother as Muḥammad's father 'Abdallāh, and is said to have been the person who took over the leadership of the Hāshim clan – said to predominate at Mecca at this time – after his father's death.

The story goes that Abū Ṭālib sometimes travelled into Syria leading a caravan. On one occasion, at least, he is said to have taken his nephew. They came to the town of Bostra (Buṣrā), the first big junction on the caravan route travelling in this direction, a meeting place of five important roads, and a great centre of Christianity. A fine cathedral had been built there not long before, and there were other impressive monuments, such as the Roman theatre which can still be seen today, and also no doubt the poor-house erected by Justinian. It was also the official residence of the Monophysite bishop, whose authority extended over the desert Arabs and whose appointment the Ghassānid phylarch al-Ḥārith had obtained from the Empress Theodora in 543. It was at Bostra that an incident is said to have taken place, one version of which the historian Ṭabarī recounts as follows:

When the company halted at Bostra in Syria, there was a monk named Baḥīrā, who dwelt in a hermitage there and who was well-read in the learning of the Christians. There had always been a monk in this hermitage, who used to extract this learning from a book which, they claimed, had been handed down as an heirloom from one to another. This year, when the caravan halted near Baḥīrā, he prepared much food for them. While he was in his hermitage, he had seen the Envoy of Allah among his companions; and a cloud covered him with its shadow. They came forward, and halted in the shade of a tree that was near Baḥīrā. He looked at the cloud, but the tree gave shade and its branches leaned down over the Envoy of Allah so that he was always in their shade. When Baḥīrā saw this, he came out from his cell and sent word to invite them all. When Baḥīrā saw the Envoy of Allah, he watched him very closely, and noted the details of his person. . . . When the party had finished eating and were about to take their leave, he questioned the Envoy of Allah about the things he felt when he was awake or asleep. The Envoy of Allah answered him. Baḥīrā found all this according to the description which he had in his possession. Then he examined his back and found the seal of prophecy between his shoulders. Then Baḥīrā said to his uncle Abū Ṭālib: 'What relation is this boy to you?' And Abū Ṭālib answered: 'He is my son.' Baḥīrā said to him: 'He is not your son. This boy's father cannot be living.' 'He is my nephew,' Abū Ṭālib told him then. The monk asked: 'What became of his father?' 'He died while his mother was pregnant.' 'You speak the truth. Go back then to your own land and keep him safe from the Jews. By Allah, if they see him and get to know what I know about him they will try to harm him.'[6]

The uncle, much impressed, hurried back to Mecca with the precious child. Is there any kernel of truth in this story? We cannot be sure. There can be no doubt that some of the motives behind it are apologetic. It was important to have the Prophet recognized as such by one of the great monotheistic religions from which Islam claimed descent. The Christians took up the legend, seeing the supposedly heretical monk as the Arab prophet's inspiration, so as to deprive him of all originality. There is nothing intrinsically improbable in the journey to Bostra or in any other journeys. Attempts have been made to gather evidence that Muḥammad was acquainted with many lands; but on the other hand it has been observed that he seems to have had no first-hand knowledge of the rites of the Christian faith. If he had been present, even once, at one of its services, it would certainly have left some impression. The Arab poets who visited Ḥīra and its churches describe them with much more animation.

Tradition lays great stress on Abū Ṭālib's fondness for his nephew and his good care of him. It has been suggested that here, too, hagiography may have twisted the facts. At all events, Muḥammad no doubt had to perform the small services expected of a child. One day, long afterwards, when some people passed the Prophet carrying the fruits of the *arāk* tree, a thorny bush used to feed camels and other animals, Muḥammad is supposed to have told them: 'Take care of the black fruit. It was those I gathered when I used to lead the sheep out to graze.' They said to him: 'Envoy of Allah, were you then a shepherd of sheep?' He answered: 'Yes, and so have all prophets been.'[7] The story was told to humble the pride of the great nomad camelherds, who despised the shepherds of more humble flocks.

This is virtually all we know about the childhood and young manhood of the future Prophet, at least from earlier sources, before the proliferation of legends of all kinds grew out of all reasonable control. Obviously it is not very much, and we are on very shaky ground. And yet it would be interesting and, from a historical point of view, extremely valuable to know what kind of education he had. Muslim tradition insists that he had no dealing with the pagan cults of his native city. This seems unlikely, and there are clear indications in his later life to suggest that, like everyone else, he practised the religion of his fathers. We are told elsewhere that he sacrificed a sheep to the goddess al-'Uzzā. One little-known tradition has him offering meat which had been sacrificed to idols to a monotheist, who refused it and rebuked him.[8] He is said to have belonged to the *ḥums*, a brotherhood which practised its own special rites at Meccan ceremonies and observed additional taboos. Whatever Arabic tradition may have assumed from a wrong interpretation of a word in the Koran, it seems certain that Muḥammad learned to read and write. But except for a few vague and unreliable pointers in his life and work we have no way of knowing the extent of his learning. More will be said of this further on.

Muḥammad seems to have remained a bachelor for longer than was usual among his people. The reason for this was probably poverty. He asked, it is said, Abū Ṭālib for the hand of his cousin Umm Hānī. Marriages between cousins were approved of in Beduin society; but the suitor was rejected, probably in favour of a more illustrious rival. Long afterwards Umm Hānī, then widowed, would have been glad to have her cousin renew his offer, but Muḥammad was no longer inclined; they remained, however, on good terms. He was sleeping in Umm Hānī's house the night he made his nocturnal voyage to heaven.

Fortune soon favoured him. Without falling into the traditional exaggerations which make him as early as this period a model of physical, intellectual and moral perfection, the qualities he displayed later are enough to show that he must have made a favourable impression on those with whom he came in contact. Even at this stage, people must have been struck by his intelligence, and his calm, confident and balanced manner of conducting himself both in his own affairs and in his dealing with others. It was probably this quality which led Khadīja bint Khuwaylid, a widow no longer in her first youth, who had already been twice married and had several children, to engage him in her employ. She was rich, and equipped caravans to travel into Syria to bring back Byzantine merchandise for sale on the Mecca market. Khadīja seems to have sent her new employee with the caravans to deal with purchasing. If this was so, Muḥammad must have revisited Syria; and this has provided an opportunity for the traditions to introduce more monks, who comment once again on the miracles attending the young Qurayshite's passage and predict a brilliant future for him. What is quite certain is that Muḥammad's exertions on Khadīja's behalf aroused in her the wish to marry him. She may already have been aware of Muḥammad's charm when she engaged him. In any event the lot of unmarried women among the Arabs was not an enviable one. Her father, if he were still alive, could act as her protector, but she had every reason to regard the future with apprehension. Khadīja is said to have been forty, but she had no lack of suitors. Muḥammad would then have been twenty-five. The inevitable go-between, Nafīsa bint Munya, is credited with saying:

> Khadīja sent me to Muḥammad to sound out his feelings after he came back from Syria with his caravan. I said to him: 'Muḥammad, is there any reason why you should not marry?' He told me: 'I possess nothing to marry on.' I answered him: 'And suppose there was someone who had enough for two? And suppose you were summoned to beauty, wealth, and to a position of honour and ease, would you not accept?' 'Who is the woman?' 'Khadīja.' 'What must I do?' 'I will attend to all.' 'And I too will do my part.'

Nothing remained but to complete the necessary formalities. Some accounts added that this was not easy and that Khadīja had to get her father drunk in order to obtain his consent; but most traditions say that by this time her father was long dead and it was her uncle who represented her family in the marriage.

His marriage to Khadīja was the saving of Muḥammad and opened the door to a brilliant future. He had no further material anxieties. From the poor relation of a great family, earning his living in the service of others, he became a person of importance. He must have seen God's hand at work in this; and, one day, he heard Allah say to him:

> Your Lord has not taken leave of you, nor despised you . . .
> Did he not find you an orphan and give [you] shelter?
> He found you erring and guided you.
> He found you poor and enriched you.
>
> (Koran xciii)

It is unlikely that he felt for Khadīja the physical passion which was later to procure him, in his old age, the young and lovely women of his future harem. But he always had a great respect for her and a firm affection and gratitude which never wavered. A psychoanalyst has suggested that the frustrations of an orphan, deprived of his mother's warmth at an early age, may have strengthened this attachment to an older woman. Muḥammad used to say that she was the best of all the women of her time, and that he would live with her in paradise in a house built of reeds, in peace and tranquillity. He spoke of her often after her death, much to the fury of his beloved 'Ā'isha. 'Ā'isha described her jealousy of the dead woman, whom she had never met, as beyond what she felt for anyone in the world. One day Khadīja's sister Hāla came to the Prophet's door, and asked to be let in. He recognized her voice and was thrilled. He cried out: 'My God, it's Hāla!' 'Then', said 'Ā'isha, 'I was seized with jealousy and screamed: "Why do you have to be always remembering that toothless old Qurayshite with her red mouth? Fate made her die and God has replaced her with a better!"'[9]

Khadīja gave Muḥammad several children. There were four daughters of whom we shall have more to say, Zaynab, Ruqayya, Fāṭima and Umm Kulthūm. But what for an Arab was then, and still is, a great misfortune, all her sons died at an early age. Tradition lists them variously. One was al-Qāsim, who is said to have died when he was two and from whom his father took the *kunya* of Abū l-Qāsim, which he was to retain. There also seems to have been an 'Abdallāh, who may in fact have been named 'Abd Manāf, in token of respect to the deity Manāf whom his parents were soon to reject. At about this time Muḥammad adopted his young cousin 'Alī, whose father, Muḥammad's uncle Abū Ṭālib, was experiencing some business difficulties. Khadīja also made Muḥammad a present of a slave whom her nephew had bought in Syria – a young man from the tribe of Kalb, of strong Christian affiliations, whose name was Zayd. Muḥammad gave him his freedom and adopted him as a son.

Now that he was prosperous he certainly continued in business. His language was always studded with commercial terms. He was well thought of by his colleagues. His daughters later made respectable marriages – right and proper, and according to custom. Ruqayya, and perhaps Umm Kulthūm as well, married their cousins on the father's side, sons of Abū Lahab. He was one of Muḥammad's uncles and later to become one of his greatest enemies. However, he seems at this time to have been in an excellent social position, taking over from his brother Abū Ṭālib as leader of the clan of Hāshim. Another daughter, Zaynab, married her maternal cousin, Abū l-ʿĀṣ.

The following story, if true, would be an indication of the regard in which Muḥammad was held. Unfortunately it has certainly been embellished and may even be an outright invention, whose purpose was apologetic. The Kaʿba had fallen into disrepair and people had taken advantage of its dilapidated state to steal its treasures. The Qurayshites, at the height of their financial prosperity, decided to rebuild it, but hesitated to touch the sacred stones in order to carry out the demolition work initially required. Moreover they lacked materials and skilled workmen. The timely wreck in the Red Sea of a Greek ship, carrying wood to Abyssinia for the building of a church, seemed to them like a sign from heaven. They appropriated the cargo washed up on the shore of the Hejaz and also a Coptic carpenter named Pacomius who happened to be on board. The rebuilding proceeded at a good pace, after the initial panic when a bold man took it on himself to strike the first blow with his pick at the old building. The whole town spent an anxious night expecting him to be struck down by supernatural powers; but in the morning he was still in excellent health, and the work went on. At last the time came to replace the Black Stone at the corner of the building. The four tribal groups all laid claim to the honour and in the heat of the argument were on the point of coming to blows. They decided to appeal to the first man who came into the sanctuary as arbiter. This was Muḥammad. He sent for a cloak and, placing the sacred stone inside, made a representative of each tribe hold one of the four corners. They raised the cloak and carried the stone to its place. Then he himself set it in position.

Muḥammad would then have been thirty-five years old. He was given, it is said, the name of *al-amīn* – the sure man, in whom one could trust. He was rich, or at least comfortably off, surrounded by affection, respected by all and with a part to play in his own small sphere. He might have gone on living like this, quietly and happily. Everything was in favour of it.

And yet he was not satisfied with this humdrum existence, day in, day out. He had an underlying restlessness. He wanted something more. His fundamental psychology in every detail will always be a mystery; but, while laying no claim to any impossible and almost certainly misleading analysis, yet, taking into account the trends of human behaviour pointed out for us by Freud, it is possible to make some observations on which to build some kind of psychological hypothesis.

In general, Muḥammad gave the impression of a sensible, deliberate and well-balanced man. All his life we find him thinking before taking a decision, conducting his public and private business efficiently, knowing when to bide his time and when to retract, and capable of taking the necessary action to ensure the success of his plans. His physical courage, although perhaps acquired rather than instinctive, was adequate to enable him to figure creditably in the various battles of his lifetime. He was a remarkably able diplomat, and capable of reasoning with clarity, logic and lucidity. And yet, beneath this surface, was a temperament which was nervous, passionate, restless, feverish – filled with an impatient yearning which burned for the impossible. This was so intense as to lead to nervous crises of a definitely pathological kind.

Muḥammad had, as the phrase goes, everything to make him happy, and yet he was not happy. Happiness, with its limitations, its calm or eager acceptance, its resignation to things as they are, is not made for those who are always looking beyond what they are and what they have, whose questing spirit is always reaching out for the next thing to be desired. And a poor, deprived, orphan childhood such as Muḥammad's was bound to foster the growth of this endless capacity for desiring. Only success on an extraordinary, one might even say superhuman, scale, would satisfy it.

Muḥammad was certainly dissatisfied. Were there more tangible reasons for an attitude of mind without which his later development cannot be understood, and if so what were they? We can glimpse them faintly. Strange as it may seem to us, one of the things which affected him most was the fact that he had no male heir. With the Arabs, as with the Semitic peoples in general, this was a source of shame; and men who suffered it were called by the name of *abtar*, which means roughly 'mutilated'. One day, in the early days of his prophecy, Muḥammad the *abtar* heard a voice from heaven declaiming to him these vengeful lines:

> Yes, we have given you abundance.
> So pray your Lord and sacrifice;
> It is your enemy who is the *abtar*!
> (Koran cviii)

Khadīja's inability to give him male heirs no doubt provided an additional reason for some dissatisfaction with his excellent wife. One recalls Ammianus' comments on 'the passion with which the two sexes abandon themselves to love among this nation [the Arabs]'. And, of the doctors of the Talmud, Rabbi Nathan declared that nowhere in the world was there such a propensity towards fornication as among the Arabs, just as nowhere was there any power like that of Persia, or wealth like that of Rome, or magic like that of Egypt. The same observed that, if all the sexual licence in the world were divided into ten parts, then nine of these would be distributed among the Arabs and the tenth would be enough for all the other races.[10] All around him Muḥammad saw the wealthy Qurayshites using and abusing the pleasures of love. Each man, merchants and travellers especially, was allowed by custom to take wives for a limited period. Polygamy was perhaps less widespread than has been suggested, but divorce was simple and frequent. Outright prostitution, not readily distinguishable from temporary marriage, also occurred. Religious rites seem to have involved occasional ritual copulation. Young and beautiful slave-girls were easily bought. But Muḥammad was wedded to Khadīja and to her alone. It is possible that their marriage contract involved an obligation on his part to take no second wife. The wealthy Khadīja was in a position to make demands. But, as a man known for his belief in fairness and moderation, Muḥammad was bound to the mother of his children by ties much stronger than any written undertaking. Even so, knowing what we do of his amorous proclivities later on in life, we can scarcely imagine that there were not plenty of times when he, in the Gospel phrase which would probably have astounded him, 'committed adultery in his heart'. He must have thrust away temptation many times, perhaps even with deceptive ease. But whether they appeared easy or hard, we know now what these victories may have cost him and what a sense of frustration they may have left behind.

Yet another cause of dissatisfaction, and one less often remarked, was the driving spur of ambition – legitimate ambition, due to a very clear consciousness of his own worth. Muḥammad no doubt considered himself an exceptional person from a very early age. He saw few of the people around him take any interest in the religious, moral and intellectual questions which occupied him. The rich Qurayshites, his relatives and friends, acquired political influence by virtue of their wealth, their capacity for intrigue and their apparent competence in dealing with public affairs. Muḥammad's interests at the time must have gained him the reputation of an inoffensive idealist, quite unfitted to cope with practical matters. And yet he had a deep inner conviction that what he knew and what he foresaw was more important than all the complex calculations of political men, even in the worldly perspective of effective guidance of the Meccan community, and perhaps beyond it, in that of the Arabs as a whole.

The troubles of a man mocked for his lack of male heirs, the frustration of a highly sexed man whose own moral conscience prevented him from realizing his desires, the suppressed fury of a man fundamentally sure of himself but treated with contempt by practical politicians – all these things were capable of creating a personality thirsting to turn the tables in each particular, but still keeping strictly within the normal bounds of the society in which he lived. There was something in Muḥammad which made him overstep those bounds.

This something was a certain pathological element in his make-up. Perhaps the stories about the angels who came and took him and opened his heart while he was pasturing flocks belonging to his nurse's family actually developed from accounts of some kind of seizure. Ḥalīma is said to have come up on him one day standing amazed and stupefied. When questioned, he told a story of two men in white robes who came to him and opened his breast and touched 'something, I know not what'. His foster-father was worried and said: 'Ḥalīma, I fear that this boy may have had an attack. Take him back to his family before his disease declares itself.' Muḥammad, it will be remembered, was no more than six years old.[11]

This story may be a complete fabrication. It may be, too, that as a child Muḥammad had some mental experience of the kind known to many shamans of north and central Asia, and also to Australian magicians: at the moment of their initiation they feel that a spirit has taken away their internal organs and replaced them with fresh ones. However that may be, the Prophet certainly suffered from attacks of some kind in adult life. Hostile Christians put it down to epilepsy. If this were so, it was a benign form. What is much more probable is that Muḥammad's psycho-physiological constitution was basically of the kind found in many mystics.

In all societies and among all races individuals are found who, because of something in their constitution or their personal history which it is the psychiatrist's job to unravel, find it difficult or even impossible to adjust to the roles which society expects of them. In some cases their behaviour brings them into violent conflict with their environment. Others succeed in making some kind of adjustment, especially since many societies have allotted exceptional roles to these exceptional people. This often takes the form of making those with a particular kind of abnormality responsible for contacts with the supernatural world, the world of gods and spirits.

Some of these individuals possess exceptional gifts. They see things which others do not see, hear things which others do not hear. A feeling they cannot explain makes them utter words and gestures which are quite outside the normal behaviour patterns of ordinary people. All this is naturally put down to their contact with another world – the world of powers which, while they cannot normally be seen or heard, can perform what to the common run of mortals is impossible. Some of these extraordinary beings are, of course, very far from normal; while in others the strangeness and abnormality manifests itself only rarely, in particular circumstances, and in the course of everyday life they behave just like everyone else. There are some whose inferior mental capacities are not enhanced by their special peculiarities; others, on the contrary, possess complex and powerful personalities with a capacity for rich and original thought.

Pre-Islamic Arabia had its own share of such men. Arab poets were believed to be inspired by a spirit. Above all, there was the *kāhin* or soothsayer, a word etymologically related to the *kōhen* or priest of the Jews. The *kāhins* had visions; but, what was more important, they also possessed familiar spirits, which they called companions or friends or 'seers' and which spoke through their mouths. The spirits' inspiration took the form of a vague mumbling or of short, staccato rhymed phrases, with repeated oaths which called freely on the names of the stars, morning and evening, plants and animals – all delivered in a breathless, rhythmic voice which made a great impression on the audience. While they were prophesying in this way, the *kāhins* would cover themselves with their cloaks. They were highly respected, appealed to and consulted as oracles and advisers in both public and private matters.

Muḥammad had many traits in common with the *kāhins*, as his contemporaries could not fail to notice. Physiologically and psychologically he belonged, undoubtedly, to the same type.

Like them, he was liable to emotional attacks, with a tendency to see, hear and feel things beyond the reach of other people's senses. It may be that the deep-rooted dissatisfaction, which was both the cause and effect of his temperament as he approached the age of forty, helped to strengthen his natural predisposition. But because he was endowed with a vastly richer and more powerful personality than that of the average *kāhin*, this dissatisfaction also led him to think deeply. Alongside the effects of his innate temperament and of his private emotional life, a complete intellectual structure was developing. And this intellectual development was something quite exceptional.

Muḥammad was not a *kāhin*. He did not find lost camels or interpret dreams. Nor did he set himself up as a professional seer, adviser in supernatural matters to a particular tribe or prince, although such a post might carry a good deal of prestige. But again, this would have been to associate himself and his particular psychic gifts with the whole social and intellectual framework of Arab society, which, unconsciously, he was trying to transcend. He remained an ordinary trader, a good husband and father and a prudent sensible man; but he was learning and thinking all the time. Little by little his spirit was advancing along the road which was to lead him far beyond the limits of his own time and place.

The questions he asked himself came to him above all in their religious aspects. Once again war had broken out between the great powers of the day, Persia and Byzantium, and this time the conflict was assuming unexpected proportions. To a highly placed civil servant like Procopius its political and economic foundations were perfectly clear, but in the eyes of the masses the struggle was first and foremost an ideological one. As we have seen, the war had begun again in 572; but in 591 the new Persian King of kings, Khusrō II, called Abharwēz, 'the Victorious', who had gained the throne with the aid of the Romans, had made peace on terms highly favourable to his protectors. Before long he was burning to get back what he had ceded. Khusrō's friend, the basileus Maurice, had been deposed and killed in 602 by a revolt of the army which brought to power a brutal and quick-tempered officer named Phocas. The king of kings seized on this as an excuse for reopening the war. The Persians made rapid and astonishing progress. One army overran Roman Armenia, went on to invade Asia Minor and, in 610, its advance scouts reached the Bosphorus within sight of Constantinople. Another army moved into Syria, and the cities of northern Mesopotamia fell one after another. Antioch was under siege. The Monophysites of Syria were up in arms. The Jews took advantage of the confusion and of the Persian advance to take their revenge. Acting in collusion with the political and sporting anti-government faction, they killed the pro-imperial Patriarch of Antioch. Faced with imminent disaster, the malcontents raised to power another soldier, this time a man of real ability, Heraclius; he entered Constantinople in October 610. Phocas was put to death. While Heraclius was slowly gathering his army for the counter-attack, the Persians continued their successful advance. Antioch fell in 611 and then, the ultimate disaster, on 5 May 614, the holy city of Jerusalem itself. The Patriarch and the inhabitants were taken into captivity, the churches burned and the most sacred relic of the True Cross removed with great ceremony to Ctesiphon. In 615 the Persian general Shāhēn took Chalcedon, across the strait from Constantinople. Between 617 and 619, the Persians occupied Egypt, the granary of the empire and of the capital in particular. The Avars and the Slavs were menacing in the west. Byzantium was at the lowest ebb.

There were some Christians on the Persian side. Khusrō had a favourite, a Christian girl from Syria whose name was Shīrēn; the story of their love has provided material for endless romances in every language of the Muslim east. The Nestorians continued to support him. His high treasurer, Yazdēn, was a Christian who was constantly building churches and monasteries. The Monophysites, who were the dominant sect in Syria and Egypt, if they did not actually help the Persians because of their alliance with the Nestorians, made no effort to defend the empire. For two centuries at least they had been in a state of moral secession, religious differences serving to accentuate and bring out purely local difficulties such as the quasi-nationalist feelings of rebellion against Greek dominance, feelings which were encouraged by a progressive economic decline. However, viewed from a distance, it was the attitude of the Jews which more than anything gave the conflict, to some extent at least, the appearance of a war of religion. This was how the tale was told with embellishments in distant Gaul.

A Burgundian chronicler, writing some thirty or forty years after the event, described Heraclius as 'pleasant to look on, with a handsome face, tall and very active and a valiant warrior. Alone and unarmed, he would often kill lions in the arena and wild boars in remote places.' When the Persians came in sight of his capital, he proposed to their emperor, Cosdroës, to settle the quarrel by single combat. Cosdroës sent a gallant nobleman to fight for him; Heraclius killed him by a cunning trick, whereupon the Persians fled. But Heraclius was 'well versed in letters', and had therefore studied astrology. Thanks to this art he had learned that his empire would be devastated by peoples who practised circumcision. Concluding that this must refer to the Jews, he 'sent to Dagobert, king of the Franks, to entreat him to give orders that all the Jews in his realm should be baptized in the Catholic faith; this Dagobert instantly performed. Heraclius ordered that the same thing should be done throughout all the imperial provinces; for he had no idea whence this scourge would come upon his empire.'[12]

There can be no doubt that in Arabia, too, these events made a great impression. Among the Jews and the various Christian sects, propaganda was rife. The social conditions which favoured its growth have already been described. Anyone in Mecca who was interested could easily find Jews and Christians who were only too ready to explain the basic tenets of their faith. In the case of the Christians it was unfortunate that they knew very little about their own religion. They were for the most part poor folk – traders, butchers, smiths, bloodcuppers, pedlars, wine-sellers, adventurers and slaves. They had no organized community, no priests or churches. They belonged to different sects, each convinced that the rest were heretics. They were certainly none too well up in theology. Their religion was the popular faith of simple people. They probably had a few prayers, and were certainly acquainted, in somewhat garbled versions, with the beautiful stories of the Old and New Testaments. The Jews, on the other hand, whose activities as agricultural settlers have already been noted, were numerous and well organized throughout Arabia. But their communities were tightly knit and closed. In Mecca – where people suffered from their commercial competition and feared the potential power of such busy and energetic bodies, and where they wondered at their curious habits, such as their reluctance to eat such foods as camel-hump lard, which everyone else liked, and mocked their clumsy Arabic, full of words culled from Hebrew or Aramaic – Jews seem to have been comparatively rare. Even so, they too were not averse to recounting, for the benefit of curious idolaters, the biblical tales we find in the Talmuds and the whole body of Midrashic works, which had been expanded and embellished by writers of Hellenistic and Roman times. Some of them seem to have had the idea of bringing the revelation and its sequels within the reach of Arab hearers by giving some events an Arabian setting, or by giving a Jewish angle to popular Arab tales.

We have irrefutable evidence from the text of the Koran itself that Muḥammad was accused of listening to men who spoke a foreign language (Koran xvi, 105) and who told 'legends about the ancients' (Koran xxv, 5). These were certainly stories that he listened to most carefully. By their light he gradually pieced together a picture of the world and its history. Jews and Christians told him about the same God, Allah, 'the Divine One', who was also worshipped in Arabia alongside other gods. He it was who had created heaven and earth; to him were due the wonders of nature, such amazing phenomena as storms, lightning and rain. His were the miracle of the human body, the mysteries of animal reproduction, the secrets of the vegetable kingdom. He would resurrect the bodies of men after death and be sovereign judge of all mortals, rewarding them according to the manner of their lives on earth, either with the delights of a celestial garden or the sufferings of a place of torment. In this way the mysteries of the world were resolved around us, and its injustices set right. This vision of the world was clearly superior, both intellectually and morally, to that of the pagan Arabs in which dozens of minor gods contended capriciously, yet without decisive influence upon the decrees of Allah or Fate, and, above all, where Justice did not emerge triumphantly from all this universal anarchy.

Moreover, Allah had thought to make himself known to men and to make known his will. Several times he had sent men, the prophets, to expound his revelation to his chosen peoples. Already Adam had received such a message, and after him the patriarchs listed by the Hebrews – not all of whom were, strictly speaking, Jews, as the Christians did not fail to point out: Noah, the ancestor of all living men, Abraham, who, according to the accepted explanation of the story of Ishmael and Agar, was the ancestor not only of the Jews but also of the Saracens (hence the name of Agarenians, by which they are designated in the writings of the period). Jacob, Joseph and above all Moses had all been charged with messages for Israel. The great prophets had made little impression on the popular imagination, but it did retain from Jewish sacred history the kinds of things simple folk would remember: David overcoming Goliath, the wisdom of Solomon, Lot disputing with the Sodomites, Jonah and the whale, Elijah contending with the prophets of Baal, Job on his dungheap . . .

The Christians, too, spoke of Jesus, whom they believed was the son of God and a god himself, and of other highly involved and, to unsophisticated minds, incomprehensible matters. In addition, they argued furiously among themselves as to the divine and human natures of the Messiah, even going to the point of waging war over it. Yet Jesus too had been charged with Good News, a Gospel for mankind. He was very like the prophets; he had associated himself with them and had been regarded as such. He was, to be sure, a highly remarkable prophet, a most superior prophet, when one thought of all the delightful and fascinating stories that were told about his mother, Mary (and wasn't there a virgin Mary who sang hymns of praise in the story of Moses? Surely she would be the same?), and of his miraculous birth. Why reject such a good story, as the Jews did? If it was hard to believe that he was the son of God, without falling back into the Arabic polytheism which was just what one was trying to get away from, or plunging into incomprehensible theological arguments on nature, person, essence and hypostasis, could one not simply look on him as one of the prophets, the greatest and most wonderful of them all?

There was another belief very widespread throughout the east which added still more prophets to all these. Mānī (216–277), a native of Babylonia, was the founder of a new religion, Manichaeism, which also had its days of glory and expansion. Mānī claimed to be one of a series of messengers sent from God to the different peoples. In his own words:

> Wisdom and good works have been brought in perfect succession from age to age by the messengers of God. They came in one age through the prophet called Buddha in the region of India, in another through Zarādusht [Zoroaster] in the land of Persia, and in yet another through Jesus in the lands of the west. After this came the revelation, and prophecy manifests itself in this latter age through myself, Mānī, the messenger of the True God in the land of Babel.[13]

Mānī inherited his ideas from those of various dissident Christian sects of Gnostic inspiration. According to the apocryphal Acts of the Apostles, the Apostles had divided the different regions of the world between them so that each should have its share in the Gospel.[14] It seemed a flagrant injustice for one country to have escaped the teaching of the divine word.

The Arabs who listened to all these tales would then recall the legendary stories of the former inhabitants of the peninsula, to whom were attributed the ancient monuments found there. They talked of vanished peoples, of 'Ād and Thamūd and of the catastrophes which had struck them. Surely it was conceivable that these catastrophes might have come as a punishment for rejecting the prophets who were sent to them? In just this manner had the Flood punished those men who were deaf to Noah's warnings; and Jesus had threatened Jerusalem, 'that killeth the prophets', with a similar fate.

Arabs like Muḥammad heard these stories, and reflected upon them. Jews and Christians were sustained by world-wide empires and belonged to rich and powerful organizations. Their claims rested on sacred books sent from heaven in ancient times, revered for their antiquity, their worth proven by miracles. They knew the secrets of Allah, they knew how he wished to be worshipped, what prayers and sacrifices, what fasts and processions he required if he was to look kindly on men. The Arabs did not know these secrets, the Arabs were set apart from Allah. They must learn from those who knew, from the People of the Book, and so try to come closer to Allah.

There must have been some at least who thought in this way and yet did not become either Christians or Jews. We have seen the considerations of national pride which prevented many Arabs from accepting such a conversion. Perhaps they were already becoming known as *ḥanīfs* towards Allah – a word derived, most probably, from a misinterpretation of an Aramaic word meaning 'unbelievers'. This came to mean that they were seeking to draw closer to Allah without becoming enrolled in the ranks of the recognized religions. They may already have begun to observe that, by the Jews' and the Christians' own accounts, before the foundation of Judaism by Moses, men like Abraham (Ibrāhīm in Arabic) whom they revered had held much the same attitude. The Bible itself said that Abraham was the ancestor of the Arabs through his son Ishmael. Surely it was natural therefore for the Arabs to follow their ancestor's example and worship Allah independently of the established religions?

Both Jews and Christians despised the Arabs, regarding them as some kind of savages who did not even possess an organized Church like civilized people. It may have been pride that made the Arabs adopt the name of *ḥanīf* ('pagan' or 'infidel') put upon them by their 'civilized' neighbours. They were infidels, and as infidels they sought God. Many of them were actuated by a certain spirit of revolt against the pretensions of the other nations who humiliated them at every turn. On a political plane, too, as we have seen, the Byzantine emperor Maurice had demolished the Arab phylarchy of the Ghassānids. Across the border, Khusrō Abharwēz had grown suspicious of his Arab vassal in Ḥīra, Nuʿmān III, a Christian famous in Arab poetry, and in 602 or thereabouts he had him imprisoned and put to death. The crown taken from the Lakhmid family was bestowed on a man chosen from a remote tribe with no tradition of government, with, in addition, a Persian inspector to keep a close eye on him. However, the new 'king' of Ḥīra promptly sent word to the shaikh of the Arab tribe of Bakr, which was also an auxiliary of the Persians, to ask for money, weapons and a thousand shields which had been left with him by Nuʿmān before his imprisonment. The Arab chief refused. Khusrō sent a large army against him, made up of Arab auxiliaries with a thousand Persian horse. The battle which took place near the well of Dhū Qār, not far from what was later to be Kūfa, resulted in the rout of the Persians, who lost both their generals, and of their Arab allies. On learning the news at Mecca Muḥammad was said to have exclaimed: 'This is the first time the Arabs have avenged themselves on the Persians.' It was not to be the last.

However, both the Arabs' mortifications and this first flicker of revenge were only incidents in an overall picture rich in apocalyptic hues. The struggle between the two great powers was reaching its climax. The fall of the Second Rome might be the outcome. The Jews were taking their revenge on the Christians. Everywhere foreign war was accompanied by internal troubles. All this was known in Arabia. As so often in history, many people thought it heralded the end of the world.

The Arabs themselves were humiliated abroad while wickedness triumphed at home. The rich and powerful oppressed the poor. The immemorial laws of tribal solidarity were broken daily. The weak and the orphan were sold into slavery. The old unwritten code of decency and morality was trampled underfoot. The people no longer even knew which gods to worship. Were not matters worse than in the days of Noah? Was not all this a foretaste of another imminent catastrophe – perhaps even of the great Last Judgement described by Jews and Christians?

The Jews had prophecies which forecast that the end of the world would come at the end of the fifth century, and then, when the date had to be put forward, in the year 531. This new date too had to be deferred. But the great wars between empires, coupled with a fresh rising of the Jewish people, seemed sure signs. People said: 'When you see kingdoms fighting among themselves, then look for the footsteps of the Messiah. Know that it will be so because so it was in the days of Abraham. When nation made war against nation [Genesis xiv] then was redemption granted to Abraham.'[15] There were a number of texts forecasting that a great war between the Romans and the Persians would come just before the end. One Targūmic text ran:

> Rejoice, exult, O Constantinople, city of wicked Edom [another name for Rome and the Romans], built on the soil of Romania, possessed of the countless armies of the people of Edom! For thou also shalt be chastised. The Parthians [the Persians] shall ravage thee, the accursed cup comes to meet thee and thou shalt be made drunken and cast out. And then shall thy sin be expiated, O community of Zion! Thou shalt be delivered by the Messiah thy King and by Elijah the priest.[16]

How could anyone doubt that these things were about to come to pass?

Whenever such a situation occurs, there are always men ready to get up and proclaim that the catastrophe is imminent and to urge sinners to make their peace with God in readiness for the great day. There was no shortage of such prophets among the Arabs. Two names that crop up are those of a Khālid ibn Sinān, who was sent to the tribe of 'Abs, and a certain Ḥanẓala ibn Ṣafwān. One of the best known was Maslama of the tribe of the Banū Ḥanīfa in the Yamāma, in the very middle of Arabia. Muslim tradition has set out to ridicule him, attributing his success to conjuring tricks and putting the date of his emergence as a prophet very late. But information preserved by Arab historians contradicts this picture. Maslama preached in the name of a God he called Raḥmān, which means 'merciful'. We know now from inscriptions that this was the name given by the South Arabians to the God of the Jews and to God the Father in the Christian Trinity (following the Hebrew and Aramaic usage), using the form Raḥmānān, that is, with the South Arabian definite article as a suffix, 'the Merciful'. We are told that Maslama himself was called by the name of Raḥmān, after his God. Now Muḥammad was accused of obtaining his knowledge from someone called Raḥmān of the Yamāma. Some sources also claim that Maslama began his work before Muḥammad and later made him a proposal to divide authority between them. It would seem, therefore, that we have here evidence of another prophet who was also preaching in Arabia at this time, with ideas very similar to those of Muḥammad.

All this had its effect on him. Dissatisfied, he was on the verge of something which would give meaning to his life and guarantee his revenge on the rich and powerful. He was familiar with the basis of the new ideas brought by the Jews and Christians, and sympathized with the tendency towards monotheism; but he remained an Arab with no intention of cutting himself off from his Arab brethren. He was horrified by the evils which had resulted from the recent social changes and by the sorry state of prevailing moral standards. With his own vivid memories of his years of poverty and humiliation, he could feel for the sufferings endured by the victims of these changes. He was appalled by the great upheavals which were shaking the world, and wondered if they should not be seen as signs of the approaching end of time and the great heavenly reckoning. He saw prophets arise, claiming to be sent from God to summon men to repent. Pride, and a real sense of his own worth, combined to suggest to him that he too might have his part to play in the drama of the Last Days. His natural predisposition made him ready for the great cataclysm which would reveal God's ways to him.

4

Birth of a Sect

THUS, Muḥammad's spiritual development was enriched by a myriad outside influences and, little by little, came to include a great many concerns. But, at the same time, he was fighting a spiritual battle of a different kind, embarking on a different journey through the innumerable rooms of that inward castle, which, in the words of St Teresa of Avila, 'is built entirely of a single diamond or of purest crystal'. At a very early stage his eyes were turned to the very centre of the castle, 'the place, that is the palace wherein dwells the king'.[1]

It is not known for certain when he began his habit of withdrawing for periods of retreat to a cave in the hill of Ḥirā, a few miles north-east of Mecca. It was one of those bare and arid uplands, 'devoid of all beauty', its 'dull, monotonous colouring' varying 'from dirty yellow to dirty light brown and muddy grey', as Charles Huber described it shortly before his death.[2] Certainly there was nothing there to distract the mind from contemplation. The inspiration for this practice had come from the Jewish and Christian ascetics. A few *ḥanīfs* probably followed their example and devoted themselves to nocturnal meditation. 'And the night time', to quote Jean Gerson, 'is the most suitable for this, being more intimate, more quiet and private and without the temptations of the vain glory of this world.'[3]

What was Muḥammad after? What was he seeking and what precisely was he doing? There are no reliable documents to tell us. He was certainly troubled by all he heard about Allah and his revelations, and was seeking some kind of spiritual truth. But what? The behaviour of the Christian hermits of the desert, reading the scriptures by the light of a lamp shining in the darkness, praying to God with tears and loud lamentations, appealed strongly to the imagination of Arab poets. Anxious pagans might be moved to imitate them, like the future bishop of Arbela in Mesopotamia who, before he was baptized, 'entered into a cavern and meditated on the vanity and frailness of the world'.[4]

Muḥammad, then, was certainly meditating and praying to Allah for enlightenment. And then one day, according to the most credible account we possess of the matter – one which is said to go back to what Muḥammad himself confided to his beloved 'Ā'isha – something happened. 'The beginning of the revelation for the Messenger of God', 'Ā'isha declared, 'was the True Vision which came like the break of day [*falaq aṣ-ṣubḥ*].' The Arabic word implies a sudden break – the abrupt rending asunder of the darkness of those lands, where there is no twilight of dawn or dusk, by the rising of the sun. Just so came the vision of the Being, the pervasive feeling of, perhaps, someone present; 'God establishes himself within the soul in such a way that, when it comes to itself, it can have not the least doubt that it has been in God and God in it' (Teresa of Avila).[5] Or was it a sudden imaginative vision? Teresa of Avila again:

> The soul is far from the expectation of a vision, it has not even the smallest thought of it, when suddenly the image of Our Lord appears in its completeness, overpowering all the senses and filling them with fear and apprehension, only to translate them presently to a delightful peace. Just as, when St Paul was struck down, there was at the same instant a tempest and a great turmoil in the air about; so, in that inner world of which we are speaking, first a great shuddering occurs, then in an instant, as I have said, all is peace once more.[6]

'After this,' 'Ā'isha continues, 'solitude became dear to him. His place of solitude was a cave on the hill of Ḥirā. He passed a number of nights in holy retreat before returning to his family. Then he returned, and he took provisions for a similar length of time.' This must have gone on for some time. Then one day, just as suddenly and unexpectedly, the great call came.

One day without warning a voice spoke to him. It must have been the first time that the sense of something extraordinary had come to him so clearly; there can be no other explanation for its effect on the devout Meccan. The Voice said three words in Arabic which were to shake the world:

'You are the Messenger of God.'

'I was standing,' Muḥammad is reported to have said, 'but I fell on my knees and dragged myself along while the upper part of my chest was trembling. I went in to Khadīja and said "Cover me, cover me!" until the terror had left me.'

How this and the following revelations fitted together in chronological order we cannot tell for sure. They certainly took on a more clearly defined shape as time passed. The sensations of a supernatural presence, the vague visions and awareness of simple spoken phrases were followed by long sequences of words in intelligible order, bearing a clear meaning, a message. Without doubt there were some interruptions, and recurrences of earlier things. The traditions mention this. At first there was fear of the sudden divine manifestation, and of whatever mysterious purpose the unknown power from which it came might have for the recipient. Later, when Muḥammad had got used to the idea of his remarkable destiny, there was terror in case he should be mistaken, and, especially when the supernatural manifestations ceased for a while, fear of being abandoned by his God. All mystics have had these phases of anguished doubt. 'The moment the soul hears the word,' wrote Teresa, 'it is quite sure that it comes from God; but when a long period of time has passed since then, and it is no longer under the first impression, a doubt rises in it, and it wonders if it has been deceived by an evil spirit or is the victim of its own imagination; and yet, the moment it hears the word, it has no doubt and would die to maintain the truth of it.'[7] Muḥammad was deeply distressed. 'I considered throwing myself from the top of a mountain scar,' he said. Perhaps from the heights of Mount Ḥirā itself, which ends in a steep, slippery crag.

Later on he heard God himself proclaim the truth of the

visions he had at this time to those who denied it, and give an account of them:

> Your companion is not in error, nor is he led astray,
> He does not speak out of his own fancy.
> This is none other than a suggestion suggested,
> Taught to him by One strong in power
> And wise, who stood straight,
> On the highest part of the horizon.
> Then he drew near and let himself down
> Till he was two bows' lengths off or closer.
> Then he suggested to his servant that which he revealed . . .
> He saw him also at a second descent
> By the jujube-tree of al-Muntahà
> Near which is the garden of al-Ma'wà
> When the jujube-tree was covered with that which covers it.
> His eye did not wander, nor did it turn aside.
> He saw one of his Lord's greatest marvels.
>
> (Koran liii, 1–18)

And again:

> By the oncoming of the night,
> By the morning when it breathes;
> This is indeed the word of a noble messenger,
> Powerful, beside Him of the Throne, established,
> Obeyed there and faithful also.
> Your companion is not a possessed.
> He saw him on the clear horizon.
>
> (Koran lxxxi, 17–23)

Muslim tradition has identified the being who appeared to Muḥammad as an archangel, Gabriel (*Jibrīl* in Arabic) or Sirāfīl. It seems highly probable that Muḥammad did not at first identify him at all except as a powerful messenger from Allah, possibly an emanation of his own being, of the same kind as those vague entities referred to by the Christians – the Spirit, the Word or the Breath of God.

At length, by Muḥammad's own account, a time came when the Mighty Being said to him: 'Recite!' 'I said: "What shall I recite?" He took me and tormented me thrice until I was overcome with exhaustion. Then he said to me: "Recite: In the name of thy lord who created thee . . ." And I recited.' The words he had uttered constituted what, chronologically speaking, are the first words of the Koran.

This probably took place one night, that of the 26th to 27th of the month of Ramaḍān, a night which was later to be called the night of destiny; a night which, in the words of a later passage of the Koran, was worth a thousand months. Year after year Muslims look forward to this night, believing that at a given moment the heavens will open and a mysterious light appear, and that whoever sees it will have his wishes granted. The date was about A.D. 610, or a few years after.

Still Muḥammad doubted. Who was this being who appeared to him? Perhaps it was an unclean spirit or a figment of his imagination. Perhaps, for all his contempt of seers, he was behaving like a typical *kāhin*. He confided in Khadīja. She had a cousin, an old man, a *ḥanīf* who was also seeking God. His name was Waraqa ibn Nawfal and he was a scholar with a wide knowledge of the scriptures, both Jewish and Christian. He was even said to know Hebrew. Khadīja sent her husband to him. 'She told him,' Muḥammad's account runs,

> 'Listen to your brother's son.' He questioned me and I told him my story. He said, 'This is the *nāmūs* that was revealed to Moses. Ah! if only I were young! If only I could be still living when your people drive you out!' I said to him: 'Will they drive me out?' He answered: 'Yes. No one who has brought what you bring has ever failed to make enemies. If your time had come in my lifetime I would have helped you with all my strength.'[8]

This *nāmūs* was new to the Muslims; they identified it with the archangel Gabriel. In fact, it was the Greek word *nomos*, meaning Law, which was the name given to the Torah, the Pentateuch revealed by God to Moses; the word had passed into Aramaic dialects. Waraqa meant that this was one of the series of great revelations by which God made his will known to mankind.

Khadīja, too, reassured him. At first they kept the matter

a secret. As the months went by the revelations continued, now causing less surprise and terror. But it was still a painful and agonizing experience. We are told that Muḥammad's face was covered with sweat, he was seized with a violent shuddering and lay unconscious for an hour as though in a drunken stupor. He did not hear what was said to him. He perspired copiously, even in cold weather. He heard strange noises, like the sound of chains or bells or rushing wings. 'Never once did I receive a revelation', he said, 'without thinking that my soul had been torn away from me.'[9] For the most part, at first, he felt something like an inward inspiration not expressible in words; and then, when the crisis was past, he uttered words which obviously corresponded for him to the inspiration he had received. In other words it was what Catholic mystics have called an 'intellectual revelation', and was also accompanied, undoubtedly, by 'intellectual visions'. 'Since you see nothing,' Teresa of Avila's confessor asked her, 'how do you know that it is Our Lord?' 'And she answered', she wrote, referring to herself, 'that she did not know, that she saw no face and could add nothing to what she had said: that she knew it was Our Lord who spoke to her and it was no illusion. . . . As for the words he spoke, she did not hear them when she willed, but at times when she was not thinking about them and when it was necessary.'[10] 'One sees nothing, either within or without,' she explains elsewhere, 'but while seeing nothing the soul understands what it is and where it is more clearly than if it saw him. . . . The soul hears no word, either within or without, but understands quite clearly who it is and where he is and sometimes even what he means to tell it. How and by what means it understands it does not know, but so it is; and while this is happening it cannot fail to know it.'[11]

At other times, and it appears with increasing frequency, Muḥammad had what the same mystics call visions or imaginative utterances. He saw an angel who spoke to him, and he understood. This awareness of the image and the words came from within himself and, likewise, spasmodically, when he was least expecting it – sometimes when he was engaged in conversation, or as he rode his camel on a journey. Sometimes the visions or words were even externalized, exactly like real beings speaking real words, although none of those present saw anything.

Muḥammad gradually grew accustomed to a certain way of receiving these visions and messages. Sometimes he even attempted to summon or induce them. From the first, when they came to him, he covered himself with a cloak in the manner of the *kāhins*. Initially Muḥammad seems to have tried to hasten the expression of what he heard by stammering and mumbling. The odd consonants which occur at the beginning of certain *sūras* of the Koran, about which many theories have been advanced, may have something to do with this confused attempt. At all events he earned a reprimand from God:

> Do not wag your tongue when you are reciting so as to do it more quickly.
> It is for us to collect it and recite it.
> When we recite it, follow the recital.
> Afterwards it is for us to explain it.
>
> (Koran lxxv, 16–18)

Later on God was to tell him again:

> Be not hasty in your recitation before the suggestion of it to you is finished.
>
> (Koran xx, 113)

These passages are somewhat obscure, but they clearly imply that the Prophet was to let the inspiration take its tumultuous course before giving it outward expression.

This raises a question, unavoidable in any discussion of Muḥammad, to which I have already given a sketchy answer but which must now be dealt with in more detail. This is the question of his sincerity.

We have passed the period when incredulity towards any form of religious message seemed to make it obligatory to regard all those who transmitted them as liars. Eighteenth-century rationalist philosophers for instance, like Christian apologists and theologians, looked on Muḥammad as the example of a perfect fraud. It was even said of him, from certain dubious accounts of his life, that he actually resorted to conjuring tricks in order to impress his contemporaries. The only difference was that the philosophers extended this explanation to cover all founders of religions, and some, like Voltaire, managed to find some extenuating circumstances for Muḥammad in his legitimate ambition to raise his people to a less ignoble position on the stage of history. The times he lived in and the rough nature of the Arabs he had to lead obliged him to resort to fraud if he was to make any impression on such people. Hubert Grimme, a great German Arabic scholar of the late nineteenth century, also revived a similar theory by crediting Muḥammad with still more praiseworthy objectives. According to Grimme, Muḥammad believed that some remedy had to be found for the social conditions in his native city of Mecca, and that the only way to do this was, in the modern idiom, to soak the rich. He conceived a plan of assisting the poor by means of a heavy tax on income, which would strike principally at the very rich. But he realized that he had no chance of getting them to agree to this solution. However, Muḥammad clearly had no conception of a fierce class war of the type known in the nineteenth and twentieth centuries. Consequently, he hoped to frighten the rich into accepting a programme which Grimme, writing at a time when the Social Democrat Party in Germany was making spectacular advances, described as socialist. To do this Muḥammad invented a 'mythology', actually reduced to the barest minimum, incorporating a Last Judgement in which the rich would come off very badly unless they placated the Celestial Judge by paying the 'purification' tax (*zakāt*), which Muḥammad prescribed.

Modern advances in psychology and psychiatry have made short work of such simplistic explanations of fraud, whether justifiable or otherwise. The reaction may even have gone too far in the other direction, for there have been, and still are, cases of real fraud. But their number is limited. At all events, it is now generally understood and admitted that certain individuals can sincerely believe that they are the recipients of visual, auditory and mental messages from the Beyond; and also that their sincerity is no proof that these messages really come from where they are claimed to come. It is the concept of the unconscious which has enabled us to understand these things. This is now sufficiently well known and accepted to need no detailed explanation here, not even of the distinctions and qualifications introduced by psychologists. One has only to dip into psychology text-books to find a hundred perfectly bona fide cases of people in a state of hallucination hearing things and seeing visions which they claim quite genuinely never to have seen or heard before. And yet an objective study of their cases shows that these are simply fresh associations produced by the unconscious working on things which have been seen and heard but forgotten. Facts of this kind we now take for granted. It is therefore conceivable that what Muḥammad saw and heard may have been the supernatural beings described to him by the Jews and Christians with whom he talked. It is understandable that, in the words that came to him, elements of his actual experience, the stuff of his thoughts, dreams and meditations, and memories of discussions that he had heard should have re-emerged, chopped, changed and transposed, with an appearance of immediate reality that seemed to him proof of some external activity which, although inaccessible to other men's minds, was yet wholly objective in its nature.

A study of Muḥammad's earliest messages, coupled with a perusal of accounts of the crises of doubt or despair which preceded or accompanied them, can only produce a sceptical attitude towards the theories which see them as evidence of a coolly calculated plan carried out ruthlessly from motives of either ambition or philanthropy. And these accounts do seem to be authentic. Tradition, concerned to stress the supernatural affiliations of Muḥammad's personality, would not have invented from scratch such very human traits. A genuine

Muḥammad is much less difficult to explain than a fraudulent one.

It is true that, later on, some disturbing characteristics did appear. Muḥammad had to take day-to-day decisions, decisions of a political, practical and legislative nature, which could not wait for some unspecified moment when the spirit might see fit to breathe on him. He was constantly under fire, bombarded with questions and requests for advice. The divinely inspired nature of his replies gave them a solid basis of authority. Did he yield to the temptation to nudge the truth a little? Some of the revelations correspond a little too closely to what might have been the Prophet's own human desires and calculations. Or was it, once again, his unconscious at work? We shall never know. But the problem will be examined once more in Chapter 6.

Supposing he was sincere, that he really had what, for the sake of frankness, we can call visual and auditory hallucinations, does this mean that he was in some way abnormal, sick or mad? To begin with, the whole concept of madness is one which has long been discounted by experts. The borderline between what is considered as normal and so-called 'abnormal' behaviour is much more flexible than was once thought. Some 'abnormal' characteristics are to be found in most people. The neurotic or insane are simply those in whom such characteristics occur in a more intense and lasting form.

Given the right conditions, Muḥammad had, from the first, exactly the temperament to become a mystic. The circumstances of his childhood, his adolescence and even of his adult life had combined to steer him in this direction. He had begun to devote himself to the practice of asceticism, which, for all mystics, is one stage on the road to the objective towards which they are moving, voluntarily or involuntarily – a means of freeing themselves from the contingent and corporeal self, of severing as far as possible all ties with the external world, with its attendant temptations, attractions and desires, and submitting themselves in all humility to the Being whom they seek. When his soul was thus plunged into the void, the impassioned prayer which filled it brought him still closer to what he sought. As with many others who have followed the same path, Muḥammad then attained periodic states of ecstasy in which he felt that he had been stripped of his own personality, submitting passively to the invasion of a mysterious force, of whose nature he was in some ineffable, untranslatable and quite incommunicable fashion aware, and experiencing an inexpressible joy in so doing. In this state, again like many other mystics, he experienced the phenomena described above – seeing and hearing things, either inwardly or outwardly, in the mind or the imagination.

We find these ecstasies and sensory phenomena in a very similar form among persons suffering from recognized mental conditions such as hysteria, schizophrenia and uncontrolled verbalization. Whether the great mystics are men and women naturally prone to such abnormalities, who experience them without previous preparation and, with the practice of asceticism, experience them again, but in a purer and nobler form, or whether the practice of asceticism artificially reproduces the psycho-physiological conditions which induce such phenomena in the mentally ill, is a matter best left to psychiatrists and psychologists to determine.

The great mystics, both Christian and Muslim, have not stopped here. Generally they have gone on to experience a long period of barrenness, or drought, in which the ecstasies and sensory phenomena cease and God abandons them. In terror at this apparent desertion, the mind begins to doubt its own experience, while at the same time longing for the return of the unutterable joys it has lost. This agonizing state may last for several years, after which the ecstasy recurs, but this time in a calmer and more definitive form. This is what has been called, following H. Delacroix, the theopathic state. The Christian or Muslim mystic feels calm and happy, in a permanent state of quiet communion with the Being for whom he has sought with such labour. For the Christian mystic this is a union, a special kind of marriage with God. For the Hindu mystic, it is the experience of an ineffable, non-personal absolute which is the basis of all reality and attained through knowledge of Self, 'since it is none other than the mystery and infinite richness of *my* own act of being' (L. Gardet).[12] For the Muslim mystic, whose frequent heterodoxy enables him to express himself more freely than Catholic mystics who are bound by their own dogmatic theology, it is a total union between what was apparently two distinct beings. In the words of the tenth-century poet Ḥusayn ibn Manṣūr al-Ḥallāj, who was later to suffer for his opinions:

> I have become the one I love, and He whom I love has become me.
> We are two spirits, compounded in a single body . . .
> When you saw me, you saw Him
> And when you saw Him you saw us. . . .
> And so to see me is to see Him, and to see Him is to see you.[13]

As we have seen, Muḥammad probably went through the barren period familiar to other mystics. But he never reached the theopathic state. He always felt himself to be separate and even infinitely removed from God, who spoke to him and sent him messengers, who chided, comforted and commanded him. They were in two such different worlds, with such a gulf between, that emissaries were needed to bridge it.

Muḥammad, therefore, stopped at the first stages of the mystic's journey. The 'graces', as Catholic theology would call them, which he had received, both auditory and visual, might seem impressive to ordinary mortals. But to the great mystics they were no more than ephemeral transitory signs, and perhaps even suspect and perilous. One could never be sure they were not machinations of the devil or even natural products of the imagination. They might encourage self-love, pride and covetousness. At the best they were simply stages to be passed through. The great heterodox Muslim mystics have tended to look down on the Prophet as being simply a robot, a kind of primitive recording machine or gramophone, a loudspeaker for transmitting God's messages.

Those modern psychiatrists who hold religious beliefs are troubled, too, by these hallucinations and ecstatic states since, in all honesty, they are forced to admit that no clear distinction exists between the experiences of the mystics and those of the mentally ill. In the last analysis, the real distinction lies in the personalities of those who undergo the experience. On the one side are weak personalities with impoverished and disconnected ideas, whose mental activity is petty and blundering. On the other are great minds with a forceful, well-integrated personality, capable of broad, far-reaching ideas and often of intense, constructive mental activity, who use their mystical experiences as a basis for their own fresh and boldly individual philosophy. Muḥammad, needless to say, whatever his shortcomings from a mystical point of view, belonged to the second type. Like the great mystics, he strove hard for self-discipline, the conquest of himself.

The necessary coming-to-terms with these strictly personal experiences can only be achieved within the given framework of society. Muḥammad had followed the pattern of ascetic discipline derived from the Christian hermits, which may have been that already adopted by the *ḥanīfs*. He was unprepared for the extraordinary sensory manifestations which these exercises triggered off, and he reacted to them by following the only example that his experience of society had given him: the trances of the poets and *kāhins*. When he hurried to Khadīja to be covered with a mantle, he was copying instinctively the behaviour of the *kāhins*. As it happens the model was repellent to him; but it was the only one he had.

As a matter of fact, in the earliest revelations which he attributed to his God the form of the words he heard and repeated is identical to the words which the spirit breathed to these desert seers who were also beginning the same mystical ascent, although, in their case, their journey would carry them only a very little way. As in the case of the *kāhins*, the words fell into short, disjointed phrases, probably thrown out in violent convulsions, more or less fully rhymed. This is what is called in Arabic the *saj*ʿ, or rhymed prose. As with the *kāhins*, these utterances were full of oaths invoking in turn all the objects of the natural world. The spell-binding effect of this kind of primitive poetry remains remarkably strong even after thirteen centuries.

Muḥammad did not, then, introduce any formal innovations. But the content of what he said was quite new. In this he was far beyond the poor *kāhins*, who merely did what was traditionally expected of men of their kind. His unconscious, for that is what these contents reveal, was far richer.

The nature of his upbringing we have already seen. The ideas which came to him from his Qurayshite background – inculcated, in the way of such societies, by the process of education by example, by which the child is gradually assimilated into his cultural surroundings – had been revised, deepened and reinforced by the effects of the great current of monotheism which was sweeping Arabia at that time. Muḥammad's own difficulties led him to adopt a critical attitude towards the rich and powerful, and consequently towards conformists in general. As a result, he reacted to novel ideas with an open mind. He was to identify himself with the victims of society and make their suffering his own; and he rounded on the men of the existing establishment to call them to account and break down the ideology which served as the justification for their position.

Muḥammad's attitude was therefore implicitly a revolutionary one. The mystic stood in direct relation to the Being of Beings, who showed himself to him and spoke to him. His own, individual experience had an absolute value which to him was not in doubt and which had nothing to do with the rules governing social life, even if these were only an extension of some previous revelation of the same kind. Like the rational theorist who sees no flaw in his reasoning, he could not feel bound by the blind force of habit, even if disguised by secondary and transparent rationalizations. In the same way, Leszek Kolakowski has described mysticism as the revolt of the individual conscience against the system, the 'apparatus'.

Mysticism is certainly a private experience which has an

absolute value for the person involved, and so where the 'system', that is the established framework of ideas and institutions, is opposed to its revelations it can indeed be such a revolt of experience. So, given the same conditions, can pure science or philosophy. But there are systems – the Catholic Church is one – which are sufficiently flexible and intelligent to have been able to channel this spontaneous mystical activity so as to give it a place, a role, even to make use of the vital impulse as something which feeds it and to which it in turn gives rise. This is how Teresa of Avila and John of the Cross have remained great Catholic mystics, and ornaments of a Church they might have shaken.

No similar institution existed in Arabia to channel Muḥammad. There was nothing to stop him attacking the beliefs and institutions of his country, beyond a certain native caution which often made him temporize, without, however, preventing him in the long run from pursuing the realization of his plans. At first he kept his revelations a secret, but the Qurayshites lost nothing by waiting.

Muḥammad's first message may be identified with reasonable certainty. In this connection, one or two things should be made clear to those readers unfamiliar with Islam. The revelations, the groups of words uttered by Muḥammad as inspired by Allah, formed what was called a 'recitation', *qur'ān* in Arabic. They were taken down in his lifetime on a variety of materials such as scraps of leather, flat camel-bones, potsherds, palm-fronds and so forth. In his lifetime, too, these fragments began to be collected and grouped into *sūras* or chapters and became known collectively as 'The Recitation', in Arabic *al-qur'ān*, from which came the English 'Alcoran' and later, with the dropping of the Arabic article, simply the Koran. At some later date, a number of eminent Muslims made what they hoped were complete collections and of which in the end only one has survived. In this the *sūras* were, all except the first, placed automatically in diminishing order of length, and consequently the textual order found in modern editions of the

Koran and in the majority of translations bears no relation to chronological sequence.

However, Muslim scholars had already assembled traditions indicating the period at which this or that part of the Koran had been revealed. European orientalists, for their part, have been able, from the study of style and internal criteria, to arrive at a more accurate picture of this sequence and where necessary to modify it. They have then been able to divide it roughly into periods. Translations of the Koran in chronological order have appeared, the most recent being the French version by Régis Blachère, a work of such remarkable erudition that it must supersede all previous translations into French. Richard Bell's English translation places the *sūras* in the traditional order; however he gives precise details about the chronology of the entire text; the work is altogether a very fine achievement. It is consequently possible, nowadays, to study the Prophet's earliest messages, as represented by a somewhat limited collection of *sūras* and verses whose age is generally agreed on, even if serious differences exist on matters of detail.

Nothing is more infuriating to the revolutionary, or to the reformer even, than the complacency of the establishment: its assumption that good consists in its own continued existence and in that of its time-honoured habits, its unawareness of the dangers threatening the world it holds dear and its contempt for all warnings. It is against such people, who take their own strength for granted and who, having amassed great wealth, believe they can do just as they like regardless of anyone else, that the earliest revelations are directed. Allah reveals to them how little they are:

> We have created man in trouble.
> Does he think that none will have power over him?
> He says: I have wasted great riches.
> Does he think that none has seen him?
>
> (Koran xc, 4–7)

Can these people not see that they are no more than transitory beings, made from a drop of sperm, destined for annihilation?

Confound man! How ungrateful he is.
From what did He create him?
From a drop He created him and fixed his destiny,
Then He laid down his path for him.
Then caused him to die and laid him in the grave.
(Koran lxxx, 16–21)

What a miserable creature is man beside the glory of Allah!

All that is on [earth] shall pass away,
But the face of your Lord shall remain, glorious and revered.
(Koran lv, 26–27)

It is Allah ('your Lord' as he invariably describes himself) who has created all things and who, even now, 'each day is employed in some work' (lv, 29). He made all created things, the heavens, the sun, the moon, the earth and sea, the mountains. The continuing miracle of the vegetable kingdom by which mankind is fed is his work:

Let man consider his food.
We have poured down water in showers,
We have broken up the earth in cracks,
And have caused to sprout up in grain,
And vines and green shoots,
Olives and palms,
And orchards luxuriant,
Fruit trees and pasture
For you and your flocks to enjoy.
(Koran lxxx, 24–32)

But more than anything else, his power is displayed in the unfathomable mystery of procreation. It is mentioned in the very first revelation:

Recite in the name of your Lord who created,
Created man from a blood-clot.
(Koran xcvi, 1–2)

And the theme recurs more than once:

> Let man consider from what he was created.
> He was created from a fluid issuing
> Which comes forth from between the loins and the ribs.
>
> (Koran lxxxvi, 5–7)

Both man and the invisible spirits, the jinns, are his work therefore. He it is who has ordained their fate. He it is who created animals which serve men; first among them is the camel. He it is who directs their doings. From him comes the wonderful sight of

> The ships towering up in the sea like mountains.
>
> (Koran lv, 24)

And, whatever their private opinions, it is to him the Qurayshites owe the success of their trading ventures:

> For the sake of the covenant of Quraysh,
> Their covenant for the summer and winter caravans,
> Let them worship the Lord of this Temple
> Who has provided them against hunger
> And kept them safe from fear.
>
> (Koran cvi)

And so Muḥammad, the champion of the poor and the orphan, of whom he had been one, rebukes the hated Qurayshites in the name of the one Being whose power can override them, the Being and the power that his own meditations, conversation and experience have taught him to know. He is not content merely to show them. He threatens, as well. The Lord has shown man the way to follow:

> Have we not shown him the two ways?
>
> (Koran xc, 10)

But the men Muḥammad had in mind had rejected the steep way, the hard and difficult climb. They believed that everything was over after this life and so all they had to do, all their days, was to make hay while the sun shone, only keeping within the limits of honour, and then resign themselves to the inevitable suffering and death that was their lot. In their view, although the gods lived and moved somewhere between heaven and earth, the one God had not been born and a great deal was permitted. Now Muḥammad was telling them that death was not the ultimate end. So let them – these proud, rich men – beware of the day when, miraculously resurrected, they would have to face the dreadful Judgement:

> When the sky shall be rent asunder,
> And shall hear its Lord in submission.
>
> (Koran lxxxiv, 1–2)
>
> When the trumpet shall sound
> That shall be a day of horror
> Beyond bearing for the ungrateful.
>
> (Koran lxxiv, 8–10)
>
> Streams of fire and molten brass shall come upon you and you shall have no help . . .
> When the sky shall split, and become scarlet like red leather . . .
> On that day shall neither man nor demon be asked about his sins . . .
> But the sinners shall be known by their marks, they shall be seized by their forelocks and their feet.
>
> (Koran lv, 35–41)

Then these sinners would spin between a hell of fire and an abyss of boiling water (lv, 44). Those who, on the other hand, had feared Allah in their earthly lives would go to two gardens full of dark green foliage, where two springs of water flowed, gardens overflowing with palms and pomegranates and fruit trees of all kinds. There the elect would lie upon soft green cushions beneath branches heavy with fruit, just within reach, and enjoy (in every sense of the word, without a doubt) young, modest-eyed virgins, beautiful as coral and rubies, kept apart in tents, innocent of any touch of man or jinn (lv, 46 f). We can understand the Lord's promising the ardent husband of the elderly and already twice married Khadīja that:

The life to come shall be better for you than the first.
(Koran xciii, 4)

But where did Muḥammad get such pictures from? Were they derived solely from visions and hallucinations, which were so suspect and so similar to those experienced by the poets and seers who were regarded with such universal suspicion? No, he had stronger proof, in those excellent scriptures which had not yet been made available to the Arabs but which lay in the keeping of the highly civilized peoples who were the great world powers. From the very first, the Lord's messages to Muḥammad invoked these.

Recite in the name of your Lord who created,
Created man from a blood-clot.
Recite! Your Lord is the most bountiful,
He has taught by means of the Reed,
He has taught mankind those things he did not know.
(Koran xcvi, 1–5)

The reed (*qalam* in Arabic, the Greek word is *kalamos*) is the pen with which the earliest messengers had transcribed the revelations from on high, and which were written down somewhere

On honoured pages,
Exalted and purified,
By the hands of scribes
Noble and virtuous.
(Koran lxxx, 13–15)

What then should men do in order to escape the infernal torments awaiting them? They should 'purify' themselves (*tazakkā*), that is, lead a morally just life. And this just life, in all the passages of the oldest layer of the Koran, is defined almost exclusively by the right use of wealth. Wealth must not be amassed for its own sake, but a part given to the poor:

Whoso gives, and shows piety,
And professes the truth of the most excellent [reward],
We shall smooth [his way] to ultimate happiness.

Whoso is mean and bumptious on account of his wealth,
Who denies the most excellent [reward],
We shall smooth [his way] to ultimate misery.
His fortune shall not profit him when he falls into the abyss.
(Koran xcii, 5–11)

First and foremost it is the behaviour of the selfish rich which is condemned:

Beware! You do not honour the orphan,
Nor urge to feed the poor.
Greedily you devour the inheritance [of the weak],
And you love riches inordinately.
(Koran lxxxix, 18–21)

This, by contrast, is the conduct of the just during their life:

They were sleeping but little at night,
At first light they were praying for forgiveness.
Their goods they shared with the beggar and the destitute.
(Koran li, 17–19)

To Muḥammad himself, a very early revelation prescribed a code of conduct applicable to others:

You, that are covered with a mantle,
Arise and warn!
Your Lord, magnify.
Your garments, purify.
All pollution [*or possibly* anger], shun.
Do not fear in giving alms to give too much.
For your Lord, wait patiently.
(Koran lxxiv, 1–7)

But the injunction to warn was for him alone. This was the chief duty laid on him by his Lord, although this role had not yet assumed the importance it was to acquire in the later revelations. However, Muḥammad already had one privilege. Promises were given him, and he was comforted in his times of doubt:

By the morning brightness,
By the night, when it reigns:
Your Lord has not abandoned you, nor has he hated you.
The life to come shall be better for you than the first life.
Indeed your Lord shall give to you in the end, and you shall be satisfied.
Did he not find you an orphan and give you shelter?
He found you erring and guided you.
He found you in poverty and enriched you.
So as for the orphan, do not wrong him,
As for the beggar, do not reject him,
As for the goodness of your Lord, discourse of it.

(Koran xciii)

It is clear, then, that this modest duty of warning involves not only certain equally modest privileges, a particular attention from the Lord, but also some obligations. A misdemeanour earns him a rebuke. The nature of this misdemeanour is interesting. A blind man, who was certainly poor and may have been a beggar, came to seek him while he was engaged in conversation with an important person, one of the 'bumptious' rich men he was anxious to win over, one of those who believed that everything was possible to them without the help of Allah. The blind man insisted, no doubt with the persistent importunity usual among oriental beggars. Muḥammad lost patience, and frowned and scowled at him. Evidently he blamed himself for this momentary impatience and worried about it, in the same way that upper-class reformers since his day have often worried, when their old habits have led them instinctively to choose the company of those who share their way of life rather than those to whom they feel a duty. And naturally the revelation came, and the pricks of conscience took the form of an admonition from on high:

He frowned and turned away
When the blind man came to him.
What would make you know? It may be that he would purify himself,
Or mend his ways, and the reminder profit him.

But to the complacent wealthy
You give all your attention.
And yet if he did not purify himself the fault would not be yours;
But to the one who comes to you eagerly
Being in fear,
You pay no heed.

(Koran lxxx, 1–10)

This, then, was the substance of the first message which Muḥammad undoubtedly believed himself to have received from his Lord. The degree of originality contained in the ideas expressed is a matter for later consideration. But was its form at all unusual? This raises substantial problems.

No Arabic prose dating from before Islam has come down to us. According to the classic picture of Arabic literature, in the beginning there was only poetry. The sudden appearance of a new literary form (or even of a constellation of new literary forms), and this, moreover, of a kind which they regard as perfect, with no previous preparation, antecedents or precursors, could not be explained except by a miracle. Muslim apologists see this as proof of the divine origin of these words and phrases. They go on to point out that there was nothing in Muḥammad the man to suggest the presence of any literary gifts whatsoever.

As is so often the case with ideological argument, whether religious or secular, this thesis is put forward with an assurance of irrefutability, which is all the greater because it may be reversed by a flick of the finger. Throughout the world prose literature certainly comes after poetry, and Arabia is no exception. The prose of the Koran is prose of a very special kind, and Arab authors themselves tell us that discourses in the same form existed before it; these literary fragments were however never written down. It needed the specific nature of the recitations contained in the Koran to make men note them down (and even then only in part, especially to begin with), or to make any attempt to remember them. There was no incentive to preserve in writing the other pieces that were more or less in the same vein; and if, even so, some of them were written down, the triumph of Islam prevented them being handed on, or even destroyed all record of them.

As for the stylistic perfection of the Koran, this has become an article of faith for Islam, which teaches that no one else is capable of doing anything like it. Great stress has been laid on this incapacity (*iʿjāz*) by numerous theologians, who have drawn from it all kinds of theoretical conclusions.

But there has been no lack of independent spirits in Islam to shed doubt on the incomparable nature of the Koranic text. Some have actually set out to write imitations of the Koran. One of these, in medieval times, faced with the objection that his text did not produce the same mesmeric effect as recitations of the Koran, retorted: 'Have it read out in the mosques for centuries and then you will see!' Here in fact is the heart of the matter. A text on which one has been brought up from infancy and heard recited with great fervour in the most solemn and moving circumstances, which one has studied word for word so that it has become almost a part of oneself, sets up, after a time, a special kind of reaction. It becomes quite impossible to hear it with a fresh ear or look at it with a fresh eye so as to see exactly how it would appear to us if the bare text, free of all associations, were to be put before us for the first time without warning. For Catholics, it is the same with certain scriptural passages and latin hymns used in the liturgy, and for Protestants with the Bible as a whole. It is not surprising that so many Muslims should be convinced of the inimitable perfection of the Koranic text and amazed and indignant that anyone could doubt it. Nor is it in any way surprising that outsiders, confronted for the first time with the texts in question, should often see in them nothing which appears to them to justify the admiration of those who were brought up on them.

And so the beauty of the Koran has been hotly contested by those who for one reason or another failed to fall under the collective spell. In medieval times a number of free-thinking

Muslims wrote books entitled *muʿāraḍat al-qur'ān*, which can be roughly translated as the Anti-Koran. The apologists felt bound to refute them and, especially on a literary level, to produce a painstaking defence of the style and images of the Koran, point by point and word by word. In our own day the great German semitic scholar Theodor Nöldeke, a learned student of Arabic, has written at length about the stylistic defects of the Koran.

Muḥammad had not the least intention of producing a work of literature. The experience he was seeking and which he underwent was, as we have seen, initially a non-verbal one. Words came at a later stage; and from then on the experience was, in this respect at least, comparable to the inspiration of the writer – of the writer, that is, whose aim is to communicate not simply words alone but intelligible meaning. In this it differed from the automatic writing of the surrealists, which in other ways it resembled. It was André Breton who described 'the moment of inspiration when a man in the grip of some strong feeling is suddenly seized by something "stronger than himself" which thrusts him into immortality against his will'. And he was clearly aware of this as a kind of prophecy. 'The surrealist voice which shook Cumae, Dodona and Delphi was none other than that which dictates my least furious words to me.' Only what the Voice dictated to Muḥammad was not phrases like: 'There is a man cut in half by the window.' It was coherent messages. It may appear from what has been said above that the babblings and stammerings accompanying the revelations resembled, at least in their elements, those exquisite phrases revelled in by modern poets, alongside pure sounds justifying the 'sound-poetry' hypothesis I have put forward. Earlier prophets had accepted the surrealist verbal messages of their unconscious in their entirety. So it was, for instance, in the first Christian communities, where it was called 'speaking with tongues', *glosso-lalia* in Greek. St Paul advised that adepts be allowed to 'speak with tongues', and he thanked God, writing to the Christians of Corinth, that 'I speak with tongues more than ye all'.

Muḥammad was on Paul's side, not André Breton's. Paul was seeking consciously to control his surrealist gifts.

> Yet in the church I had rather speak five words with my understanding, that by my voice I might teach others also, than ten thousand words in an unknown tongue.

Indeed, he added (1 Corinthians xiv, 2–3):

> He that speaketh in an unknown tongue speaketh not unto men, but unto God: for no man understandeth him; howbeit in the spirit he speaketh mysteries. But he that prophesieth speaketh unto men to edification, and exhortation, and comfort.

Muḥammad too had to sort out and eliminate, unconsciously no doubt, and retain only that which 'edified, exhorted and comforted'. Probably his finest poems were never written down. He was waiting for messages from God of a specific kind, and this expectation shaped the words which tried, unsuccessfully, to be 'stronger than himself'. Beyond the Christian speakers with tongues, he rediscovered the tradition of the great prophets of Israel.

His words, therefore, were not pure poetry. Nor were they literature in the usual sense of the word. He was not, as Régis Blachère has pointed out,[14] in command of his medium; or, more accurately, he only succeeded in mastering it in part and unconsciously. He was in no way trying to create a work which would make him famous like the poets of the desert for its style and content. But, with prophets as with pure poets, his private experience, the 'supreme moment', in its entirety incommunicable, that ineffable personal contact with pure being, was already expressing itself in an ordered linguistic form whose purpose was communication, and in a style that was aesthetically striking. In spite of itself, at least at first, it was both a message and a poem, because again the Voice adhered faithfully to the models stored up in the unconscious mind of its mouthpiece and reverted to the language of the inspired soothsayer, the *kāhin*. It followed the usual stereotyped formula in such things as the invocation of heavenly bodies; but, what was more important, it fell back on the use of rhythm and on the methods dictated by the laws of rhythm when adapted to the demands of spoken language. Arabic is perhaps of all languages that best suited to the growth of spontaneous poetry. It possesses a vast fund of words of parallel formation, with the same alternation of strong and weak stresses punctuated by the recurrence of the same vowels in corresponding positions; and, among these assonances, it allows of a wide choice of rhyming words. For this reason it encourages the development of the *saj'*, a rhymed and rhythmic prose divided into short metrical units of generally no more than eight to ten syllables, grouped together in rhyming strophes with identical rhythm.

Of course, in this similarity to the language of the *kāhin* the Voice was a long way from adopting the forms used by that other inspired speaker, the *shā'ir*, or poet. Starting from what may have been an experience of the same kind, either verbal or purely existential, the *shā'ir*, like the majority of poets of any period or place, endeavoured by methods developed with great skill over a long period by his predecessors consciously to communicate the incommunicable. Moreover, in many cases he was only using the same methods to versify a message quite unconnected with the living well of pure poetry. The form employed was a complex one, the *qaṣīda*, a poem consisting of lines made up of two half-lines, rhymed internally and with corresponding rhythms based on one of the traditional 'metres', somewhat in the manner of Greek, Latin or English verse. The *shā'ir* was an artist, or rather a craftsman, in command of his tools and committed to a task which he had mapped out in his mind and which he then carried out according to a proven method, putting into it either more or less of his own heart and mind, and making it live or not by reference to the springs of all human feeling.

Thus the message intercepted by Muḥammad was the more faithful to pure poetry the further it was removed from poetry of the traditional kind. The Voice itself insisted:

We have not taught him poetry, nor does it beseem it.
(Koran xxxvi, 69)

Views may differ as to the poetic merit of the early messages; here too it is not easy to look at them with a fresh eye. The imagery has been criticized as arid; but again, it is difficult not to be captured by the verbal resonance, or by what Régis Blachère calls the 'hammering rhyme' and 'breathless, bumpy and uneven tempo'. The convolutions of idea and expression, the assonances and repetitions, induce in the reader, in the words of Max Eastman, an almost hypnotic state,[15] a trance-like condition of suggestibility in which he is ten times more receptive to words, rhythms and images.

But then again, as has been said already, the Voice itself laid stress on preaching and exhortation, on the intellectual content of its message; and this tendency increased. As Muḥammad's circle of mesmerized listeners grew larger and his words attracted more attention and began to cause something of a stir, so did the need for explanation and description, and then for refutation and argument, increase. It was no longer enough simply to play on people's emotions. The message became more explicit, although for a long time yet it was deeply imbued with the pure poetry from which it sprang, lofty and eloquent. But the overt content was to gain an ever-increasing prominence.

There was nothing at all revolutionary or shocking in the message – or not, at least, at first sight. It did not appear to involve any major religious innovations and, from the point of view of its immediate reception in Mecca, it was appearances that counted. Strangely enough, in fact, Muḥammad's Lord did not, in his first revelations, attempt to deny either the existence or the power of the other divinities. He was content merely to ignore them. There are no denunciations as there are in later messages of 'those who assign companions to Allah', no insistence on the uniqueness of the supreme deity. It is probable enough that while Muḥammad was at this period convinced of the infinite power of his God, who was also the God of the Christians and the Jews, he also believed in the possible existence alongside him of a host of minor divinities, of no great importance since they were in all things dependent on the supreme Master, and only a little higher than the jinns or demons whose existence as God's creatures, as we have seen, he openly admitted. This exaltation of one God above all others – who are not so much denied as simply passed over – is a common phenomenon in many polytheist religions. It has been called 'henotheism'. Henotheism was accepted by many people in Arabia and no one thought anything of it. Muḥammad may have been torn between henotheism and the outright monotheism preached by the Jews and Christians. There is, as we shall see, some evidence which points to it.

Consequently, Muḥammad's insistence on the power of his Lord was not likely to upset the Meccans. Attributing to him the intention of judging mankind in the manner of the Jewish and Christian God, with its implied suggestion of his power to resurrect the dead, might be a matter for scepticism but nothing more. The practical proposals were already widespread among the Meccans. Criticism of the 'complacency' of the rich and of their conviction that their wealth entitled them to 'be independent' (*istaghnā*) of all authority was perfectly acceptable in moderation. Insistence on the necessity of almsgiving was nothing out of the ordinary and could be backed up by the old tribal ideal of putting generosity among the foremost of the virtues, which was still very much alive in men's consciences although its practice was not much in favour among the wealthy inhabitants of Mecca. His message also corresponded to current religious beliefs about the importance of making sacrifices so that the divinity might share in any unexpected blessing, and so as to divert his possible wrath. Clearly, none of this involved any vital innovations of a moral nature either. The Arab national colours under which current Judaeo-Christian ideas were presented were bound to appeal to the audience to whom they were preached.

There was nothing in all this unacceptable to the Meccans. That, certainly, was Muḥammad's belief as we have seen him endeavouring to win over an eminent man to his ideas. It contained nothing that could appear at all revolutionary. The deeper implications, which did represent a radical change of outlook, went unnoticed and were in any case not yet fully developed. Muḥammad's preaching might have been simply one direction among many within the general pattern of Arabic moral and religious beliefs, about which there was nothing set, rigid or canonical. And yet this preaching also had the power to attract a number of people who from their age or social position were receptive to a message which answered to their deepest needs. We have seen the reason. The ideas Muḥammad had to offer, while not apparently particularly original in themselves, formed a novel synthesis based on the highly personal way in which he believed the Presence from the Beyond had made itself known to him. In this, the individual assumed a very special importance. The concern of the Supreme Being was for him. He had created him and would judge him without consideration of kinship, family or tribe. In this way the individual whose value as a social unit had been enhanced by economic progress acquired an ideological value and became significant for his own sake, by having access to eternity. On the other hand, to reiterate: the Judaeo-Christian beliefs, which had attractions for all from their association with the prestige of the higher civilizations and powerful empires where they were held in honour, became perfectly acceptable to Arab pride when presented in Arabic and reduced by an Arab messenger to their basic and easily assimilable essentials.

The ideological movement founded by the new preacher, the men he attracted, might, at first sight, seem to slip easily into place among the multifarious movements, schools of thought and confraternities which blossomed all over western Arabia. It was, however, to explode into violent conflict, for reasons which we shall attempt to explain.

First to accept Muḥammad's message were naturally the people of his own household: his wife Khadīja, of course, and also his young teenage cousin and ward, 'Alī. Another was the freedman Zayd ibn Ḥāritha, who may have played a large part in informing Muḥammad about Christianity, which was as we have seen widespread among his tribe, the Kalb. Who were the first outsiders to join this small family group? In later years heated arguments developed on this subject, because an early conversion to Islam represented a claim to honour and prestige which counted for a good deal in the fierce political struggles of the early days of the Muslim empire, especially since this glory reflected on the convert's descendants. But without paying undue attention to precise dates which, to the historian, are of no great moment, however much they mattered to the priority-conscious political men of the time, we can claim to know roughly the names of the forty or so who were converted in the first few years.

One of the earliest converts, even if he was not actually, as has been claimed, the very first after Khadīja, was a merchant known by his *kunya* as Abū Bakr. He was some three years younger than Muḥammad and apparently quite prosperous in a small way, a man of courage and steadiness, with sound judgement and strong common sense, who, having made his choice, never went back on it. He remained unconditionally loyal to Muḥammad while at the same time exerting a moderating influence on his decisions. 'Abū Bakr', writes Margoliouth,

> was a hero-worshipper, if ever there was one. He possessed a quality, common in women, but sometimes present in men, i.e. readiness to follow the fortunes of someone else with complete and blind devotion, never questioning nor looking back; to have believed much was with him a reason for believing more.[16]

A tradition which is said to go back to Zuhrī, a Meccan born some forty years after the death of the Prophet, a man who devoted a lifetime to research into the early days of Islam, tells how:

> The Messenger of God sent out the call to Islam both openly and in secret. Those whom God willed among the young and

weak listened eagerly so that the number of those that believed in him was great. The infidel Qurayshites did not find fault with what he said. When he passed by their parties, they would point him out among themselves saying: 'That is the young man of the Banū 'Abd al-Muṭṭalib who talks of heaven.'[17]

The text should perhaps be altered following Buhl's emendation to read: 'to whom spoke one out of the heavens.'[18]

Who were these young and 'weak'? Montgomery Watt has made valuable and extremely detailed biographical studies of these first forty of the faithful. Here is the gist of his results.

First, there were young men from the most influential families of the most influential clans in Mecca, related to those who wielded power. One of these was Khālid ibn Sa'īd ibn al-'Āṣ, of the clan of 'Abd Shams, at the time one of the two ruling clans, and, within that clan, of the family of Umayya, which as we shall see was to become increasingly prominent. He had a dream in which he saw himself standing on the edge of a lake of fire into which his father was pushing him. A man, whom Abū Bakr seems to have identified for him as Muḥammad, held him back and saved him, and from then on he became his follower and was joined not long afterwards by his brother 'Amr. When their father died, a third brother, Abān, composed some verses in which the dead man was heard bemoaning the errors of his sons. Khālid replied, also in verse:

> Let the dead be: he has followed his fate.
> Take heed for your neighbour: his need is greater.[19]

It is tempting to see this as a case of youthful rebellion, of the sort: 'Families, I hate you!' Another belonging to the same background and the same family was 'Uthmān ibn 'Affān, a man of about thirty destined for a high and tragic fate. For the present, however, he was a handsome young dandy, more interested in his clothes and appearance than anything else – idle and not very brave, but with a good head for business. It has been suggested that his conversion was largely due to his love for Ruqayya, one of Muḥammad's daughters.

A second category was made up of men belonging to less aristocratic and influential clans. These were for the most part young men under thirty; but they also included one or two individuals between thirty-five and fifty. Some of these possessed a degree of influence in their own clans or families. Into this group, for example, comes Abū Bakr, already mentioned, who was rising forty, and also the young Ṭalḥa ibn ʿUbaydallāh, an ardent, brave and ambitious youth who cannot have been more than eighteen at the time of his conversion.

Both these belonged to the clan Taym. From the Zuhra clan came an exceptionally able businessman of just over thirty – ʿAbd al-Kaʿba ibn ʿAwf, later known as ʿAbd ar-Raḥmān.

Those whom Zuhrī calls 'weak' may well come into this category; but the term certainly applies to a third group as well. This was made up of men who were not Qurayshites, who belonged to no clan by birth but were affiliated to a Qurayshite clan as 'confederates'. The clan to which they were affiliated owed them protection in theory but sometimes disdained to afford it or, if it were itself too weak, was unable to. Among these was one of the earliest believers, one of those under thirty, Khabbāb ibn al-Aratt, a smith and a maker of swords, the son of a woman who performed circumcisions, and an adopted member of the Banū Zuhra. Below these were freedmen such as Ṣuhayb ibn Sinān, a lad of twenty or so who was also called the Rūmī, that is the Roman, or Byzantine, on account of his fairness ('red' to the Arabs), and also perhaps because he had some connection with Byzantine Syria, like his friend ʿAmmār ibn Yāsir, an adopted member of the Banū Makhzūm, whose father-in-law was a freedman of Byzantine origin.

At the very bottom of the ladder were the real slaves. The most famous is Bilāl, a black Abyssinian, tall, thin and hollow-cheeked, with a stentorian voice. Like another slave, ʿĀmir ibn Fuhayra, he was bought from his master by Abū Bakr and given his freedom.

On the whole, those who turned to Muḥammad were among the most independent-minded in Mecca. The religious aspect of the doctrine was undoubtedly a decisive factor in their choice; but what inclined them to look favourably on this new teaching was their own freedom of mind compared with the conformist attitude of the ruling classes in Meccan society. This open-mindedness was itself due to different causes in different individuals; to an adolescent craving for new ideas, to contacts with foreign parts, to some degree of dissociation from the Meccan social system, to moral indignation or even to ambition and envy which led to criticism of those in power and thence of their system of values, and lastly and quite simply to the needs of individual psychology. It was therefore linked to a more or less confused awareness of the critical social and ideological state described earlier. Muḥammad and his message were closely bound up with this crucial state, and it was this which drew these people to him.

As the above quotations from Zuhrī show, the Qurayshites regarded the new group, which was gradually shedding its cloak of secrecy and emerging into the open, with amused tolerance, very much as Londoners today might watch a Salvation Army meeting on a street corner. They were harmless visionaries and there was no need to take them seriously. At the most, there was a certain contempt for the low social status of those involved.

According to Ibn Is'ḥāq, when the Messenger of God took his seat in the sanctuary (near the Ka'ba), the 'weak' among his Companions were accustomed to sit near him. The followers of Muḥammad who roused the Qurayshites' scorn were Khabbāb, 'Ammār, Abū Fukayha Yasār, Ṣuhayb and others of the same sort. 'There, you see,' they said to one another, 'those are his companions! And of all of us, would Allah have chosen them to show the right way and to teach the truth? If what Muḥammad brings us were something good, such people would not have got hold of it before us!'[20] Muḥammad, who was after all of better birth than the majority of his disciples, cannot in his heart of hearts have been wholly insensible to this argument, and unconsciously he welcomed the justifications and precedents cited by his Lord. It had been just the same with Noah when he warned his people of imminent catastrophe:

> The senate [the *mala'*, the name of the Meccan council of elders], the ungrateful among his people answered: 'We see in you only a man like ourselves and we see among your followers only the basest and most foolish of us all. We see no virtue in you more than in ourselves. Rather, we look on you as liars.'
>
> (Koran xi, 29)

Noah and his humble followers were vindicated by the Flood. Before long, Muḥammad and the weak would have their revenge and be similarly justified.

But neither scepticism nor mockery constituted serious opposition. In the end, however, this came. What brought it about? A few accounts which have filtered through a tradition tending rather too much towards hagiography throw some light on what may have happened, and allow us to hazard a guess.

The new movement must have caused many Qurayshites some anxiety. The reassuring character of its doctrine and the fact that it involved apparently few changes in the previously accepted world picture were not enough to make everyone regard it as harmless. In all situations and walks of life, we have known people who are often in principle most open to new ideas, to be so hidebound that they automatically dread change of any kind – even when aimed at nothing more radical than a superficial adjustment of outdated forms – in any organization or ideology with which they are concerned. What must these have been like in western Arabia in the seventh century, in what was still a strongly traditionalist society in spite of all the structural changes it had already undergone, but which, at a conscious level, it had refused to recognize? We are familiar, too, with the sentimental arguments of the conservatives, the lachrymose appeals to old-established custom, the indignant attacks on all who dare to take a fresh look at established beliefs, and the reminders of the sacrifices made in their defence, the contemptuous attitude to youth and inexperience, the lack of weight in society carried by reformers – we also know that all this works with powerful effect on the nerves, hearts and minds of an unprepared crowd. It is also more than likely that the young enthusiasts made mistakes, and that their blunders and excesses added to the uneasiness of the conservatives.

And yet, as we have seen, Muḥammad was by no means an extremist. Among those who regarded his movement with anxious perplexity there were also men of judgement, who were carefully weighing up the advantages and disadvantages from the point of view of Meccan high society. Two crucial points, one doctrinal, the other mainly practical, must have seemed to them somewhat obscure; and their attitude would depend on how Muḥammad cleared up these points.

First, what was the role assigned to the various gods worshipped by the Qurayshites? Were they mighty gods? Small, minor gods? Jinns? Above all – and this was the most important from the devotional point of view which is not greatly concerned with theological subtleties – was Muḥammad a threat to their cult? Were their shrines to be abandoned, their symbols destroyed, their offerings neglected? What had Muḥammad's mysterious Lord to say on this score?

And how did Muḥammad see his own role? As is often the case, his opponents seem to have seen more clearly than he himself what lay beneath his surface modesty. He accepted with humility the modest role of herald which the Lord assigned to him. But it cannot have been difficult to discern the legitimate pride underlying the humility which he honestly endeavoured to acquire; and, above all, intelligent politicians could readily understand how the logic of his position was inevitably bound to push him, in spite of himself, to supreme power. How could a man to whom God spoke directly ever submit to the decisions of any council? How could the dictates of the Supreme Being be subjected to discussion by the aristocracy of Mecca? In a society which drew no clear line between the sacred and the profane, it was quite obvious that the logical outcome would be a situation in which God would dictate his commands personally through Muḥammad, in the sphere of internal and external affairs as well as on strictly religious matters. Was Muḥammad aware of this logic, and how far was he prepared to go?

That some attempts at compromise were made is clear from documentary evidence which, while certainly contrived, probably had some foundation in fact. An old man named ʿUtba ibn Rabīʿa, one of the leaders of the ʿAbd Shams clan, whose young son was among the earliest of Muḥammad's followers, was said to have stood up in the council one day and remarked: 'Assembly of Quraysh! Suppose I go to Muḥammad and speak to him? I will make him some proposals. Perhaps he will accept some of them. We will give him what he wants and he will leave us alone.' His colleagues agreed and he went to Muḥammad who was sitting a little way off, and said to him: 'Well, nephew! You are one of us, you know that, you are of good birth in your tribe and your descent is noble. You have faced your tribe with a considerable problem, you have divided their community and made light of their dreams, you have belittled their gods and their religion. You have proclaimed their deceased forebears pagans. Listen! I am going to give you some proposals to think over. You may perhaps accept some of them.' Muḥammad replied: 'Speak, Abū l-Walīd, I am listening.' Then the old man went on to say: 'Nephew, if all you want out of this business that you have stirred up for us is money, we will club together and give you enough to make you richer than all of us. If it is prestige you want, we will make you our leader, so that we will decide nothing without consulting you. If you want sovereignty, we will make you our king. If what obsesses you is a ghost you cannot be rid of, we will seek out a doctor and lay out our own money to cure you, for often a man may be possessed of a familiar spirit until he is cured of it' – or words to that effect. Muḥammad's answer was to recite some verses from the Koran. ʿUtba listened carefully and went back to his companions with this advice: 'Leave him alone. By God, his words will have vast consequences. If the Arabs [that is, the Beduin] kill him, then you will be delivered from him by others. But if he triumphs over the Arabs, his sovereignty will be your sovereignty and his glory will be your glory, and through him you will be the most prosperous of men.'[21] 'Utba's speech is undoubtedly apocryphal; this is clear from certain arguments he uses, and in any case the author does not vouch for the exact words. But, as we shall see, it had an element of truth in it.

There was one incident, in fact, which may reasonably be accepted as true because the makers of Muslim tradition would never have invented a story with such damaging implications for the revelation as a whole. 'When the Messenger of God saw his people draw away from him,' wrote Ṭabarī,

> it gave him great pain to see what a distance separated them from the word of Allah which he brought to them. Then he longed in his heart to receive a word from Allah which would bring him closer to his people. Because of his care for them and the love he had for them, he would gladly have seen those things that bore too harshly on them softened a little, so much so that he kept saying it to himself, and desiring it and wishing for it. It was then that Allah revealed to him the *sūrah* of the Star . . .

When he came to the verse:

> Have you considered Allāt and al-'Uzzā
> And Manāt, the third, the other? . . .
>
> (Koran liii, 19–20)

the demon put upon his tongue what he had been saying to himself and would have liked to hand on to his people:

> They are the Exalted Birds
> And their intercession is desired indeed.

According to Muslim lore, when the Qurayshites heard this verse they were highly delighted and all prostrated themselves, Muslims and non-Muslims alike.[22] It was only later that the archangel revealed to Muḥammad that he had been deceived by the Devil – although, he added as consolation, that was no wonder because the earlier prophets had experienced similar difficulties and for the same reasons.

The additional verses were taken out and replaced by others rejecting the cult of the 'three great aquatic birds' (the word which I have rendered 'birds' is actually cranes or herons); and after this splendid but temporary display of unanimity the Meccans were once more divided.

Obviously (Ṭabarī's account as good as says so in fairly clear words) Muḥammad's unconscious had suggested to him a formula which provided a practical road to unanimity. It did not appear to conflict with his henotheism, since these 'great birds' were, like angels or jinns, conceived of as subordinate to Allah. Elsewhere they were called the 'daughters of Allah'. On the other hand this provided a clear indication that the new teaching was in no way revolutionary, and that the new sect honoured the city's divinities, respected their shrines and recognized their cult as a legitimate one.

But Muḥammad must very soon have realized the implications of this concession. It meant that the sect renounced all claim to originality. Jews and Christians pointed out maliciously that Muḥammad was reverting to his pagan beginnings. Besides, what force had the threat of the Last Judgement if the daughters of Allah, propitiated by traditional offerings and sacrifices, could intercede on behalf of sinners and save them from eternal damnation? Above all, what authority was left to the herald sent by Allah if any little priest of al-'Uzzā or Manāt could pronounce oracles contradicting his message? All this was probably underlined by rebelliousness and indignation within Muḥammad's own small group of followers and by the no doubt all too evident relief of the conservative Qurayshites. 'In the end, it pleased Ibn Abī Kabsha [a name he was popularly known by] to speak well of our goddesses,' exclaimed the rich and powerful Abū Uḥayḥa Sa'īd ibn al-'Āṣ, the father of the young convert who dreamed he was trying to push him into the fire.[23] We can imagine how pleased he must have been, and how great must have been the indignation of the young rebel.

Also, if he went back on what had been said, it would mean taking what had until then been a somewhat doubtful leap; it would mean an open break – putting himself in a position to win or lose all. Ideologically it would mean denouncing the gods of Mecca as lesser spirits or mere names, void of any objective meaning, and denying the validity of their cult and alienating their priests and their followers. It would mean casting off everything relating to the traditional religion as the work of pagans and unbelievers, consigning the Meccans' pious ancestors and relatives to hell fire. On another level, Muḥammad would henceforth be freed from any necessity to acknowledge the authority of any pagan in any way whatever. It would remain to be seen whether he would retain his independence as an Arab prophet or join up with the foreign churches.

Was he going to become a Christian? The people of Mecca recalled an incident which had occurred during his youth, when an ambitious Qurayshite named 'Uthmān ibn al-Ḥuwayrith had been converted to Christianity and had tried to make himself king of the city under Byzantine protection. He had almost succeeded when a sudden democratic revulsion of feeling on the part of his fellow citizens brought about the failure of his plans. The Qurayshites may have feared that the same danger would occur again.

At all events, they responded to the break by counter-attacking fiercely. One apparently reliable source even states categorically that the persecution of the members of the sect started 'when Muḥammad mentioned their idols'. It goes on to say, an interesting detail which somehow rings true, that: 'Qurayshite landowners from Ṭā'if came and reproached him for this; they behaved violently towards him and showed their dislike of what he said and so roused up those who served them.' It is tempting to think that these Qurayshite landowners from Ṭā'if (the cool, shady mountain resort not far from Mecca, where the rich Meccan merchants had pleasant country houses) acted from the desire to protect the cult of Allāt which had an important shrine at Ṭā'if. 'Then,' our text continues,

> the people abandoned Muḥammad, except those whom Allah preserved, and they were not many. Matters rested in this state

for as long as Allah willed it. Then their leaders conspired together to draw aside their sons, their brothers, and members of their tribes who were among his followers, and turn them from their belief in Allah. It was a very great ordeal for the Muslims who followed the Messenger of God. Those who were led away were led away, and Allah strengthened those among them whom he would.[24]

The actual persecution was on the whole comparatively mild. Ibn Is'ḥāq sums it up quite well in the few lines he devotes to the activities of one branded in Muslim accounts among the Prophet's fiercest opponents. This was Abū Jahl, a trader and one of the most influential leaders of the Banū Makhzūm.

It was the villain Abū Jahl who roused the men of Quraysh against them. Whenever he heard that an honourable man, with a host of supporters, had been converted to Islam he would berate him soundly so as to shame him. 'You have abandoned the faith of your father, although he was a better man than you,' he would say. 'We will show that you have acted like a fool and lack judgement. We will ruin your reputation.' If the man were a merchant, he would tell him: 'By Allah! We will boycott your business so that you will lose all you have.' If he was a person of no influence, he beat him and turned people against him.[25]

There was, then, an attempt to make Muḥammad's followers give up their faith by, as happens in the case of men of no social standing, a combination of moral and economic pressures. In the majority of cases nothing more could be done, since according to the prevailing social system these men were protected by their clan. We are told that some of the persecutors who were anxious to make trouble for al-Walīd ibn al-Walīd – a man of the clan of Makhzūm who had become a Muslim but who feared the violent temper of his brother Hishām – went to him first to warn him:

They said, 'We only want to teach these young men a lesson, because of this new religion. Then we will be at peace with the rest.' 'Very well,' was the answer, 'deal with him and teach him a lesson. But have a care to his life.' And he quoted these lines:

> For so it is. Let not my brother 'Uyays be killed
> Or there will be an exchange of curses [i.e. war] between us forever.

'Beware of his life. I swear, by Allah, if you kill him, I will kill all the noblest amongst you to the last man.' Then they said to one another: 'Allah's curse be on him. Now who is going to embark on the business? By Allah! if the man dies at our hands, he is quite capable of slaying our leaders to the last man.' So they left him alone and did not touch him.[26]

As usual, therefore, it was the poorest and most deprived members of the movement who suffered most, and first and foremost the slaves. Bilāl, for instance, was exposed by the folk of his master's clan at the bottom of the dry valley of Mecca in the full glare of the sun at the hottest part of the day with a great rock bound on his chest. (It was at this time that Abū Bakr purchased a number of Muslim slaves in order to give them their freedom.) This ill treatment may have been exaggerated later on in order to enhance the virtues of the earliest believers and also, most probably, to provide excuses for apostates.

They persecuted [the Muslim], striking him and making him suffer hunger and thirst until he could not keep upright where he sat because of the pains he had endured. In the end he agreed to abjure as they demanded of him. They asked him: 'Are Allāt and al-'Uzzā your gods, not Allah?' And he said, 'Yes.' He had reached the stage where, had a beetle gone by and had they said: 'Is that beetle your god and not Allah?', he would have said 'Yes' to that too, only to escape the tortures they had inflicted on him.[27]

In this situation, Muḥammad himself escaped any ill usage because his clan, the Banū Hāshim, stuck by him. The reason for this was that his uncle, Abū Ṭālib, under whose protection, as we have seen, he had been brought up, still retained considerable influence among them, in spite of the decline in his fortunes. He by no means approved of the ideas which his unaccountable nephew was putting forward; but the honour of the clan demanded that even its most culpable members should be protected. This reflection was calculated to rally the whole clan solidly behind him. The conservative Qurayshites were furious, seeing their most desirable victim elude them. They tried to put pressure on the Hāshim clan as a whole to make them withdraw the protection they were according their black sheep: no one was to do business with, or form marriage ties with, any members of the clan or of the allied clan of al-Muṭṭalib. In fact, quite apart from the need to combat the new movement, this boycott seems to have had distinct practical advantages for the Makhzūm and the ʿAbd Shams, by this time the ruling clans in Mecca, since it served to isolate the once powerful clan of Hāshim from nearly all the clans which, during the time of Muḥammad's youth, had been allied with it to form an alliance which had carried considerable political weight.

The boycott lasted for two years, although it does not seem to have been very strictly enforced. In a society where no central authority could impose itself by force it was not easy for any alliance of individuals or clans to endure for very long. The clans persuaded by the Makhzūm and ʿAbd Shams to join in the boycott must quickly have realized that the elimination of Hāshim merely strengthened the economic and political domination of its initiators. Besides, in practice, this show of solidarity was not without its cracks. On the Hāshim side, one of the leading members of the clan had deserted – an uncle of Muḥammad's named Abū Lahab. He broke off the marriage (or it may have been only the betrothal) of his two sons to two of Muḥammad's daughters and sided with the boycotters, led by his wife's powerful clan, the ʿAbd Shams.

Pressure was also brought to bear by means of what we should nowadays call propaganda. Public heckling and mockery of Muḥammad's message was stepped up. The resurrection of the body, which was the chief basis of the new teaching of the Last Judgement, was laughed to scorn. Muḥammad was called on to provide more information as to the date of this event, which he may have hinted was closer than it seemed. They pressed him closely on the most important question, already mentioned above, of whether they were to abandon the faith of their fathers and consign them to everlasting fire. More than ever Muḥammad was called a visionary, possessed maybe by a spirit of a lesser order like the *kāhins* (soothsayers), magicians and poets. Names of Christians and Jews were quoted, from whom he was said to get his information and whose teachings he was supposed merely to repeat. It was pointed out that the Supreme Deity was unlikely to have chosen as his messenger a man of such little weight as Ibn Abī Kabsha. Besides, where were the supernatural signs, the miracles which Allah would naturally bestow on his messenger to establish the authenticity of his mission? Here was nothing more than an ambitious man trying to thrust himself in among the leaders of Quraysh. The offers of compromise, which were, it is said, repeated at this stage and of which a typical example has been cited above, may also have been in part a cunning move to discredit him by proving to the world that his aims were purely political.

Muḥammad succeeded in swiftly organizing a defence against this persecution. In this he was notably assisted by a member of the hostile clan Makhzūm, al-Arqam ibn ʿAbd Manāf – an indication of how little unity prevailed within these social groups. Al-Arqam was young, not more than twenty-five and most probably less; but he was, it seems, the head of his family, because he was able to offer the new sect a refuge for its meetings in his house, which was large and conveniently placed. The less well-protected or less intrepid members slipped in there under cover of darkness, keeping close to the walls. There were more conversions. One of these, dating from the beginning of the persecution, carried a good deal of weight since the man concerned was Ḥamza, one of Muḥammad's uncles, who, while admittedly of no great social standing, being poor, quick-tempered and over-fond of drink, was none the less brave and energetic. Moreover it was losing his temper which led to his conversion. He came home from a hunting trip to hear from a crony, who had watched the scene from a window, that Abū Jahl had insulted his nephew. He flew into a rage and, hurrying off to find the persecutor and call him to account, hit him with the bow which he still held in his hand. A general free-for-all was only averted thanks to the good sense of Abū Jahl, who admitted that he had gone rather too far and that Muḥammad's clan had every right to take offence. He restrained his supporters, and in a spirit of bravado Ḥamza was converted. This penniless ruffian was however a useful recruit. The disciples stood in great need of some strong physical support.

At this time there probably occurred an important event, the history of which has been so much rewritten to fit the ideas and interests of later times that it is hard to see it in its true light. (Similar instances abound today, and are indeed common practice in the historiography of those states and movements which keep a tight hold over the minds of their subjects or followers.) This particular episode concerns the emigration of the first Muslims to Abyssinia, which is generally thought to have occurred before that of the verses inspired by Satan; although there is a case for believing (as Montgomery Watt does) that it took place afterwards, since according to our oldest reliable source it followed the persecution which, in turn, occurred after Muḥammad's attack on the 'idols'. The beginning of this hostile attitude was marked by the revelation abrogating the 'satanic verses'. Let us, therefore, refer back once again to this source, the beginning of which has already been quoted:

Then the people turned away from Muḥammad except for those whom Allah preserved and they were not many. . . . This was a very great ordeal. . . . Those who were led away were led away and Allah strengthened those among them whom he would. When this took place among the Muslims, the Messenger of Allah commanded them to depart to Abyssinia. There was in Abyssinia a good king called the *najāshī* [*nagāshī* in Ethiopian]. Nobody was oppressed in his land and through him prosperity reigned there. Moreover, Abyssinia was a market for the

Qurayshites who traded there because they found food in plenty, security and good business. The Messenger of Allah bade them do this, and for the most part they went there when they were oppressed at Mecca. He feared they might be led astray. But he remained there all the time. In this way, years passed during which [the Qurayshites] dealt harshly with those amongst them who embraced Islam . . .[28]

It is clear from this that the emigrants were those whose faith Muḥammad considered the least steadfast and that the fact of having emigrated to Abyssinia cannot, as it was thought later, be regarded as a claim to distinction, although some of those who went seem to have been good believers. It is also possible, as Montgomery Watt has suggested, that Muḥammad was using the escape from persecution as an excuse to get out of the way a section of his following whom he suspected of being likely to disagree with himself in certain particulars. The chief figure in the little band of emigrants was ʿUthmān ibn Maẓʿūn of the clan of Jumaḥ. He was a man who had taken to an ascetic way of life, even before Islam. He would not drink wine and, later on at any rate, made a vow of chastity about which his wife complained to ʿĀʾisha. He even applied (unsuccessfully, it goes without saying) to Muḥammad for permission to castrate himself. When he joined the movement he brought with him his son, his two younger brothers and his three nephews; these went with him to Abyssinia. It therefore seems likely that quite independently he may have had ideas similar to those of Muḥammad, and, having gathered round him a small circle of monotheist *ḥanīfs*, joined forces with the stronger personality, ʿAbdallāh's son.

In any party there will be suspicion of those who, having arrived at the same truth as the leader independently of him, join as a coherent group and then, still as a group, show a tendency to criticize the party line, to pass judgement on the leadership and in short not to acquiesce automatically, in spirit and in practice, in every one of the leader's changing decisions. Our sources furnish anecdotes indicating a measure of hostility between ʿUthmān and the active leaders Abū Bakr and ʿUmar, whose counsels Muḥammad followed. Long afterwards, ʿUmar scoffed at ʿUthmān for dying in his bed, and picked a quarrel with one of the emigrants by insisting that the Abyssinian exile had been a rest-cure amounting virtually to desertion. In this one can recognize the usual reproaches addressed by the man of action to the theorist. ʿUthmān ibn Maẓʿūn was a sincere believer but he was independent and an extremist. (According to one story, he once caused a scene at a literary party by taking exception to the excessive materialism of the famous poet Labīd.) He was unable to bow readily to the tactical fluctuations of more politic leaders.

Scarcely any of the information we possess about the stay in Abyssinia is at all reliable. Did the exiled Qurayshites, who included, among others, the elegant ʿUthmān ibn ʿAffān and his wife, Muḥammad's daughter Ruqayya, and the Prophet's cousin, and brother of ʿAlī, Jaʿfar ibn Abī Ṭālib, really make a strong impression on the Negus (or *nagāshī* as one called him then) of Axūm and on his bishops and chief officials, and did the Qurayshites really send an ambassador to demand their extradition? It would be equally rash to answer yes or no to these questions. Later historians have embroidered a good deal on both suppositions and extricated themselves from the resulting mass of contradictions by assuming two successive migrations, the suggestion being that some of the emigrants returned to Mecca on hearing of the episode of the 'satanic verses' which they took to mean a general reconciliation of the Qurayshites. This is clearly unacceptable if that episode is placed before the emigration. Whatever the truth, the emigration itself remains a certainty.

It must also have a significance in the sphere of international politics, although the precise nature of this is not easy for us to pinpoint. The choice of Christian Abyssinia ('God's country' as one woman emigrant called it),[29] Monophysite but an ally of Byzantium, as a refuge was certainly significant. For at this time Heraclius and the Byzantine armies were withdrawing on all fronts before the victorious Persians, and men could foresee an imminent end to the Christian empire which, so short a time before, they had believed to be universal and eternal; the triumph of the Mazdaean Persians and their Jewish and Nestorian allies was building up to a political upheaval on a considerable and perhaps even a cosmic scale. Was this a clear choice in favour of Christianity? Moreover, was the decision really Muḥammad's or was it taken by dissident elements and only later, when dissension had been smoothed away by victory and conveniently forgotten, confirmed and sanctified by being attributed to the Prophet? The evidence we have is too scanty and unreliable to enable us to judge clearly.

The list of emigrants to Abyssinia has certainly been added to at a later date. There may have been no more than fifteen originally. The little community remaining in Mecca amounted to some forty men and ten or twenty women. They endured patiently the cold-shouldering of their enemies, the jibes and insults and occasional ill treatment – all the petty irritations of the cold war which was all that tribal solidarity allowed. They achieved one notable success in the conversion of a man of some standing who, after Muḥammad, was probably the person to do the most for Islam. ʿUmar ibn al-Khaṭṭāb was about twenty-five years old and a member of a minor Qurayshite clan. He was a man of naturally violent temper, but he also possessed an iron will and the ability to dominate and control his impulses and use them in order to further rational designs.

He had sided against the new sect with his customary energy, but his sister Fāṭima and her husband Saʿīd had joined it secretly. It is true that a few Muslims had suspected him of some sympathy for the emigrants who had left for Abyssinia, but his general attitude was so uncompromising that they said: 'He will be converted when his father's ass becomes a Muslim.' One day, he drew his sword and set out in a fury for the meeting place of the sect in the house of al-Arqam. He was met by a cool man of his tribe who asked where he was going. 'I am seeking Muḥammad,' he replied, 'that Ṣābi'an [a baptist monotheist sect of Babylonia] who has sown dissension in Quraysh, who mocks at their beliefs, disparages their religion and insults their gods. I am going to kill him.' 'You are making a mistake,' the other man told him. 'Do you think for a moment that the Banū ʿAbd Manāf [the group of clans related to Muḥammad's] will let you walk the earth once you have killed Muḥammad? You would do better to go home and put your own house in order.' Surprised, ʿUmar asked what he thought was going on in his house. The man told him what everyone knew, whereupon ʿUmar turned round and went home again where, as it happened, the humble Muslim smith Khabbāb was reading a leaf of the Koran to his sister and brother-in-law. When they heard ʿUmar coming they were panic-stricken. Khabbāb hid in another room while Fāṭima sat down cross-legged and hid the leaf of the Koran under her skirts. ʿUmar came in, demanding to know the meaning of the noise he had heard. Fāṭima and her husband pretended not to understand. At this, ʿUmar lost his temper completely; he told them what people were saying about them, and struck his sister a blow on the head. However the sight of the blood brought him to himself, and he asked to see the leaf they were looking at before he came in, promising to give it back safely. An exclamation of wonder was forced from him as he read the words. Then Khabbāb came out of his hiding place and very cleverly told ʿUmar that he had heard Muḥammad praying for his conversion only the day before. ʿUmar, much moved, insisted on being taken to the house of al-Arqam, this time with his sword in his belt. They were a trifle nervous about letting him in; but he delighted the hearts of all by announcing his conversion.[30] This, as G. Levi della Vida says, was the beginning of the 'compass swing by which, knowing no middle course, the same uncompromisingly single-minded attitude brought to bear an equal impetuosity and intensity whether in hatred or devotion'.[31] ʿUmar's adherence encouraged the disciples who, we are told, were emboldened to the extent of saying their prayers in public close by the Kaʿba.

Meanwhile, all this time the revelations were continuing. Slowly, painfully, a doctrine was taking shape. There, in the strange atmosphere of Mecca, on the edge of the magnificent civilized world of the great powers, just then engaged in an apocalyptic struggle, the faith was growing up which was later to overflow into the world at large and endeavour to mould it. All this was taking place within the brain of a single man, but stirring within it were the reflected problems of a whole world; and the historical conditions were such that the results of all this mental activity were calculated to shake Arabia and beyond.

Force of circumstances, that is, in this case, the force of Meccan conservatism, together with Muḥammad's deep-rooted conviction of the importance of his message and the burning desire for a new deal on the part of his disciples, had made compromise impossible. From then on, the ill-assorted group of individuals, all more or less in sympathy with the message of one inspired spokesman, became welded into a community, its unity only strengthened by the hostility which surrounded it. This transformation involved a profound alteration in the content and even the form of the message, and in the general attitude of the master and the disciples towards everything around them.

This group had to distinguish itself clearly from everything outside itself. To do that, it first had to have its own clearly defined ideology. Essentially this was based on divine unity, since this had brought about the rupture and was a watchword by which friends could be clearly divided from enemies. This cut right across the Meccan cult of the three 'Exalted Birds', called the daughters of Allah, about which the revelation from on high is quite clear:

> Is he to have daughters and you sons? . . .
> Do they know the Unknowable, do they set it down in writing? . . .
> Have they any God but Allah? How far is Allah above those they associate with him.
>
> (Koran lii, 39–43)

And rather later perhaps:

> Invoke the name of your Lord and dedicate yourself wholly to him,
> The Lord of East and West. There is no god but he.
> Take him for your protector.
>
> (Koran lxxiii, 8–9)

The message is explicit. There is only one god. No other being may be 'associated' with him as an object of worship because all other beings of whatever kind are far below him. The Being who inspired Muḥammad and who referred to himself simply in such modest terms as your Lord, or their Lord, finally named himself clearly. It was indeed Allah, the one God, the Supreme Deity, well known to the Meccans who were merely ignorant of the extent of his power and his divine solitude. However he had another name, ar-Raḥmān, meaning the Beneficent. But ar-Raḥmān was used as a proper name. It was foreign to the Hejaz and regarded by the Meccans with particular dislike. It was the name of God used by the Jews and, in the form Raḥmānān, by the Christians of South Arabia to signify God the Father. It was the name of God used by Maslama, the prophet of the Yamāma, in his teachings and it must have been the name used in certain Jewish and Christian circles in Mecca to whom Muḥammad was urged by his inspirer to apply for information, notwithstanding their distastefulness to the Meccans:

> He who in six days created the heavens and the earth and all that lies between them, and then seated himself in majesty upon the Throne, is ar-Raḥmān, ask one who knows about him.
>
> When it is said to them: 'Prostrate yourselves before ar-Raḥmān,' they answer: 'Who is ar-Raḥmān? Shall we prostrate ourselves at your command?' And this increases their repulsion.
>
> (Koran xxv, 60–61)

The Supreme Lord called himself Allah or ar-Raḥmān indifferently.

> Say: 'Pray to Allah,' or 'Pray to ar-Raḥmān.'
> To whomsoever you pray, his names are the most beautiful.
>
> (Koran xvii, 110)

This God was all-knowing and all-powerful. One should turn to him; other so-called gods had no power, and Fate, that first metaphysical incarnation of the laws of nature to which Meccan ideology clung, was subject to the Deity. God gratified those whom he would, and humbled and raised men at will. At the end of time he would deal out reward and punishment according to his own lights, which were beyond human understanding, to those who had pleased or displeased him. These things would be decided at the Last Judgement, which already figured in the very first revelation and which emerged as a basic dogma, putting the new community in direct opposition to the dominant religious beliefs of its society. With the passage of time, however, the descriptions of the Judgement and of what was to follow, the delights of paradise or the torments of hell, became increasingly condensed and lost their more picturesque elements. It was, by then, less a matter of describing than of replying to the Meccan arguments. As with the Jews and early Christians, a resurrection for the Judgement which did not involve a reconstitution of earthly bodies was inconceivable. Consequently the Meccans pointed out the improbability of this process when anyone could see how bodies decayed in the tombs and bones crumbled under the desert sands. Muḥammad's retort was that the infinite power of God who had created them once from a drop of sperm was quite equal to recreating them from dry bones. And then, when would this fantastic event take place? At first, the Voice from on high declared that it was imminent.

> The reckoning draws near for men, yet they turn away from it, heedlessly.
>
> (Koran xxi, 1)
>
> They say: 'If what you say is true, when will this threat come to pass?'
> Answer: 'A part of that which you are in haste for may be already close behind you.'
>
> (Koran xxvii, 73–74)

It is worth noting in passing the commercial language

employed by this God, speaking through a merchant to merchants.

In order to justify itself in the face of a powerful and aggressive opposition – an opposition on the alert for every weak place in the new doctrine, based first and foremost on the conservatism of the few and of the masses and quick to make extensive use of the argument of loyalty to the ancestral faith and to denounce Muḥammad as an ambitious troublemaker – the new faith had to create a tradition for itself which would also explain its difficulties in making its way, difficulties which, it might be thought, supernatural assistance should surely have avoided. To this end, the Voice, profiting from all that Muḥammad was learning, and all that he already knew, told the story of the prophets of the past. This was what it was to call later 'the seven narrations' (*mathānī*), using the same Aramaic word which was used by the Jews to signify the Repetition, the pre-eminent Oral Tradition (*mishnah* in Hebrew, *mathnīthā* in Aramaic). All these narratives followed the same pattern. A prophet was sent to call a people to repentance and to the worship of the one true God, but the people would not listen and were then doomed to destruction. As we have seen, this pattern had been suggested to Muḥammad by an eastern tradition of Judaeo-Christian origin. But that it applied first, in these narrations, to purely Arab peoples is without doubt from the tales, one half or three quarters legend, which were well known in the Hejaz and were inspired by the ruins which the caravans had many opportunities to observe on their routes.

There were the 'Ād, a race perhaps believed to have been giants, who had left enigmatic monuments on the peaks. A messenger named Hūd had been sent to them, but he was rejected; then a violent wind had blown for seven nights and seven days, leaving in its wake only empty ruins. There were the Thamūd who, as we know from the evidence of (among others) Greek and Roman authors, were a real people. The Thamūd had built castles in the plain and dug out dwellings in the mountain-sides. These were very probably the handsome

Nabataean tombs in Hellenistic style, which could be admired in the region of al-ʿElā, in the north of the Hejāz, at the beginning of the seventh century, just as they can today. Why were these fine monuments no more than deserted ruins? The reason was that another prophet, Ṣāliḥ, had brought the word of Allah to this people, producing as the sign of his mission a camel, possibly held to be miraculous, which was to be allowed to graze 'on the land of Állah' and given a share of water. But the elders (*mala'*) of the Thamūd, like those of Mecca later on, were unimpressed; they cavilled at the prophet and mocked the humble believers. They sacrificed the camel. Then, after a space of three days, they were destroyed by a cataclysm, apparently an earthquake accompanied by thunder and a shattering din. Similar tales were told about the people of Midyan, in north-western Arabia, and their prophet Shuʿayb, and about the people of the Well, the people of the Thicket, the people of Tubbaʿ (who were probably South Arabian), and the Sabaeans whose fertile fields were overwhelmed by a flood. Some of these stories are mere allusions, so that we do not even know exactly who were these people of the Well and people of the Thicket. But these essentially Arab tales were very soon tied up with Old Testament stories carrying a similar moral. Noah, also, preached in vain, and the Flood engulfed those who had paid no attention to his words. Lot reproached the inhabitants of Sodom for their homosexuality; but instead of listening to him they grew angry and drove him out, and so their city was destroyed and only he and his family were saved, 'except for one old woman who stayed behind' (Koran xxxvii, 135). Pharaoh – bizarrely referred to as 'the master of boar-spears' – was warned, along with his *mala'*, by Moses and Aaron. They would not believe them and were destroyed by Allah. Korah, who in the Bible rebelled against Moses in the desert for reasons of priestly supremacy, and for that was swallowed up with his family when God made the earth crack beneath them, reappears, under the name of Qārūn, placed, by an astonishing anachronism, along with Haman, 'the impious Aman, of the Amalekite race' (in the words of Jean Racine) in the story of

Esther, and with Pharaoh, among the proud men who would not listen to Moses and were therefore severely punished. In the same way, Abraham (Ibrāhīm in Arabic) tried to persuade his father and his people to give up the cult of idols. He was not listened to either, and had to emigrate because of the threats against him. It was the unbelievers who were 'the worst losers' (Koran xxi, 70).

These stories, drawn from Arab tradition or from the sacred books of the Jews, distorted at some stage in the transmission, are not told for the mere pleasure of the telling. Parallels with Muḥammad and his own situation emerge more or less clearly at every turn. Ṣāliḥ, Hūd, Noah and Moses are himself. 'Ād, Thamūd, the proud Pharaoh, the rich Korah, their people and their *mala'* are the senate and people of Quraysh. Muḥammad's people refused to listen to him: that is the normal rule. As to what will befall them, one has only to refer to the precedents:

> We carried off each of them for their sins. Against some we unleashed a whirlwind. Others were carried off by the Clamour. Others we caused to be swallowed up in the earth. Others we drowned. It was not Allah who wronged them: they wronged themselves.
>
> (Koran xxix, 39)

The same doom was bound to fall on Mecca. Muḥammad and his followers would be saved in one way or another from the punishment that would strike the proud and unbelieving city. Precisely what punishment, the Voice did not say. Possibly Muḥammad thought that Allah would make use of the fortunes of the war between Byzantium and the Persians; this may have had something to do with the emigration to Abyssinia. We cannot tell for certain. At all events, it is noticeable that the threat of the end of the world and the Judgement to follow was employed only in the early stages; it later gave way to the promise of a temporal and purely localized punishment.

Alongside these stories, with their direct morals, were others which seem to have been intended primarily as a general demonstration of the power and greatness of Allah. They came from the treasury of legend common to the whole of the Christian east, handed down by way of Syriac literature.

One such was the story of the Seven Sleepers of Ephesus, young Christians who took refuge in a cavern to escape persecution by the Emperor Decius and slept there for several hundred years. Another was the legend of Moses and his mysterious servant, who went in search of the Spring of Everlasting Life – a legend in which one can find echoes of the old Sumero-Akkadian epic of Gilgamesh, recast into the Hellenistic story of Alexander. The same Alexander reappears in another tale under the name of Dhū l-Qarnayn, the two-horned (because his 'father' Jupiter-Ammon had two horns); in this tale he is building a wall at the world's end to keep out the mythical races of Gog and Magog.

Having by this means acquired illustrious precedents, and a venerable tradition, in part Arab and in part Judaeo-Christian, the community had still to answer all kinds of questions and criticisms. The demands made upon it were heavy – and quite rightly so, since it claimed to be acting on divine inspiration and offering a higher way of life. Muḥammad pondered, meditated and learned. His thoughts germinated in his mind; and one day the Voice from on high gave the answer. And so, little by little, an embryo theology emerged, a rough and ready affair as befitted the society and the individual minds for whom it was intended.

While a man is, so to speak, an organic part of his clan, tribe, village or city and simply one interchangeable element in a rigorously hierarchical society, fixed in the place that fate has assigned to him for a purpose which is always the same, he finds himself inevitably adopting the idea of an after-life which is the same or similar to this one. There, too, the pale ghosts would continue to lead their shadowy lives within the same social framework as in this world. In these lands beyond the grave, shadowy servants would serve phantom masters, spectral peasants cultivate their fields and ghostly craftsmen produce their wares. The merits or demerits of this world made little difference there. Such were men's earliest ideas about what happened after death, although their details no doubt varied a good deal. But when races, men and ideas began to mingle with the growth of trade between the nations, and societies were formed in which money became the measure of all things – in which an economy based on money broke through the ethnic barriers and each man was able to make his own fortune, and where the individual's place in the world was determined by the worth of his own efforts – when all this came about, then people began to hope for a fate according to each man's deserts. From that time prophets began to arise; these men, while deploring the end of the old social order in which each man's livelihood at least had been guaranteed by the group and denouncing the rich and their extortionate demands, told them of the certainty of the individual punishment awaiting them first in this world and then in the next. From that time organized communities were formed to teach their members how to attain a blessed state in the world to come and how to win individual salvation.

These religions based on individual salvation had already spread through the ancient world between the eighth and the fifth centuries before Christ. Now, after a substantial time-lag, the wave was reaching western Arabia. There, too, men were asking what they must do to be saved.

The answer given by the Voice which spoke to Muḥammad may be deduced from the foregoing. Men must turn to Allah. Allah is, as has been shown to us, infinitely powerful; but he is also infinitely good. The signs of his power described at the very beginning of the revelation – the creation of the whole world, of all vegetable and animal life, of human intellect and emotions – these are also 'signs' or proofs of his goodness. It is man's duty to be grateful for all this, and that is why the ungrateful (this was almost certainly the original meaning of the word *kāfir* which came to acquire the sense of infidel or unbeliever) will be punished, and the grateful, that is the faithful, rewarded.

The Voice sometimes resorted to crude, commercial terms,

presenting the right way as a good bargain, but at other times it spoke in more elevated language and appealed to nobler instincts. In this one can already feel the contradiction between the purely human aspirations to salvation, which the prophets and religious founders were coming to see in terms of a reward, and the moral attitude which had long denied all merit to what is done from interested motives. This contradiction, which went unnoticed by Muḥammad, spread rapidly among Muslim as well as Christian mystics, who would have extinguished hell and set fire to paradise for the sake of finally purging the love of God of all trace of interest.

There is another striking and still more serious contradiction, which no religion has succeeded in resolving. Granted that God is all-powerful, it is therefore he who determines every detail of human behaviour. It is his will which causes some men to listen to his voice and others to turn away from it.

> He whom Allah leads is on the right way and he whom he leads astray shall find no protector to guide him.
>
> (Koran xviii, 16)

> If you strive to guide those who disbelieve [it is useless], for he whom Allah leads astray shall not be guided; for them there are no helpers.
>
> (Koran xvi, 39)

> What think you? The man who has made perdition his god, the man whom Allah has knowingly led astray, whose ears and heart he has sealed up and whose eyes he has bandaged, who but Allah shall guide him?
>
> (Koran xlv, 22)

But in that case what is the use of warning people and calling on them to repent? Why do anything at all? And by what right, according to what moral principles, are punishment and reward meted out? Muḥammad never asked himself this question, which has troubled so many theologians before and after him; and the Voice never answered it. He was keenly aware of divine omnipotence as being beyond all rational thought. How could it fail to direct the opinions, actions and decisions of mankind? The Qurayshites' disbelief demanded an explanation; and there was none other than the will of Allah. The punishment was equally indispensable. It was unthinkable that those who rebelled against God could be treated the same as the faithful. Action and preaching were no less vital. The attempt had to be made to enlighten mankind, to give the faithful guidance. The success or failure of his Messenger's efforts was in the hands of Allah. Beyond these simple facts they did not go.

Gratitude for Allah and his goodness had to be shown outwardly, first by faith, by believing in him, in his Message and his Messenger, and secondly by a cult, a form of worship. The Koran repeatedly prescribed the expression of general gratitude to Allah; but for a community it is best that such manifestations take a definite form, a specific order of their own, so as to distinguish the group from others around it. These are then rites, in the true sense of the word. At the time that we are considering, the community had not yet acquired more than a very few rites; and those were clearly based on the devotional exercises performed by eastern Christians, from whom the name (*ṣalāt*) which was used to describe them was borrowed. Consequently the faithful were exhorted to devote themselves to the performance of such pious acts as prostrating themselves, bowing deeply from the waist in salutation, and reciting sacred texts, in this case extracts from the Koran, the word of Allah as revealed to Muḥammad. The recital was to be made in a low voice, with becoming modesty. All this was done with the face turned towards Jerusalem, like the Jews and Christians. As in the Nestorian Church, these exercises were to be carried out at sunset and sunrise and also during the night. The word *ṣalāt* is usually translated as 'prayer', but this is only acceptable if it is clearly understood to apply to words and gestures previously laid down by divine command, and not to a private appeal requesting the divinity for special favours. Such an appeal (*du'ā'*) may, however, be slipped in among the gestures and recitations of the *ṣalāt*. Apart from this, the believer was not bound by any observances that could properly be called rites. The Voice from on high merely recommended such universal moral virtues as charity, piety towards God, comparative restraint in sexual matters, honesty and so forth.

It is true, as the Japanese arabist Toshihiko Izutsu has recently demonstrated from semantic analysis,[32] that the moral code put forward by the new sect represented a radical departure from existing Arab morality. The men the Arabs admired were careless, arrogant, afraid of nothing and ready to sacrifice their lives and goods for nothing – for the sake of a fine gesture, without a thought for the consequences. What did they care for such incidental matters as reducing their families to poverty and ruin! In their eyes it was a noble thing to give way to one passion after another, to run to meet death merely to avenge the smallest insult, to treat with open contempt those whom nature or society had spurned, to spare oneself the trouble of the hard work needed to scrape a little extra from a life that at best was a transitory thing, yet to sacrifice all one's worldly goods and those of one's kindred for the reputation of being a paragon of hospitality. Against this lofty ethic of the chivalrous kind which, in similar conditions, has been the ideal of a good many societies and which crops up so often among members of the younger generations, for whom life's more realistic demands are for the time being rather vague and distant, Muḥammad set the presence of God. God was there, as a fact, and that changed everything. God existed and he cared for men, even for the humblest. He did not wish for lawless outbreaks of violence, regardless of the peace and even the very lives of others. Above all else, the believer must take life seriously and show consideration for others, for morality and for the demands of God. Morality was practically identical with religion. Faith must always, should always, be expressed in works. Every 'social' act was a way of worshipping God. Carelessness and mockery were especially condemned. Courage and generosity should be kept within bounds. Men who knew no fear had been highly praised; but it was right to be afraid. Yes, however shocking this might seem to people brought up to the chivalrous ideal, men must fear God. Vengeance as far as possible must be left to God who would not fail to accomplish it in the next world with a circumspection which men often disdained. Indiscriminate generosity must be replaced by organized charity, preferably administered by the community as a whole. Nobility in this world was mere vanity. The humble and the outcast must not be ignored. There must be no more of these tempestuous passions, these fits of blind frenzy when the senses overcame the reason, in the course of which all else was forgotten. In short, once again, it was important for men to become earnest.

Outwardly, therefore, the community was distinguished only by the practice of the *ṣalāt*. But, little by little, in other ways, it was gaining autonomy. It was developing its own organization, defining itself in relation to the outside world. But this process as yet was only beginning. The group had not yet acquired a name. Its members could only call themselves the faithful (*mu'min* in the singular) and, probably not until a good deal later, those who had surrendered (*muslim*, or *moslem*) to Allah. But these qualities did not necessarily apply to them alone. In particular, the same words were used to describe those who had followed the call of the prophets of the past. There are no signs of a truly organized community. They followed Muḥammad, who was inspired by Allah. Even so, it is clear that an 'inner circle' was already forming, a small group of the faithful who were closest to the inspired leader and whose advice he would ask. There were decisions to be taken on tactical matters, about what attitude to adopt in relation to the outside world, to the Qurayshites, when the Voice remained silent. The principal member of the circle was Abū Bakr, but, after his conversion, the energetic 'Umar was also a considerable influence. On another humbler level, the beloved freedman Zayd also played his part. Independent spirits who had been led to join the group by some intense, private experience, like Khālid ibn Sa'īd and 'Uthmān ibn Maẓ'ūn before their departure to Abyssinia, were no doubt consulted and, as we have seen, it may have been divergences of opinion during these discussions which brought about their departure. Those of humbler status or disposition, such as Khabbāb or Bilāl, filled the modest but indispensable role of ordinary believers, what we should call the 'basic' following. Their tireless devotion, total selflessness and absolute lack of mental doubts and soul-searchings, coupled with the invaluable service they rendered in practical matters, made them examples to be held up to cavilling opponents.

In the end, everything came back to Muḥammad, whose personality was, all in all, the one real pillar unifying the group. To the Qurayshites, he maintained modestly but steadfastly that he was indeed the envoy to whom Allah had entrusted a message intended for them. In response to their criticisms, the Voice became more specific about his function. Muḥammad was simply a human being who needed to eat and drink, have wives and children, and so could not be expected to produce miracles in proof of his mission. Allah performed miracles as and when he would. If the earth had been inhabited by angels, Allah would have sent them an angel. But the man he sent, Muḥammad, was an upright man, driven by no political ambition and not possessed by a demon or any lesser spirit. It was true that he was not one of the great ones of the city and that many of his followers were men of lowly condition, but so were prophets before him; and the Qurayshites might remember that they held Muḥammad in some esteem before the revelation came to him.

Even so, he was no ordinary man. People were beginning to look on the words which had been given to him as something valuable, comparable to the writings handed down by earlier prophets and preserved by the Jews and Christians; comparable and even substantially the same. And the very fact that this revelation, addressed to Muḥammad 'in pure Arabic', existed already in ancient writings was in itself a sign of its authenticity. The fact that it was in good Arabic refuted the slanderous imputations that Muḥammad had drawn his information from foreigners, whether Jews or Christians.

Just as, in the Syrian Church, readings (*qeryānā* in Syriac) from the holy scriptures filled a liturgical role, so the faithful devoted a part of their devotional exercises to recitation (*qur'ān*, Koran, a parallel word to the Syriac one) of the Arabic revelation. From this moment they began assembling together the parts of that revelation. The smaller fragments, as we have said, were put together, to form *sūras*, something like chapters. The name may be derived from a Syriac word for 'writing'. Rhymes were adjusted, and cautionary and explanatory notes added. The Koran as we know it bears signs of revision (the credit for revealing this belongs to Richard Bell), suggesting that some work has been done on the written texts. This work was certainly carried out, if not by Muḥammad himself at least under his direction. Even so, it was not done without some errors and inconsistencies. Allah repeated his revelations, amplifying and altering them, as the enemy were delighted to point out. But Allah replied that he was free to do as he liked and that included altering his message. He might, for instance, lighten an obligation he had previously imposed, out of pity for the human weakness of his faithful. In this way, the revisions and the final version were, like the original inspiration, guaranteed by Allah. And so the revelation as a whole flowed into a unified mould and a certain order and pattern began to emerge. It has been suggested that the influence of the usual form taken by the Homilies (famous in the Syrian Church) of St Ephraem, one of the Fathers of that Church, can be detected in a recurring Koranic pattern. Some (admittedly later) writers do tell us that Muhammad heard a Christian, Quss ibn Sā'ida, said to have been a bishop, preaching at the great Arab fair of 'Ukāẓ and dilating, in rhymed prose and verse, on the theme of human frailty and the coming judgement. Could there be a connection here between Syrian Christianity and the Koran? There are some impressive points of similarity; but Quss may well be a legendary character and his sermons apocryphal.

While it was becoming set in this way, the style of the revelation underwent a change. The Voice spoke now in a more composed, less nervy and breathless fashion. The verses were longer and the rhymes less varied. The oaths and invocations in the manner of the *kāhins* had disappeared. The statements and instructions were more explicit. The language, however, was still elliptical. The pieces were often put together in dramatic form with different speakers answering one another. Since the text was intended to be read aloud in public, there is no indication of any change from one to the other. God speaks to his messenger, the messenger speaks to his people and the actors in the drama each take their cue. This is very lively and, while still aimed at preaching a sermon, sprinkled with slogans for the faithful to utter as responses. But the grim, oppressive proclamation of the approaching end had given way to a more relaxed preaching. The cry hurled at a hostile world became a call sent out by a small but close-knit band of disciples to a society which, for all its reservations, seemed open to conversion. Now Allah had time before him.

The community had become 'us', as the sociologists would say, a group sharing a common attitude towards those outside it. The Meccans associated other gods with Allah and were therefore to be condemned. Tradition has it that the 'surrendered' ones venerated the sacred Kaʿba and, although their intentions were different, shared in its cult like the other Qurayshites. This is most probably a mistaken view of the religious history of Islam, a reconstruction drawn from later events. In fact, the revelations of this period make no mention of the Meccan holy place or of the cult which must have surrounded it. As for the Jews and Christians, neither is singled out expressly. The only references are to those 'to whom knowledge was given before' (xvii, 108), to the 'keepers of the Reminder' (xvi, 45; xxi, 7), to 'those who recited the [revealed] scriptures [literally "the Book", *al-kitāb*] before you' (x, 94), or 'who possess knowledge of the scriptures ["the Book"]' (xiii, 43). For Muḥammad at this period they were clearly the mouthpieces of a message that was substantially the same. After all, they shared in part the same sacred books, told the same stories about the Jewish prophets and about the Creation and the Flood. It is unlikely that he did not realize that there were divergencies between them; but this seemed to him unimportant, at least on an ideological plane. These divergencies pointed to a good many different political attitudes; but the same was true of the divergencies between Christian sects themselves – the Monophysites, Nestorians and Melkites. The ideological basis of each of these sects was in differing ideas about the relations between the divine and human natures of Christ – questions which when viewed from the outside appeared supremely unimportant. Even their supporters must often have failed to grasp them properly. They supported not this or that theory but this or that party, which had gained their sympathy for temporal reasons far removed from the ideas it maintained. Thus it was hatred of foreign domination, and the sense of an Egyptian character standing firm against Byzantium, that drove the peasants of the Nile valley to fanatical belief in the single nature of Christ. So it has always been.

For Muḥammad, these differences, about which he was very ill-informed by the uneducated Christians and Jews he met, had no more importance than the difference between Catholic and Protestant, or between the various Protestant sects, has for the majority of the prophets who have appeared in black Africa in recent times. He was convinced, not unreasonably, that the Voice which spoke to him was repeating essentially the same message as that which had been given to the 'Peoples of the Book' and which was common to them all. The rest was mere detail. Moreover, the Voice does not seem to have mentioned Jesus at this period. It may already have mentioned John the Baptist, but this is not certain.

And so, with successive revelations, the little community saw its limits and its objects becoming more defined and its doctrinal capital growing. Once the boycott aimed at the Hāshim clan was lifted it enjoyed a measure of peace, owing to the protection of Abū Ṭālib and to the political situation at home in general. A few conversions must certainly have been recorded, although not very many because, with the few emigrants who returned from Abyssinia (some remained there for a few more years), the group cannot have comprised more than a hundred persons.

They might, perhaps, have continued to lead a quiet, unremarkable existence – helping to popularize a few new ideas among the Meccans but, as a group, becoming lost in the crowd, thinning out and finally disappearing like so many other small sects in history – if unforeseen events had not occurred which were to fling Muḥammad and his followers back into a state of insecurity.

Khadīja and Abū Ṭālib both died within a few days of one another. This happened in 619; we are now entering the period when the chronological order of events can be traced with comparative safety. The death of Khadīja undoubtedly affected Muḥammad a great deal. He was bound to the mother of his children by their mutual fidelity and by the memory of what she had been to him in the early days of his mission. She had chosen him even before Allah himself, and had believed in him before anyone else. Considering the relationship of employer to employee, and wealthy widow to poor orphan, which had overshadowed the beginning of their union, it seems likely that she retained a certain amount of authority in the house. He had been nurtured and protected by her. For him, the fact of emerging from this downy nest and having to shoulder his own responsibility acted as a stimulant. No Arab, especially one with children, would remain long without a wife. A few days, a few weeks at most, after being left a widower, Muḥammad married one of the faithful, a widow named Sawda. She had gone with her late husband to Abyssinia, where he had become a Christian. She was not a young woman and was running to fat, but she was a good housewife and took good care of the children. This was what Muḥammad had taken her for. She had no influence over him. He was certainly the master. She did not satisfy him sexually or in his wish to consolidate his position.

At about this time, the faithful Abū Bakr decided it would be a good idea to strengthen his own ties with the master and bethought him of his daughter 'Ā'isha. She was, admittedly, only six years old, which was too young, even for Arabs; but Muḥammad had seen her twice and she was a pretty little girl. They were betrothed. In those days there seemed nothing extraordinary in such an arrangement.

The death of Abū Ṭālib was a serious business. Even on his deathbed he had refused to be converted. He was succeeded as head of the Banū Hāshim by his brother Abū Lahab, who had already evinced towards his nephew a hostility which has probably been exaggerated by tradition, since we are told that in his new position he was moved by Muḥammad's misfortunes and by the grief Muḥammad felt at them. He went to Muḥammad and told him that he would protect him as Abū Ṭālib had done; but before long Muḥammad's enemies had succeeded in changing his mind. They explained to him, what he must surely have known already, that, according to his nephew, his grandfather, 'Abd al-Muṭṭalib, and Abū Ṭālib himself, were suffering the pains of hell. Abū Lahab went and asked Muḥammad about this and the Messenger could only confirm that such was indeed his doctrine. Abū Lahab was furious at such want of family feeling and withdrew his protection from the black sheep.

From then on things went from bad to worse. Muḥammad's enemies were able to indulge themselves to their hearts' content. The petty irritations increased. His neighbours threw a sheep's womb at him while he was praying and even into his pot just as he was about to eat. On the day this last insult occurred, he got up angrily and, grabbing a stick, went out on his doorstep shouting: 'O Banū 'Abd Manāf, what kind of protection is this?' The culprits must have laughed behind their walls, at having succeeded in making him lose his temper. A ruffian threw sand at his head. When he reached home one of his daughters washed it off in tears. 'Do not weep, child,' he told her, 'Allah will protect me.'[33]

Allah's protection was certainly needed. The community's future prospects in Mecca looked hopeless indeed. There were no more spectacular conversions, and it may have been at this period that considerable defections occurred. Muḥammad was furiously angry. The Voice comforted him with promises of punishment:

> When our verses are recited to them, these striking proofs,
> They say: 'This man is only trying to turn you away from the things your forefathers worshipped.'
> They say: 'It is nothing but a tissue of lies he has invented. . . .'
> We have given them no scriptures that they might study,
> We have not sent them any warner before you.
> Those who were before them also called it lies . . .
> They accused my Messengers of lying. Great was my disapproval.
> Say: 'One thing only, I would urge you.
> Stand up before Allah, in pairs or singly,
> And then reflect that your fellow is not mad;
> He is only sent to warn you
> Before a fearful scourge. . . .'
> If you could only see them when they shall be snatched up in terror, with no way of escape!
> They shall be taken from a place near at hand.
> They will say: 'We were believers . . .',
> When they did not believe in it before.
>
> (Koran xxxiv, 42–52)

Since the unbelieving city to which he had been especially sent was hardening in its refusal to understand, he could only think again that its punishment was not far off. The international situation was still doom-laden. The Second Rome, still besieged by the Persians from across the Bosphorus, and by the Avars on the European side, was suffering the ravages of famine. Heraclius humbled himself to sue to Khusrō for terms, but to no avail. The terms were quite unacceptable. Jerusalem fell; to many Christians this seemed like a foretaste of Doomsday, 'when angels will tremble, when thrones will be set up, when the books will be opened, when the unquenchable, darkened river of fire will appear; like lead, or pitch smelted by fire, does this fire appear – a fire bereft of all light.'[34] Muḥammad's enemies, we learn from a later source, rejoiced at this defeat of the monotheists. But the Voice answered (if the difficult, obscure and much-abused text does in fact belong to this period):

> The Romans have been defeated on the borders of our land,
> But in a few years after their defeat, they will be victorious.
> Their fate, in the past as in the future, is in the hands of Allah.
> Then shall the believers rejoice.
>
> (Koran xxx, 1–3)

Muḥammad must have thought it high time to leave the doomed city, whether the catastrophe in store for it was of a general or a particular nature. Where should he go? Where would his community be safe? Where should it go to await the Last Days; or rather, in the shadow of the cataclysm that awaited Mecca, where should it go to find a better place to grow and prosper?

He thought first of Ṭā'if, the cool, green, hillside town where the rich Qurayshites had lands and property which was held by the Thaqīf tribe. He went there and stayed for ten days, doing the rounds of all the most important citizens. For some reason we do not know, he tried particularly hard to convince three brothers; but they only answered him with jokes and unkind remarks. 'If you were sent by Allah as you claim,' one of them told him, 'then your state is too lofty for me to address you, and if you are taking Allah's name in vain, it is not fit that I should speak to you.' Another said: 'Could Allah find no one else but you to send?' They called on slaves and bullies to throw stones at him. Muḥammad took refuge in a garden belonging to two Qurayshites, who belonged to the clan of 'Abd Shams which was hostile to him. Even so, they took pity on him.

He went back to Mecca in a state of abject depression; but before entering the city it occurred to him that he might easily be attacked or thrown out, now that even his own clan was against him. Even the strongest or most influential of his followers – Abū Bakr, Ḥamza, 'Umar – were evidently in no position to give him adequate protection and his temporary absence might well have encouraged his adversaries. In accordance with Arab custom he sent messengers to a number of Qurayshites asking them to protect him. In the end one of them, Muṭʻim ibn ʻAdi, agreed. He was one of those who had done most to get the boycott against the Hāshim lifted. With an armed escort of the men of his family, he accompanied the Messenger on his return to his native city and publicly proclaimed him under his protection.

The Meccans were still stubbornly against him, although Muḥammad pointed out to them the political advantages of joining him. Abū Ṭālib, on his deathbed, was said to have made one last attempt to reconcile the Messenger and the Qurayshite leaders. 'Nephew,' said the dying uncle, 'here are the leaders of your people gathered together on your account. They will make some concessions to you if you will make some concessions to them.' 'My uncle, let them give me only one word and with it you will rule the Arabs and strangers will obey you.' 'By your father, speak!' Abū Jahl exclaimed. 'Ten words even!' But Muḥammad answered: 'Say only: There is no god but Allah, and abandon those you worship besides him.' Then they clapped their hands. 'Would you make all the gods into one, Muḥammad? What an idea!' And they went away disappointed.[35]

Muḥammad tried to dazzle the influential members of the Beduin tribes who came to Mecca or whom he met at the fairs of the Hejaz with the prospect of political power, but the Qurayshites denounced him and the Beduin said to him: 'Your family and your clan know you better than we do and they do not follow you.'[36]

One ambitious man who was tempted said: 'If I were to take this fellow of Quraysh at his word I could "eat up" the Arabs with his help.' To 'eat up' a particular people – in other words to live off them – was the dream of plenty of desert chiefs. So he asked him: 'If we follow you and Allah makes you victorious over your enemies, do you think we should succeed to your authority?' This was a serious question and Muḥammad was not anxious to commit himself. He answered:

'Power is from Allah. Allah gives it where he will.' The shaikh answered: 'Then, our breasts will be a target for the Arabs and, for your sake, when Allah has made you victorious, it will be others who command! We have nothing to gain from your offer.'[37] This was the crux of the matter. The bargain was a hard one.

It was at about this time that Muḥammad's eyes lit on another possible refuge and base for his operations. Some two hundred miles north-west of Mecca was the town of Yathrib. It was evidently an old town, since mention of it has recently been discovered in a Babylonian text of the sixth century B.C.; but it had been repopulated at a comparatively recent date. There were Jews there, who seem to have been partly settlers from the north of true Israelite descent, with an addition of Arab proselytes. At all events they had to a great extent adopted Arab customs and spoke a dialect of Arabic. They were divided into three tribes: the Qurayẓa, the Naḍīr and the less important Qaynuqā'. There were in addition two dominant Arab tribes, said to be of Yemeni origin: the Aws and the Khazraj. Some other, smaller Arab tribes who had been there before them were closely connected with the Jews and partly judaized. The Jewish name for Yathrib was the Aramaic *medīntā*, which means simply 'the city'; this became in Arabic *al-madīna*, from which we get Medina. That the Koran itself calls it by this name is proof that Yathrib did not, as has often been claimed, take its second name from the phrase *madīnat an-nabī*, 'the city of the Prophet'.

Properly speaking, it was not really a city at all according to our modern ideas. Rather it was an oasis, rich in underground water supplies which accumulated in the rainy season from numerous *wādīs*. There were therefore many springs and fountains, which made it remarkable in Arabia. The houses were spread over a wide area, standing singly or occasionally in more compact groups of small fortified huts amid dense plantations of palms and other fruit trees. The Jews had developed these plantations and the Arabs had learned from them, earning the contempt of their Beduin brothers who retained all their old scorn for the peasants. Even so, they had kept only too many of their desert ways.

At the time we are speaking of, relations between the different groups in Medina had, in fact, reached a very low ebb. As so often with the nomads, unimportant quarrels between clans and tribes had gradually grown in bitterness. Each side cast about for allies. Violent attacks ensued and the cultivated fields suffered. We can get some idea of the state of affairs by a glance at conditions in, for example, Wādī 'Amd, in the Ḥaḍramawt, in South Arabia in recent times. Freya Stark, crossing this region some thirty-five years ago, came in sight of two fortified houses and was offered hospitality by the occupants. They were people who, like many South Arabians in modern times, had made their fortunes in Java, in the hotel industry.

> In Batavia you may see them, fathers, sons and nephews, attending successfully to the intricacies of finance and running establishments with lifts and taps of running water; but here they carry on a hundred years' war with their neighbour, a town visible two miles or so away under the cliff.
>
> Into this Montague and Capulet feud outsiders have been drawn; the little town to the north, also under the cliff, was on the Buqri side, and harassed its southern neighbour. The Buqri family itself, explaining the geography of their war from their own roof, pointed to a white square tower on the edge of the precipice as an outpost of theirs, from which – as they declared – one could shoot straight down on the town. The odds seemed to be fairly even. The Buqri house, though completely isolated with a sand-dune approach on every side, was not an easy attack without artillery: it was composed of two tower-like buildings, one for the men and the other for the harim of the family, and a smooth mud wall with only one gate ran round them. Some years ago the whole valley had been a garden of palms, but the 'town' had allied itself with the Beduin of the Jōl, who came by night and poured paraffin over the roots of the trees and killed them. . . . Now only a few patches of millet were sown in the hollows, and would be watered and grow green in the soil . . .
>
> When the Sultan of Makalla came up to visit his lands of

Shibam, a six months' truce had been arranged between the Buqris and the town, so that he might pass by in comfort. . . . Even when the truce ended, they told me the daytime would be more or less quiet, for raids are made by night and ordinary intercourse continues through the hours of daylight.[38]

In an agricultural community, where prosperous harvests depend on a measure of tranquillity, such a situation cannot be tolerated for very long; but in Medina this little war had been going on for years on end with varying success for both sides. In 617 or thereabouts a great 'battle' was fought at Buʿāth, two days' march from Medina. The Aws in alliance with the Jewish tribes defeated the Khazraj, who had been uppermost in the period immediately before. A kind of equilibrium was established, but it was clear that the defeated were preparing for their revenge and that war would break out again before long.

There were a number of sensible men anxious to prevent this; but within the traditional framework of Arab society, inherited from the laws of the desert, it was impossible to break free of the vicious circle of feuds and counter-feuds. The workings of group solidarity, and the constantly changing alliances made by the clans among themselves, meant that a pointless quarrel between two members of different clans could lead to a general war that would prove disastrous for all. To maintain the peace would have needed a superior authority to impose a peaceful solution on any dispute arising between the clans, by force if need be. In other words, what was needed was a state.

On the other hand, the cohabitation of Jews and Arabs had had its influences on the latter. The chief divinity of Medina was Manāt, goddess of Fate, but already there were some there who placed Allah above all the rest. There were even some *ḥanīfs* who went further and became outright monotheists, seeking God by devoting themselves to the kind of asceticism practised elsewhere in Arabia. Here, as elsewhere, this development was linked to the increasingly high value put upon the individual personality. Why be forced to lose one's life for a ridiculous quarrel started by some hothead, merely because he happened to be related to you?

Clan rivalry was unendurable. Each individual must be judged by his own actions without dragging the whole of his group with him into what was his own responsibility. And if men were to be judged individually in this world, with how much more reason should the same hold good in the next, before Allah. Allah, who had created all men, should also be just to all his children and not show favouritism towards one clan or tribe, as could the lesser gods honoured by one particular group or another.

Then the rumour spread that there was a man of God at Mecca who received revelations from Allah himself and had authority to speak in his name. He was being persecuted by the Qurayshites; this was bound to be a recommendation in the eyes of the people of Medina, who were irritated by the arrogance of the Meccans and by the superior claims of the great trading centre. Moreover, Muḥammad had personal connections with Medina. His father had died there on the way home from a trading venture and was buried there among his father's mother's people, the Banū 'Adī ibn an-Najjār, a Medinan clan of the Khazraj. Muḥammad's mother, Āmina, had taken him there on a visit to these relatives when he was a child, and had died on the way back.

The people of Medina made frequent visits to Mecca, especially to take part in the rituals connected with the holy places near the Qurayshite city. Muḥammad talked to them, as he did to other visitors to his native city. But this time he found some common ground. The first he won over were six people belonging to the tribe of Khazraj, that is to the side which had been the losers at Bu'āth. Two of them were put on the track of Muḥammad by something said by the aged 'Utba ibn Rabī'a, the notable who had once tried unsuccessfully to come to an understanding with Muḥammad. 'We are much concerned with this "praying" person, who proclaims himself on the slightest provocation to be the

Messenger of Allah.'[39] They sought out the cause of the trouble and all six went to see Muḥammad.

He said to them: 'Won't you sit down and let me talk to you?' 'Certainly,' they said, and they sat with him. He called them [to accept faith in] Allah, talked to them about Islam and recited the Koran to them. Allah had set them on the road to Islam, for there were Jews with them in their own country – people who had scriptures, and were endowed with knowledge, while they themselves were polytheists and idolaters. The Jews had the upper hand of them in their country. Whenever there was a dispute among them, the Jews said to them: 'Now, a prophet will be sent, his time is almost come. We shall follow him and with his help we shall obliterate you as the 'Ād and Iram were obliterated.' When the Messenger of God spoke to them and called them to Allah, they said to one another: 'People! Understand! By Allah, this is surely the prophet with whom the Jews threatened us. We must not let them get ahead of us with him.' They answered the things he asked them, they believed him and accepted the Muslim dogmas which he explained to them. They told him: 'We renounce our people. No other is so divided by hatred and rivalry. It may be that with your help Allah will bring them together. We will go to them and call them to your party. We will tell them all that you have told us in your answers about this religion. And, if Allah unites them in this faith, there will be no man more powerful than you.'[40]

They went back to Medina and told of their interview. A few were won over. Negotiations were begun and seem to have continued for two years. Secret conferences took place. In 621 five of the first converts brought seven more, three of whom belonged to the Aws. This brought the number up to twelve, like the Twelve Apostles of Jesus; a slightly disturbing piece of information. They pledged themselves solemnly to Muḥammad. The traditional version of this oath is certainly inaccurate; but some dealings there must have been. The people of Medina probably pledged themselves to acknowledge Muḥammad's authority, to observe to some extent a certain moral code and to break with polytheism. Muḥammad sent Muṣ'ab ibn 'Umayr, one of the ablest of his followers, back to Medina with them to recite the Koran to the people of Medina and teach them the doctrine. At the end of June 622 there was another secret meeting – this time a decisive one – at 'Aqaba, not far from Mecca. This time there were seventy-five Medinans, two of them women, representing all the converts from the oasis. 'We are yours and you are ours,' they declared solemnly in the name of those they represented. 'If some of your companions should come among us, or if you come yourself, we will defend you against all things as we defend ourselves.' Twelve delegates were appointed, three from the Aws and nine from the Khazraj, to supervise the execution of this pact.

From that moment, the Muslims' haven of refuge was settled. All that remained was to get there and re-organize. The faithful set out for Medina in small groups. The Meccans do not seem to have interfered. The worst we hear is of their preventing a wife (and her child) from following her husband. They did not let her go until a year later. The departures took place over a period of roughly three months – July, August and September. At Medina, the emigrants, who, we are told, numbered about seventy, were welcomed by the local adherents. A few individuals seem to have disobeyed the word to emigrate; they remained at Mecca and left the community. Muḥammad was the last to leave. He had no wish to arrive in Medina as a solitary fugitive whose followers might or might not follow him. For once the Master was far away who could tell whether each man's ties with his Meccan background might not prove the stronger? On the spot, he kept watch over them and persuaded them to go, overcoming their objections and, if necessary, beginning his attempts afresh. When it seemed that no one else would leave, Muḥammad resolved to make his own way to Medina.

Among the Qurayshites there must have been a great deal of hesitation, deliberation and argument as to what attitude they should take. A great many must have been frankly delighted to find themselves rid of their dissident fellow-tribesmen and have looked for a return to unity. The more far-sighted probably realized the threat which the new community would constitute once it was established at Medina. But the laws of tribal society made it difficult to oppose the emigration by force. Everyone was 'protected', like Muḥammad himself. Taking positive action might well mean embarking on a period of vendettas and counter-vendettas. There may be some truth in the tradition which has it that the Qurayshites finally resolved on a scheme whereby Muḥammad was to be attacked simultaneously by representatives of every clan; this would make virtually all Quraysh jointly responsible and would present a united front to the inevitable avengers. Muḥammad's clan could not face up to such an alliance and slay all the murderers, and would be forced to accept a pecuniary settlement or blood price. But apparently they were unable to reach agreement.

Muḥammad had kept Abū Bakr with him. In preparation Abū Bakr had purchased two camels for eight hundred dirhams and also engaged a guide, 'Abdallāh ibn Arqaṭ, who was actually a pagan. (Both men's families remained temporarily in Mecca.) One day in September they left stealthily with their guide. They travelled southwards in the opposite direction to Medina. They hid in a cave in Mount Thawr, one hour's march south of Mecca; there they remained for three days. Abū Bakr's family and servants brought news from the city.

The Meccans must have been aware of their departure and instituted some kind of search; but they soon gave up. When it was clear that the worst of the danger was over, the guide led the two men first to the Red Sea coast and then back up north by devious routes, cutting across the main road to Medina. The journey must have taken a good ten days. The heat was overpowering. At last they reached Qubā', on the outskirts of the oasis of Medina. It was midday. They sank down exhausted in the shade of a tree. A Jew ran to take the news to the followers.[41] According to most of our sources this was on the twelfth of the month of Rabīʿ I; 24 September 622 according to our reckoning.

A new era was indeed beginning, because it was from the start of this year, otherwise 16 July 622, that the Muslim era was later dated – the era of the *hijra* or, in its usual English transliteration, 'hegira'. (This in turn is mistranslated as 'flight', much to Muslim fury, since its real meaning is emigration.)

At Mecca the man Muḥammad had been born and grown up in poverty to become an honourable citizen. Then his ideas had developed until the day came when they acquired an outward form and came back to him in the authoritative likeness of a voice from heaven. He proclaimed these ideas to his fellow citizens; some, he found, welcomed them because they answered to needs which were profoundly felt by them. The first of these was the need to get away from a form of society which, in the light of the developments brought about by progress, had become archaic, oppressive and unjust, and which had proved incapable of adapting itself to meet new conditions. They also answered to men's need for a new ideological synthesis incorporating their deep aspirations to a recognition of the value of the individual personality. However, in spite of his willingness to compromise, the strata of society to whom Muḥammad addressed himself refused to make any change in their traditional modes of thought and behaviour; as a result, a separatist group developed within the framework of Meccan society which, while it shared in the general social life of that society and did not yet form a completely separate organization on its own lines, none the less subscribed to a quite different system of values. It conformed to the laws, customs and decrees of the city only conditionally, in a provisional way, since the supreme authority remained the Word of Allah as expressed by his Messenger, Muḥammad.

This group, then, was ultimately dedicated to the formation of a community, a wholly separate society, complete in itself and obedient only to its own laws. This prospect began to become a reality when the group withdrew in a body from its city of origin and went to settle in a rival town where, together with local supporters, it formed a community that was from the outset quite different in kind. A combination of historical events was to give a far-reaching significance to these changes in the social relationships of a tiny group of people in two Arab towns situated on the remote borders of the desert, at the very edge of the civilized world. Because of them, hundreds of millions of men and women would date their era from that torrid summer of 622, when a Jewish peasant saw two weary men urging their camels towards the cool shade of the palm trees.

5

The Prophet in Arms

WHAT plans Muḥammad and Abū Bakr were making on the road that led them to the city we do not know. It is unlikely that they had any clear vision of the future or that they reckoned all the consequences of their emigration. They were certainly glad to be able to settle down at last in an environment friendly to their beliefs and to their action. Their ambitions probably went no further than making Medina a centre from which the belief in Allah as the One God should spread out to cover a large area of Arabia. They may also have dreamed – pending the just punishment which Allah would surely inflict on the unbelieving city – of exacting a more limited and human vengeance on their account.

First, there were the practical details of settling in to see to. The honour of providing a lodging for the Messenger may well have been disputed among several different clans and individuals. He decided, after a few days spent at Qubā', to leave the choice to Allah. His riding camel was allowed to roam free; it came to a halt near the middle of the oasis, on a piece of waste ground belonging to two fatherless brothers where dates were laid out to dry. Muḥammad dismounted. Allah showed that this was to be his home. He let his belongings be taken charge of by the man whose house stood nearest to the chosen site whose name was Abū Ayyūb Khālid ibn Zayd of the Khazrajite clan of the Najjār. Abū Ayyūb and his wife resigned the ground floor to their illustrious guest and themselves withdrew upstairs. It was they who prepared his food for him.

The site chosen by the camel was purchased scrupulously from its rightful owners. Then building began. The faithful worked with a will and Muḥammad encouraged them by toiling with his own hands. As they worked the impromptu masons sang those work-songs which are one of the earliest forms of poetry to appear in any time and place.

> If we sit down while the Prophet works,
> It could be said that we had shirked.

Others sang in a more religious vein:

> There is no life but the life of the next world.
> O Allah, be merciful to the Helpers and to the Emigrants![1]

This song, we are told, the Messenger took up, changing the order of the words and so doing away with the rhyme. The object of this anecdote was to make it clear to us that he had no gift for the diabolical art of poetry and that all the literary appeal of the Koran comes from Allah.

The humblest, who were most accustomed to manual labour, naturally did most work. Tradition has recorded for us the complaints of ʿAmmār ibn Yāsir, whose load of bricks was too heavy: 'Messenger of Allah! They are killing me! They make me carry a load they could never carry themselves!' ʿAmmār would have appreciated the lines attributed to young ʿAlī, and taken them up with vigour:

> They are not equal, the one who builds the place of worship
> And does his utmost, on his feet or on his knees,
> And the one who can be seen turning away out of the dust.[2]

There were hints that the shirker in question was none other than the Prophet's elegant son-in-law, ʿUthmān ibn ʿAffān.

The building erected in this way is regarded in Muslim tradition as the first shrine, or *masjid*. In its Nabataean and Syriac form, *masgedā*, this meant a place where people prostrate themselves, in other words a place of worship. Thence, following the ancient pronunciation (*masgid*), still current in Egypt, and via the Spanish form, we get our own word 'mosque'. It was, in fact, the centre for the secular as well as the religious life of the community. It was a rectangular courtyard, enclosed by a wall of sun-dried brick set on a few courses of stone. On the northern side was a row of palm trunks, set up parallel to the wall, supporting a roof of clay and palm fronds. Next to the eastern wall, two cabins were built, one for each of the Prophet's two wives. (He married the little girl 'Ā'isha while the building was in progress.) Carpets were laid where these cabins opened into the courtyard. The Prophet had no place of his own but lodged with each of his wives in turn. Most of his time was spent, after the Arab fashion of the time, in this courtyard; it was here that he received ambassadors, conducted business and addressed his followers. There prisoners were confined, the sick cared for and even, on occasion, mock battles fought. There, too, communal prayers were said. The poorer Companions slept there. It was, in short, both the Master's seat and a general meeting place for the whole community.

This is perhaps the moment to describe the physical appearance of the man who, at the age of fifty or so, was now embarking on a new life. All the portraits we have of him are, it is true, most unreliable; but in so far as they retain any true features, they certainly relate to this period of his life. We are told that he was of medium height, with a large head but a face that was neither round nor at all plump. His hair was slightly curly and his eyes were large, black and well-opened beneath long lashes. His complexion was fair, with a tendency to ruddiness. He had only a few fine hairs on his chest while those on his hands and feet were, in contrast, very thick, and his beard luxuriant. He was big-boned and broad-shouldered and walked with a strong, swinging stride, like one going downhill. He turned all at once, in a single movement.

A few months after the hegira, Muḥammad and Abū Bakr decided to bring their families from Mecca. Muḥammad's two freedmen set out with two camels and five hundred dirhams and brought back Sawda and the girls without any trouble. Another of the faithful carried word to Abū Bakr's son 'Abdallāh, who likewise brought his mother and small sister

'Ā'isha to Medina. All this was done with no opposition from the Meccans.

Muḥammad's wedding to the little girl followed soon afterwards. This is what 'Ā'isha apparently had to say about it:

The Messenger of God married me when I was six years old and the wedding was celebrated when I was nine. We came to Medina and then I had the fever for a month. Then my hair, which had fallen out because of my illness, began to grow thickly again. [The archaic word thus rendered may, however, according to other interpretations mean 'remained thin'.] Umm Rūmān [her mother] came to find me while I was playing with my friends on a swing. She called me and I went to her, not knowing what she wanted of me. She took me by the hand and stopped me on the threshold. I cried out 'Oh! Oh!' until I was out of breath. She took me into a house in which were some women of Medina, who said 'Happiness and blessings! Good fortune!' My mother gave me into their keeping and they washed my head and made me beautiful. I was not frightened, except in the morning when the Messenger of God came and they gave me to him.

The ceremony was reduced to its simplest form. The little girl was allowed to keep her toys and her dolls and sometimes the Prophet would play games with her.

But life could not be all play. There were the Emigrants to be taken care of. Most of them were not at all well off. They were obliged to seek employment with the Jews or with the Faithful of Medina, who were now called the *Anṣār* or Helpers, as opposed to the *Muhājirūn*, the Emigrants. Since they were for the most part quite ignorant of the elementary principles of date farming, they were generally forced to work as common labourers. They drew water from the wells and watered the palm trees. Not all of them had the commercial bent of 'Abd ar-Raḥmān ibn 'Awf, who, when a man of Medina offered him assistance, simply asked to be directed to the market. He made a small purchase on credit, resold it at a small profit, bought something else and so on. In a little while he was able to afford to marry a girl of Medina, giving the usual bride-price to her family besides defraying the costs of the wedding.

The Messenger of God was prevented by his dignity from doing the same; and so, when his followers failed to invite him and his family to eat, or to bring them a few dates, they went hungry. Most of the time they lived on dates and water. They had no fuel to make a fire in winter. After the dryness of their native city the Emigrants suffered from the unaccustomed humidity. They caught fevers and dysentery.

Organization was necessary if the community was to survive. Muḥammad's position in Medina had to be clearly established. Relations among the various groups which now made up the population of Medina had to be clarified. An agreement was concluded, the text of which, by quite extraordinary good luck, has been preserved for us by Muslim tradition. It is certainly authentic because it contains certain conditions which run contrary to later views of the original Muslim community. Montgomery Watt has shown that the document as it has come down to us is a composite one, containing some clauses dating from the initial settlement at Medina with others of a later date.

According to this agreement, which is referred to in the document itself as the Leaf, or perhaps the Writing (*ṣaḥīfa*), 'the believers and Muslims of Quraysh and Yathrib and those who follow them and are attached to them and fight alongside them . . . form a single community [*umma*], distinct from other men' (paragraph 1). 'It is clearly stated that the Jews form a single community with the believers' (paragraphs 25 ff.). The *umma* or community was therefore the people of Medina as a whole, presenting a united front to the outside world. 'Those Jews who follow us are entitled to our aid and support so long as they shall not have wronged us or lent assistance [to any enemies] against us' (paragraph 16). (The text here is obscure and open to another interpretation.) 'The Jews shall contribute to expenses along with the believers as long as they fight side by side' (paragraphs 24 and 38). 'To the Jews their own expenses and to the Muslims theirs. They shall help one another in the event of any attack on the people covered by this document. There shall be sincere friendship, exchange of good counsel, fair conduct and no treachery between them' (paragraph 37).

One article of considerable interest even incorporates the pagans of Medina in the community. For the present, Muḥammad was content to live in peace with the pagans. Their conversion would come later. What mattered was to prevent them making common cause with the Meccans. 'No pagan is to give protection to any person of Quraysh, either his goods or his person, or take his part against any believer' (paragraph 20). Other articles, however, made a certain distinction between believers and 'unbelievers' (*kāfirs*), who cannot have included the Jews (paragraphs 14 and 15).

The community was made up not of individuals but of a number of groups. Of these, the Qurayshite Emigrants were one while the rest were made up of each of the clans of Medina and of the allied Jewish clans attached to them. The three largest Jewish tribes must each have formed an additional group of their own, although all mention of their names was probably erased from the text of the Agreement when they vanished from the scene. Each group formed a single unit for the purpose of paying the blood-price, should one of its members kill anyone from outside. The Emigrants acted as a single group to ransom any of their members who were taken prisoner, as did the individual tribal units of the Medinan clans (paragraphs 2 ff.).

All the believers (with the exception of the Jews and pagans) were, however, bound by a variety of obligations, some of which have already been mentioned. They were to succour any of their number who were crushed by an overwhelming burden of debt (paragraph 11). They were not to take the side of an unbeliever against a believer, or kill a believer on account of their connections with an unbeliever (paragraph 14). All believers, even the humblest, were assured of the 'protection' of Allah and so owed one another exclusive aid and protection (paragraph 15). In the event of war, believers were not to make peace individually with the enemy (paragraph 17). If one of their number were killed, they were to make common cause against the murderer and those who helped him, and either fight them together or accept the blood-price together (paragraphs 19 and 21). They were not to give aid or shelter to any evil-doer (*muḥdith*, literally 'innovator', in other words anyone infringing the common moral code) (paragraph 22). They were to maintain their own internal law and order, themselves punishing any wrongdoers amongst them (paragraph 13).

Muḥammad's role in this extensive community was a modest one. He was simply Allah's intermediary in settling disputes and quarrels between its members. 'Wherever there is anything about which you differ, it is to be referred to Allah and to Muḥammad' (paragraph 23). 'Whenever any incident or dispute arises among the people of this document which it may be feared will bring harm to them, they shall refer to Allah and to Muḥammad, for Allah is the most strict and faithful guarantor of the contents of this document' (paragraph 42). A further, somewhat obscure clause apparently forbade members of the community to undertake any military expedition without the Messenger's consent, although there was nothing to stop anyone seeking vengeance for injuries he had suffered (paragraph 36).[3]

This, then, was the framework of the community of Medina. There was as yet no question of a state with a supreme authority, able to enforce a degree of order by means of a public force set apart from society. Each ethnic group had its own head, whose own power of action was limited to his personal authority and the extent to which this was recognized by his followers. Order was maintained only by the threat of vengeance, which ensured that wrongs inflicted were clearly paid for.

But into this typical Arab structure a new and quite different element had been introduced. This was Muḥammad himself, a man with no personal power, whose only distinction was that he spoke with the voice of Allah. This gave him certain privileges. In the first place he was the leader of the exiled Qurayshites. He was also – in a purely religious sense – an authority recognized by all the believers, which meant in practice the majority of the non-Jewish population of Medina. They chose him in preference to any other as arbiter in settling disputes and quarrels. Moreover, having been called upon to perform the function of arbiter so as to maintain peace within the oasis, he went one further and saw to the adoption of suitable measures to prevent the endless chain of vendettas and counter-vendettas. The actual conditions of the Agreement are in some doubt. We know too little about the circumstances involved. But the revelations of the Koran belonging to this period may suggest some plausible explanations and help towards an understanding of Muḥammad's initial policy in this respect. It is made quite clear where the blame lies in cases of murder or injury and that no believer may, for considerations of kinship or friendship, impede the course of justice in any way. Neither, on the other hand (this is explicitly laid down in the Koran), was he permitted to initiate a vendetta, take more than one life for a life, or perpetuate the feud by exacting fresh vengeance for vengeance once taken. The avenger of an unprovoked crime was to be, as it were, an executioner, and so immune from future vengeance.

In this way Muḥammad, inspired by Allah, was able to carry through measures to ensure internal peace, which were in the interests of all. But only the swearing of solemn oaths and the force of public opinion guaranteed that these rules would be observed. No police force existed, any more than the public funds to maintain one. It was to take all the wits and adroitness of Muḥammad and his counsellors, further aided by circumstances and pressure of social forces of which they were unaware, to turn this moral authority into an effective, practical power. Even so, the power of the state never reached a level comparable to that of neighbouring rulers.

On the whole, the people of Medina accepted Muḥammad's role as arbiter. The movement began with the weakest clans, who had suffered from the activities of the more warlike chiefs. They wanted peace in the oasis and the cost was very small. They recognized Allah as the One God but they already knew him as the most powerful. The difference was not so very great.

The minor gods were simply demoted from the status of lesser gods to that of jinns or genies. They acknowledged that the words uttered by Muḥammad were transmitted to him by the voice of Allah; this too was not hard to accept. The Messenger's sincerity was obvious, and the words of Allah were good and accorded with the aspirations of the community as a whole. There was no reason why they should not be accepted as authentic. The man was intelligent, good-natured and likeable – in short, a valuable addition to the community of Medina. It was their good luck that his Qurayshite neighbours had been stupid enough to deprive themselves of such a remarkable character.

The dominance of the belief in Allah as the One God was assured by the conversion of certain leading chiefs. Their precise reasons are not easy to ascertain. We should have to know much more about their individual psychology. The attractions of a new religion certainly had something to do with it, as did the wish for peace, motives of ambition and dislike of Quraysh. The conversion of two chiefs of the powerful Awsite clan of ʿAbd al-Ash'hal, Usayd ibn al-Ḥuḍayr and Saʿd ibn Muʿādh, was of vital importance. It is told that immediately after their conversion they went to the meeting place of their clan and Saʿd asked the chief members of the clan what they thought of him. They answered: 'You are our leader, you are the most gifted of us and the one best able to judge.' Then he said: 'Let none of your men or your women speak to me until he believes in Allah and his Messenger.' The whole clan was converted.[4]

Another important conversion was that of ʿAbdallāh ibn Ubayy, of the Khazrajite clan of ʿAwf. He took no part in the battle of Buʿāth, and had quarrelled with another important chief over the latter's unjustified execution of some Jewish hostages. He may have realized the need for unity among the people of Medina and we are told that at the time of the hegira his supporters were preparing to make him king of the city. His reason for joining Muḥammad was probably that having seen the strength of the wave of conversions to the Messenger's doctrine, he thought it wiser to join than to stand out against it.

He may have had some hopes of using the movement and making himself its temporal leader while Muḥammad's part would be simply to proclaim the doctrine sent by Allah. Finally we must not exclude the possibility of a genuine sympathy with monotheist ideas fostered by his friendly relations with the Jews.

The opposition was not significant. A group of clans belonging to the Aws tribe who were particularly associated with the worship of Manāt and were actually known as the Aws Manāt ('Gift of Manāt'), refused to recognize the exclusive nature of Allah or Muḥammad's mission, but they merely retreated into a sullen, passive and ineffectual aloofness.

More dangerous were those with the gift of poetry, in particular a woman 'Aṣmā' bint Marwān, and also an old man named Abū 'Afak, supposedly a centenarian belonging to a Khazrajite clan related to the Aws Manāt. Abū 'Afak proclaimed:

I have lived a long time, but I have never seen
Either a house or gathering of people
More loyal and faithful to
Its allies, when they call on it,
Than that of the Children of Qayla [the Aws and the Khazraj] as a whole.
The mountains will crumble before they submit.
Yet here is a rider come among them who has divided them.
[He says:] 'This is permitted; this is forbidden' to all kinds of things.
But if you had believed in power
And in might, why did you not follow a *tubba'* [a South Arabian ruler]?[5]

'Aṣmā' was even more forceful, when she wrote a short while afterwards:

Fucked men of Mālik and of Nabīt
And of 'Awf, fucked men of Khazraj [clans and tribes of Medina]:
You obey a stranger who does not belong among you,
Who is not of Murād, nor of Madh'ḥij [Yemenite tribes].

Do you, when your own chiefs have been murdered, put your hope in him
Like men greedy for meal soup when it is cooking?
Is there no man of honour who will take advantage of an unguarded moment
And cut off the gulls' hopes?[6]

Both were dangerous and we shall see how Muḥammad dealt with them. But they were isolated cases and, for the moment, their rantings were more or less harmless.

There was also the case of Abū ʻĀmir who had become a monotheist of his own accord before the hegira and had taken to living an ascetic life, which had earned him the name of ar-Rāhib, 'the monk'. Muḥammad, on arrival, conversed with him; ar-Rāhib asked him a great many questions and accused him of corrupting monotheism with false ideas. In other words, he refused to recognize the authenticity of Allah's message as transmitted by Muḥammad. Rather than submit he emigrated to Mecca with fifteen, or it may be fifty, of his followers. He took up arms against the Muslims and, when they finally triumphed, he departed indomitably for Syria where he was fortunate enough to die before the conquest.

However, Medina contained a great many more potential enemies who were very much more dangerous. These were the Jewish tribes already mentioned. As we have seen, Muḥammad had no prejudice against them. On the contrary, he regarded the contents of the message he brought as substantially the same as that received long ago by the Jews on Sinai. He was even impressed by the antiquity of this revelation and the fact that the Jewish scriptures so far antedated those of the other religions, all of which contained references to them, even where they superimposed matter of their own. The parallel message which he brought to the Arabs could not conflict with an earlier revelation from the same source.

When he was preparing to set out for Medina, he seems to have been counting on the wholehearted support of these local monotheists. No doubt he reckoned that he and his followers would close ranks with the Jews and form a united front against the paganism of the Qurayshites and of the Arabs in general. At this period, he seems to have been making a closer study of the customs of the Israelite people and to have decided on a closer approach to them. He instructed his followers (was this a new thing?) to turn towards Jerusalem to pray. However, the Voice from on high rejected the idea that God had needed to rest after the six days of creation, thus dismissing the Jewish concept of the Sabbath. In this there may have been, as Goldziher has suggested, some influence of Mazdaean ideas on the subject. In any case, before the hegira, Muḥammad was writing to Muṣ'ab, his representative in Medina, telling him to organize meetings of the faithful, including 'prayers' on Fridays – that is, the day when the Jews were preparing for their own festival on the morrow. The intention would certainly appear to have been to associate them with these preparations on the part of the Jews. Similarly, Muḥammad was much struck by the great fast observed by the Jews on the tenth day of the month of Tishri, *yōm kippūr*, the Day of Atonement. In arabized Aramaic it was called the *'ashūrā*, 'the tenth'. Muḥammad decided that his followers should observe it also. A time was also set aside for prayer in the middle of the day, according to the Jewish custom. A revelation gave the faithful permission to eat the food of the People of the Book and to marry their women. It does not appear that Muḥammad ever considered making his people follow all the strict dietary rules observed by the Jews. He followed the line of Christian, Gnostic and Manichaean belief in regarding these as a punishment imposed on them by God for their sins. But he did go so far as to introduce a limited version of these restrictions; it was roughly the same as that adopted by the early Christians and was based on what was expected by the rabbis, in principle, of those strangers admitted to live among the people of Israel and of the partial converts. This involved eating no pork or blood, or any animals that had either died a natural death, had their necks wrung or been sacrificed to idols. In fact, as we shall see, the effort to adapt had gone so far that the Muslims had even adopted certain Jewish modes of dress.

The Jews did not on the whole respond to these advances as Muḥammad expected. We do not know exactly what was the attitude of the Jews of Arabia to semi-proselytism. In Graeco-Roman times, Judaism regularly accepted *sebomenoi*, or 'God-fearing' sympathizers with Jewish monotheism who were yet under no obligation to observe all the rituals demanded of the true Children of Israel. The great calamities which had befallen the chosen people had resulted in the adoption of a much more rigid and uncompromising attitude and a greater distrust of outsiders. Only final and complete conversions were now acceptable. However, here and there, where conditions were more favourable, semi-proselytism had begun to reappear. In any case, the Jews of Medina, having been long content to live side by side with outright pagans, should have been glad, from a strictly religious point of view, to find the monotheist followers of Muḥammad settling alongside them, since these came much closer to Judaism than the *gērīm*, the foreigners dwelling in the land of Israel, who were pagans who had renounced their idols and who were theoretically admitted by the rabbis to the enjoyment of equal rights with the Jews. All that was asked of them was to observe 'the seven commandments of the sons of Noah': 'to practise fair dealing, to refrain from blaspheming against the Name, and from the practice of idolatry, immorality, murder or theft; and to refrain from eating limbs taken from a living animal'.

Muḥammad's followers for their part – quite apart from their adherence to the fundamental ideas of Judaism and to the precepts of Noah – showed perfect willingness to conform to a number of Jewish rituals. In theory, therefore, there was no reason why the two communities should not have lived peaceably together. But the Jewish tribes of Medina had probably not abandoned the idea of exerting a considerable political influence over the oasis as a whole. It was quite obvious to them, probably before very long, that Muḥammad's behaviour and the importance he was assuming were likely to interfere with this objective. Still more important, Medina was an intellectual centre. There can be no doubt that the Jewish intellectuals were extremely unwilling to endorse the validity of the revelation received by Muḥammad. It was to them, as the repositories of the ancient scriptures, that people turned for a verdict on this new message and whether it conformed to the criteria of divine inspiration accepted by experts. Even if they had been well disposed towards the new movement, it was not easy for them to sanction what in their view were the incoherent ramblings of an illiterate, nor was it easy to avoid pointing out the way in which the Koran distorted the Old Testament stories and the errors and anachronisms of which it was full. It may have occurred to some of them even then that a concern for truth did not always accord with political expediency. Certainly a great many saw no difficulty and opposed a man whom they regarded as a false prophet and at the same time a political menace. It took some time for the options to become clear; but the day was coming when Muḥammad would be obliged to face up to the situation and adjust his position accordingly.

But this day was not yet. Certain other decisions had already been taken which were to have serious consequences. Less than a year after his arrival in Medina, Muḥammad gave his uncle Ḥamza a white flag, put him at the head of seven Emigrants and sent him off 'to intercept the caravans of Quraysh'.[7] What was in his mind to make him do this?

It is possible that Muḥammad and his advisers may have foreseen some of the consequences of the situation they were creating. But it must be realized that their attitude was simply a response to the demands of the situation in which they found themselves. The members of the new community had only the scantiest means of subsistence. We have seen the extremities to which they were reduced. The life of a labourer held few attractions, while the commercial talents of a man like 'Abd ar-Raḥmān ibn 'Awf were exceptional; and none of the Meccans had the wherewithal to purchase a plot in the oasis where all cultivable land had already been divided up. The result was that most of the Meccans had no regular source of income. Muḥammad himself only scraped a bare living thanks to public charity and, what was probably even more serious, the community as a whole possessed no funds of its own. This situation had to be remedied; and among the Arabs brigandage, for it can hardly be described according to our norms as anything else, was the normal method of survival when all else failed. On this, all non-Arab writers are agreed and the fact is abundantly confirmed in pre-Islamic Arab literature itself. The obvious victims of the attacks mounted by Muḥammad were his own fellow tribesmen, the Qurayshites. Nothing was to be gained by making enemies of other tribes, and the rich Qurayshite caravans were an egregious prize (indeed, it would have been hard to find a better prey); besides which, in attacking them the exiles were assuaging their legitimate grievances against the very people who had forced them to leave their land, and the city which had presumed to scoff at the warnings of Allah. Medina was remarkably well placed to be a centre for such expeditions, since the Meccan caravans travelling between Syria and Mecca were obliged to pass within sixty miles of the oasis.

Private wars were a perfectly accepted custom. In this society, in which the idea of a state was wholly unknown, each petty chieftain was in a position to send his men to attack any objective he cared to set them. All he had to do was to take the consequences, which, if he was wise, he measured well beforehand. There was therefore nothing, beyond possible considerations of expediency, to prevent Muḥammad from indulging in such warlike activity. His people, for the most part, followed him as a matter of course, although the only pressure he could bring to bear on the cautious or the faint-hearted was a moral one. As the business began to show a profit they were joined by volunteers from the people of Medina, in spite of the fact that their agreement with Muḥammad carried with it no obligation to take part in his campaigns.

The first attacks were no great matter. They were not particularly profitable and, as was usual with Arab forays, fighting was avoided when it was clear that the victims were numerous and on their guard. They were careful to refrain from bloodshed as far as was possible, for fear of becoming entangled in the vicious circle of vendettas with very little to show for it.

In the month of Rajab of the year 2 of the hegira (January 624), about fifteen months after the arrival at Medina, the first blood was spilled under circumstances worth noting. Muḥammad sent out ʿAbdallāh ibn Jaḥsh at the head of some seven to twelve men, bearing sealed orders which he was not to open until after two days' march. This was probably so as to keep the matter a secret and so secure the effects of surprise. ʿAbdallāh's instructions were to take up a position in ambush at Nakhla, south of Mecca, on the road between there and Ṭā'if, and there to attack a Meccan caravan, which would obviously not be expecting trouble so far from Medina and in the opposite direction from it. In the event, ʿAbdallāh ibn Jaḥsh and his men succeeded in capturing the caravan and two of the four Meccans who were escorting it. Another was killed and the fourth made his escape. Plunder and prisoners were borne back to Medina in triumph. But then a wave of feeling arose because the murder had been committed in the month of Rajab, one of the holy months during which, according to pagan Arab conventions, bloodshed was forbidden. Had Muḥammad deliberately intended to flout this pagan prohibition, had he relied on the business going off without bloodshed, or had his lieutenant perhaps exceeded his instructions by taking it on himself to launch the attack before the end of Rajab, since the incident appears to have occurred towards the end of the month? It is impossible to say. He certainly bowed to what may have been for him an unexpected public reaction and refrained from laying a finger on the booty until a timely revelation from God assured him that 'to fight [during the holy months] was certainly serious' but that the sins of Meccans were much more so (Koran ii, 214). Then he accepted a fifth of the booty, thus establishing a rule for the future, while the remainder was shared out among the Companions. The two prisoners were released in return for a ransom of 1,600 dirhams each, paid by their families, although they were held, even then, until after the return of two members of the band who had gone astray and might possibly have been killed by the Meccans. One of the two prisoners joined the followers of Muḥammad and remained in Medina.

This incident, while it was a blessing to the Muslims financially, had, on the other hand, infuriated Quraysh. Those Meccans who had the broadest political vision realized that Muḥammad represented a constant threat to their city's trade and that he must be got rid of as soon as possible. This was, in particular, the view of the powerful head of the Makhzūm clan, Abū Jahl, whose fierce opposition to Muḥammad we have already seen. Two months after the Nakhla raid, in Ramaḍān of the year 2 (March 624), a very large caravan was on its way back from Gaza to Mecca, led by Abū Sufyān ibn Ḥarb of the Qurayshite clan of ʿAbd Shams. All Quraysh had an interest in the goods carried by this caravan. It was accompanied by nearly seventy merchants (some sources say only thirty) from all the clans of Quraysh.

'When the Messenger of God heard about them,' runs the oldest account of the affair, a letter written by the traditionist ʿUrwa ibn az-Zubayr to the Caliph ʿAbd al-Malik sixty years after the event, 'he summoned his companions and told them of the great wealth they were bearing with them and how few were their numbers.' We are told that the merchandise being conveyed was worth in all 50,000 dinars. It was a splendid prospect and this time there were plenty who were interested. Altogether some three hundred men came forward, fewer than ninety of them Meccan Emigrants. The rest were all Medinans who were anxious to take part in the dash for the spoils. 'They set out,' the aged ʿUrwa puts it bluntly, 'not seeking [to attack] anyone other than Abū Sufyān and those who rode with him, with no thought in their heads but of the booty to be won from the Qurayshites, and they did not expect the encounter to lead to any serious fighting. That was God's revelation concerning it [in these terms]: You wished that the band unarmed might be yours [Koran viii, 7].'[8] They laid an ambush near the well of Badr, where the road from Syria left the coast and ran a little way inland on the way to Mecca and from which point a road branched off towards Medina.

Abū Sufyān had foreseen the danger, whether from his own deductions (he was, as we shall see, a highly intelligent man) or from the reports of his spies. He dispatched a strongly worded request to Mecca for reinforcements: 'Defend your merchandise.' The summons was answered. A troop which apparently numbered as many as nine hundred and fifty men, or practically every man able to fight, was raised in Mecca. Evidently the intention was to make a strong impression on the dissidents who had fled to Medina, and to put an end to this ever-present threat to the vital interests of the entire Meccan population.

But Abū Sufyān was not relying unduly on the Meccans. He thought it safer, once within reach of Medina, to avoid the usual caravan route. At the risk of suffering from thirst he did not turn off towards the watering-place of Badr which lay on that route, but kept straight on, keeping as close as possible to the shore of the Red Sea. According to one account he reconnoitred alone as far as Badr, where he learned that two men had come into the area to fetch water. Abū Sufyān examined the droppings left by the men's camels and noticed date stones in them. 'By Allah, this is the fodder of Medina,'[9] he exclaimed. The two men were spies sent by Muḥammad. He went off again at a gallop and continued leading his caravan along the road by the sea.

The caravan was soon safely out of reach in Meccan territory. A messenger was sent to inform the army marching to the rescue. Many of its members wanted to turn back. There was now no point to the expedition except to avenge 'Amr ibn al-Ḥaḍramī, the man killed at Nakhla. A good deal of disagreement arose. Muḥammad's sworn enemy Abū Jahl cried shame on those who were preparing to desert. Did they want to be called cowards? That is an argument which has always been able to drive men to pointless acts. Most stayed. The members of two clans departed, but even this meant a loss of some hundreds of men to the Qurayshites.

Muḥammad and his followers, unaware of the existence of

the relief expedition, were still lying in wait for the caravan near the wells of Badr, where it should, in the normal way, have passed. The capture of a young Meccan water-carrier told them what had happened. The odds against Muḥammad were heavy, but he knew that the Qurayshite army, concealed from him as it was by a sand-dune, was unaware of his presence, and he believed it to be numerically smaller than it really was. He prayed and Allah gave him encouragement. A convenient shower of rain hardened the ground and enabled him to advance quickly. He reached the wells before the Qurayshites and, acting on the advice of one of his men, had them all filled in except for one. Before this one he drew up his men. The Qurayshites were forced to fight for water and to fight on ground of the Messenger's choosing.

The course of the battle is somewhat confused. There seems no doubt that tactically Muḥammad's army was greatly superior. It was drawn up in neat lines and rained arrows on the enemy without breaking ranks. As always in Arabia, single combats took place with champions from one camp hurling challenges to those on the other side to come out and try their strength. What, more than anything, gave the men of Medina the advantage seems to have been a unified command. The Qurayshites fought as individual clans and the disputes which had occurred before the battle showed how little agreement there was amongst them. They were facing east and so had the morning sun in their eyes. They were thirsty. Their principal leaders had been killed, probably near the beginning of the battle, some of them in single combat. They had seven hundred camels and a hundred horses but they made no use of the advantage which their superior cavalry should surely have given them.

Muḥammad and his advisers, on the other hand, made sure of a strictly unified command. It is true that throughout most of the battle Muḥammad remained in the rear, in a hut which had been erected for him, praying with anxious fervour. At one point he emerged and flung a handful of pebbles in the enemy's direction, crying out: 'Evil look on their faces!'[10] He followed up this ritual gesture with religious exhortations. 'By him who holds Muḥammad's soul in his hands,' he said, 'not one who fights this day, if he has borne himself with steadfast courage, if he has gone forward and not back, shall meet his death without Allah's bringing him to paradise!'

'Umayr ibn al-Ḥumām, who was eating a handful of dates, heard this and shouted out: 'Fine! Fine! Have I only to get myself killed by these men to enter into paradise?' He threw away his dates and, grasping his sword, plunged into the thick of the battle and was very soon killed.[11]

The Meccan merchants were not expecting such fury. They had probably imagined that a mere show of force would be enough to put Muḥammad's followers to flight. Many shrank from killing men who were related to them and giving rise to a new round of vendettas. Shortly before midday panic swept through them and they fled. Their dead numbered between fifty and seventy; chief among them were the two leaders, Abū Jahl and 'Utba ibn Rabī'a. Another seventy or so were taken prisoner. On the other side there were only some fifteen killed. The spoils, while admittedly not worth nearly as much as might have been made from Abū Sufyān's caravan, were still not to be despised: a hundred and fifty camels, ten horses, a great quantity of arms and armour, as well as various things belonging to the fugitives and even some merchandise which they had brought along with them in the hope of transacting a little business on the way. Disputes arose between those who had personally laid hands on the booty and others who had been unable to do so, especially those who had remained in the rear to guard the Messenger's hut. Muḥammad restored peace by ordering all the spoils to be piled into a heap and then by dividing it equally among all those present.

The prisoners were herded together. 'Umar wanted them all slaughtered, but Muḥammad decided that ransoms should be demanded first, after which they could kill any for whom no one was prepared to pay. He even went so far as to release two of them on the spot. On the other hand he gave free rein to his anger against two men who had attacked him on an intellectual level. They had studied Jewish and Persian sources and had asked him awkward questions. They had scoffed at him and at his divine messages. They could look for no mercy. He ordered their execution. When one of them asked, 'But who will take care of my sons, Muḥammad?' he answered him: 'Hell!'[12]

They returned in triumph. At Rawḥā', thirty-five miles from Medina, the followers had come out to welcome the victors, one of whom, Salama ibn Salāma, was heard to grumble: 'Why do you congratulate us? By Allah, we were only up against bald old women; we cut their throats like the camels offered up for sacrifice with their feet tied together.' The Messenger of God smiled, and then added: 'Yes, but nephew, they were the chiefs!'[13]*

The practical gains were enormous. The ransoms paid for the prisoners were heavy, varying from one to four thousand dirhams according to individual means. But the gain in prestige was much more important. This was the new sect's first real success and it was a considerable one. The great city of the Hejaz, which had been undefeated for generations, had suffered a major reverse. It was no longer possible to ignore the importance of Muḥammad and his followers. They were now a power to be reckoned with.

In particular, it confirmed Muḥammad's position in Medina. One of those who had not accompanied him to Badr hastened to make his excuses. He had thought it was simply a matter of picking up a bit of plunder. Had he known it to be a serious matter he would naturally have come. As usual, those who had been sitting on the fence rallied to the side of the victor. The Beduin tribes of the neighbourhood also began to offer friendship to the Muslims.

The effects of the victory were especially noticeable on Muḥammad himself. He had suffered and struggled, a butt for mockery and disbelief. He may even have doubted himself. And now Allah was giving him clear sign of his support. An army bigger than his own had been overcome. The hand of

* Literally 'the *mala'* [senate]'.

Allah was clearly at work. Inside his lattice shelter, in fear and trembling amidst the shouts of the warriors and the clash of arms, the screams of the wounded and the groans of the dying, Allah had spoken to him again. Perhaps whenever he glanced that way his fevered eye had seen on the field of battle the legions of angels hastening to the aid of his men, of which so much is made in later writing. Indeed it was Allah who had caused the encounter to take place, although none of the participants had, strictly speaking, intended it. Allah revealed this himself:

When you were on this side of the slope and they on that, with the caravan below, had you arranged to meet in battle you would never have agreed about the encounter [and it would not have taken place], but [everything happened] so that Allah accomplished this thing that was to be. . . . When Allah made you see them in a dream as being few in numbers, had he shown them as being many, you would have been downhearted, and argued the matter amongst yourselves; but Allah kept you in peace. He knows what is in men's hearts. When, at the moment of meeting, [Allah] made them appear few in your eyes, [also] he made you to appear few, so that he might accomplish this thing that was to be.

(Koran viii, 43–6)

Surely this was decisive proof, like that which he had once given to Moses when Pharaoh's armies were swallowed up beneath the Red Sea waves? For Moses and Aaron, that had been a 'salvation' (*furqan*, in Aramaic *purqān*), a word which Muḥammad connected with the Arabic meaning of its root and which he therefore saw at the same time as a 'separation': a separation of the just from the unjust, the good from the bad, the saved from the rejected. Surely this was the catastrophe, so long awaited, which was to fall on the Meccans and a decisive proof that they belonged among the latter? Decisive proof, besides, that Muḥammad's opponents in Medina, Jews, Christians, sympathizers with them, and pagans alike, were in the wrong. Allah was abandoning the Jews, for all their former virtues and their scriptural learning. Muḥammad returned to

Medina sure of himself and of his cause and determined to go forward and to overcome all opposition.

He was now rich and powerful, providing one more instance of the truth of the great Florentine's dictum that 'all well-armed prophets have conquered and the unarmed failed'.[14] Muḥammad's superiority, owing to circumstances and to the customs of his country, lay in being a well-armed prophet. Little by little the community was beginning to develop the characteristics of a state. Soon after Badr, Allah justified Muḥammad's share of a fifth of the spoils by laying on him the obligation to provide for orphans, for the poor and for travellers. He began to call for voluntary contributions and this was the beginning of a public treasury. The emergence of that other typical state institution, a police force, will be seen in due course.

Before Badr, the cool or actively hostile attitude of the Jews towards his advances had begun to cause Muḥammad some annoyance. The mockery and criticism of their intellectuals had become a source of irritation, for he was, as we have seen, extremely sensitive to attacks of this kind.

Even before Badr he was apparently preparing for a split without actually bringing matters to a head. He decreed that there was to be no more turning towards Jerusalem to pray. The Jews had drawn their own conclusions. It is worth noting that not one of them volunteered for the expedition. The rift was virtually a fact. Badr did away with the Prophet's remaining doubts. It was at this time, according to Richard Bell's extremely plausible theory, that he inaugurated the fast during the month of Ramaḍān, the month in which the battle had taken place. The Jewish fast of *'ashūrā*, on the day of *kippūr*, was no longer obligatory and soon ceased to be observed, or indeed if it was, it was better done either on the day before or the day after the Jewish fast. It became an object with the Muslims to distinguish themselves in all things from the people of Israel. The Jews let their hair flow loose, while the pagans combed theirs into a parting. Muḥammad had followed the

Jewish fashion; but now he reverted to the parting and charged his followers to do the same.[15]

The return from Badr signalled the hour of reckoning. The pagans were the first to be dealt with, and, as ever, the professional word-spinners, the poets. 'Aṣmā' bint Marwān's highly coloured verses have been quoted already. When these or similar verses were reported to the Messenger, he said aloud: 'Will no one rid me of this daughter of Marwān?' There was a man present who belonged to the poetess's clan. His name was 'Umayr ibn 'Adī, and neither he nor any of his clan had been at Badr, an excellent reason for giving proof of his zeal. That very evening, he went to the poetess's house. She was sleeping with her children about her. The youngest, still at the breast, lay asleep in her arms. He drove his sword through her, and in the morning he went to Muḥammad.

'Messenger of God,' he said, 'I have killed her!' 'You have done a service to Allah and his Messenger, 'Umayr,' was the reply. Then 'Umayr asked: 'Shall I have to bear any penalty on her account, O Messenger of Allah?' He answered: 'Two goats shall not come to blows for her!' Then 'Umayr returned to his own clan which was in a great uproar that day on account of the daughter of Marwān. She had five sons. 'Umayr said: 'Banū Khaṭma! I killed the daughter of Marwān. Decide what is to be done with me, but do not keep me waiting.' [The words are taken from the Koran.]

No one moved. The chronicler continues:

That was the day when Islam first showed its power over the Banū Khaṭma. 'Umayr had been the first among them to become a Muslim. On the day the daughter of Marwān was killed, the men of the Banū Khaṭma were converted because of what they saw of the power of Islam.[16]

The move had succeeded. Assassination, like the war which is an extension of it, is the pursuit of political ends by different means. 'Umayr's exploit is listed by the chroniclers among Muḥammad's 'expeditions'.

The following month, the centenarian poet Abū 'Afak was

killed in the same way, in his sleep. We have seen his quotation attacking Muḥammad. Once again the Prophet merely remarked: 'Who will avenge me on this scoundrel?' One Sālim ibn 'Umayr, another who had not fought at Badr, undertook the task.

In the course of the same month Muḥammad began to attack the Jews seriously. He took as his target the Jewish clan of the Banū Qaynuqā'. They were probably the weakest of the Jewish groups in Medina, not because of numerical weakness but because they were made up largely of craftsmen, in particular goldsmiths. Even so they could, in emergency, put seven hundred soldiers into the field, four hundred of them with armour. Muḥammad's decision to attack them was probably the result of a political calculation. They were allies of 'Abdallāh ibn Ubayy, the powerful Medinan chief who, as we have seen, had supported Muḥammad's cause without serving it heart and soul with the absolute devotion demanded by political leaders. Ibn Ubayy retained a measure of independence which made him dangerous and gave rise to the suspicion that he might one day turn against the cause. As a preventative measure it was necessary to render him harmless; this meant depriving him of forces which might offer potential support.

The pretext which came to hand was a trivial incident, common enough in Arab wars (which are not without their occasional element of spicy humour). A Beduin girl, who was married to a man of Medina who was a follower of Muḥammad, went to the market place of the Qaynuqā' to sell some of her farm produce. She sat down by a goldsmith's stall. Some young Jews started teasing her and trying to make her lift her veil. She objected vehemently. Then the goldsmith, who obviously enjoyed a joke, managed to fasten her skirts without being seen in such a way that when she stood up all the lower part of her body was exposed. The bystanders hooted with joy while the victim swore vengeance on all and sundry. The honour of everyone connected with the woman, however remotely, was at stake. A Muslim who happened to be by sprang forward and killed the goldsmith. The Jews fell on the Muslim and killed him. The quarrel was on.

The Qaynuqāʿ withdrew inside the fort which was their refuge. They probably believed that their friends and allies in Medina would intercede for them and that the matter would be settled with some indemnities on both sides. But Muḥammad meant to make the most of the incident. He sent his private army to blockade the tower and prevent the Jews from taking in supplies of food. Several Medinan allies of the Qaynuqāʿ abandoned them and took sides against them, loyalty to the cause taking precedence over their sworn word. The other Jewish tribes, for one reason or another, failed to intervene. Probably they, too, put their faith in mediation; and the various Jewish groups may well have had differences of their own. The blockade lasted for fifteen days before the defenders gave in. Muḥammad wanted to put all of them to death; and this time Ibn Ubayy did make a strong move to intercede on behalf of his allies. Muḥammad made to turn away without answering, whereupon Ibn Ubayy seized hold of the top of his breast-plate. The Messenger's face became black with rage. 'Let me go,' he said. 'No, by Allah!' came the answer. 'I shall not let you go until you deal kindly with my allies. Four hundred men without armour and three hundred with, who have always defended me from both Red and Black [that is to say against all-comers]. Will you slay them all in the space of a morning? By Allah, in your place I would fear a reversal of fortune!' This was a threat and Ibn Ubayy was still powerful. Muḥammad yielded.[17] He spared the lives of the Qaynuqāʿ on condition they left Medina within three days, leaving their goods for the victor. Ibn Ubayy and others renewed their efforts to obtain a more merciful sentence, but this time Muḥammad was implacable and one of his guards actually struck the Medinan leader. Even so, it seems as though the Jews might have tried to remain. Domestic politics were apparently taking a new turn, bringing together all those who were becoming conscious suddenly of the excessive power which this *coup* had given to Muḥammad. But the Jews no longer trusted either the steadfastness or the real effectiveness of their allies. They departed for the oasis of the north where many of their co-religionists were settled, the women and children mounted on camels, the men on foot. The spoils were enormous and Muḥammad kept a fifth.

The news of the disaster at Badr was received in Mecca first with incredulity, then with a grief which soon hardened into fierce resolution. The deaths of the old leaders had made way for younger men, less stubborn perhaps but more active and intelligent. The chief place in the city's councils went to Abū Sufyān ibn Ḥarb of the family of the Banū Umayya or, as they are called in English, the Umayyads, of the clan of ʿAbd Shams. His abilities have been seen in his conduct when the great caravan was endangered at Badr. The remarkable rise of his family under Islam had yet to appear. He forbade all show of mourning and made a vow not to touch a woman until he had led an expedition against Muḥammad. (It is however true that he was accused of effeminacy and of suffering from what would be called nowadays an anal fixation.) In raising Meccan morale he had the invaluable assistance of a brilliant propagandist. Kaʿb ibn al-Ashraf was a Medinan of Arab origins (but with a Jewish mother) and he was accepted as a member of her tribe, the Banū n-Naḍīr. Enraged by Muḥammad's success at Badr, he set out for Mecca to rouse the people against him. He sang of the nobility and generosity of the dead and cried out for vengeance:

> The mill of Badr ground for the slaughter of its people.
> For such battles as Badr, tears and rain flow in torrents.
> The flower of the people perished round its cisterns.
> Stay close, O victims! The princes are slain!
> So many of noble fame have been cut down,
> Men of goodly bearing, a present help for those in want,
> Whose hands were ever open when the stars were niggardly of rain.[18]

Abū Sufyān proposed that the profits of the caravan which he had led to safety should be set aside for the conduct of the war.

Three months after Badr he led a flying raid on Medina at the head of a small troop of some two to four hundred men, travelling by unfrequented ways. His object was probably to revive Meccan morale and to teach Muḥammad not to overestimate the extent of his victory. He appeared unexpectedly on the outskirts of the oasis, conversed briefly with two Jews who informed him of the situation there, burned a few young palm trees, killed two Medinans who were working in the fields and departed as quickly as he had come. When Muḥammad heard the news, he hurried out in pursuit but only succeeded in picking up a few cakes of roasted barley (*sawīq*), the soldiers' provision in the field, which had been dropped by the fugitives. This engagement – for Allah promised that those who took part in the chase earned the same merit as that attaching to a real engagement – was called by the Muslims the expedition of the *sawīq*.

The situation was none the less extremely serious for Quraysh. From his refuge in Medina, Muḥammad was making the roads to Syria, the principal source of Meccan revenue, impassable. The court poet, the Medinan Ḥassān ibn Thābit, whose talents had previously been employed in the service of the Ghassānids and whose services Muḥammad had recently acquired (every ruler needed such a propagandist), was able to taunt them with their loss:

> Say farewell to the streams of Damascus, for the road that way is barred
> By battle, like the jaws of great camels glutted with *arāk*! . . .
> If they take the road to the valley over the back of the sand dunes
> Then tell them: There is no road that way.[19]

They did in fact make the attempt to send a caravan by the road to Mesopotamia and hired an experienced guide for the purpose. The rich Qurayshites invested a great deal of money in the business, but it could not be kept secret. Someone told the story in a Jewish tavern in Medina. Muḥammad heard of it and sent a hundred men under the command of his freedman Zayd ibn Ḥāritha. The caravan was attacked during a halt and its escort, taken by surprise and with the dreadful memory of Badr fresh in their minds, took to their heels. The captured merchandise was valued at 100,000 dirhams. Muḥammad's treasury was becoming well filled. Two months later he was able to take a third wife. This marriage was to ʿUmar's daughter Ḥafṣa, a girl of eighteen who was already a widow. She made an excellent complement to Sawda, the housewife, and ʿĀʾisha, who was still a child. Muḥammad's frustrations were well on the way to being satisfied. Although he still had no male child, his daughter Fāṭima, who had married his young cousin ʿAlī, had given birth to a boy, Ḥasan, and was soon pregnant again.

The poet Kaʿb ibn al-Ashraf, after working the Meccans up to a pitch of excitement against Muḥammad by his verses, had returned to Medina. He was protected by the powerful Jewish clan of the Banū n-Naḍīr, to which he belonged through his mother. He lived in their quarter, in a fortress the remains of which are still visible today. As we have seen, Muḥammad could not endure satire or vituperation. As before, he indicated that the man should be eliminated; but the half-Jewish poet was on his guard. The volunteer who undertook his assassination explained to the Prophet that it would be necessary to resort to cunning, trickery and lies. Muḥammad saw no objection. The next move was to recruit accomplices, one of whom was a foster-brother of Kaʿb. They sought him out, posing as discontented followers of the Prophet who were ready to conspire against him. On a night of bright moonlight they went to his house on pretext of holding a secret conference, Muḥammad himself going with them for part of the way and giving them his blessing. Then they lured Kaʿb from his refuge, despite the gloomy forebodings of the young woman he had in bed with him, and killed him. They made their way back to Muḥammad's house uttering devout cries and flung the head of Kaʿb at the Prophet's feet.

There were a few more incidents of the same kind.

Muḥammad was, by this time, too powerful for anyone to seek vengeance for them. The more fanatical members of his party therefore acted as a kind of police force. With the removal of the remaining elements in the Medinan community possessed of sufficient power to interfere to some extent with the activities of this police force, they would have something approaching a real state.

The Jews were beginning to feel seriously alarmed. It may be true, as the chroniclers maintain, that at about this time they made an agreement with Muḥammad extending or revising the conditions of the original pact, but as a body they were still too powerful and inassimilable to permit matters to continue as they were. Even so, not all the bridges were down and, taken as a whole, the people of the Medinan oasis still placed their common interests before their internal differences.

Their unity was soon to be tested. The Quraysh were bound to strike back; and this time the blow would be well prepared. Negotiations were begun by the Meccans with the allied tribes of the neighbourhood; they sent contingents. Ṭā'if sent a hundred men. Abū 'Āmir, the Christian convert who emigrated from Medina to Mecca, brought fifty of the Medinan tribe of Aws. Besides this there were a fair number of slaves. In all, three thousand men were assembled, seven hundred of them with mail-coats and two hundred on horseback. There were three thousand camels. According to Beduin custom, a dozen or more women of the Meccan nobility were to urge on the combatants with singing and shouting. They were led by Abū Sufyān's wife, Hind, who had lost her father – none other than the venerable 'Utba ibn Rabī'a – one of her sons, her brother and an uncle at Badr. She had made a vow neither to wash nor to sleep with her husband until they had been avenged. Her fellow-wife, Umayma, was there also.

It took the army ten days to reach Medina, skirting the oasis to the north and returning to take up a position to the west of the low hill of Uḥud. Uḥud is two or three miles north of the centre of the oasis and overlooks a kind of broad gorge, which lies between two virtually impenetrable fields of volcanic rock (*ḥarra*). Warned of their coming, the Medinans had withdrawn inside their fortified dwellings, taking with them their domestic animals and farm implements. Between their camp and the city proper, the Qurayshites held the most fertile plain of the whole region, with its fields of barley, now in the ear but still fresh and green; and on these empty acres they released their horses and camels to gorge themselves on the unexpected pasture. The people of Medina could only look on helplessly at the ruin of their harvest. The most they could do was to set spies to observe the enemy from a distance and to count their numbers.

The heads of all the different groups in Medina were agreed on the proper tactics to pursue. They must not attack the enemy but withdraw for safety inside the strongholds formed by the clusters of dwellings belonging to each clan. Those forts, which were within easy reach of one another, had been hastily connected by stone walls, thus forming a network of fortified buildings beyond which it was perilous to venture but from which it would be possible to defy a numerically superior enemy for a long time. The Qurayshites' strong force of cavalry would be of no benefit to them.

The Qurayshites had reached Uḥud on the evening of Thursday, the fifth of Shawwāl in the year 3 (21 March 625). Early on Friday morning the Medinans held a council of war and determined to adhere to the plans already made. Some young hotheads, however, fired with ambitions of glory and plunder, objected angrily to this wait-and-see policy; they were supported by those whom the news from Uḥud had wrought to a pitch of anxiety about the fate of their crops. The would-be attackers demonstrated their feelings at the usual assembly at midday on Friday in the courtyard of Muḥammad's house. Muḥammad gave way and went into one of his cabins to put on his armour. In the meantime, some of them calmed down and began to wish they had not forced his hand. They told him they would abide by his decision, whatever it might be. Unable to offer them a spectacle of indecision and possibly having received some reassurance from Allah, Muḥammad answered that he would stand by the plan finally agreed on. 'Once a prophet has put on his armour,' he said, 'it is not fitting he should take it off until the battle is fought.'[20]

They set out after the afternoon prayer in the direction of Uḥud. Muḥammad had about a thousand men, a hundred of them with armour, and only two horses. The Jews, with the exception of a few individuals, remained at home. Friday evening marked the beginning of the Sabbath and all movement was forbidden. 'We can do without them,'[21] Muḥammad is reported as saying. Half-way to Uḥud, he paused and sent back a number of boys, too young and inexperienced, who had attached themselves to his company. At this point 'Abdallāh ibn Ubayy declared his intention of turning back. He made off towards the centre of the oasis, followed by about a third of the army. In all likelihood he had never abandoned the first plan decided on by the council of war, and was simply making a show of goodwill by leading his men as far as the outer limits of the Medinan territory to be defended. To attack beyond this point would merely satisfy a few hotheads and further Muḥammad's private ambitions, as well as the interests of the two Medinan clans whose lands the Qurayshites were busy ravaging. The agreement between them was for a defensive and not an offensive alliance. Furthermore, it will be remembered, Ibn Ubayy had already escaped involvement at Bu'āth and had come out of it very well. If Muḥammad were to suffer a defeat, it would take him down a peg and enable the Medinan chief to recover a measure of influence. Those who followed Ibn Ubayy were probably inspired, more simply, by an unwillingness to pull any chestnuts out of the fire for the Meccan Emigrants or for the two clans whose property was in danger.

At nightfall, the seven hundred men who remained with Muḥammad pitched camp in the *ḥarra* among the mass of basalt rocks which offered protection from the Meccan horsemen. Ibn Ubayy and his followers were encamped at no great distance. On Saturday morning, Muḥammad's troops crossed the *ḥarra* and took up a position on the slopes of Mount Uḥud where the Qurayshite horsemen could not easily follow. The Medinan archers were given orders not to leave the hill. Meanwhile, the Qurayshites with their cavalry were manoeuvring on the flat, getting in between Medina and the Medinan army, which watched, seething, as the horses galloped hither and thither with impunity over their fields of barley.

Abū 'Āmir, the Christian from Medina living in exile in Mecca, came to plead with his countrymen to give up the fight and abandon Muḥammad, their evil genius. He had no success. After this the customary round of single combats began. The man who bore the Meccan standard advanced and the battle began in earnest. The Muslim warriors, probably encouraged by some slight success which tradition has greatly exaggerated, allowed themselves to be drawn further and further away from the slopes of the hill. The women urged on the Qurayshites with singing, rattling tambourines and calling out the names of the dead of Badr who must be avenged. Abū Sufyān's wife, Hind, led the chanting:

> If you advance, we will embrace you,
> We will spread cushions for you;
> If you retreat, we will leave you
> And in no way that is loving.[22]

Some of the Muslim archers may have believed the battle already won and gone on to the plain to take a share in the plunder. Whatever the cause, a good deal of confusion began to develop. The commander of the Meccan horse, Khālid ibn al-Walīd, who was later to show his outstanding qualities of generalship in the service of Islam, took advantage of the situation to drive right through the Muslims' left flank with his men and fall upon the mass of the combatants from the rear, creating total panic. The Muslim standard-bearer was cut down within a few yards of Muḥammad. The fighting broke up into scattered groups. Fifteen-odd warriors formed up about the Prophet and slowly fought their way back with him to the shelter of the hill. For the first time, Muḥammad himself was forced to take part in the fighting, wielding a spear and drawing a bow. A stone split his lip and broke one of his teeth. Another smashed into the cheekpiece of his helmet. There was blood on his face. A Qurayshite dealt him a great blow which sent him reeling backwards into a hole. They hauled him to his feet but he was so badly shaken that he had to lean on two of his Companions. Someone cried out that he was dead, adding to the panic. At last, he and the little group about him reached safety on the slopes of Mount Uḥud. Others of his supporters fled across the plain making for the *ḥarra* and Medina. A great many were killed. One who escaped in this was the Prophet's elegant son-in-law 'Uthmān. The Qurayshites ranged over the plain, finishing off the wounded. Muḥammad's uncle, the valiant Ḥamza, was transfixed by a javelin thrown by an Abyssinian slave named Waḥshī, an expert with this weapon, who pursued him doggedly. The slave's Meccan master, whose uncle had been one of those killed at Badr, had promised him his freedom if he killed Muḥammad's uncle. With Ḥamza dead, there was nothing more for him to do and he calmly left the field of battle.

The Qurayshites celebrated their triumph in the fashion of the barbarians of their times. The women mutilated the corpses and made themselves bloody necklaces from the ears and noses. Hind carved open Ḥamza's breast, tore out the liver of the man who had killed her father at Badr, chewed it up and spat it out.

By this time night had fallen. Would the victorious Meccans march on Medina? To the surprise and relief of many, they did not do so but went away in the direction of Mecca. They had won a great victory. Muḥammad's army had been literally decimated. There were about seventy dead (only ten of them Emigrants) against a score of Qurayshites. It could therefore be fairly said that vengeance had been taken for the dead of Badr. To embark now on the difficult siege of the labyrinth of forts in Medina, an operation for which the Qurayshite army was ill-prepared, would be to hazard their great success to no purpose. Moreover it would stir up the whole population of

Medina, including the Jews, against them, when they had set out only to fight Muḥammad's private army. It would reforge the unity which had been imperilled by that very Meccan victory which might be expected to strengthen all the Messenger's opponents, not only the Jews and pagans, but also the Muslim opposition led by 'Abdallāh ibn Ubayy which had refused to fight outside the bounds of the city. It was wiser not to precipitate the worst by attempting too much, especially since the Meccan army had, after all, its own casualties. There were a number of wounded and nearly all the horses had been hit by the arrows of Muḥammad's archers.

Muḥammad himself, with the little group of fifteen or so who had stayed with him, spent the night among the rocks of Mount Uḥud. In Medina, where the news of the Messenger's death had spread, people waited in a fever of anxiety. In the morning, Muḥammad had the dead buried in huge trenches. Then the company of the survivors, emerging from the various crannies in the rocks where they had been hiding, wounded and bleeding, made their way slowly back to Medina where they were greeted by the shrill cries with which the Arab women are used to mourn the death of their kinsfolk.

Almost before his wounds were dressed, Muḥammad, with his Companions who were scarcely in a better state, set out bravely on the road to Mecca in pursuit of Abū Sufyān's forces. They kept at a distance, lighting big watch-fires to signal their presence, in the hope, no doubt, that the Qurayshites would imagine them to be a large army strengthened by reinforcements, and so be deterred from returning to attack Medina if that had been their intention. It may be that Muḥammad's main object was to impress the neighbouring tribes and convince them that his case was not nearly so desperate as the Qurayshites were certain to make out. This done, he returned to the oasis.

The situation there was a critical one for him. The Jews, pagans and non-believers were pointing out unkindly that if Muḥammad had hailed the victory at Badr as proof of the genuineness of his mission, it was only logical to deduce from his present defeat a sign of the vanity of his claims. If Allah was now on the side of the Qurayshites, it meant that Muḥammad could not be accepted as a prophet. Who had ever heard of a prophet who had heaven on his side being so humiliatingly worsted?

Ibn Ubayy and his followers were equally jubilant. They had said it was a mistake to go rushing out to meet the Meccans, as those young fools whose advice the Prophet had seen fit to follow had insisted on doing. Ibn Ubayy did not repudiate the Constitution, but he did demand that the council of the Medinan community should in future pay more attention to the advice of experienced men like himself. He and his people remained faithful to their monotheist leanings and do not appear to have questioned the fact that Muḥammad's revelations came from Allah. This had been the very foundation of all their actions for a number of years and it was not easy for them to repudiate it entirely. But they were uneasy about accepting certain of his revelations, arguing over details, pointing unhappily to contradictions in the words from on high and asking for more explicit texts. They seem to have hinted at the possibility of Muḥammad's manipulating the revelations in his own best interests by elaborating some – it is not known whether they went so far as to suggest that he added to them off his own bat – and keeping others to himself.

On the day after the battle, Ibn Ubayy came to the Mosque where his son, an ardent follower of Muḥammad, was engaged in cauterizing his wounds with a red hot iron by a large fire, and lectured him for taking part in such a foolhardy venture. The next Friday, at the great weekly assembly, he endeavoured to speak, as usual graciously extolling the Prophet to the people; but the most zealous, full of indignation for what they regarded as desertion in the face of the enemy, came and took hold of him by his garments. 'Sit down,' they told him, 'enemy of Allah. You are not worthy to speak here after behaving as you have done.' He went away grumbling: 'By Allah, anyone would think I had said something wrong when I got up to give him my support.' 'Go home,' someone called out, 'and may the Messenger of God forgive you.' 'By Allah,' was his reply, 'I don't want his forgiveness!'

He was insulted to such an extent that he gave up going to the meetings. This only made him angrier than ever, and in the months that followed his attitude became increasingly hostile. Up to a point, Muḥammad allowed his henchmen a free rein, but he would not let them take ultimate measures although, in his zeal for the cause, the Meccan leader's own son offered to go and kill his father with his own hand.

Inevitably, the Voice of Allah provided an answer to all doubts and questionings.

Do not grow faint or grieve. It is you who triumph because you believe. If you have suffered hurt, so also have they. We alternate the days [good and evil] between the people so that Allah may know the faithful and choose witnesses from amongst you (for Allah does not love the wrong-doers), so that he may let the believers shine forth, and cast the infidels out into darkness. (Koran iii, 133–5)

What befell you on the day when the two armies met was by the permission of Allah so that he might know the Believers and so that he might know the Doubters. . . those who stayed quietly at home and said of their brothers: 'Had they obeyed us they would not have been killed.' (Koran iii, 160–62)

The Arabic word translated here as 'Doubters' (*munāfiqūn*) – usually translated as 'Hypocrites' – is one borrowed from the language of the Christian Church of Abyssinia. In Ethiopic, it meant doubters or sceptics, those with reservations, men who were in two minds, people of little faith. In Arabic, however, it had the further connotation of the action of a jerboa diving into its hole. To the younger Muslims it seemed a fitting description of those who had 'deserted' at Uḥud.

The protests of the Jews and the Doubters were reaching a peak. Some answer had to be made. As we have seen, Muḥammad had moved away from the Jews after the brief period in which he had thought he would be able to make converts among them. He had adopted different rites and customs. He had forced the Qaynuqā' to emigrate and seized their possessions. He was also obliged to answer the sharp and knowledgeable attacks of Jewish intellectuals. If Muḥammad recognized the Jewish prophets as inspired by Allah, and the Old Testament as a holy book, why did he not adhere to the faith of Israel? How could the revelations he claimed to receive contradict the Torah? And, if he was not a Jew, what was he?

Muḥammad's and his followers' acquaintance with the scriptures, while it was never very profound, had grown enormously since their coming to Medina. The handful of Jews who had joined the Meccan prophet's ranks must have had a good deal to do with this. One of the prophets mentioned in the revelations received at Mecca as having been sent to the different peoples was Abraham, or Ibrāhīm as he was called in Arabic. He had broken with his own people, idolaters, and with his father in particular, after vainly preaching monotheism to them. Later, when he was an old man, mysterious visitors had promised him a 'prudent son' (Koran li, 28). The Voice from on high referred to the 'early scriptures, the scriptures of Ibrāhīm and Moses' (Koran lxxxvii, 18–19). All these details are taken from the Old Testament and from more or less distorted versions of later Jewish legends.

As time went on these vague ideas were expanded. Even during Muḥammad's Meccan period there was mention of another prophet, Ismā'īl, who had also preached truth. At a given moment, whether while still in Mecca or after the Emigration, it emerged that Ismā'īl was the son of Ibrāhīm, that he was the father of the Arabs (as the Bible had said), and brother to Isaac, the father of the Jews. This was a new and highly important fact. The stories of the prophets, which had hitherto belonged to some chronological limbo, now acquired a time and place. Ibrāhīm, the forefather of both Jews and Arabs, grandfather of Jacob, the father of the twelve tribes of Israel, and distant forebear of Moses who revealed the Law to the Israelites, was not therefore strictly speaking a Jew at all. His faith in the one almighty God, which went much further back than the tenets of Judaism or Christianity, could surely be defined best by regarding it as a similar step to that taken by the *ḥanīfs*, men who, as we have seen, sought an approach to Allah without becoming either Jews or Christians? If this were so he could surely be regarded as the first man who surrendered to the will of Allah, in fact the first Muslim? From then on Muḥammad had his answer ready for those who called him to follow Judaism or Christianity. 'Rather follow the community of Ibrāhīm like a *ḥanīf*! For he was not of those who associate other gods with Allah [that is, the polytheists]' (Koran ii, 129).

This was not a very original view. St Paul had already written to the Romans, in about A.D. 58, that Abraham was 'the father of us all' (Romans iv, 16) that he was 'the father of all them that believe, though they be not circumcised . . . and the father of circumcision . . .' (Romans iv, 11–12). It was a rabbinical maxim that 'the father of all proselytes is Abraham', and, whenever a proselyte was given a Hebrew name, he was hailed as 'son of Abraham'.[23] But Muḥammad went further in discovering a special relationship between Ibrāhīm and his own land and people.

Perhaps he had never entirely abandoned his reverence for the central shrine of his native city, the Ka'ba with its Black Stone, however much he may have turned against the idols which were set up there beside Allah for the worship of the faithful. Jewish and Arabic legends may have existed already about the adventures of Ismā'īl in the wilderness of Pāran, where Genesis sets the scene of his exile and where it declares that Yahweh will 'make him a great nation' (Genesis xxi, 18–21). Jewish tales told how Abraham his father went secretly to visit him in the wilderness, unknown to Sarah, the stepmother of the ancestor of the Arabs.[24] However that may be, the Voice from on high came to Muḥammad one day to explain that Ibrāhīm had 'settled some of [his] offspring in a barren valley' near a holy Temple of God (Koran xiv, 40). He and his son Ismā'īl had built this temple and purified it, and made it a place of pilgrimage and asylum. He asked Allah to send one of the future inhabitants of the City which would grow up around this temple as a messenger (*rasūl*) to tell his people of his revelations, the scripture and the wisdom (Koran ii, 118 ff.). When the decision was made not to turn any longer to Jerusalem to pray to mark the break with the Jews, the Voice commanded them to turn towards Mecca and the Kaʿba instead (ii, 139).

From then on, from an ideological point of view, the situation was reversed. It was no longer Muḥammad, the untutored son of a barbarous and idolatrous people without scriptures or Law, who was entering into the community of the keepers of the revelation of Moses. It was the Jews, the faithless children of those to whom that revelation had been addressed, who were called upon to confess the truth of the messages which Allah sent to a descendant of their common ancestor in the very same spirit as the message which, on the evidence of their own tradition, had been communicated to that ancestor, Abraham or Ibrāhīm. With a biblical knowledge that was quite new, they were accused of having rejected and persecuted the prophets among their own people, of having rebelled against Moses, of having disobeyed the commandments which had been given them, and in many cases of continuing to disobey them. Had they not also, as the Christians could testify, failed to believe in Jesus? Had they not killed him, or rather had they not tried to kill him; and had they not slandered Mary his mother? If they claimed that the coming of Muḥammad was not foretold in their scriptures, then they were deliberately falsifying their meaning or concealing some part of it.

Why, moreover, did their Law deny them so much that was perfectly good to eat, if not because of their great sins? It was a punishment for their wrongdoing (Koran iv, 158). The faithful for their part had no cause to abstain. They had merely to avoid eating blood, pork or meat which had been sacrificed to pagan idols and carrion (ii, 168). To each his own food. These dietary regulations were the ultimate parting of the ways. It must not be forgotten that the first universal rule laid down by the Christian Church to mark its beginning as a distinct community had been very similar. 'For it seemed good to the

Holy Ghost and to us,' the Apostles and Elders assembled in Jerusalem wrote to their non-Jewish followers in about A.D. 48, 'to lay upon you no greater burden than these necessary things; That ye abstain from meats offered to idols, and from blood, and from things strangled, and from fornication' (Acts xv, 28–9).

And so, little by little, Muḥammad's group of disciples became a definitive sect. It was at about this time that the name by which they were most generally known became, once and for all, the 'surrendered' to the will of Allah, in Arabic *muslimūn*, more familiar to us in its singular form *muslim*. The corresponding infinitive, *islām*, 'surrender', was destined for far-reaching influence.

But, after Uḥud, danger loomed over them. Abū Sufyān, the new leader of Quraysh, was, as we have said, a highly intelligent man. He was well aware that the threat represented by Medina and the Muslims must be destroyed, and that it was now or never. He set about achieving just that. To do so it was necessary to assemble an even larger army than at Uḥud and wipe out the enemy stronghold completely. Only the Beduin tribes were in a position to provide men in sufficient numbers. Qurayshite emissaries were despatched to sound out potential allies and solicit their support.

Muḥammad, for his part, was now the possessor of money and a large, devoted following; he too sent agents, whose business was to counter the efforts of the Qurayshites. This diplomatic tussle was productive of a good deal of plotting. The Beduin chiefs, predictably in the circumstances, took advantage of the situation to sell to the highest bidder. Rival chiefs contending for leadership of a particular tribe endeavoured to make use of the help proffered by Meccans or Muslims to gain their ends. All this is the familiar and everlasting stuff of politics.

Sometimes it had tragic results. The tribe of the Banū Liḥyān had long ago laid the foundations of a powerful kingdom. Now it formed part of the confederacy of Hudhayl, which was under Qurayshite ascendancy. Apparently, Muḥammad learned that their chief, Sufyān ibn Khālid, was gathering men to attack him. He sent one of his followers, ʿAbdallāh ibn Unays, to him with permission to say whatever he liked: even to abuse the Prophet if necessary, in order to win the confidence of the Liḥyānite shaikh. Everything worked perfectly. Sufyān was so taken with his new recruit that he invited him to sleep in his tent. He had a camel milked and offered fresh milk to his guest. 'I sipped a little,' the man recounted, 'but he plunged his nose right into the froth and lapped it up like a camel.'[25] Ṣuch manners were only fit for an enemy of Allah. Like Judith, ʿAbdallāh cut off his head in the night and succeeded in making his escape in spite of the screams of his victim's wives. Travelling only at night, he came to Medina and flung Sufyān's head at Muḥammad's feet. The Prophet was well pleased and gave ʿAbdallāh ibn Unays a rod. The man took it and thanked him; but he was a killer and not over-intelligent. When people asked him why Muḥammad had given him such an apparently pointless gift, it emerged that he had not thought to ask. His questioners persuaded him to go back and find out. Muḥammad told him: 'It shall be a sign between you and me on the Day of Judgement. There will be few then who shall hold a rod.' From then on Ibn Unays refused to be parted from his rod and had it buried with him.[26]

The Banū Liḥyān took this murder harder than Allah was to do. They began negotiations with two clans of the tribe of Khuzayma, offering them a number of camels in exchange for their assistance. A delegation from the Khuzayma went to Medina and asked Muḥammad to send them some of his followers to teach them the new faith. Muḥammad, pleased and unsuspecting, gave them seven men. When they came to the well of Rajīʿ, the pretended converts slipped away. Suddenly the Muslims found themselves surrounded by a hundred archers of Liḥyān, who called on them to surrender. They wanted them alive in order to sell them to Quraysh. Four refused, rushed the enemy and were killed. Of the remaining three, one tried to escape and was stoned to death. The two survivors were bound, taken to Mecca and sold to the Qurayshites eager to avenge their dead. In this way, with true Beduin realism, the Banū Liḥyān were at once sure of their own revenge and of raising a large sum of money. One of these two was apparently put to death fairly quickly. The other, Khubayb ibn 'Adī, had rather more to suffer – at least according to tradition which, here again, seems to have expanded what was probably a real incident in a tendentious way. He was crucified, which probably means that he was tied to a stake. A child, the son of a man who died at Badr, was encouraged to jab at him with a spear, but could not strike hard enough. A crowd of women, children and slaves had gathered round to see the spectacle. They marvelled at the courage of martyrs who, right to the end, refused to recant. Apparently they had to be finished off with spear thrusts. Before he died, Khubayb prayed to his God: 'Allah,' he cried, pointing at those about him, 'count them well. Kill them all, one by one, and let not one escape!'[27]

Among those present was a youth who, twenty years later, was to become the supreme head, the Caliph of all the Muslims. He was Mu'āwiya, the son of Abū Sufyān. His father quickly threw him to the ground to escape the effects of the curse. Muḥammad's poet composed a great many verses in honour of the martyr and his companions.

The head of 'Āṣim ibn Thābit, one of those killed outright at Rajī', was cut off and sold by the Liḥyān to a Qurayshite woman whose two sons he had killed at Uḥud. She had made a vow to drink wine from his skull. But 'Āṣim, while he lived, had sworn never to have anything to do with an idolater. By a miracle, Allah permitted him not to break this vow. On the night of the execution a swarm of hornets prevented the woman from getting at the skull; and by next morning the whole *wādī* where it lay had been flooded, and the gruesome relic had been swept away.

Some time after this (or it may have been before, as the chronology of these incidents is very vague), Muḥammad, somewhat against his inclinations, allowed himself to be persuaded by one Abū l-Barā', a shaikh of the Banū 'Āmir ibn Ṣa'ṣa'a, to send them forty or so of his disciples to instruct them in the faith. Another of the chiefs of this tribe, 'Āmir ibn Ṭufayl, who was an enemy of Muḥammad and possibly also a rival of Abū l-Barā', had the Muslims murdered at the well of Ma'ūna – not by men of his own tribe who refused to break their given word, but by members of a neighbouring tribe. Muḥammad was deeply grieved. He was not at that time in a position to avenge the dead, but he called down the vengeance of Allah on 'Āmir ibn Ṭufayl.

Only one Muslim escaped the massacre. On his way home he came across two of the Banū 'Āmir lying peacefully asleep, and killed them to avenge his companions. He had been saved from the slaughter because he had wandered some way away from his party; the first he had known was when he saw the vultures wheeling over the bodies. He did not know that the Banū 'Āmir had taken no direct part in the massacre.

Muḥammad was responsible for the two murders committed by his henchman and, in spite of the greatly superior losses he had himself suffered in the business, he was obliged by virtue of his pact with the tribe to pay the blood money. He set about collecting funds.

Among those in Medina he approached for contributions was the Jewish tribe of Banū n-Naḍīr, who lived on the extreme south-east corner of the oasis. He appeared at the council of the Banū n-Naḍīr on the Sabbath, accompanied by a number of the more important men of his community, among them Abū Bakr, 'Umar and the Medinan chief Usayd ibn Ḥuḍayr.[28] The council, having declared its willingness to contribute to the expenses, went on with its business, requesting the noble visitors to sit down outside and wait for the outcome. While they thus waited sitting against a wall, the council, it is alleged, discussed whether this was not the longed-for moment for getting rid of Islam and its founder. Suddenly Muḥammad got to his feet. Allah had warned him, he explained afterwards, that some such conspiracy was being hatched at that very moment. In fact it was a not altogether unlikely assumption and one which, given a minimum of political intuition, anyone less intelligent than the Prophet might have suspected. Ka'b ibn al-Ashraf, the half-Jewish poet assassinated a few months previously at Muḥammad's instigation, had belonged to the Naḍīr through his mother. However that may be, Muslim accounts claimed to know who at the council had proposed dropping a large boulder, a millstone, from the rooftop on to the Prophet's head, who had agreed to do it and who had opposed it. At all events, Muḥammad slipped quietly away 'as though answering a call of nature'.[29]

After a while his Companions began to wonder where he was. Someone told them: 'I saw him going back to Medina.' At this, they also went back and found their leader at home. He described what Allah had revealed to him, and then sent one of his people, Muḥammad ibn Maslama, a Medinan belonging to a tribe allied to the Naḍīr, to present them with an ultimatum. They were to leave the oasis within ten days upon pain of death. They must take their goods and chattels with them, and would receive a part of the produce of their palm trees. But the tone of the message was stern: 'Leave my city and live with me no longer after the treason which you have plotted against me.' When they expressed surprise that a man allied to their clan should have agreed to carry such a message, Muḥammad ibn Maslama answered them: 'Hearts have changed and Islam has wiped out old alliances.'

The Naḍīr were prepared to temporize, but the 'Doubter' Ibn Ubayy, who was becoming increasingly impatient with Muḥammad, advised them to resist. He would support them, and so would the remaining Jewish tribe in Medina, the Qurayẓa; his nomad allies, the Ghaṭafān, would also come to the rescue. The Naḍīr shut themselves up inside their fortresses. Muḥammad came with his men and sat down outside with a wooden hut to protect him from their arrows. No one made a move, not the Qurayẓa, nor the Ghaṭafān nor Ibn Ubayy himself, who looked on grimly as his Muslim son came to arm himself for the fight.

Muḥammad began felling the Naḍīr's palm trees. This was

an act that went strongly against all Arab principles although, as always, these were frequently subordinated to the demands of war. Not so many years ago, in the Ḥaḍramawt, Freya Stark was able to observe the same infringement of the rules and the (pointless) recriminations it produced. All the same this act of total war, coming on top of the desertion of their allies, broke the Naḍīr's nerve. They registered a solemn protest, and some of the besiegers felt a twinge of conscience. But a revelation came from Allah to assure them that the Prophet's warlike behaviour was perfectly right. The siege lasted for a fortnight and then the Naḍīr surrendered. The conditions, naturally, had grown much harsher. 'Leave this place. You have your blood [in other words, your lives] and what you can carry on your camels, except for your weapons.'

They went, defiantly proud and perhaps glad to escape so lightly from such a perilous situation. They had friends and relatives and, some of them, land at Khaybar, the great Jewish centre in the north of the Hejaz. They loaded six hundred camels with their possessions, even dismantling their houses and carrying away the doors and roof-trees. The women decked themselves in their jewels and their finest clothes. And so, with drums and tambourines, the endless column of the defeated tribe wound its way joyously as though in triumph, through the oasis on the way to Khaybar or to Syria. The 'Doubters' saw it go with sorrow. One more counterweight to the power of Muḥammad was vanishing with it.

Muḥammad himself was adding up the spoils: fifty coats of mail, fifty helmets and three hundred and forty swords would be very useful. And then there were the Jewish lands, their palm plantations and what was left of their houses. Muḥammad explained to the Medinans that so far the Meccan Emigrants had been a burden to them because they were unable to supply their own needs. It was in their own interests that the Emigrants should have these lands, so that they would be able to make a living without begging from their brothers. As a result of this reasoning, the Jewish lands were divided up solely amongst the Muslims of Qurayshite origin. Exceptions were made only in the case of native Medinans who were very poor and deserving. The Prophet did not forget himself in the division. He got some good land with barley growing between the palm trees. From now on he had his own share and need be dependent on no one. He used the produce of his land to support himself and his family and also for the needs of the community. Among those needs it is only right to say was the maintenance of the destitute.

Moreover his family was growing. Some six months after these events, Fāṭima gave him a second grandson, Ḥusayn, who was destined for a tragic fate. In addition he had married two women of Quraysh (either by birth or by marriage) both aged about thirty, whose husbands had been Muslims killed at Badr and Uḥud. Their names were Umm Salama and Zaynab bint Khuzayma. The latter died not long afterwards.

Arab opinion reacted in various ways to the expulsion of the Banū n-Naḍīr. The propagandist poets, who were the journalists of the time, engaged in violent controversy. The Jew Sammāk lashed back at the versifiers in the pay of the Prophet:

Since you boast – and for you it is a boast –
Of having murdered Ka'b ibn al-Ashraf,
Coming to kill him in the early dawn,
Him who was incapable of treachery or bad faith,
It may be that nights and changing fortunes
Will bring their vengeance on the 'Just' and the 'Fair'
For attacking and driving out the Naḍīr[30]
And felling the palm trees before the crop was gathered.
As I live, we will meet you with spears at the ready
And with all our swords sharpened
In the hands of warriors who use them to protect themselves.
When they meet an enemy, they will be sure to slay him.
Ṣakhr [Abū Sufyān] and his companions stand with the
people.
He does not weaken when he attacks the foe,
As a lion of Mount Tarj in defence of his lair
As a son of the bush, mighty in stature, crushing his prey.[31]

The Jews then were pinning their hopes on the coalition which Abū Sufyān was in the process of forming. It could be a formidable one. But on the domestic front, Muḥammad's enemies could look for nothing more from the opposition in Medina, which had proved itself both timid and incompetent. Allah had remarked on this with pointed irony from heaven.

> Have you not seen the Doubters saying to their brothers, those impious among the People of the Book: 'If you are driven out, we will go with you; we will never serve anyone against you and, if you are attacked, we will come to your aid.' Allah can bear witness that they lied. If they are driven out, they will not go with them. If they are attacked, they will not aid them or, if they do, they [will quickly] turn their backs, and they shall have no help. . . . They all will never fight you except from strong fortresses and from behind high walls. They are very valiant among themselves: you would think them united. But their hearts are divided. They are men of no judgement.
>
> (Koran lix, 11–14)

Moreover, Muḥammad was losing no time in strengthening his position, both morally and materially. On the battlefield of Uḥud (on 23 March 625), Abū Sufyān had flung his challenge to the Muslims: 'In one year at Badr!' Badr was the scene of a great, yearly fair, which went on for a week. The Muslims duly put in an appearance in April 626 with fifteen hundred men and ten horses to make a show of strength. They did some good business there and their profits amounted to as much as a hundred per cent. The Meccans brought two thousand men and fifty horses to within sight of Badr but did not enter the fair itself. Each side had shown its colours.

It was probably at about this time also, after the expulsion of the Banū n-Naḍīr, that a group of Muslims from the Medinan tribe of Khazraj combined to assassinate the aged Jew Abū Rāfiʿ. The suggestion is that they were motivated by the desire to prove themselves as valiant as the members of the Aws tribe who had killed Kaʿb ibn al-Ashraf. The 'expedition' had the blessing of Muḥammad who had, however, enjoined the commando force to kill no women or children. They returned from Khaybar ten days later with their mission accomplished. The old man had been killed in his bed and his murderers had succeeded in making their escape. There was some argument as to who had struck (so gallantly!) the fatal blow. Muḥammad decided the matter by examining the swords. It was the one with traces of food on it. Abū Rāfiʿ must still have been digesting his dinner.

This was already the fifth year of the hegira (June 626). Muḥammad spent a fortnight on an expedition aimed at frightening two tribes that were massing troops for use against him. They fled and the Prophet returned to Medina, having shown his strength and captured a few pretty girls who had been left behind. In August of the same year an expedition set out for the great oasis of Dūmat al-Jandal, a long way to the north, where a famous fair was held. Muḥammad had learned that an army was mustering there also. Once again, the enemy fled and the force from Medina returned, without even reaching its goal, having captured a few animals and one prisoner.

In December the Prophet set out on another expedition which was to produce one or two especially noteworthy incidents. He scattered the Banū l-Muṣṭaliq, another tribe which was apparently mobilizing for an attack on Medina. Taken by surprise at the well of Muraysīʿ near the shore of the Red Sea, the army was swiftly put to flight. The Muslims lost one man killed, their enemies ten. But they took two thousand of their camels, five thousand head of sheep and goats and also two hundred women. One of these, Juwayriyya, was the daughter of the chief of the Banū l-Muṣṭaliq, and very beautiful. No one could set eyes on her without loving her. In the division of the spoils she fell to the lot of Thābit ibn Qays. She haggled with him about her ransom and demanded to be set free in return for signing a promissory note. He must have refused because she went and complained to Muḥammad. As ʿĀʾisha recounted later: 'By Allah, I had scarcely seen her in the doorway of my room before I detested her. I knew he would see her as I saw her.'[32] And so it was. Muḥammad heard her plea and immediately offered to buy her from Thābit and marry her himself. She agreed at once. From then on her tribe was related to the Prophet, and it was not long in trying to make the most of it.

The captured women were all intended to be returned on payment of a ransom. But they seemed very desirable to warriors on the night after a battle. As Abū Saʿīd Khudrī put it:

> We were lusting after women and chastity had become too hard for us, but we had no objections to getting the ransom money for our prisoners. So we wanted to use the *ʿazl* [*coitus interruptus*.] . . . We asked the Prophet about it and he said: 'You are not under any obligation to forbear from that. . . .' Later on women and children were ransomed by envoys [who came to Medina]. They all went away to their country and not one wanted to stay, although they had the choice.

The narrator goes on to recount how he went to the market with a young girl to sell her (she must have been a poor girl for whom no one would pay the ransom):

> A Jew said to me: 'Abū Saʿīd, no doubt you want to sell her as she has in her belly a baby by you.' I said: 'No; I used the *ʿazl*.' To which he replied [sarcastically]: 'Then it was the lesser child-murder!' When I repeated this story to the Prophet he said: 'The Jews lie. The Jews lie.'[33]

He was to be obliged to command his temper. Immediately after the fight, a Medinan and a Meccan Emigrant got into an argument at the well where they were watering their horses, and came to blows. The Medinans must have grudged the assignment of all the spoils from the Naḍīr to the Emigrants more than the sources admit. Ibn Ubayy, who happened to be on the scene, lost no time in exploiting these seeds of dissension and burst out angrily: 'Did they so? They are trying to outdo us, seeking to outnumber us in our own land! By Allah, I think that between us and these dregs of Quraysh it is like the saying "Fatten your dog and he will devour you." But when we get back to the City, by Allah, the stronger will drive out the weaker!'

He went and talked to the men of Medina, and told them:

'See what you have done to yourselves. You have laid open your lands to them, you have shared with them all you possess. If you had kept your own for yourselves, then, by Allah, they would have gone somewhere else.'

These words were reported to the Prophet. 'Umar said to him: 'Command 'Abbād ibn Bishr to kill him.' Muḥammad answered: 'What, 'Umar? And let men say that Muḥammad slays his Companions?'

At this point Ibn Ubayy, knowing that word of his angry outburst had reached the Prophet, went to him and denied everything, swearing an oath to prove it. The Medinans who were present bore him out. 'Perhaps the lad [who had reported the scene] had been mistaken; he might not have remembered exactly what the man said.' Muḥammad agreed to forget the matter, but he could not get it out of his mind. On the way home he spoke of it to another Medinan chief, Usayd ibn Ḥuḍayr. Usayd told him: 'But you are the one who will drive him from Medina if you like! By Allah! you are the strong and he the weak. And yet deal gently with him. When Allah brought you amongst us, the people were threading pearls to make him a kingly crown. And now he thinks that you have robbed him of kingship.'[34]

Ibn Ubayy's son, a devout Muslim as we have seen, also came to the Prophet and spoke to a quite different purpose. 'If you really want him killed,' he told him, meaning his father, 'command me to do it and I will bring you his head. By Allah, the Khazraj know there is no better son than I. I am afraid that, if you order another to kill him, I shall not afterwards be able to endure the sight of Ibn Ubayy's murderer preening himself among the people. I shall kill him – and then I shall have killed one of the faithful for the sake of an infidel, and I shall go to hell.'[35]

Muḥammad calmed him down. He also succeeded in mastering his own anger which was certainly great. But the voice of reason spoke louder. As time went on he observed that, whenever Ibn Ubayy made some false move, the very Medinans who had saved him were the ones who rounded on him most fiercely. He remarked one day to 'Umar: 'What do you think, 'Umar? By Allah, if I had killed him that day when you advised me to, the chiefs of Medina would have been shaking with fury; but now if I commanded them to kill him, they would kill him.'

Muḥammad soothed the exacerbated nerves of the Medinans and the Emigrants by striking camp as fast as possible and proceeding by forced marches, which left his men too exhausted for further bickering. But the expedition was not to end without one more incident which was significant in more ways than one.

Muḥammad had taken the youngest and best loved of his wives, 'Ā'isha, with him on the expedition. 'Ā'isha was then thirteen years old. Arab women had reached the age of maturity then, and the marriage had been consummated long since. Instructions had begun to come down from heaven prescribing a certain respect due to the Prophet's wives (he now had five, in addition to Juwayriyya whom, as we have seen, he had recently married). 'Ā'isha used to be carried in a closed litter mounted on the back of a camel. She did not weigh very much at the time owing to her tender age and also to the frugal rations distributed while on campaign. Men were assigned to saddle the camel and place the litter on its hump after every halt. One night, the last before they reached Medina, as 'Ā'isha related afterwards

I went away to fulfil a need. I was wearing a necklace of shells from Ẓafār. When I had finished, my necklace slipped off my neck without my noticing. When I got back to the camp, I felt my neck and found it gone. The men had begun to strike camp. I went back to the place where I had been and felt about [in the sand] until I found the necklace. Meanwhile the men whose job it was to load my camel came along, and, when they had finished saddling it, they took up the litter thinking that I was inside it, lifted it up and fastened it on to the camel. They had no idea that I was not inside. Then they departed, leading the camel by the head. When I came back to the camp there was no one there. I wrapped myself in my cloak and lay down where I was, telling myself that when they noticed my disappearance they would come back to look for me. As I was lying there, Ṣafwān ibn al-Mu'aṭṭal as-Sulamī came by. He had dropped behind the army for some reason, and had not slept with the rest. He saw me and came towards me, and stopped near by. Now he had seen me before when we were instructed to wear the veil. When he recognized me, he cried out: 'We are Allah's and to him we shall return! The wife of the Prophet!' I was wrapped in my garments. He said to me: 'Why have you been left behind?' But I spoke no word to him. He led his camel forward and said to me: 'Mount.' Then he stood aside. I mounted, and he led the camel by the head. And he departed quickly, looking for the army. But we did not catch up with it, and no one noticed my disappearance until the morning. Then the army halted, and, while they were resting, the man came up leading me. Then the liars said what they do say, and the army was in a state of turmoil. But by Allah, I knew nothing of it.[36]

There was a terrific scandal. It was and still is true to say of the Arabs, as Carlo Levi says about the Lucanian peasants, that

love or sexual attraction is regarded by the peasants as a force of nature of such power that no will is strong enough to fight it. When a man and a woman find themselves alone together without witnesses nothing can keep them from each other's arms. No amount of resolution, chastity or any other obstacle can restrain them and if by any chance they do not actually make love, they might just as well have done. Simply being together amounts to making love.[37]

The usual scandal-mongers were against 'Ā'isha at once. It was said that she had been seen talking to Ṣafwān on several occasions before that. There were those who were jealous of her father, Abū Bakr, and their friends. There were the relatives and friends of the Prophet's other wives, who hoped to profit by 'Ā'isha's disgrace. The Doubters too found this a good opportunity to make capital out of the Prophet's domestic troubles. Lastly, there were all who had been irritated by the rough edge of 'Ā'isha's tongue and her capricious behaviour. There had been another incident involving a necklace when the whole caravan had gone thirsty at a waterless halt while she looked for it. Chief among her accusers was naturally ʿAbdallāh ibn Ubayy, followed by a kinsman of Abū Bakr by the name of Misṭaḥ, and finally Muḥammad's propagandist poet, Ḥassān ibn Thābit.

Muḥammad was deeply distressed. He loved his child-wife, but he was not entirely convinced of her innocence. Had she perhaps been deceiving him with the young and handsome Ṣafwān? A great chill fell on his heart. ʿĀʾisha was ill; she said she knew nothing. Could not this be a trick? She claimed that all she knew was that, to her surprise and grief, her husband was behaving with unusual coldness to her in her illness. Her mother had come to nurse her; *he* merely dropped in and said: 'How are you?' Next she asked him to let her go to her mother's, where she could be better looked after. 'No harm in that,' was all he said. Apparently it was a mere accident which informed her of the truth some three weeks later. (This is not to say, however, that the account attributed to her may not be a later interpolation by some mischievous Persian, glad of the chance to show up the primitive habits of the Arabs.)

We are Arabs and do not have in our houses such closets for the relief of nature as foreigners have. We loathe and we abhor them. We go out into the empty places of Medina. The women go out every evening to relieve themselves. I went out one night for that purpose with Umm Misṭaḥ bint Abī Ruhm, whose mother, the daughter of Ṣakhr, was the maternal aunt of Abū Bakr [my father]. She was walking beside me when she tripped over her skirts and cried out: 'Curse Misṭaḥ!' I said to her. 'By Allah, that is an evil thing to say of an Emigrant who was a martyr at Badr [a fighter].' She said to me: 'What? Have you not heard the story, daughter of Abū Bakr?' I said to her: 'What story?' Then she told me what the liars were saying. I said to her: 'Is it indeed so?' And she answered me: 'By Allah, it is so.' By Allah, I could not finish what I was about, and I went home; and by Allah I could not stop crying until I thought my liver would burst with my sobs.

She went and told her mother, who remarked philosophically:

There, there, my child, don't take it to heart. It is not often you find a pretty woman married to a man who loves her and who has other wives, without them telling heaps of stories and tales about her, and other people as well![38]

Like any deeply worried man, Muḥammad went round asking for advice and counsel. Young Usāma ibn Zayd spoke up for 'Ā'isha. The servant-woman Buraya was questioned. 'I know nothing but good of her,' she declared. 'I have only one thing to say against her. When I was kneading dough and told her to keep an eye on it, she went to sleep and then the lamb came along and ate it!' His son-in-law 'Alī was unsympathetic. 'Women are plentiful,' he said bluntly. 'All you have to do is change her.'[39] We may wonder if he was put up to it by his wife, Fāṭima, who did not care for her young mother-in-law, or whether there was already some hint of political rivalry between 'Alī on the one hand, and the clan of Abū Bakr and 'Umar on the other – a rivalry which in its later developments was to lead to the formation of the two parties whose strife was to echo through the history of Islam. Whatever the reason, 'Ā'isha never forgave 'Alī for that remark – a remark which finally led to his death by an assassin's sword twenty years later.

The excitement mounted. Usayd, a member of the Aws, told the Prophet he would deal with the slanderers in his own tribe and that if any came from the tribe of Khazraj his friends would be very happy to cut off their heads. This brought protests from the Khazraj. 'You lie!' 'Liar yourself.' The poet Ḥassān ibn Thābit, a Medinan from the Khazraj, lampooned Ṣafwān and the Emigrants. It became a matter of vital importance to allay the various emotions triggered off by the incident.

Allah came to the rescue just in time. Muḥammad had gone to the house of his parents-in-law to beg 'Ā'isha to repent if she had done anything wrong. She turned to her parents, but they, deeply distressed and none too sure at heart of their daughter's virtue, said nothing. She wept and refused to say she was sorry because that would have been an admission of guilt. She had nothing to reproach herself with. She would endure this ordeal patiently like that patriarch whose name she could not remember – but, anyway, he was Joseph's father. Then she started to cry again.

Muḥammad was at his wits' end. He fell into a trance. He was wrapped in his mantle and a leather cushion was placed under his head. The Voice from on high spoke to him. Abū Bakr and his wife held their breath with anxiety. Was Allah about to reveal their daughter's guilt? 'Ā'isha herself was perfectly calm, trusting as she said in her innocence. Then it was all over. The Prophet recovered from his trance and wiped the sweat from his streaming forehead, 'and it ran from him like drops of water on a cold day'. He spoke: 'Good news, 'Ā'isha; Allah has revealed your innocence.' Then he went out and recited the revelation he had received.

The slanderers were a small group among you. That is not a misfortune for you; it is for your good. Each of them shall bear the guilt he has earned for himself. And for the one who bears the chief guilt, his punishment will be terrible indeed. Why, when you heard it, did the faithful men and women not of their own accord think the best and say: 'This is a manifest lie'? If they had even produced four witnesses! But they produced no witnesses. So they are the liars in Allah's eyes. . . . Why, when you heard it, did you not say: 'It is not for us to speak of this. Praise be to you! This is a monstrous slander.'

(Koran xxiv, 11–15)

The reprimands were followed by rules for the future. 'Ā'isha's case was to act as a precedent. Accusations of adultery and fornication must in future be supported by four witnesses. If the accusation were shown to be true the guilty parties were each to receive a hundred lashes. But if the accusers could not bring four witnesses, they were to be regarded as bearing false witness and themselves punished with eighty lashes. It was a rule which was to prove a blessing to Muslims intending to commit adultery. It was not easy to produce these famous four witnesses, especially since – at least in those cases where scandal was to be avoided, and unless the authorities had any reason to hold a grudge against the accused – the judicial authorities came to demand that they must bear ocular testimony of anatomical precision. But the jealous customs of the peoples who adopted Islam eventually proved stronger than the indulgence of the Prophet and his God, and in spite of the texts they had no compunction in sanctioning their own harsh standards.

The scourging decreed by Allah was apparently meted out to the chief scandal-mongers, although Ibn Ubayy was probably spared on account of his advanced years. This episode completed his downfall, and effectively deprived him of all political influence. The poet Ḥassān had insulted Ṣafwān; and one day Ṣafwān struck him a blow with his sword, wounding him seriously. The poet's tribe, the Khazraj, kept the young man prisoner until Ḥassān was fully recovered. If he had not done so, according to the laws of the vendetta, Ṣafwān would have been put to death. Fortunately the poet recovered and, on Muḥammad's intervention, forgave Ṣafwān in exchange for some land and a Coptic female slave. Ḥassān, with all the address common to poets, obtained ʻĀʼisha's forgiveness by sending her some verses celebrating her chastity and domestic virtues. ʻĀʼisha herself carried the affair off with her head held high. She thanked Allah for exonerating her, having no reason, as she pointed out to her shamefaced husband, to give any thanks to *him*. She went on to add that Ṣafwān in any case was now known to be impotent. The last shadows disappeared.

The outcome was a general feeling that the Prophet's wives ought to be given more protection from the mass of his followers than had previously been the case. In the Mosque of Medina, which was in practice Muḥammad's headquarters as well as his house, the great courtyard, where the huts occupied by each of his wives stood, was constantly thronged with visitors. Revelations came to say that it was forbidden to enter unannounced or to talk with the women except through a curtain. In addition they were to keep their faces covered.

Moreover, another incident involving a woman was to occur before very long to demonstrate the value of such precautions as it were from the other side. According to one possible chronology, this took place some two months after the 'affair of the necklace'. One day, Muḥammad was looking for his freedman, Zayd ibn Ḥāritha, the one-time Christian slave who had been given to him by Khadīja. Muḥammad had given him his freedom and adopted him as a son, and he was often known as Zayd ibn Muḥammad. His adoptive father, the Prophet, placed great trust in his judgement and courage; not long before this he had made him his secretary and asked him to learn Aramaic so that he would not be obliged to employ Jewish secretaries. He had married him to one of his cousins, Zaynab bint Jaḥsh, who was, it is said, a girl of great piety, some say a widow, and certainly very lovely in spite of her age which, at rising thirty-five, was by no means young for an Arab. The household does not seem to have been a very happy one. One day Muḥammad knocked on the door, looking for Zayd. He was not at home; but Zaynab met him in a state of undress and asked him in. After all, he was as father and mother to her. Muḥammad declined but the wind lifted the curtain, evidently while she was hurriedly dressing. He fled in some confusion, muttering something which she did not quite catch. All she heard was: 'Praise be to Allah the Most High! Praise be to Allah who changes men's hearts!'

Not long after this Zayd came home, and his wife told him all about it. He went to the Prophet and said to him: 'Messenger of Allah, it has come to my ears that you went to my house. Why did you not go in? Are you not father and mother to me, O Messenger of Allah? Can it be that Zaynab found favour with you? If that is so, I will part from her!' Muḥammad answered him: 'Keep your wife for yourself.' Nevertheless Zayd ceased to have any intercourse with her and even lived apart from her. Still Muḥammad refused to marry the wife of his adoptive son, for fear of the scandal it would cause. Adoption among the Arabs was regarded as being to all purposes the same as natural fatherhood. Marrying Zaynab would be equivalent to marrying his daughter-in-law, almost his daughter, and dreadfully incestuous. It is however by no means certain that Muḥammad, as an individualist who had already revised many of the common beliefs of his people, did not in his heart of hearts entertain some doubts about this identification of artificial kinship with natural fatherhood. Elsewhere, the Koran makes a point of insisting on the observance of a period of continence on the part of the woman in cases of divorce and remarriage, so as to avoid any possible confusion about the paternity of the children. However, in the matter of Zaynab he clearly felt himself to be in the wrong. He himself, in the first year of his sojourn in Medina, had introduced an artificial 'brotherhood' between the people of Medina and the Emigrants; did not that have legal consequences? But, as always in cases of difficulty, Allah came to the rescue. One day when Muḥammad was with 'Ā'isha he went into a trance. When it was over he smiled and exclaimed: 'Who will go to Zaynab and tell her the good news, that Allah has married me to her?' And he recited the revelation which had just 'descended on him'. The Koran text from which it is quoted probably belongs to a slightly later date, however.

> It is not for the faithful, men or women, to make their own choice in a thing when Allah and his Messenger have decided the matter. . . . When you told the man whom Allah has favoured and whom you have favoured yourself: 'Keep your wife and worship Allah,' you were concealing within yourself what Allah was to reveal. You feared [the judgement of] men but you should rather fear Allah. When Zayd ceased having intercourse with her we gave her to you in marriage, so that the Faithful should suffer no anxiety on account of the wives of their adoptive sons when they have ceased having intercourse with them. Let Allah's will be done in this. . . . Muḥammad is the father of no man among you. He is the Messenger of Allah and the seal of the prophets.
>
> (Koran xxxiii, 36–40)

Admonished by Allah, but happy, Muḥammad hastened to proceed with the marriage which was the occasion of a spectacular feast. He made the incident a precedent for what was to become a general rule. Present-day Muslim authors, with whom on this point W. Montgomery Watt is curiously in agreement, have endeavoured to maintain the asexual nature of this episode. At thirty-five, they say, Zaynab could not be desirable as a woman. What Muḥammad was really doing, therefore, was to contract the marriage for political reasons (to ally himself with the kin of Abū Sufyān) and also as a legal test-case directed against the accepted valuation of adoption. It is western Christians (they continue) or Voltairians who have emphasized, with such heavy irony, the Prophet's highly inflammable passions. However, it is enough to read the sources, the Arabic histories and traditional texts, to realize that this interpretation was not a western invention. It is these texts which lay such stress on Muḥammad's disturbed state of mind after his glimpse of Zaynab in a state of undress; it is they that describe her remarkable beauty. The verdict of public opinion, which as we have seen is mentioned in the text of the Koran itself, could not have been so severe unless it suspected motives other than legal ones for the proposed marriage. Tradition confirms this. The intervention of Allah, which should have been above suspicion, ought to have cut short these rumours, at least among the Faithful. However, a *ḥadith* credits the jealous ʿĀʾisha with the following caustic allusion to the accusation put about by some Doubters that Muḥammad had failed to divulge certain of the verses which Allah revealed to him, and had kept them to himself: 'If the Prophet had concealed anything of the revelation, it would have been those verses he ought to have kept hidden.'[40] Clearly they were thought to be a great deal too much to his liking. It was not, of course, that his amorousness aroused any adverse comment. No one saw anything beyond what was perfectly normal in that. What struck them as odd was that the rule should have been so exactly calculated to satisfy desires which were for once in conflict with social taboos. As for thinking, with that most learned Muslim apologist Muhammad Hamidullah, that Muḥammad's exclamations at the beauty of Zaynab merely signified his astonishment that Zayd should not have managed to get on with such a lovely woman, this is out of the question since it is in flat contradiction to the obvious meaning of the text. Even the passage from the Koran, brief though it is, implies that the Prophet certainly wanted to do what the revelation did not command him to do until later, and that only fear of public opinion prevented him. Hamidullah's theory only shows once again the over-subtleties which can result from the desire to prove theories the truth of which has already been proclaimed by dogma.

Must we conclude from this that Muḥammad invented these verses and that he put into the mouth of Allah what he wanted him to say, that he was, in fact, a classic impostor in the Voltairian sense of the word? I do not think so. But this is a problem of which more will be said later.

More serious matters were to arise to distract the Prophet from his domestic problems. As we have seen, he had dispersed the concentration of troops being raised against him by a series of small raids. Assassination had relieved him of the problem of a number of influential enemies. The expulsion of the Banū Naḍīr and the fall from power of Ibn Ubayy had secured his rear. But Abū Sufyān, on the other hand, had not been idle. A great coalition was in the making. Muslim tradition assigns a major role in its formation to the Jews of the Banū Naḍīr who had sought refuge at Khaybar. Whether that is so or not, Quraysh and the Jews certainly obtained the support of a number of the great nomadic tribes and in particular of the Ghaṭafān, who had driven a hard bargain over the price of their assistance. At the end of March 627, apparently not long after Muḥammad's marriage to Zaynab, three armies amounting in all to some ten thousand men with six hundred horses and some camels, under the supreme command of Abū Sufyān, marched on Medina.

Muḥammad, who had his own means of acquiring information, learned that a move by the coalition was imminent. He himself could assemble a force of at most about three thousand men. There was no question of facing the coalition in a pitched battle, or even of going out to meet them as at Uḥud. In any case, it was no longer necessary to defend the fields of barley, because the enemy was in no hurry and there had been time to gather the harvest and get it in. The important thing was therefore to be able to withstand a siege of the oasis in reasonable order. An Arab army could not remain for long in the position of a besieger. The chief thing was to prevent them from getting inside the oasis, an operation for which they were probably better equipped than at the time of Uḥud. As we have seen, Medina was well protected to the west, south and east by basalt plains (the *ḥarra*) and hills, the whole presenting a considerable obstacle to the progress of a mounted army. It was also easy to block the few roads leading into the most thickly populated built-up area. The city was exposed only to the north, where the houses were scattered over open ground. To secure this breach, Muḥammad ordered the digging of a fairly deep ditch, which was called by the Persian name of the *khandaq*. Tradition has it that such a work seemed an astonishing innovation to the Arabs and that it was a Persian freedman, Salmān, who suggested this method of defence to Muḥammad. Such fortifications are, however, known to have existed in Arabia – at Ṭā'if, for example, not to mention the Yemen.

The work went with a swing. Everyone joined in, even the children. Muḥammad set the example. Even the members of the last Jewish tribe left in Medina, the Qurayẓa, co-operated. The women and children were gathered for safety inside the forts which were dotted about the oasis. In six days the ditch was finished and Muḥammad set up his headquarters close by, on Mount Sal'. It was time. The enemy was approaching.

They set up two camps, to the north and the north-west of the oasis. What happened next seems very surprising to us with our notions of military tactics. We may well hesitate to believe that this siege can really have taken place as tradition, in its fragmentary, uncertain and often contradictory fashion, records. But recent and well-attested instances of siege warfare in Arabia show that things could very well have happened in this way. All the thirteen thousand men gathered on either side of this trench spent two or three weeks exchanging insults in prose and verse, backed up with arrows fired from a comfortable distance. In all, there were three dead among the attackers and five among the defenders of the oasis.

The harvest had been gathered and the besiegers had some trouble finding food for their horses. These horses were no use to them in the attack; they could not be used on account of the ditch. Most of the men had come tamely expecting to take part in a general assault in which the cavalry would have played the major role. It now became clear that they would have to attack an enemy who was well dug in behind the embankment made from the earth which had been taken from the ditch. They had to face bombardment with stones and arrows.

All this promised a great many casualties, which Arab warfare in the old style tended to avoid wherever possible. The attackers had no ladders or siege engines and despised manual labour too much to build any. According to one source 'They swore at the ditch', which they said was an unworthy trick in war, and un-Arab.[41] One poet is credited with the following lines:

> But for this ditch to which they clung
> We should have wiped them all out,
> But it was there before them, and they,
> Being afraid of us, skulked behind it.[42]

At one point they do seem to have attempted a general cavalry attack but were driven back. From time to time a few horsemen endeavoured to leap the ditch. On one occasion some of them succeeded, but were driven back by the Muslims. ʿAlī killed one of them, an old man of ninety, in single combat. The others got back over the ditch, except for one who fell into it and was finished off with stones. During this incident ʿUmar found himself face to face with his own brother who was still a pagan, but he refrained from killing because he had made a vow to kill no Qurayshite, and confined himself to holding the point of his spear under his nose.

The real battle was a diplomatic one. The allies were trying to persuade the Jews of the Banū Qurayẓa, who lived in the south-east of the oasis, to attack the defenders of the ditch from the rear, after first massacring their women and children who were sheltering in the forts. This was Muḥammad's greatest fear. The Jews debated the matter. According to the tradition, they were tempted to intervene and a body of eleven men [*sic*] actually went into action, but at all events nothing serious occurred and tradition had every incentive to exaggerate the incident as an excuse for the massacre which followed.

None of the attackers seems to have thought of assailing the city from the south, although this would surely have been possible, notwithstanding the difficulties of the terrain. Probably it would have involved too many casualties.

Muḥammad countered by trickery. It was not difficult to go from one camp to the other and he made attempts to win over the Ghaṭafān and the allied tribe of the Fazāra by promising them a third of the date harvest of Medina. The Medinan chiefs however refused to pay this price for the withdrawal of not unduly bellicose contingents. Muḥammad also sowed the seeds of suspicion between the Qurayẓa and the coalition.

The siege dragged on. The horses were hungry, and the men too, in all probability, in spite of the supplies sent from Khaybar. Nothing was being achieved and nothing could be done about it. The Beduin contingents must have been feeling that they had stayed too long away from their flocks already. The coalition decided to go home.

For Muḥammad, this was a great triumph. It had been proved before the watching eyes of all Arabia that he was not to be defeated by force. What the coalition with their ten thousand men had failed to achieve, no one could. The Muslim state of Medina was a force to be reckoned with.

This force still had one weakness in the presence of the Banū Qurayẓa, who had been a constant source of anxiety to Muḥammad during the siege. It was clearly necessary to be rid of this dangerous element. Muḥammad wasted no time. On the very day that the coalition withdrew he turned his troops against the fortified village belonging to the Jewish tribe. The Jews dug themselves in, exchanging reproaches and abuse with the attackers. When Muḥammad accused them of taking sides against him, they denied it flatly. They protested indignantly at the ingratitude of the Aws, who had been their allies, and the confederates for whom they had fought gallantly at Bu'āth against the Khazraj; but they received the usual answer that Islam had altered all that. After twenty-five days they lost heart. Some escaped with their families and were converted to Islam. Their leader suggested killing their women and children and flinging themselves into one last desperate sortie against Muḥammad, pointing out that for this attack they would be able to take advantage of the fact that the enemy, trusting in the Jewish respect for the holy day, were known to relax their watch on the Sabbath. All these proposals were rejected. They asked Muḥammad to let them go free on the same conditions as the Naḍīr. He refused. This time he meant to have unconditional surrender.

The Qurayẓa hesitated. Muḥammad allowed them to consult with one of their Aws allies, Abū Lubāba, who, questioned as to the Prophet's intentions, touched his throat, indicating that it would be a massacre. He regretted this indiscretion at once, and went and bound himself to one of the pillars of the Mosque by way of punishment. The Jews either failed to understand, or simply did not believe it, or may perhaps have been resigned to anything. At all events they capitulated, probably putting their trust in the intercession of their old allies, the Aws.

These did, in fact, besiege Muḥammad with requests for mercy from the moment of surrender. He had certainly been merciful to the Qaynuqā' at the request of a man of the Khazraj, Ibn Ubayy. The Prophet had his answer ready. Would they agree to one of their own men, an Aws, being appointed to decide the Qurayẓa's fate? They agreed and he immediately appointed as arbiter Sa'd ibn Mu'ādh, a man dying of wounds received during the siege. He was brought, riding on a donkey with a leather cushion, with his Aws fellow-tribesmen urging him to spare their allies. His indistinct answer was not encouraging. When it came to the point, he demanded an oath from them all that they would carry out his sentence. Then he pronounced it. All adult males were to be slain, the women and children sold into slavery, and their property divided. Muḥammad cried out: 'You have judged according to the very sentence of Allah above the seven skies.'

The next day he had great trenches dug in the market place of Medina. The Jews were led out tied together in groups, and beheaded, one by one, on the edge of the trenches and thrown in. According to some there were six or seven hundred of them; while others say eight or nine hundred. Some individuals were spared at the request of one or other of the Muslims. One woman only was executed. She had killed one of the attackers with a millstone. She laughed a great deal during the massacre and chatted with 'Ā'isha right up to the moment when her name was called:

> 'By Allah,' she said, 'that is me.' I said to her 'You poor soul, what is to happen to you?' She said: 'I must be killed.' 'Why?' I asked her. 'For something I did,' she answered. She went away and was beheaded. By Allah, ['Ā'isha adds] I shall never forget her cheerfulness and her great laugh when she knew that she was to be killed.[43]

After this the women and children were sold. The money they fetched and the chattels were divided up, two extra shares being given to the horsemen. The Prophet took a concubine for himself, the lovely Rayḥāna, the widow of one of those who had been executed. She was converted to Islam. Sa'd died shortly after passing judgement. He was such a holy man that his death shook the throne of Allah in heaven.

It is not easy to judge the massacre of the Qurayẓa. It must be remembered that the customs of the time were extremely primitive. Even so, the care taken by the texts to exculpate Muḥammad shows that it must have aroused some feeling. Details emerge even from these very texts which make it difficult to accept the Prophet's innocence. How are we to explain the episode of Abū Lubāba if not by the assumption that the fate of the Jews had already been determined? A tradition handed down by the earliest Muslim historians says that the wounded Sa'd made this prayer: 'O Allah, if you make the war with Quraysh last a little longer, spare me so that I may join in it . . . and do not let me die before I have comforted myself at the expense of the Banū Qurayẓa.'[44]

It is scarcely possible to imagine that Muḥammad did not know of the vindictive feelings nursed by the stout Medinan, as he was cared for in a tent in the courtyard of his house by Rufayda, the Florence Nightingale of that primitive society. From a purely political point of view, moreover, the massacre was an extremely wise move. The Qurayẓa were a permanent threat in Medina. To let them go would be to strengthen the hot-bed of anti-Muslim intrigue at Khaybar. Only the dead do not return. Furthermore, the killing would help to frighten and discourage the enemy. Politically speaking, the chosen solution was undeniably the best. Politicians are notorious for disregarding considerations of humanity except when these in turn become political factors, or when they have no choice.

As the red dawn of May 627 rose over the freshly filled trenches in the market place of Medina, Muḥammad was in a position to face the future with confidence.

6

Birth of a State

MUḤAMMAD the child and Muḥammad the restless young man became Muḥammad the Prophet. Owing to a certain personal, religious and sociological appropriateness, his message met with an enthusiastic response from a group of disciples who then became a community, a sect. In Medina the Prophet had found himself in a position which enabled – indeed even compelled – him to play a part in the struggle for power within the oasis. He found himself the leader of a party. Little by little this party, partly religious and partly political, had grown. By nature and by origin, it was bound to become a totalitarian party. It had acquired an independent army and its own treasury while at the same time eliminating those elements it was unable to assimilate and silencing opposition within the fold. Five years after the hegira it had transformed itself into a state respected by its neighbours, and with Allah himself as its supreme ruler, speaking through the mouth of his Messenger, Muḥammad ibn 'Abdallāh.

History, and the history of Islam especially, has known many other preachers of religious reform who have found themselves in a position to play a political role, but they have frequently proved unfitted to adapt themselves to the interplay of political forces. They have failed to act where and when necessary, they have not known how to keep their eyes on distant objectives (which must indeed never be lost sight of, even when circumstances enforce an apparent deviation from the direct road to their goal), and also failed to pursue a practical programme of action which is bound to vary continually, in order to meet the ever-changing needs of the immediate situation. Sometimes the ideologist or the religious leader has had to run in harness with a man of action familiar with the difficult art of manipulating people and making things happen. But Muḥammad found within himself all the resources necessary to fulfilment of this dual role.

In Medina the preacher of eternal truths emerged in addition as a shrewd, patient and able politician, capable of controlling his feelings and not allowing them to appear until the right moment, capable of waiting for a long time and striking quickly when the moment came. He may perhaps have surprised himself. But he would always fall back on seeing this as yet another mark of Allah's grace on him. In the same way he revealed himself an excellent general, able, for the most part, to plan a battle or a campaign intelligently and take the appropriate action in the course of a battle.

With all this, Muḥammad remained a deeply religious man, convinced that he was in direct communication with Allah and that the mission which had been laid on him was essentially to bring the Arabs to a knowledge of the greatness, the oneness and the Law of Allah. Surrender to Allah, Islam, would resolve all problems, make men good, just and faithful, enable them to live in harmony together in a society as perfect as human weakness would allow. But, in order to reach this most desirable of goals, it was necessary to use means which, the Prophet quickly realized, could not be confined to mere preaching. It was necessary to use the means of political warfare. The material strength of the unbelievers, who in Mecca had succeeded in preventing the widespread diffusion of the message of truth, must be opposed by the material strength of the faithful. And it was understood long before Clausewitz that the normal means of political warfare covered almost everything, including war, and murder – which is only war on a small scale. In this there was not even a conflict of ends and means. Arab society, like any other, had its moral code. Respect for hospitality and for a sworn oath, for example, was a categorical imperative to be observed in all circumstances. But it had nothing against war and murder and was extremely open-minded about the methods employed in war and murder.

Muḥammad treated the moral code of his people with the mixture of invincible respect and impatient irritability common to all those who have discovered a superior ethical principle which deserves to take precedence over all others. For him it was the triumph of Allah. But his respect for the moral code in operation did not constitute a great impediment to his actions. This was an essential condition if that respect was to be, on the whole, maintained.

In Medina the preaching of supreme truths concerning divinity, the world and man, the call to the spiritual reform of the individual and the teaching of the history of divine intervention in the lives of men became less paramount. What was needed above all was to mobilize men's energies for immediate action, to denounce the enemy, reassure the armies of the faithful, justify the decisions taken, brand traitors and irresolute people for what they were, and give the community of the Faithful some rules by which to live. The Voice from on high conformed to these altered perspectives and to a great extent the character of the revelations changed. As Caetani puts it, the Koran became a kind of newspaper, publishing the orders of the day to the troops, passing judgement on domestic affairs and explaining the ups and downs of the conflict.[1] Moreover Allah's style altered in consequence. Even in Mecca the disjointed verses of the early days – terse and abrupt to the point of considerable obscurity, full of striking poetic images – had become, in the account of the lives of the prophets of ancient times, much longer, more pedestrian and more precise. The narrative could not retain the lyrical style. But in Medina, alongside fragments which still recall the happier Meccan flights, we find a great many more endlessly long-drawn-out laws, exhortations, protestations and proclamations, often painfully prosaic and cluttered with repetitions and stylistic errors. It needs the faith of Muslims to continue to see in them an unparalleled work of universal rhetoric whose very perfection is enough to demonstrate its divine origin.

May any Muslims who happen to read these lines forgive my plain speaking. For them the Koran is the book of Allah and I respect their faith. But I do not share it and I do not wish to fall back, as many orientalists have done, on equivocal phrases to disguise my real meaning. This may perhaps be of assistance in remaining on good terms with individuals and governments professing Islam; but I have no wish to deceive anyone. Muslims have every right not to read the book or to acquaint themselves with the ideas of a non-Muslim, but if they do do so, they must expect to find things put forward there which are blasphemous to them. It is evident that I do not believe that the Koran is the book of Allah. If I did I should be a Muslim. But the Koran is there, and since I, like many other non-Muslims, have interested myself in the study of it, I am naturally bound to express my views. For several centuries the explanation produced by Christians and rationalists has been that Muḥammad was guilty of falsification, by deliberately attributing to Allah his own thoughts and instructions.

We have seen that this theory is not tenable. The most likely one, as I have explained at length, is that Muḥammad really did experience sensory phenomena translated into words and phrases and that he interpreted them as messages from the Supreme Being. He developed the habit of receiving these revelations in a particular way. His sincerity appears beyond a doubt, especially in Mecca when we see how Allah hustled, chastised and led him into steps that he was extremely unwilling to take. But it is said that in Medina, as Buhl has very aptly expressed it,

> when we see how his later revelations sometimes come to the aid of his less elevated inclinations, when we observe how he becomes increasingly cautious in producing revelations to back him up, and how these, obviously enough, often contain conclusions at which he has himself arrived after reflection and meditation on the needs of the situation or even as a result of suggestions made by those close to him, it is very hard for us to believe that they appeared in the same innocent fashion as in the earlier period.[2]

Had the inspired visionary been transformed into an impostor, driven by necessity to produce a convenient revelation at the appropriate moment and at no other, in the way that mediums have been known to resort to fraud in similar cases? ʻĀʼisha certainly remarked sarcastically on one occasion on the Lord's readiness to answer her husband's wishes.[3] There are also a number of difficult occasions, when we find him hesitating to make up his mind, asking advice and thinking things over, before the revelation suddenly descends from heaven and solves the problem along the lines of what human (sometimes all too human) cogitation might have suggested. ʻUmar boasted innocently of having three times given advice which turned out miraculously to correspond with the dictates of heaven. And on one occasion after the Prophet's death, he exclaimed, with regard to a question of some delicacy: 'If God's Prophet were still alive, I daresay a Koran would have been revealed about this.'[4] Even Muslim tradition tells the story of a secretary of the Prophet's, ʻAbdallāh ibn Saʻd, who was taking down the sayings of the Koran at his dictation. At one point, when the Prophet broke off, the secretary continued aloud to the end of the sentence as he thought it should read, and Muḥammad absentmindedly incorporated ʻAbdallāh's suggestion into the divine text. (A prey to doubts of the Prophet's inspiration, ʻAbdallāh abjured Islam and fled to Mecca. When the city fell the Prophet wanted to kill him, but he finally escaped with his life after his foster-brother ʻUthmān interceded for him.)[5]

All this is true, but does not necessarily imply any deliberate deception. Men's capacity for self-deception is infinite. It is obvious to non-Muslims that the words which Muḥammad heard, by which his experiences (in themselves almost inexpressible) were translated in so miraculously perfect a fashion, were dictated to him by his unconscious. He himself suspected it; he had doubted their source, he was afraid that human inspiration might have formed some part of it, and, as we have seen, he even admitted at a later stage that Satan himself had managed to insert his own orders.

With success achieved, his own faith acknowledged, strengthened and confirmed by thousands of disciples, it was only natural that he should have fewer and fewer doubts about the promptings of his inner voice; and that these, too, should have conflicted less and less with the results of his conscious deliberations and with the urge of those strong instincts which were fostered by the relative comfort of his position, by the intoxicating influence of success and by the consciousness of power. But there is plenty of evidence that, to the end, he remained convinced that what spoke within him was the voice of that implacable and omnipotent Master who directed him from above the seven skies, for whom he had dared and endured so much and for whom he was ready to endure again. There was nothing surprising in the fact that Allah should suddenly command him to take reasonable decisions which his own human reflections, or the advice of shrewd companions, had already urged. Besides, what could be more natural than that the Master's orders should correspond with the lawful wishes of his faithful servant? To quote the beautiful lines which Hugo puts into the mouth of the Prophet of Islam:

Celui qui prodigua
Les lions aux ravins du Jebel Kronnega,
Les perles à la mer et les astres à l'ombre
Peut bien donner un peu de joie à l'homme sombre.[6]

('He who lavished lions on the ravines of the Jebel Kronnega, pearls on the sea and stars on the firmament can well give a little joy to dejected man.')

As we have said, Medina was now a state: a state of a rather special kind, but indubitably a state. It was a theocratic state, that is to say the supreme power belonged to Allah himself. Allah made his will known through Muḥammad and through him alone. If we consider that the Voice of Allah was in fact the voice of Muḥammad's unconscious, the inference is that what we have here is, in principle, an absolute monarchy. Who could moderate, bend or alter or contradict the will of Allah?

In practice, however, this was not altogether the case. Allah only made his voice heard on important occasions. The numerous decisions which had to be taken to direct and organize life in the Medinan community still depended, in principle, on the same authorities as before: the leaders and councils of each tribe and each clan. Theoretically, by the terms of the constitution of the community which has been examined in an earlier chapter, Muḥammad was only the arbiter in legal disputes. In fact his influence was so great that no important decision could be taken without his consent. This did not mean, however, that the old authorities became entirely powerless. In practice a delicate balance was established, in which nothing was fixed, statutory or definite, between the temporal powers – themselves, as we have seen, to a great extent dependent on public opinion – and the sacred charismatic power of the Messenger of Allah. Moreover, Muḥammad possessed in the highest degree the essential virtue of the *sayyid*, or Arab chieftain: *ḥilm*, that is, a patient and tireless cunning in the manipulation of men through the knowledge of their interests and their passions. Ultimately he was able, intelligently and without resorting to force or drama, to obtain his followers' agreement to the decisions he had taken. But he had to manoeuvre and even, on occasion, to give way for a while. Even then the established customs and authorities often won the day. Muḥammad, for example, had wanted to release Ṣafwān, when Ṣafwān had lost his temper and wounded the poet Ḥassān ibn Thābit at the time of the accusation of adultery against 'Ā'isha. But as we have seen, Ḥassān's clan had kept Ṣafwān prisoner in spite of Muḥammad's intervention until the poet's wound had definitely been cured; for should he have died, they would have had to avenge the young man's death. Later on, after the victory over the tribe of Hawāzin and the distribution of the booty and prisoners, the tribe suddenly announced its conversion to Islam. Muḥammad agreed that the booty should be kept, but he wanted the prisoners to be released. He succeeded in this only after lengthy negotiations with his disciples and even then two chiefs in his army refused. It was their right and Muḥammad had to buy their prisoners from them.

Before taking a decision on any matter whatsoever Muḥammad surrounded himself with advice. His chief advisers seem to have been Abū Bakr and ʻUmar. The first of these was more measured, with a more moderate temper, content to take a back seat, while the second was more violent and more radical. But both the Prophet's fathers-in-law got along perfectly. There was never any clash between them. Their daughters provided them with an easier means of working on the Prophet's mind. Muḥammad never seems to have made a decision which really went against their views and, as we have seen, Allah himself more than once endorsed ʻUmar's counsel. Lammens[7] has claimed that these two men, with another, also a Meccan called Abū ʻUbayda, formed a kind of triumvirate which worked on the Prophet and in actual fact directed his policies. There may be some truth in this theory, although it should not be carried too far. Muḥammad was no puppet ruler and, in the last resort, it was he who made the decision.

In contrast to this inner circle, certain opposing factions can be discerned which were to remain in embryo during the Prophet's lifetime, but which broke out later, leading in the end to civil wars. Certainly at a very early stage the Prophet's cousin and husband of his daughter Fāṭima, ʻAlī ibn Abī Ṭālib, had evident reservations about Abū Bakr and ʻUmar. We have seen how he sided against ʻĀʼisha. Among the reasons for this attitude Fāṭima's dislike of her step-mothers must certainly be included, but there must also have been some clash of personalities and aims. To all appearances, young ʻAlī (he was about twenty at the time), whose enemies described him as narrow-minded, regarded the two 'old men' as a great deal too opportunist. He stood out in defence of principle, spoke up against manoeuvres that savoured too much of political cunning and opted for piety, purity and the literal observance of the divine commands. No doubt he seemed a young enthusiast with no experience and no grasp of reality. It may be that, while the Prophet was still alive, the Medinans, who were allowed no part in Muḥammad's immediate counsels and were jealously watching the Meccans alone keeping a tight hold on all real power, tended to support the young son-in-law. When the policy of seeking a reconciliation with the Qurayshites became definite, many people would have no wish to put their former persecutors back in the saddle, or to reforge the tribal links between Muslims who had formerly been driven out and new converts who had once done the driving. Rather, they would have a motive for putting forward one who by blood was, so to speak, the incarnation of the new principle, since the prophetic mission did away with tribal relationships. Then, for the father of the Prophet's grandsons, they would rediscover the principle of hereditary legitimacy, which existed, for example, among Persians. But as yet all this was no more than a possibility, a seed. All these men were equally devoted to Allah and obeyed blindly the orders that came to them from the lucid brain and firm hand of the Prophet.

He it was who decided peace or war. But there was nothing resembling a standing army. For each expedition it was necessary to summon the chiefs of the Muslim tribes, who then appealed for volunteers from their ranks. The Prophet reviewed them and ruled out those who were weak or undesirable. He either appointed a leader or took command himself. He seems to have had a gift for military as he had for political strategy. He was continually inventing all kinds of stratagems and was especially fond of pretending to send his forces somewhere other than their real objective. The saying 'War is cunning' has been attributed to him. Once the expedition was over, everyone went home with his share of the booty.

The means by which Muḥammad could carry out his foreign policy were only provided, therefore, by the free adherence of his followers. But this adherence was sufficiently certain for him to appear to outsiders as the real centre of Muslim power. He it was who conducted negotiations, by means of envoys selected by him and furnished with written messages and instructions from him. It was to him that similar messengers and similar messages were dispatched.

We have seen that Muḥammad had at his disposal a number

of fanatical young henchmen, who were virtually prepared to strike down any opposition whenever necessary. But it must not be thought that this was in any way a permanent police force. Every time a special summons was required, however discreet. Every time it was necessary to reckon the consequences of the projected action. Would the victim's family be sufficiently loyal to Islam, or so weak or intimidated not to seek vengeance? The government of the community could only act in the traditional Arab fashion: negotiating with all those who possessed a fraction of authority – the heads of tribes, clans and families – and even with individuals. Nobody could be constrained except by the observation of a number of customary rules and the exercisc of great shrewdness and adaptability.

This meant that legal decisions could only be carried out with the endorsement and consent of public opinion and under its pressure. As we have seen, the Prophet was the great arbiter of the community in all disputes. But he seems to have been called upon only in the last resort, or in matters of great importance. Here, again, it was the old Arab system which worked in the normal way, with its absence of written law or any supreme authority and its consideration of ethnic groups and individuals as autonomous powers.

No regular police force and no real administration. Muḥammad had his advisers, who possessed no powers of coercion, and his secretaries, who were mere instruments. He delegated certain of his functions to individuals who acted as his personal agents. Whenever, for example, he left Medina, he used to leave a representative behind him. Later on, at the time of his conquests, he appointed men to be a type of governor; they were often chosen from among the chief men of the local tribes. Wherever there was a mixture of ethnic groups, including Muslims, unbelievers and others in between, he sent someone from Medina. But even these governors were not supported by any public body. They achieved the results prescribed by their instructions by means of persuasion, by the authority derived from their position as the Prophet's representatives and, even more, by long delicate negotiations with the tribal leaders.

There was no distinction between the public exchequer and Muḥammad's private fortune. At the beginning everyone earned his living in his own way. Muḥammad merely appealed to those of his followers or sympathizers who were better off, on behalf of those who were less so. The Jews seem to have made a substantial contribution to this work of charity. It was not until shortly before his death that Muḥammad compelled, by a formal treaty, certain newly conquered groups to hand over a fixed portion of their property or income each year. A special tax was imposed on Christian Arabs who did not go over to Islam; but this was not necessarily higher than the more or less voluntary contributions made by the Muslims. Some taxes in force before Islam may have continued to be levied in some places. Lastly, the Prophet received private gifts, either from living persons or as legacies.

Apart from taxes and such gifts as came to him directly, Muḥammad, as we have seen, received a fifth of all spoils taken from the enemy. This was a modest levy since Arab chiefs were in the habit of taking a quarter. Like any other chief, Muḥammad had, in addition, a right to a share equal to that of the others and also to the thing or person he liked best before the share-out. When the plunder had been won not in battle but as a result of negotiation Muḥammad took it all – as happened in the case of the property of the Banū Naḍīr, which he re-distributed among the Emigrants alone. After the capture of Khaybar, it will be seen that he left the former owners in possession, but sequestered more than half the harvest-produce on behalf of the Muslims. He kept a fifth, perhaps even a third, of the lands for himself. This made him extremely rich.

His position moreover saddled him with a number of financial obligations, some of which were very heavy. Increasingly he devoted all his time to public affairs and to the service of Allah. He could not earn his living from 'business', like his commercially gifted disciple 'Abd ar-Raḥmān ibn 'Awf.

He was, like the *sayyid*, the chief of his community and, as with the *sayyid* of a tribe, this involved extensive hospitality, generous gifts to those around him and conspicuous expenses for display. The Voice of Allah commanded him, like other men, to give generously to his relatives, and to orphans, beggars and travellers (this is almost certainly the proper meaning of the term 'son of the road' which was later given a different interpretation), and to contribute towards the ransom of captives. At a later stage in Muḥammad's rise to power, the Voice added to the expenses which the Prophet was called upon to meet from the income he received from taxation, the payment of the agents who collected these taxes, expenses 'in the path of Allah' and sums distributed to 'those whose hearts are won'. There has been a good deal of argument as to the precise meaning of this last phrase. Muslim tradition interpreted it as those whose hearts 'were to be won', in other words gifts aimed at purchasing the goodwill of influential persons towards Islam. W. Montgomery Watt has put forward reasons for thinking that it meant rather presents to the heads of delegations already largely won over to the cause. Whatever the truth these were political expenses – like those incurred 'in the path of Allah', which included, for example, the purchase of weapons and horses.

Clearly this was a very fluid state with very little administrative apparatus. Its development was similar to that which can be seen, for example, among the Negro tribes of Kenya, where we find men fulfilling the function of mediators in society. In the words of Lucy Mair,

> This is a beginning of government conceived as an activity of persons whom the community authorizes to take action on its behalf. But we are still a long way from anything that could be called law enforcement.[8]

However, far from 'withering away', the Muslim state solidified and grew stronger during the first decades of its existence. To begin with, in Muḥammad's lifetime, we are dealing with an incipient state, functioning with a bare minimum of administrative organization. Even so, as we shall see, it was firmly based and, in spite of a momentary crisis, the death of the leader on whom the whole structure appeared to depend did not shake it. This solidity stemmed to a large extent from the preservation of the essentials of the tribal structure, in spite of the comparative disintegration which had begun before Islam and the individualistic spirit which the faith had introduced. The state, with its charismatic leader and his individual advisers, its volunteer army raised only in case of need, its small, rudimentary and purely occasional police force, its paucity of administrators and its public funds inextricably mixed up with the private fortune of its leader, worked only as a conglomeration of ethnic groups; and the normal heads of these played a vital part in transmitting orders from the highest authority downwards and in passing up aspirations from below. Everything depended on them, and they in turn depended on the goodwill of their theoretical dependants. In this rudimentary mechanism, which was to all intents without powers of coercion, at least to those within it, everything in the last resort depended on public opinion. The stability of the régime came from the total hold of Muslim ideology over the minds of the people. It should be added that this hold was gained partly by the practical and material advantages which accrued from the choice of Islam.

In the last resort therefore, if we insist on applying our own criteria, executive and judiciary authority rested with Allah and Muhammad. Legislative power was also theirs, but here again it is necessary to be particularly careful to take into account the extreme fluidity of the situation. The Voice from on high had laid down a number of legal principles for Medina, either on matters which it apparently regarded as having a particular importance or which were the subject of argument within the Muslim community. But these were widely differing matters and amounted to no kind of system. In theory, obedience to the rules laid down by Allah in person was imperative; but J. Schacht[9] has shown that the earliest generations of Muslims paid very little attention and either got round or quite simply disregarded them. In everything else, at all events, custom reigned supreme. It was accepted later that a great many legal precedents, which were afterwards handed down by tradition as authoritative, were established by the Prophet, either by precept or by example. Schacht again, following I. Goldziher,[10] has made it abundantly clear that this was a much later view and that the use of legal traditions, and even their formulation, was an innovation dating from the second or even the third century of Islam. It is none the less possible that the Prophet may have given advice on matters of law or custom on his own authority and without reference to Allah. But nothing certain has come down to us, and his community does not appear to have taken a very great or sustained interest in the matter.

All the same, some coherent tendencies can be discerned in the legal precepts laid down in Medina. It would take too long to analyse them here other than in very broad outline, based chiefly on W. Montgomery Watt's excellent summary. The new laws were concerned primarily with the kind of problems with which society was most concerned: the protection of the safety, lives and property of its members. We have seen that this elementary public order was assured in tribal society by the custom of the vendetta. A man hesitated to kill his enemy because he knew that his enemy's tribe would be ruthless in taking vengeance on the murderer or one of his kin, being perfectly free not to accept a 'blood-price'. In future, the Muslim community, the *umma*, would act as a tribe in protecting its members from outside attack; but within the Muslim community Allah insisted that two rules must be strictly observed. The avenger, whatever his social position, was not to inflict a greater injury than that which he had himself suffered and the vengeance taken was not to be made the occasion of a reciprocal vengeance in its turn. If the murder had been unintentional it was obligatory to accept the blood-price and not to insist on an eye for an eye. In the absence of any proper police force, the avenger was still, as a matter of course, the relative traditionally designated to fulfil this role.

In this way the old system was perpetuated; but it avoided the exaggerated vengeance and endless chain of vendettas which could disrupt society for years on end. Moreover, rather than risk trouble, Muḥammad himself often paid the blood-price.

The penalty for thieves was to have a hand cut off (we are not told who performed the office). Allah also forbade killing of infant girls – a common custom among the Arabs, prompted by the appalling poverty of the desert and probably connected also with some lost element of pagan religion. This prohibition was actually linked in the Koranic text with the question of food. Allah would provide. In fact, Islam was to provide the Arabs with sufficient resources to obviate any malthusian considerations.

The newly revealed precepts dealt, above all, with marriage and the family. These were clearly vital matters for the small new community. On the other hand, the new legislation did not conflict with any previous rules which had been firmly established and consecrated by former systems. It is not easy to penetrate the maze of pre-Islamic Arab customs concerning domestic relations, but it would appear likely that by the seventh century A.D. they were in a comparatively fluid and rapidly developing state. Scholars like W. Robertson Smith and G. A. Wilken[11] have held the view that traces can be found among the Arabs of that date of the so-called primitive 'matriarchal' stage of society in which women were supposed to have been the dominant sex, with descent reckoned by the mother's side and property (in so far as there was any) handed down through the female line – as, for example, from the maternal uncle to his nephew rather than to his son. The existence of any such stage, although once a fashionable theory, has long been acknowledged to be highly improbable; even the idea that the same forms of family life must have persisted in an unvarying pattern throughout the world is, moreover, discounted – in my opinion quite rightly so – by competent experts of the present day. The matriarchal theory has been modified and reduced to a few more or less certain points. It is recognized that there have been human societies in which succession through the maternal line was dominant and that this has sometimes (but by no means always) been associated with a tendency to concede a slightly greater part to women. One indication of this is what has been called 'uxorilocal' residence by the couple, that is, where the husband goes to live with the wife's people. Some accounts of pre-Islamic Arabia suggest the existence of matrilinear characteristics, especially in certain regions, such as Medina. There may be a connection between these characteristics and the traces in certain places of the existence of polyandry, that is, the marriage of one woman to several men at one time. Montgomery Watt has suggested that these disparate signs could be interpreted as an indication that Arab society, which had formerly been matrilinear, was in the Prophet's time in the course of changing to the patrilinear system, and was therefore in a transitional stage associated with the general development towards individualism. This view seems to me, as it does to J. Henninger,[12] somewhat dubious. There is evidence that the patrilinear system predominated in Arabia from time immemorial, in particular from the so-called Thamudic inscriptions. What does seem to be true is that in certain regions and localities such as Medina, this system coexisted with some types of polyandrous custom, and with the accepted assignation of a substantial role to women (several sources indicate a remote period in which there were Arab queens); even in some cases with uxorilocal residence and the inheritance of property through the female line.

The rules laid down in the Koran bear clear indications of a spirit of individualism. A period of waiting is prescribed for a woman about to remarry, so that there shall be no doubt as to the real paternity of any future child. We have seen, too, that one consequence of the Zaynab affair was to prescribe that the tie of adoption could not be reckoned as genuine affiliation. It is laid down that certain clearly specified ties of kinship constitute an impediment to marriage. It seems probable that old customs were ratified and confirmed in this way, perhaps by extending their validity according to criteria which are not clear to us. Montgomery Watt thinks, along with Robertson Smith, that there was an extension to the paternal kin of the principles previously applicable to maternal kinship. But there also remain stipulations which he interprets as 'concessions to matrilinear groups'.[13] At all events, what is certain is that the rules of the Koran were aimed at rooting out customs which did not treat individuals, and women in particular, as independent subjects. Certain prohibitions may have been intended simply to do away with such established customs as a man's automatic marriage to his father's widows other than his own mother. Similarly a bride (and not her father) was bound to receive the dowry paid by her betrothed. Concubinage with slaves and captives, and also divorce, were permitted, but subject to certain limitations. Temporary marriages, tending towards polyandry, although apparently permitted at one time, were afterwards frowned on. The insistence (of a very 'reformist' kind) on real facts rather than social fictions emerges clearly in the Koranic rule permitting a man's marriage with his step-daughter (the daughter of his wife's previous marriage), provided that the union with this wife had not been consummated.

One notorious verse of the Koran recommends marrying two, three, or four wives 'if you fear to be unfair to the orphan' (Koran iv, 3). Some present-day Muslims who, influenced by contemporary western culture, frown on polygamy have attempted to 'make excuses' for this provision on the grounds that before Islam the Arabs were in the habit of marrying any number of women, and that Allah had meant to take this custom into account. In the manner of the 'divine instruction' so popular with many modern Christian theologians, he was reluctant to impose monogamy (or monogyny to be more precise) on these primitive people at one fell swoop. 'Permission' to have four wives was a stage towards the adoption of the moral rule of monogamy. Besides, the verse goes on to say that 'if you fear that you cannot be quite fair [to all your wives] [take] only one or concubines'. Since to be entirely fair in such a case is not possible, the text amounts in practice, they say, to a recommendation of monogamy. What we see here is a typical childish example of apologetic reasoning which, as usual, runs completely counter to the historical spirit. It is, in fact, by no means certain that polygamy was so widespread in pre-Islamic Arabia. It is hard to see how an encouragement to take concubines if one is afraid of not acting fairly towards a number of wives can be a move in the direction of the supposedly more moral ideal of monogamy. Moreover, the Koranic text is clearly not a restriction but an exhortation, somewhat vaguely (for us) connected with fairness to orphans. Probably, as a result of battles and other factors, the community of Medina included more women than men. Those who had lost their fathers, and women especially, were not always well treated by their guardians, who took advantage of their position to rob them. Muslim widows and orphans had to be married off as soon as possible. Once again, in order to understand a phenomenon, it is necessary to set it in its historical context before allocating praise or blame in the name of supposedly eternal moral, religious or political dogmas.

There are a number of articles laying down fairly strict rules about inheritances. This was apparently necessary in the unsettled situation which resulted from the disintegration of the tribal structure. The stronger must have found it easy to lay hands on the family or tribal possessions of the weaker. The rule of the Koran guaranteed everyone his share, which was worked out in a somewhat complicated fashion. Women were allowed a share in the property. (This seems to have been the custom in Mecca, although not in Medina.) Admittedly their share was only half that of the men. Inheritances were divided up, which was normal practice in a pastoral community but impracticable for an agricultural population, since, of course, successive divisions rapidly tended to create holdings too small to be viable.

Slavery, naturally, persisted. People were urged to treat slaves well and encourage them to gain their freedom. It would be naïve to expect the abolition of an institution in the seventh century simply because it shocks us today. It would be equally so to regard it, like Muhammad Hamidullah, 'as a house of humanitarian correction' and laud its virtues.[14] Loans at interest or, more probably, some form of them, were forbidden. This prescription seems in practice to have been aimed chiefly at those who, in the early days of the move to Medina, refused to make loans to the needy community without interest. It affected the Jews particularly who, because they refused to grant this gratuitous loan, were deemed to have refused to regard the Muslims as co-religionists. But there seems to have been no intention of prohibiting the normal practices of Meccan trade. Wine and a particular game of chance called *maysir* were forbidden, probably on account of their connection with pagan cults. It was probably for a similar reason that a return was prescribed to the strict lunar year of 354 days, abandoning the intercalary month which made it possible to keep the calendar in agreement with the course of the sun and the seasons.

In this way a body of legislation was built up which, with all its gaps, obscurities and dependence on circumstances, was in many respects an advance on what had gone before. It answered the particular needs of a small, expanding Medinan community well enough. It protected the safety of the individual and gave protection to certain classes of persons who were particularly at risk. In general, the existing trend towards individualism was encouraged without abandoning the tribal system. Above all, out of the sea of customs hallowed by tradition and public opinion, the elements of a real law were emerging, rules of conduct that were clearly expressed and valid for everyone. But the community still had a long way to go to the establishment of a real corpus of law, and the adaptation of these few rules laid down in Medina to the needs of a vast empire or of well-ordered states would pose very many problems.

It was in Medina, also, that the ideology which was to bind together the Muslim states of the future, and the institutions by which their adherence to this ideology could be distinguished, developed in a decisive fashion.

But, to understand this ideology and these institutions, we must trace them back to their common source. It is a fact that any ideology – any system of ideas, that is, which is offered to men as a guide, to give a sense of direction to their lives by placing them in a transcendent order and cosmic pattern of development – crystallizes around a central intuition: the way in which its founder envisages his own and other men's relationships to that order and cosmic pattern of development. This basic intuition is not born of nothing, and I do not share the view of those who believe that it is imposed from without by the irruption into the human mind of some superhuman reality. It is for this reason that I have tried to portray the conditions of personal existence within the framework of a given society which could have given rise to such an idea in Muḥammad the man. But if the central intuition *does* spring from something, it is none the less something complete in itself, which leaves its mark on a whole variety of ideas and actions. This system, once set in motion, may develop and in some cases become something almost entirely different; but it seems rare for all traces of the initial inspiration to disappear, and, if there are documents to preserve it, free spirits may come sooner or later to drink from this spring.

This basic intuition was naturally a religious one. Muḥammad's enemies believed in a form of primitive humanism. They believed that it was possible for man to fight against the fear and dread of existence, and overcome them by his own strength. They did not, of course, raise this possibility to the level of a Promethean vocation to build the world to the measure of man. Their humanism was not a hopeful summons to transcend this present life, but a way of making it more comfortable. It was this which made it repugnant to those who had need of hope.

In a world where man seems very weak – or even, as his strength increases, in circumstances which force him, individually or collectively, to return to this condition of weakness

– his general attitude to the world is more likely to be a religious one. What Muḥammad, like so many others, felt was a sense of subjection to the terrible yet fascinating mysteries which surrounded him. And this mystery became crystallized for him as an awesome Presence.

Many others besides him have had this feeling. But it manifested itself in a form which was peculiar to himself. The Presence, Allah, was an almighty power which had no limits of any kind anywhere; a will which no bounds could contain. This, too, is something which others have felt. This image was, moreover, somewhat softened by various attributes. Throned in infinite majesty, his limbs, movements and gestures were nevertheless described in anthropomorphic terms. Above all, he was kind, merciful and close to man, whom he warned, loved and forgave like an indulgent father. But a great gulf divided him from his creature, a gulf which nothing could fill – not even unfailing care for a people lovingly chosen; nor the Redeemer, born of himself, so sensitive to human suffering that he came to share it. His paternal love for mankind was somewhat abstract and universal, expressed in a general goodness towards humanity as a whole or towards groups of men. It was, as has been said, the busy, organizing but not particularly affectionate goodness of the head of a family. The only possible attitude to this God was an infinite humility and total surrender (*islām*), in anticipation of a terrible judgement of which the outcome was wholly unpredictable. Faith, devotion, gratitude, worship and even trust were owing to him; but hardly ever was love expected. And so sin was a fault, a disobedience, a mark of ingratitude, an omission brought about by an unjustified preference for the goods of this world. It never elicited from God the laments of the betrayed lover, weeping to see faithless man reject his love, which run all through the pages of the Old and New Testaments. Such a piteous appeal for the love of a weak creature would be inconceivable coming from the Master of the worlds of the Koran, who reaches the uttermost limits of his goodness in himself deigning to love and to forgive. Similarly, the sinner's repentance was much more the regretful acknowledgement of a mistake, an unfortunate oversight, than the anguished desolation of a creature who, craving love, has momentarily strayed or failed to see the offer of a boundless affection until too late.

This had been Muḥammad's basic intuition from the first moment the Voice spoke to him, or even before. But now it was being worked out in a different context from its original one. It was no longer purely a matter of defining the relations between God and mankind in general, and extracting rules of universal application. To begin with, the Voice imparted to the Arabs a universal message, already known to others. Now – and, as I hope I have made clear, this situation was the result of a sequence of quite unforeseeable events, especially in the sphere of political relations – an Arab community existed and was in possession of the true message, which was unknown to or distorted by everyone else. For a single group of Arabs, alone in the world, to know the truth seemed like a sign of God's special relationship to the Arabs and with, at least, one corner of Arabia.

The message was no longer a purely doctrinal one, a concept of the world which each man might adopt individually, drawing his own conclusions about the way he ought to act – on the lines of, let us say, Immanuel Kant's ideas on pure and practical reason. It was addressed to a specific community – for the time being, at least, an Arab community – which was guided and organized in all its actions by this message. This was indeed an ideology.

This ideology became a system. The dogmas and prescriptions of which this system is composed are related to one another more or less inextricably as the case may be. If certain things are accepted as true, then it follows inevitably that certain others may be deduced from them and yet others rejected. There is a considerable intellectual fashion at present in favour of the idea of system or, as it is called, structure. There are those whose enthusiasm has rendered them incapable of seeing anything in the development of ideas beyond complete, perfect and well-ordered systems appearing mysteriously in place of others of the same kind. What I have been trying to show here is that an ideology was, on the contrary, built up from elements imposed on a man by his own situation and adopted by a society by reason of its situation. It may be added that, should the situation alter to any material extent, this must necessarily involve a modification of the ideology, not directly or all at once but in the long run and through necessary transpositions – even, sometimes, its complete rejection and the adoption of a different system.

A fitting slogan for Muslim ideology at this period might have been: An Arab religion for the Arabs. We have seen how the community had finally traced its descent from Abraham–Ibrāhīm, the supposed ancestor of the Arabs. Now Allah was revealing his demands and his truths in the Arabic tongue through Muḥammad. We have seen that from now on they turned in prayer not to a foreign sanctuary but towards the Kaʿba, an Arab shrine if ever there was one. Next Allah had commanded them to take part in the curious rites, their origins lost in the mists of time, which took place around the Kaʿba and consisted largely of circling round the sacred edifice. This was called at that time the *ʿumra* or 'cult', although it may already have been the *ḥajj al-bayt*, 'the pilgrimage to the house' (that is to the shrine). But in addition to these rites, Allah also decreed that it was obligatory to take part in certain ceremonies, the meaning of which is also highly obscure, which seem to have borne the name of *hajj* or 'pilgrimage' *par excellence*. These took place in a series of small shrines not far from Mecca. Hitherto these rites, or some of them at least, had been bound up in popular worship with the cults of various gods. Now they were all to be performed in the name of Allah alone. These prescriptions were to play an important political role. They made it possible for Muḥammad to demand that the Qurayshites allow his followers access to the shrines in and immediately around their city. Why should the Muslims be excluded from these rites when so many Arabs who lived in distant parts took part in them? On the other hand, the

Qurayshites convinced themselves that, if Islam carried the day, their city would still be an important religious centre and might even find its importance increased, which, for these merchants, was a major consideration.

By now the break with the Jews and Christians was complete. Muḥammad had gone as far as he could towards remaining on good terms with them. To begin with all he wanted was for them to acknowledge him as a prophet, alongside their own, Moses or Jesus, specially appointed by Allah to guide the Arabs towards monotheistic truth. But both had rejected him and repelled him by their exclusivity.

> They have said: 'None but Jews and Christians shall enter into paradise.' Such are their wishful fancies. Say: 'Let us have proof, if what you say is true.' No. He that surrenders himself to Allah and does what is right shall have his reward with his Lord.
> (Koran ii, 105–6)

Now it was over. To each his own faith and his own community. Abraham was neither Jew nor Christian; yet he had been a true prophet, and both acknowledged him as such. So was it now with Muḥammad; so let them acknowledge him! But they persisted in rejecting him. And yet they were very sinful. They did not live according to the precepts which Allah had sent them by Moses and by Jesus, in the Torah and the Gospel. They had added new things of their own invention to these precepts. They, who had been so highly favoured as to be called to monotheism long ago, had sinned mortally by committing the ultimate crime, by associating sons and wives with Allah, exactly like the Meccan polytheists. The Jews claimed that 'Uzayr (Esdras, or Ezra) was the son of God, a status which the Christians attributed to Jesus.

The first of these assertions begins to look less unjustified than it seems at first sight when we find, in a first-century Jewish 'Apocrypha' which later enjoyed great popularity, the fourth book of Esdras,[15] the following words spoken to Esdras by an angel:

> Thou shalt be taken up from [among] men, and henceforth

thou shalt remain with my son. . . . Let go from thee the cares of mortality; cast from thee the burdens of man.

(Koran xiv, 9, 14)

Jesus was called *al-masīḥ* (the Messiah), a word borrowed from Syriac or Ethiopic, which in Arabic could also mean 'the anointed', although the implications of this appellation were obviously not understood. His mother, Mary, the sister of Aaron and hence of Moses, had been warned by angels that she would conceive without having known a man and bear a remarkable son,

a Word from him [Allah] and his name shall be the Messiah, 'Isā, son of Maryam [Mary]. He shall be noble in this world and in the next, and shall be of those close [to the throne]. He shall speak to men from his cradle. . . . [Allah] will instruct him in the Book and in Wisdom, the Torah and the Injīl [Gospel].

(Koran iii, 40–43)

This miracle came to pass because Allah had sent some of his Spirit into Mary. This was a prophet sent by Allah to the Israelites; but an unusually remarkable one. He had come into the world and worked many miracles. Even as a child he made birds out of clay and breathed life into them. He cured the dumb and the lepers and resurrected the dead. The Jews boasted of having killed him but this was not true. They had been the victims of a mirage, a ruse on the part of Allah. They believed they had crucified him, but in fact 'Allah raised him to himself' (iv, 156). He was with his mother 'on a hill peaceful and well-watered' (xxiii, 52).

In the beginning, the revelation from on high laid great stress on this evidence against the Jews, which was probably taken from Christians who knew little of their religion or were influenced by the picturesque stories of the apocryphal gospels. Some, at least, of these Christians belonged to or were influenced by certain peculiar sects; among these were the Docetists, who did in fact deny the reality of that terrible thing, the suffering and death of God. The Docetists explained that a phantom in his shape had been substituted for Jesus on

Golgotha, and this it was that the soldiers had crucified. At a later date, when Muḥammad was at political odds with the Christians and also perhaps when he had acquired a certain amount of supplementary information concerning Christian beliefs as they were understood by the poor Christians of Arabia, the Koran added to these facts some anti-Christian polemics. The Christians were wrong in saying that Jesus, the superman, was the son of Allah; Allah, being himself uncreated, could not create. They were wrong to believe in a Trinity made up of Allah, Jesus and Mary. There was only one God, Allah. Jesus himself had condemned these exaggerations and was quite innocent of them. Like his mother, he took food. He was not God.

Islam, the last prophetic revelation, which had been granted to the Arabs, was therefore the supreme and definitive religion. Muḥammad's message picked up those of the earlier prophets and completed, set a seal on them. Muḥammad was the gentile prophet (*ummī*) in the Jewish and the Christian meaning of the word, the prophet sent to the pagans, to those who were not of Israel. (The word was in fact misunderstood and was later thought to mean that he could not read or write.) He had been foretold by Jesus. Now he must join him:

> Men were once one community. Then Allah sent the prophets as messengers to announce the good news and warners. With them, he sent down the true scripture to arbitrate between men in those things which they disputed. Only those who had received [a scripture before] opposed it, in their mutual vainglory, after the proofs had been vouchsafed to them. Allah has guided the Faithful to the truth, that [truth] which [the others] had opposed, [and all this] by his will. Allah guides whom he will to a right path.
>
> (Koran ii, 209)

> 'I shall set down [a happy life] for those that are pious . . . and believe in our signs, for those who follow the Messenger, the gentile prophet, whom they find mentioned in the Torah and the Gospel in their possession, who commands them to do what is reputable and forbids what is disreputable, who makes good

[food] lawful for them and forbids what is foul, and takes from them the burden and shackles which weighed them down . . .' Say: 'O men, I am the Messenger of Allah to you all, from him who rules over earth and sky. There is no God but he. He ordains life and death. Believe in Allah and in his Messenger, the gentile prophet who believes in Allah and in his words. Follow him, and no doubt you will be well guided.'

(Koran vii, 155–8)

So Muḥammad's message acquired a universal value.

The new ideology had therefore its supreme authority in Muḥammad, the gentile prophet who judged right and wrong, transmitting the irrefutable message of Allah. But in the absence of the Prophet the Faithful should be able to remember his words, to refer to and quote them and find arguments in them for action in any situation. Besides, it was necessary to prepare for the time when the supreme mouthpiece would be no more. The document had to be objective, a scripture that could be consulted like the Torah and the Gospel. Men had written down the messages as they were revealed and others had learned them by heart. Richard Bell has described most convincingly how Muḥammad himself undertook a revision of these writings. He arranged them in sections in chapters of varying lengths which were called, as we have already seen, *sūrahs*. The messages which had been a Recitation (*qur'ān*, Koran) now became a book (*kitāb*) like those of the Jews and the Christians.

In this book were written down, as we have seen, the precepts and rules of social behaviour which men ought to follow. There were also accounts of the ancient prophets and, in short, the whole of the sacred history which led up to the new Law and which constituted its spiritual ancestry. We have given some idea of a few of these accounts. The dogmas, the basic ideas which men were to believe in, were also set down there. Allah, the one, the creator of man and the Cosmos, the almighty, reigned alone above the skies. Heaven and earth were his. The gods of the polytheists did not exist because they were incapable of creating anything, or they might be jinns. Gathered round the throne of Allah, singing his praises, were the angels; these were his servants and his messengers, and observed and recorded the deeds of men. Among them were named Gabriel, the messenger of the revelation, and Michael. Allah acted by means of entities which were distinct from his all-enveloping personality, without being altogether separate from it. This idea was based on vague notions borrowed from the mass of speculation evolved by Judaism and Christianity, under the influence of Platonism, to explain the problem of communication between the perfect Supreme Being and the imperfect world. Thus we have the Word of God, his Breath or Spirit, his Order, his Light, his Presence. Opposed to Allah and his angels stood the Fiends (the 'satans'), with their leader, Satan, who is also called Iblīs (the Greek *diabolos*, from which comes our own word 'devil'). He had once been an angel, but was accursed because he refused to prostrate himself before Adam, Allah's creation. Allah permitted him to tempt mankind, and he succeeded very well, especially, so it seems, with those predestined to ungodliness.

Allah, the almighty, directed the thoughts and deeds of mankind, making one man pious and amenable to the preaching and admonitions of his messengers, the prophets, and another a ready victim to the temptations of Satan. As we have seen, this was no impediment to the declaration of man's responsibility, or to rewarding one and punishing another. Men owed him gratitude for his goodness and it was unlawful to reproach him. What was man before him? Did not men owe him everything? What right had they to judge him? Allah was infinitely just, far above any concepts of justice we might have. He was also implacable; this characteristic is particularly in evidence during the Medinan period, as was natural at this time of fierce conflict with the Qurayshites, the Jews and adversaries of all kinds. At such a time it was scarcely possible to threaten the enemy with anything less than those threats which the gentle Jesus himself had used: outer darkness, and wailing and gnashing of teeth. At the same time, however, Allah was portrayed as being infinitely compassionate, kind and merciful. Towards the good and pious, one assumes. It is unnecessary to stress the inextricable contradictions contained in these ideas. Ordinary humanity has never paid much attention to logic where ideologies are concerned.

One day the Hour would come. At first Muḥammad had believed it to be imminent. Then it seemed further off, yet not too far. The Hour, in other words the Day of Resurrection, the Day of Judgement, would come quite unexpectedly. There would be a great clamour, a fearful din, a sound of enormous trumpets. The sun and the stars would be darkened, walls would swell and boil and the earth tremble. Then the dead would rise from their graves, where perhaps they had already had a foretaste of the fate in store for them. Then Allah would sit in judgement with his angels around him. Considerations of wealth or kinship or social position would no longer count. Each would play his part, a little book in his hand with, inscribed in it, the reckoning of his virtues and his sins. Neither the angels nor the prophets would be able to intercede unless Allah permitted. There would also be a weighing in a celestial balance. The basic criterion for the judgement would be faith. Those who had believed in Allah and in his Prophet and had acted in accordance with this faith would be rewarded. The rest, the unbelievers, whatever their deeds, would be punished.

The description of the state of the dead after the judgement occurs somewhat belatedly in the Koran. The damned were to go to Gehenna (*jahannam*), in other words the Fire. Angels would be assigned to torture them. The wretched sufferers would be loaded with chains and iron collars, and jets of fire and molten bronze would be turned on them. When their skins were burned they would be replaced by new ones. Sometimes it would be terribly cold. They would drink foul water and some a boiling drink, and eat the fruit of the *zaqqūm* tree which was particularly bitter. All this would devour their entrails. They would beg in vain for the blessed to sprinkle a little water on them from their celestial dwellings. The blessed would mock them and refuse, with all the sadistic satisfaction of privileged people who are conscious of their own rectitude, and, as usual in such cases, who consider their privileges well deserved.

The blessed would receive their reward in the Garden of Eden, also called paradise (*firdaws*). Then they would enjoy the peace, tranquillity, joy and satisfaction of praising Allah unceasingly. But there would be other more material delights. Lying on couches in the shade of orchards and vines, dressed in green garments, made of satin and brocade, adorned with silver bracelets, they would watch youths, eternally young, moving among them, offering them dishes of meat and especially fowls, fruit and cups of delicious but innocuous wine. Streams and springs would give forth exquisite coolness which would make the Blessed forget the relentless sun and scorching dryness of their native land. For wives they would have women who were good, beautiful, amorous and seductive, dwelling in a pavilion, ever virgin, ever young, with modest looks and shapely breasts, and huge gazelle-like eyes of a beautiful black (*ḥūr al-ʿīn*, from which we get our word 'houri').

Christians, with all the puritanism inherent in their faith, were very ready to be shocked by these delights, especially of the latter kind. But Hubert Grimme has discovered a model for them in the poetical description of the delights of paradise made by St Ephraem, a Father of the Syrian Church, who lived in the fourth century and whose works were very widespread.[16] He also sang of the sweet perfumes and the soft music of Eden, its sweet-smelling springs, its pleasure tents, the crowns of flowers which bound the brows of the righteous and the airy spirits who served them as cup-bearers, and the wine drunk by the Blessed who had wisely abstained from it on earth. Admittedly all this was metaphor and poetic imagery which the Arab prophet, when the echoes of these descriptions reached him, seems to have taken for physical realities. But a great many Christians, including no doubt those who passed them on, had done the same. There was a very old and deep-rooted strain in popular Judaism and Christianity which regarded the delights of paradise as very real. Some theologians had even tried to assimilate it by limiting its application and pronouncing that the righteous dead might enjoy some pleasures of this order before the coming of the Day of Resurrection and Judgement. Only then would the time of purely spiritual bliss come.

The Swedish scholar Tor Andrae in particular has claimed to find the original of the houris in St Ephraem's own writings in the vine stocks (a feminine word in Syriac) which were to take to their immaculate bosoms the aged monks, whose chastity had never known the sweetness of earthly loves.[17] The Rev. E. Beck has disputed this last connection with great vigour.[18] Certainly it is impossible to prove, in the legal sense of the word, a connection between the Syrian deacon and the Meccan prophet; and vines are not women. But the indirect influence remains a probability, and there is no doubt that the Christian ascetics dreamed of compensations in the next world for the mortifications they inflicted on themselves in this, and that those compensations were frequently of the same order as the privations. Probably quite unconsciously they evoked objects of markedly feminine attributes as a mild reward for chaste men. In the same way, a few verses before the mention of the comforting vines, Ephraem pictured lonely virgins in their early lives, surrounded in the next by an admiring throng of angels, apostles and prophets. It would be difficult not to see a hidden sexual meaning in this, and there was certainly no shortage of Christians ready to translate these hints into the broadest reality. Origen, at the beginning of the third century, was already remarking that some people seemed to think there would be marriage contracts and the getting of children after the Resurrection. And a century before him even, Papias, bishop of Hierapolis in Phrygia, who had questioned the disciples of the Apostles themselves and who, according to early Christian writers, had even known St John in his old age, recorded that Jesus described the millennium, the rule of God on earth a thousand years after the Resurrection, in the following terms:

The day shall come wherein vines shall grow, each one having ten thousand branches, and on one branch ten thousand shoots, and on every shoot ten thousand clusters, and in every cluster ten thousand grapes. And every grape when it is pressed shall yield twenty-five metretes [rather less than a thousand litres] of wine. And when one of the saints taketh hold of one of the clusters, another will cry out: 'I am a better cluster. Take me. Through me bless thou the Lord.'[19]

It is true that Eusebius of Caesarea had no great opinion of Papias and suggests that 'he misunderstood the descriptions of the Apostles and did not see that they were using figures of speech and expressing themselves in symbolic language'.[20] That may well be so, but there were a great many who believed this witness from the first generation of Christians, even men as eminent as Irenaeus, the holy bishop of Lyon.

How could one attain these delights? Allah was implacable and had determined each man's fate in advance, in this world and the next. And yet he could exhort men to act in such a way as to merit reward. For the logic of the believer and for it alone there is no contradiction in this. Men should therefore believe in Allah and his Prophet, do good, that is what Allah commands, and shun evil, that is what Allah has forbidden. They should be generous, good, benevolent, respect their parents, be honest, courteous and just, and refrain from murder, theft, or fornication, that is from unauthorized sexual relations, and observe the rules of diet. They should show a spirit of solidarity within the community.

They must also take part in the rituals – the external manifestations by which they demonstrate their surrender to Allah and to his messenger and their integration into the community. As we have seen, they were also to take part in the ritual prayers three times a day. This figure was probably not increased to five until after Muḥammad's death. After Badr, as we have seen, it was made a rule to fast during the month of Ramaḍān. We have seen, too, that whenever possible the faithful were to make the ritual pilgrimage to the house of Allah at Mecca. Another duty of the same kind was the payment of the *zakāt* or 'purification' tax, which is generally translated as 'obligatory alms'. One contemporary Muslim apologist observed with justification that it was really a compulsory tax raised to the status of a ritual.[21] In the same way those who were able were liable for the blood tax, i.e. armed warfare 'in the path of Allah'.

In this way a loyal member of the Muslim community found himself part of a system of commandments and instruction, which the majority of men need if they are to live, which used to be called a religion but which we would now describe in a more general way as an ideology. Authorities laid down for him how he was to act and what he was to think. By believing this teaching, obeying these rules and observing these rituals, a man had a good chance of winning the ultimate Reward. On these beliefs and these observances rested the ordered running of society and the world. The ideals of the old religions of the land and the tribe, and those of the new religions of individual salvation were thus achieved simultaneously. A society so firmly based was well placed to set out to conquer the world.

After the raising of the siege of Medina and the massacre of the Banū Qurayẓa, Muḥammad seems to have turned his thoughts away from Mecca for a few months. He launched no attack on his ungrateful native city and she did not attack him. In any case events had proved that neither was in any position to inflict an overwhelming military defeat on the other side. The Meccans, driven to a standstill, were as if stunned. None of their leaders, not even the able Abū Sufyān, seems to have been capable of the imaginative effort needed to offer any effective opposition to the activities of their adversary and enemy. In fact, a slow process was taking place in their minds, the results of which were to appear before very long. It may be true that, as tradition has it, the conversion to Islam of two of its future military luminaries – both Qurayshites – dates from this period: 'Amr ibn al-'Āṣ, who later conquered Egypt, and Khālid ibn al-Walīd, whose strategic ability had been responsible for Muḥammad's defeat at Uḥud and who later became 'the Sword of Islam' and the conqueror of Syria.

But, although he launched no direct attack, Muḥammad had not forgotten Mecca. The object of his activities at this period seems in fact to have been to isolate and weaken it and, above all, to damage its commercial relations with Syria. The merchant 'Abd ar-Raḥmān ibn 'Awf, who could display some military talents when occasion demanded, was dispatched with seven hundred men to Dūmat al-Jandal, a great trading centre on the road to Syria where an important annual fair was held. The inhabitants, who belonged to the Christian tribe of the Kalb, surrendered without a fight. Their prince concluded a treaty with the Muslims and gave his daughter to 'Abd ar-Raḥmān. Zayd, the beloved adoptive son whose tractable disposition we have already seen, was sent with others to trade in Syria, but was attacked by Beduin, robbed and left for dead. Somehow he made his way back to Medina. A little while later he avenged himself hideously by having the old Beduin woman he believed was responsible for this attack torn limb from limb between four camels. Zayd himself had better fortune leading an expedition of a hundred and seventy men to attack a Meccan caravan on its way back from Syria, capturing substantial booty and two important prisoners. 'Ā'isha, to whose care one of these was imprudently committed, allowed him to escape while she was chatting with neighbours. The other turned out rather unexpectedly to be a son-in-law of the Prophet and also a nephew of his dead wife, Khadīja. His name was Abū l-'Āṣ ibn ar-Rabī'. He had already been taken prisoner at Badr but his father-in-law had allowed him to return to Mecca on condition that he permitted his wife, the Prophet's daughter Zaynab, to join him in Medina. This had been done; and now that he had been taken prisoner again he found means to gain access to his wife, who still loved him in spite of their separation. She took him under her protection, a traditional Arab gesture – perfectly lawful, but unpopular with those who had taken the trouble of capturing him and were hoping for a ransom. Muḥammad denied any part in this plot; but he supported his daughter. He had the property which had been taken from Abū l-'Āṣ restored to him and sent him back to Mecca, without however allowing him to see Zaynab again. She could not be permitted to have carnal relations with a pagan. Once back in Mecca, Abū l-ʿĀṣ indemnified those who had taken him prisoner, put his affairs in order, then returned to Medina, was converted and restored to his wife. He explained that he had been unwilling to make this gesture during his captivity in case he was suspected of being converted out of self-interest.

Alliances were made with tribes in the vicinity of Medina, apparently without any demand for the conversion to Islam of the contracting parties. Respect for the territories of the city and for Muḥammad's personal flocks and herds was enforced, with no hesitation in resorting to the torture of prisoners as an example. It was likewise necessary to intimidate any who contemplated an alliance with the Jews of Khaybar. ʿAlī made one such expedition northwards against the Banū Saʿd, from whom he captured five hundred camels and two thousand sheep and goats. A unit of thirty picked killers was sent into Khaybar itself, disguised as an embassy from Muḥammad. They negotiated with the Jewish leader, Usayr ibn Rāzim, and ended by persuading him to go to Medina with an escort of thirty of his own men, to reach an agreement with the Prophet himself. On the journey all the Jews were killed by surprise. Muḥammad congratulated the leader of the band on his return: 'It was Allah', he said, 'who saved you from the company of the oppressors.'[22]

In the following month – this was towards the end of the sixth year since the Emigration to Medina, March 628 – Muḥammad reached a decision which, although it was apparently precipitated by a dream from on high, had clearly been the subject of long and careful meditation. This decision was none the less an unexpected and surprising one. He announced that he was going to Mecca for the ritual of the *ʿumra*, the traditional ceremonies consisting principally of processions which used to circumambulate the Kaʿba. He bought animals to sacrifice to Allah, according to custom. He invited his followers to go with him; also the local Beduin, who gave little evidence of enthusiasm. The pilgrimage was to be a peaceful one. The only weapons they took were swords which, in theory, were not to be unsheathed. According to some sources the troop comprised seven hundred men; others say between fourteen and sixteen hundred. There were four women. They approached the Qurayshite city across the desert and the countryside (which this year was parched by an exceptional drought) after first stopping in the proper place to put on the traditional dress of pilgrims. Naturally the Meccans were not long in hearing that Muḥammad was approaching the city at the head of a numerous company. Excitedly they prepared for battle, first sending out two hundred horsemen in the direction of the Muslims as scouts. No less naturally, Muḥammad was aware of all this through his spies. At one time he does seem to have been tempted to take advantage of the fact that the enemy's troops were all deployed against him. By a flanking movement he could have entered the city on its undefended side, and occupied it. Abū Bakr wisely insisted on sticking to the original plan of a peaceful pilgrimage. Muḥammad took his advice. He eluded the Qurayshite horsemen by finding a guide to take him across broken, thorny ground, which the army found it hard to penetrate. In this way they came to Ḥudaybiya, some nine or ten miles north-west of Mecca, where there was a great tree and a well. This was the edge of the holy ground and Muḥammad's camel refused to go any further. The Muslims had reached this place before dawn and proceeded to light fires, making no attempt at concealment. The Qurayshite horsemen took up a position between them and the city.

The Qurayshites were divided amongst themselves. Abū Sufyān, their leader, was away on a journey. A large faction wanted to negotiate with Muḥammad. They sent envoys chosen not from their own ranks but from among their Beduin allies to sound out the Prophet's intentions. These returned much impressed by the Muslims' piety and peaceable demeanour, and also by Muḥammad's control of his army. In the course of the discussions one of the negotiators had several times stroked the Prophet's beard; and one of the Muslims present, taking offence at this familiarity, finally struck him on the hand. This Muslim had turned out to be a cousin of the negotiator's, expelled by his tribe for the murder of some members of another tribe; he had then embraced Islam and taken refuge in Medina, leaving his fellow tribesmen to settle with the tribe of his victims. They had been obliged to part with thirteen hundred camels in compensation. What the man said to Muḥammad was: 'What are you doing coming against your respectable kinsfolk with all this rabble? They'll desert you at the first opportunity.' This made Abū Bakr very angry indeed: 'Go and suck the cunt of Allāt! We, desert him?'

Now it was Muḥammad's turn to send an ambassador. He chose his son-in-law, the elegant 'Uthmān, who set out under the protection of his numerous relatives from the opposing camp. The negotiations went on for a long time. The rumour reached the Muslim camp that 'Uthmān had been put to death. Deeply upset, the men went to where Muḥammad sat beneath the tree of Ḥudaybiya and swore a solemn oath to defend him to the death. The 'pledge under the tree' became famous. It was an honour to have an ancestor who had taken part in it. However, 'Uthmān returned. The negotiations had not been broken off, but they had reached a deadlock. Muḥammad persisted, but without losing his temper. All he wanted was to perform the ritual and nothing else. Could they refuse him that? In the end the Qurayshites sent an envoy with full powers, Suhayl ibn 'Amr. The talks continued between him and Muḥammad under the tree, with the Muslims standing round – not shy of expressing their own opinions and haughtily advising the Qurayshite envoy to speak more softly. 'Umar and some others were angry at the idea of treating with these pagans. The future Caliph came to upbraid the Prophet. He declared later that if he had had a hundred men on his side he would have seceded. But Muḥammad was immovable. At last 'Alī was summoned to set down the details of the treaty in writing. The Prophet told him to begin with the Muslim phrase: 'In the name of Allah, the Compassionate [*raḥmān*], the Merciful.' Suhayl objected, 'I do not recognize that phrase. Write: In thy name, O Allah.' Muḥammad gave way. He went on dictating: 'This is the treaty of peace concluded by Muḥammad, the Messenger of Allah, with Suhayl ibn 'Amr.' Suhayl objected again: 'If I had agreed that you were the Messenger of Allah, I should not have fought you. Write your name and your father's name.' Again Muḥammad gave way. It was written simply: 'This is the treaty of peace concluded by Muḥammad ibn 'Abdallāh with Suhayl ibn 'Amr.' There followed the conditions. War was to cease for ten years. During this time all Qurayshites who might go to Muḥammad without permission from their legal guardians were to be sent back, but Muslims who might return to Mecca were not to be. The tribes were to be free to make alliances with either side. For this year, Muḥammad and his followers were to abandon their proposed entry into Mecca; but the following year the Qurayshites would evacuate the city for three days so that the Muslims could come and perform their devotions, armed only with the traveller's weapon of a sheathed sword.

The Muslims were very disappointed and showed it. But Muḥammad and Abū Bakr were more far-sighted. At the cost of a great many concessions, some of which were humiliating but not really significant, they had got what they wanted. The Qurayshites had negotiated with Muḥammad, and had therefore recognized his authority. Most important of all, they had admitted that he and his men were respectable followers of the cult of the city since they were to be allowed to come and practise it there the next year. The implications of all this were very soon apparent.

But, for the present, the non-aggression pact concluded with Mecca gave Muḥammad a long-awaited opportunity. The effective alliance between the Jews of Khaybar, Quraysh and the Beduin tribes of Ghaṭafān and Fazāra was broken up. It was vital to take advantage of this to render the enemy centre of Khaybar harmless. It was moreover necessary to provide an outlet for the energies of the Muslims who had been deprived of their booty at Ḥudaybiya. Khaybar was rich. Like Medina (some ninety miles south of it), it was a vast palm plantation in between plains of volcanic rock. By means of irrigation and assiduous cultivation, the Jews had developed the date-farming, which was the basic wealth of that part of Arabia, on an intensive scale. They lived in seven forts scattered among the gardens. Part of the harvest – as was, and still is, the custom in Arabia – went to buy protection from the militarily superior Beduin tribes of the region for the peaceful pursuit of their agricultural activities. The Jews (it will be remembered that the Jewish tribe of Banū Naḍīr, which had been driven out of Medina by Muḥammad, had found refuge in Khaybar) were divided up into tribal groups which recognized no one central authority. This was to make Muḥammad's task easier. Remaining barely a month in Medina after his return from Ḥudaybiya, he set out northwards with sixteen hundred men. The Jews' Beduin allies offered them no assistance. Muslim tradition has attempted to justify this breach of faith by citing a variety of reasons for their abstention, some of them supernatural. Probably Muḥammad had simply bribed them with promises of a share in the plunder. The siege, if it can be called that, lasted over a month. Withdrawing by night into their own camp, the Muslims attacked the Jewish forts one by one with arrows, preventing the defenders from getting out, keeping them short of water and ravaging their fields. The Jews were incapable of offering any organized resistance. Their attempts to break out were beaten back. Some negotiated with Muḥammad in the hope of saving their skins. Several forts surrendered. Muḥammad continued his blockade and waited patiently for the last three to give in. Envoys were sent to negotiate. The Muslims taking part in the siege became simply the successors of the Beduin, who had levied a part of the Jews' harvests on pretence of protection. They, however, took half the harvest. It had been foreseen from the beginning that only those who had been at Ḥudaybiya would get a share in this bonus. On the other hand the booty was considerable. The better part of all that the Jews possessed was sequestered. The men and women taken in the first forts were kept as prisoners, among them a beautiful girl of seventeen named Ṣafiyya, whom Muḥammad took for himself after killing her husband for concealing his goods. He persuaded her to embrace Islam and, being violently attracted to her, took her into his bed that very night. By so doing he was violating his own previous commands, according to which his supporters had to wait until the beginning of the next menstrual cycle before having intercourse with their captives. But she was so very beautiful! When she mounted her camel for the return journey, the Prophet of Allah went down on one knee so that she might use the other as a step.

Another Jewish girl was less easily won. Her name was Zaynab; she had seen her father, uncle and husband killed. Ordered to prepare a roast lamb for the Prophet's dinner, she found out which part he liked best. It was the shoulder. She poisoned it, and the rest of the meat with it. Thinking that the first mouthful tasted strange, Muḥammad spat it out; however Bishr, one of his Companions, swallowed the meat and died of it. The Prophet questioned Zaynab. 'You know what you have done to my people,' she replied. 'I said to myself: If he is a prophet, he will know [about the poison], and if he is an earthly king, I shall be rid of him.' Muḥammad forgave her.

The other Jewish colonies in the region, at Fadak, Wādī l-Qurā and Taymā', all learned their lesson from Khaybar. They submitted without argument and were given the same terms as Khaybar or rather better. They were allowed to keep their possessions on payment of a tax. As far as Muḥammad was concerned, the Jewish problem was practically solved.

The rest of the year was spent in routine small raids, diplomatic negotiations with the shaikhs of the tribes and manoeuvring to win over to the Muslim side one or another of the leading personages among the Beduin or Meccans. Mecca was still problem number one. After twelve months had passed, Muḥammad set out on the pilgrimage in accordance with the terms laid down in the treaty of Ḥudaybiya. He took with him two thousand supporters and a great quantity of weapons.

These were set down on the borders of Meccan territory, with a small company to guard them in case of need. Retaining their sheathed swords as their only weapons and driving before them the camels intended for the sacrifice, the Muslims advanced into the city, which had been evacuated by its inhabitants, in accordance with the agreement. This was the first time for seven years that the Prophet had set eyes on the city of his birth. He returned with head held high, surrounded by his people. He made the ritual turns around the Kaʿba without dismounting from his camel. Apparently he was denied entry to the little sanctuary. He also performed the seven ritual laps of the *ʿumra* between two low hills, Ṣafā and Marwa, which stood near the holy place, some four hundred yards apart. From the tops of the nearby hills the Qurayshites were able to watch the bulk of the Muslims imitating their master – on foot – and uttering the customary cries of '*Labbayka!*' (Behold I am yours). They saw Bilāl climb on to the roof of the Kaʿba and give the Muslim call to prayer; and they covered their faces and thanked the gods for permitting their fathers to die before they could see such sacrilege. Muḥammad took advantage of his stay to marry a sister of the wife of one of his uncles, a small banker named ʿAbbās who had not embraced his faith. This new bride, Maymūna, was twenty-seven. Muḥammad tried to use the wedding as an excuse to stay longer in Mecca. He invited the Qurayshite chiefs to the traditional marriage feast; but they answered that they did not need a feast and requested him to be gone with all speed. Muhammad did not insist and left, consummating the marriage, with his usual precipitancy, at the first halt.

The small military expeditions to avenge an insult or to compel a tribe to respect the new Muslim power continued. One in particular stands out, although its motive and the course it took are somewhat obscure to us. Traditional accounts have woven together a medley of partial and contradictory reports in inextricable confusion. This was the expedition which was sent out in the year 8 of the Emigration, September 629 according to our reckoning, northwards towards the frontiers of the Byzantine Empire. Its commander-in-chief was Muḥammad's adoptive son, Zayd ibn Ḥāritha; and since the Prophet had given him three thousand men, this was evidently a campaign of some importance. However the force seems to have been made up largely of newly converted Beduin, whose main object was plunder. For the first time the Muslims penetrated into the Byzantine Empire. Learning of the approach of what he must have regarded as a band of brigands, the controller of the area, one Theodore the Vicar, raised a force of Arab auxiliaries – both Christian and pagan – from the frontier region to the south-east of the Dead Sea, which was the old land of Edom. So says the Byzantine historian Theophanes; and this is the first time that incidents in the Prophet's life can be taken from a non-Muslim source. The armies met at Mu'ta; the affray was a bloody one, although there is mention of only twelve Muslim dead. It is possible, however, that deaths among the Beduin, who were recent and doubtful adherents, were not thought worthy of mention. Among the dead were the three successive leaders of the army: Zayd ibn Ḥāritha, who was followed by Ja'far ibn Abī Ṭālib, the brother of 'Alī and a cousin of the Prophet, and finally the warrior-poet 'Abdallāh ibn Rawāḥa. The fleeing Muslims were rallied by the former Qurayshite commander-in-chief, who had recently become a Muslim and been assigned to a subordinate position in the army. Khālid ibn al-Walīd, who came to be called 'the Sword of Allah', succeeded in restoring some degree of order and led the disgruntled survivors back to Medina; there they were met with such furious mockery and abuse that Muḥammad was obliged to take them under his lofty protection.

The three months that followed were a decisive period. Muḥammad's eyes were now fixed firmly on Mecca. The treaty of Ḥudaybiya, which he had agreed to in order to further his immediate aims, contained a number of stipulations which would not do in the long run. It has been said already that Muḥammad pledged himself, somewhat mortifyingly, to a one-sided promise to send back to Mecca anyone who embraced Islam without the permission of their legal guardian. An awkward case cropped up not long after the treaty. Muḥammad had on this occasion sent back a man named Abū Baṣīr, a confederate of the Qurayshite clan of Banū Zuhra. On the road back to Mecca, this man killed one of his guardians and made his way back to Medina. The surviving guardian hastened to complain; Muḥammad, in some embarrassment, offered to hand the man over. The guardian was horrified and refused to escort such a dangerous prisoner on his own. At this point, having twice delivered up Abū Baṣīr to the Qurayshites, Muḥammad felt that he had fulfilled his obligation under the treaty. He had done his best and it was not his fault if the man's guardians had let him give them the slip and were now refusing to take delivery of him. However he hinted to Abū Baṣīr that he would rather see him out of Medina. Abū Baṣīr took the hint and fled to a place near the Red Sea where the Meccan caravans passed by on their way to and from Syria. There he gathered together some seventy men in a similar situation to himself; and they took to a life of brigandage, preying on the Meccan caravans. The Qurayshites were apparently unable to deal with the gang by force of arms; Muḥammad declared that they were none of his business. In the end the Qurayshites begged Muḥammad to take them into his own community and agreed not to press any claim for their extradition. In this way they would at least be safe from their depredations and would know whom to blame.

All the same they were very angry. Many of them swore that they too would take advantage of the letter of the treaty and pay Muḥammad back in his own coin. Their chance very soon came. In Rajab of the year 8 (November 629), in consequence of a vendetta which had been going on for several decades, some of the Banū Bakr, Beduin allies of Quraysh, having the more excited of the Qurayshites at their rear, attacked a group of the tribe of Khuzā'a, Muḥammad's allies, not far from Mecca. One man was killed and the rest badly mauled and forced to flee into the sacred territory of Mecca. Pursued even there they took refuge in two friendly houses. Shamefully the Banū Bakr laid siege to the houses. In all twenty people of the Khuzā'a were slain.

By Arab standards this was a bad business. Muḥammad was bound to set up a cry for revenge. The differences, which had been growing greater and more serious for some months, between the Meccan leaders over the proper attitude to take with respect to the Prophet, would be brought into the open. The hard core of those who had encouraged the Banū Bakr and even, it was said, taken an active part in their exploits were for taking a firm line. But Abū Sufyān had long been convinced that the best course was to reach an understanding with the Prophet. It emerged from the discussions that the majority were with him.

This was the outcome of a lengthy mental process. The unsuccessful siege of Medina had shown that it was no longer possible to destroy Muḥammad. His power had grown too great. His victories over the Jewish colonies, his expeditions to the north, his treaties with the Beduin had all increased his power still further. His activities were seriously interfering with trade, which was the Meccans' exclusive livelihood. Then again, his solemn pilgrimage to the Ka'ba had shown his respect for the Meccan holy places. It was clear now that he had no intention of destroying the sanctuary but actually meant to encourage its cult, after first giving it a somewhat different orientation: towards the glorification of Allah alone. His formula for a theocratic state had proved its worth. The Meccans had been impressed by the discipline of the Muslims at Ḥudaybiya and during the *'umra* of the following year. Muḥammad's followers were strong and their leader had succeeded in making them rich. There seemed to be every advantage in sharing in this power and wealth, since it could not be destroyed. For practical businessmen like the rich Meccans, as well as for the poor who were attracted to the prosperity which the Medinans enjoyed, things were what they were and the ideological obstacles should be easy to overcome.

Abū Sufyān, the man of compromise, was therefore sent to Medina to pacify Muḥammad. His daughter, Umm Ḥabība, who had left him long before in order to embrace Islam, had actually married the Prophet the previous year. All Quraysh waited on tenterhooks for Muḥammad to decide what was to be done about the Khuzā'a, who were complaining bitterly. They could not bring themselves either to declare war on him, or to pay the heavy blood-price which would be demanded for the dead Khuzā'a, or to abandon the Banū Bakr to his mercy. Could Abū Sufyān arrange matters? Tradition records that he was given a very cool reception in Medina, even by his daughter; but these details are clearly inspired by the anti-Umayyad leanings of the early chroniclers. (The dynasty of Umayyad Caliphs traced its descent from Abū Sufyān.) The sequence of events would seem to suggest that, on the contrary, the Meccan leader and his son-in-law arrived at what may have been, to some extent, a tacit agreement.

Certainly Muḥammad immediately began making preparations for a Meccan expedition. He kept his preparations carefully secret, broke off all communications with the Qurayshite city and pretended to be making ready for some northern campaign. He summoned contingents from all his allied tribes. At last he set out with what was, compared to what was usual in Arabia at that time, an immense army: ten thousand men. This was on 10 Ramaḍān of the year 8; 1 January 630. All along the way he was joined by fresh contingents and by Meccans anxious to get on the right side of their probable conqueror. Among these was one of the Prophet's worst enemies from earlier days, who was now, very reasonably as it turned out, afraid of reprisal, and Muḥammad's uncle, 'Abbās the banker. The army encamped two days' march from Mecca and lit ten thousand fires. Panic grew in Mecca. What emerges from traditional accounts, which are muddled and contradictory, is that Abū Sufyān was sent into the Muslim camp by the Qurayshites, or, more probably, induced them to send him. He placed himself under 'Abbās's protection. All this had no doubt been arranged between them before 'Abbās joined his nephew's army. Abū Sufyān was formally converted to Islam and then returned to Mecca, where he proclaimed

Muḥammad's terms. These were perfectly clear. The city was in no danger if it welcomed the conqueror peacefully. In the face of his strength all resistance was vain. The life and property of all those who did not resist would be safe. All that they had to do was to lay down their arms and to shut themselves inside their houses or take refuge in the house of Abū Sufyān. Abū Sufyān's wife, the fanatical Hind, tried unsuccessfully to silence him by grabbing hold of his moustaches and crying out: 'Go on, kill this great goatskin, full of grease! A fine leader for the people, he is!' However he answered: 'Woe unto you! Do not let her lead you astray. Something unprecedented has occurred!'[23]

Muḥammad allowed the news carried by Abū Sufyān time to do its work and then, on Thursday, 20 Ramaḍān 8 (11 January 630), the Muslims made their entry in four columns into the deserted streets of the city. Only a handful of extremists offered some resistance in one corner of the city. Khālid ibn al-Walīd routed them easily, with the loss of ten or twenty lives as against two or three on the Muslim side.

Muḥammad barely rested before making his way to the sanctuary, mounted on a camel, with a long wand in his hand, in the midst of his rejoicing army and a crowd of men, horses and camels. Before the awed Qurayshites, who had climbed on to their roofs and balconies, he touched the Black Stone with his stick, crying out in a loud voice the supreme invocation of Islam: '*Allahu akbar!*' (Allah is greatest). The ten thousand men took up the sacred formula. After this he made the seven ritual circles, and had the many idols inside the temple thrown down. Then he called for the key to the Ka'ba and went in. Inside there was much treasure; this he respected, even though it was composed of gifts offered by the pagans to their gods. There were also some frescoes which he had removed except, it is said, for the images of Abraham, Jesus and the Virgin Mary. Then he made a speech and invited the Qurayshites to come and pay homage to him, acknowledging him as the Messenger of Allah and as such to swear obedience to him. In a long column, the men first and the women behind, they filed past the Prophet as he sat on the rock of Ṣafā, and swore allegiance on the hands of ʻUmar, who sat a little way below Muḥammad.

Like most sensible politicians, Muḥammad proclaimed an amnesty for past offences. He did, however, make an exception in the cases of some ten men and women whose affronts had been more than he could swallow. These were not the ones who led the resistance against him. Muḥammad was well aware that, having once played and lost, these men had learned their lesson and that in future he could count on their abilities being used in his service. But those he could not forgive were the propagandists who had mocked and made fun of him in songs and verses. These included ʻAbdallāh ibn Saʻd, the secretary who had been taking down the revelations at his dictation and who had been seized with doubts when, after writing his own words in the style of the Koran, the Prophet had not noticed the interpolation. It will be recalled that he had fled to Mecca, where he spread the story. ʻUthmān asked for mercy for this man who represented all that the disseminators of ideologies hate most: rational lucid criticism. ʻUthmān was so insistent (ʻAbdallāh was his foster-brother) that in the end the Prophet gave way; but he later said to those who had been present: 'I was silent for a long time. Why did not one of you kill this dog?' 'Why did you give me no sign, O Messenger of Allah?' one of them said. 'One does not kill by signs,' the Prophet said irritably.[24] ʻAbdallāh later reached high office in the Muslim empire. He had realised that truth is powerless in the face of myths, when these have history and strength on their side. There was more to be gained from making the best of it.

Another apostate (this time for less idealistic reasons) was not so lucky. He had composed verses against Muḥammad and gave evening parties in Mecca, at which he had them performed by two female singers. He was put to death, together with one of the singers. The other hid herself and was later pardoned. Also among the proscribed were two or three men who had ill-treated the Prophet's daughters; and another who, after receiving from Muḥammad the blood-price for his brother (who had been killed by mistake), had nevertheless gone on to avenge him on the Muslims. Hind, the wife of Abū Sufyān, who had behaved with such savage exultation at Uḥud by eating the liver of the Prophet's uncle Ḥamza, was naturally spared. Her husband and family were too valuable as recruits. Before long her son and grandson had become princes of that Islam which she and her husband had fought so bitterly.

The few instances of the Prophet's vengeance began to alarm the Qurayshites. Abū Sufyān came to express the tribe's anxiety, but Muḥammad assured him these were the last. He took the opportunity of borrowing large sums from the wealthiest Qurayshites. It was after all good policy to distribute some compensation to the Muslim soldiery who had laid hands on nothing in the way of booty. Fifty dirhams each were distributed to over two thousand men, selected from among the most needy.

Muḥammad remained a fortnight in Mecca. He introduced the administrative measures necessitated by his victory. He had the idols in the neighbouring sanctuaries smashed, and a herald warned the new believers to destroy their private idols. But no one seems to have felt under any constraint to embrace Islam. A certain number of pagans must have been left. Like his later successors on a world-wide scale, Muḥammad had the sense to create a favourable climate for the adoption of his religion and then to leave matters to take their own course without hurrying them. Conversion carried with it considerable advantages. For the future, the pagan cult had to be a purely domestic affair. Social pressures no longer worked in favour of paganism but favoured Islam instead. It was enough; in a few years, paganism in Mecca was a thing of the past.

The Medinans, the Helpers (*anṣār*) as they were called, looked askance at this indulgence on the part of the Prophet. Were his Meccan brother-tribesmen, who had fought so hard against him, to be dearer to his heart than those who supported him through his unhappiest moments? Was theirs to be the better part? Were family and birthplace ties to prevail over the comradeship created by facing common perils? They communicated their anxiety to Muḥammad, and he reassured them. 'I mean to live and die among you,' he said. He lived in a tent and said his prayers like a traveller.

From Mecca he sent a number of small expeditions into the surrounding country. But above all he had to face an unexpected danger. A large confederation of tribes called the Hawāzin had risen against the Prophet. They were in league with the tribe of Thaqīf, whose principal home was in the upland city of Ṭā'if, some sixty miles south-east of Mecca. The Hawāzin were old and bitter enemies of Quraysh. The decline of Quraysh had given a fresh impetus to the anti-Qurayshite party in Ṭā'if. The two allies seem to have been intending to profit from the Meccan defeat to assure their own supremacy in the Hejaz. Not unreasonably, what they saw in Muḥammad was essentially a Qurayshite taking command of his native city with the object of creating a Qurayshite kingdom. He had to be destroyed. Muḥammad left Mecca with twelve thousand men (the recently recruited Qurayshites were only too willing to fight the hereditary enemy) on 27 January 630. Both he and his army were full of confidence. After four days' march they met the enemy at Ḥunayn. The Hawāzin apparently numbered about twenty thousand men and had brought their women and children along with them. They were led by a gallant thirty-year-old chief named Mālik. They broke through one wing of the Muslim army and a rout threatened. Muḥammad, faced with a general panic, remained calm and, with his best troops around him, rallied the fugitives and finally made a fresh onslaught. Victory was his. He drove home his advantage by laying siege to Ṭā'if. He possessed a few catapults; but even so the siege of a fortified city was too bold an undertaking for an army such as his. After a fortnight he raised the siege. The campaign was a draw. The rest must be left to time. He led his army back to Ji'rāna, where they had left the prisoners and booty taken from the Hawāzin at

Ḥunayn. The share-out of the spoils was turned into a riot by the greed of those taking part. Muḥammad himself was pushed up against a tree and had his clothes torn. Not without some trouble, he succeeded in restoring order and making himself obeyed. In order to satisfy the greedy demands of his own people, he divided the female captives among them, including his sons-in-law in the division. But envoys came from the Hawāzin. The Prophet agreed to give them something back, on condition that they agreed to surrender and be converted. They could have either the women or the goods, but not both. After a good deal of hesitation the Hawāzin chose their womenfolk. In the subsequent share-out of the great spoils the Prophet shocked and horrified his old supporters by favouring the new converts outrageously. Abū Sufyān was given a hundred camels and each of his sons – Mu'āwiya, the future Caliph, and Yazīd – the same number. Even those Qurayshites who were still pagans received something. One of those who disapproved exclaimed: 'It is not with such gifts that one seeks God's face.'[25] Muḥammad was very disturbed by this remark, 'he changed colour', but he persisted in his policy. He made another *'umra* at Mecca. He left there a governor, 'Attāb ibn Asīd, with a stipend of one dirham a day as subsistence. This seems to be the first occasion on which there is any mention of a salaried official. Mu'ādh ibn Jabal remained with him, to teach the Meccans the Koran and the new religion. Then the Prophet returned to Medina – greatly to the relief of the Medinans, who had been afraid he would settle in his native city. On the twenty-seventh of the month of Dhū l-Qa'da in the year 8 (18 March 630) he returned to the palm grove where, with so few of his Companions, he had sought refuge eight years before, in wretchedness and exile. Now victory, glory and triumph were his for ever more.

The capture of Mecca was called in Arabic *al-fat'ḥ*, which means the opening – but also the judgement, sentence or revelation. This subsequently became the accepted word for a conquest. In fact this operation was the justification of all the

Prophet's earlier policies. Allah was vindicating him once and for all, showing that he had been right. His worst enemies had become his most zealous servants, acknowledging his superiority, confessing that he was indeed the Prophet of Allah and admitting that they had wronged him and been blind to the prodigious works of Allah. They lost nothing by it.

They gained prestige, political influence and material advantages. They were among the first in the state of Medina, which now stretched from the Byzantine frontier to Ṭā'if and whose influence covered the whole of Arabia. One tradition says that when, just before the fall of Mecca, Abū Sufyān had gone to the Muslim camp as an envoy, he saw the Muslim troops parade past him in great numbers and good order and asked Muḥammad how he had been able to gather together so many people against his native land. He ought, he said, rather to turn them against its enemies. The Prophet is said to have replied: 'I hope that my Lord will grant me to do both.'[26] Not long afterwards he did in fact subdue the Hawāzin and Ṭā'if, both enemies of Quraysh. Before long his successors were to subdue the common enemies of all the Arabs. It was as though at last Quraysh had found a natural leader in its estranged child and, in the hazy words he uttered, the watchword which would lead them on to rule Arabia and the world. The persecutions and the battles had been no more than a prolonged misunderstanding. Order was restored. Allah had finally overcome Allāt, 'Uzzā and Manāt, and there were other Arabs alongside the Qurayshites among the leaders; but these were minor details. Medina – not yet Damascus – became the capital. Mecca was emptied of its great men and the less great. But even that scarcely mattered. The Meccans were destined to become the rulers of a vast empire.

The times were prodigious. The apocalyptic period, intimated by the clash between the two empires and which seemed imminent when the Persians were laying siege to Constantinople, receded once again into the unfathomable mists of the future. The vice-like grip had relaxed and the Second Rome was saved once again. Heraclius had left the City and landed in 622 behind the Persian lines in Asia Minor. He had defeated the great Persian general Shahrbarāz, the conqueror of Jerusalem. But the alliance between the Avars with their Slavonic auxiliaries and the Persians had been renewed. Once again in 626 Constantinople was beleaguered. Shahrbarāz was once again in Chalcedon, on the opposite shore of the Bosphorus, and the army of the Avars was encamped beneath its walls. This was the final test. The courage and determination of the besieged, their religious fervour and their faith in the divine Panaghia, the all-holy Virgin, together with their naval superiority, forced their assailants to raise the siege. From then on the trend was reversed. The Byzantines would win the day. In December 627, not long after the Qurayshites had raised the siege of Medina, Heraclius won a decisive victory at Nineveh. In February 628, as he was marching on the Persian capital of Ctesiphon, the Iranian generals and nobles, who had been driven to desperation by the obstinacy of Khusrō Abharwēz in pursuing the war, deposed him and set his son Kawādh Shērōē in his place. The old king of kings was put to death and Shērōē sued for peace with Heraclius. The treaty was signed on 3 April, at almost the same time as the pact of Ḥudaybiya. A series of palace revolutions at the court of Ctesiphon followed. Shahrbarāz, who had designs on the empire, withdrew none to hurriedly from Syria and Palestine and later, from Egypt and Cappadocia. In August of 629, after an absence of six years, Heraclius made a triumphal re-entry into Constantinople. In March 630 he performed a solemn pilgrimage to Jerusalem, ceremoniously bringing back the True Cross. This was at the time when Muḥammad was returning to Medina after the capture of Mecca.

The triumph of Christ seemed assured. The echoes of Heraclius' victory resounded throughout the world. 'The ruler of India sent his congratulations,' writes Henri Pirenne, 'and the Frankish king Dagobert made peace with him in perpetuity. . . . Admittedly, the Lombards were occupying a part of Italy, and in 624 the Visigoths had re-captured the last outposts of Byzantium in Spain; but what was that compared to the impressive recovery which had been made in the east?'[27]

And yet, in a way that was totally unforeseen, the Persian defeat left the field open in Arabia for Islam, the unsuspected enemy which was slowly maturing in the desert. The Persians as we have seen occupied South Arabia, and exerted a strong influence over eastern Arabia and supported the Jews. When their power waned, what was left? The Byzantine presence was chiefly felt through Christian Abyssinia. But the Persians had eliminated the Abyssinians as a power some decades earlier, and Abyssinian strength had declined to such an extent that it seems that they were incapable of taking advantage of the situation. The power and independence of the South Arabian states had been broken by the Abyssinians and the Persians. South Arabia had been parcelled out into a host of small, virtually independent domains, whose barons, the *qayls*, were continually bickering amongst themselves. Arabia was a political vacuum. Aspirations to peace among the tribes, to a strong state which should guarantee the safety of persons and property and allow free and profitable trading – these aspirations, whose origin we have endeavoured to describe, had no alternative goal on which to set their sights than an Arab state with an Arab ideology. And it was for the best. Conversion to Islam and to the Arab state was becoming a craze, an irresistible trend. The Prophet's poet Ḥassān ibn Thābit could address a delegation from the tribe of Tamīm in these words:

> Do not give associates to Allah. Become Muslims,
> And cease to dress after the fashion of strangers.[28]

The years following the capture of Mecca were largely taken up with the military and diplomatic manoeuvres resulting from this new situation. Muḥammad had countless opportunities to demonstrate his talents in both fields. There was a constant flow of envoys into Medina from the farthest corners of Arabia. It was necessary to estimate how representative these were, since they were generally sent by one party within a tribe, and every tribe was continually in the throes of a frantic struggle for power. Muḥammad had to decide whether the particular party concerned possessed any real authority: whether any agreements made with it would be honoured or implemented by the tribe as a whole and how it would affect the attitude of neighbouring tribes, who were – as a general rule – hostile. All these considerations had to be weighed up and a sensible decision reached.

The tribes immediately around Mecca and Medina, especially those to the west as far as the Red Sea, presented few problems. They had long ago acknowledged the Prophet's power and the advantages of becoming part of his system. They were allies, superficially converted (no one could be sure what was in their hearts, but for the moment it was the surface which mattered most), and furnished contingents for the Prophet's expeditions. This was indeed, as Montgomery Watt has called it, the kernel of the Muslim state. They were the living proof of the success of his system. There were no more internecine wars but, instead, rich spoils to be won from the pagans they were sent to attack.

The desert tribes to the east of these two key cities presented some complex problems. The history of the relations of each one with Quraysh or with the tribes of Medina had generally been complicated by endless fluctuations between friendship, open war and more or less determined hostility. Men and parties within each tribe were divided for or against Quraysh.

Muḥammad, the upstart Qurayshite, had inherited the problems of Quraysh; but in order to solve them he was able to employ, besides the traditional methods, a summons to acknowledge the power of Allah, through whom he had conquered, and the lure of peace at home and spoils from abroad. The rough and ready Beduin scarcely distinguished between these various reasons for joining him. Muḥammad was able to bribe influential men with suitable presents and, like a true politician, to play on men's ambition, greed, vanity, fears and sometimes no doubt (although more rarely) on their thirst for idealism and devotion. Some were completely converted, others gave their allegiance while remaining pagan at heart. Every tribe bound itself to Medina with promises to furnish troops and not to attack the other tribes which had made alliances with Muḥammad. They smashed their idols and undertook to pay either the lawful contribution of the faithful or the tax levied on associates, as the case might be. Some among them were truly converted and observed the simple rites described above; but the majority rendered only lip service and in their hearts did not swerve from belief in the little tribal gods, while conceding perhaps that Allah might be the greatest. No more was in fact asked of them. Every conceivable attitude was there, from firm conviction to downright unbelief. But all these tribes were bound to Muḥammad as political entities. That was what mattered.

As we have seen, the Prophet raised the siege of Ṭā'if, the mountain city of the Thaqīf tribe. But, with considerable shrewdness, he encouraged the tribe of Hawāzin – who were his allies after their defeat at Ḥunayn – to harass the enemy city (where a convert to Islam had been killed): to steal the Thaqīf's herds at pasture and to cut their links with Mecca, which played a fundamental part in their economy. About a year after the raising of the siege, the Thaqīf had had enough. They sent a delegation of their cleverest men to negotiate with Muḥammad. The envoys did not refuse to embrace Islam, but they asked to be released from what were to them its more troublesome obligations. They travelled a great deal and therefore wanted to continue to have relations with women other than their wives. They wanted to be allowed to lend money at interest, to drink the wines of their famous vineyards and even to maintain a cult to the great lady and protectress of their city, the goddess Allāt. Muḥammad refused these concessions. They asked that at least they should be left this cult for three years, then two, then one. Muḥammad was obdurate. All they got was permission not to destroy their idol themselves. Others would do it for them. But the Prophet did grant them leave to observe the fast of Ramaḍān somewhat less strictly than other people. He also agreed that the holy place of Wajj –

originally the name of a divinity but later simply a place – at Ṭā'if should retain its character. It would be forbidden to hunt there and to cut down the trees called *'idāh*. The actual text of this treaty has vanished, although others have been preserved. All we know of it is that it named Muḥammad ibn 'Abdallāh with no mention of his status as Messenger of Allah, which is significant. It may well have contained something liable to prove damaging to the faith of a later age. When the negotiators returned home they seemed to have had some difficulty in getting their fellow-citizens to accept these conditions. We have here a characteristic instance of the lack of enthusiasm which conversion to Islam often produced.

South Arabia was, as we have seen, in a state of feudal and tribal anarchy as a result of the wars which had destroyed the old, well-ordered constitutional kingdoms, and also as a result of the collapse of Persian power. Moreover the Persians can never have controlled the country as a whole. The Persian governor, Bādhām, and, after him, his son were converted to Islam or at least concluded an agreement with Muḥammad. Those of mixed Arab and Persian descent, the *abnā'* or 'sons' as they were called, seem to have been receptive to Muslim propaganda. Amongst all these quarrelling tribes they must have felt a need for the protection of a strong state. Muḥammad sent no expedition into this region, apart from a few very small parties. He had agents there and he supported certain feudal or tribal chiefs who acknowledged Islam. He encouraged them to act in concert against the non-Muslims, thus at one and the same time increasing their own wealth and influence and the Prophet's sphere of action. When the need arose, he dispensed favours such as exceptional endowments, or tax exemption. There were a great many Nestorian Christians in the region who were sympathetic to the Persian Empire, and some Jews whose ties with it were still closer. Those who were not converted were, in accordance with Muḥammad's usual practice, permitted to enjoy the benefits of Muslim peace in return for the payment of a tax.

The town of Najrān in the Yemen was famous for its large

and prosperous Christian community, which a century earlier had suffered persecution by the Jewish king, Dhū Nuwās. These Christians, who, together with a certain number of pagan brother-tribesmen, belonged to the tribe of the Banū l-Ḥārith, sent an embassy to Medina, led by their bishop, the head of their Council and another important person. People were shocked and dazzled by the richness of their garments. They engaged in a theological dispute with Muḥammad concerning the divine nature of Jesus. Muḥammad, growing weary, proposed that they should settle the matter by the old Arab method of reciprocal curses. Each side was to curse the other and they would see whose divinity would fulfil the curse. After consulting among themselves, the Christians withdrew. They preferred to abandon religious argument and conclude a treaty which would allow them to keep their religion. Arab historians have preserved the text of this treaty which served as a model for future agreements with the 'People of the Book', that is, with the Christians and Jews. This text is certainly not wholly authentic, but it may retain some of the original conditions. The community was placed under Muslim protection in return for the payment of an annual tribute of two thousand garments of a specific value. In the event of war it was to provide thirty coats of mail, thirty camels, and thirty horses. It would give board and lodging to the Prophet's envoys for up to a month. The people of Najrān had only to refrain from the practice of usury. In return for this they were indemnified against any attack on their persons, property or religion. Bishops and priests would not be removed from their sees, or monks from their monasteries.

The vast region of central Arabia known as the Yamāma was dominated by the great tribe of the Ḥanīfa, whose people were allies of the Persians and seem to a great extent to have made their living by trading between Persia and South Arabia. A great many of its members were Christians. Some important members of the tribe – they are actually called kings – treated with Muḥammad, and some became Muslims. The traditional accounts are so obscure and contradictory as to make it impossible to be sure just how widespread this trend towards conversion and adherence to the Medinan system was. It seems to have been precipitated by the collapse of Persia. But in this region and in this tribe Muḥammad had a rival. This was Maslama or Musaylima, who had also proclaimed himself a prophet, possibly, according to certain sources, even before Muḥammad. He too recited revelations in rhymed prose, recalling the style of the earliest revelations of the Koran. He too appears to have organized some kind of system of prayer. He was certainly influenced by Christianity and showed marked ascetic tendencies. He forbade wine and prescribed a form of birth control along the traditional Roman Catholic lines, by abstention from sexual intercourse after the birth of one son. He made efforts to come to some arrangement with Muḥammad, but Muḥammad, claiming an exclusive right to receive revelations, rejected his advances and treated him as an impostor. It is not easy to assess the degree of success achieved by his doctrines before the prophet of Medina's death. But we do know that, immediately after this event, he was successful in raising his entire tribe against the Prophet's successors. At one time he allied himself with the prophetess Sajāḥ, who played a similar role in the tribe of Tamīm. This was a nomadic tribe from the region to the east of the Ḥanīfa and equally imbued with Nestorian Christianity. Here again we cannot tell precisely how widespread was conversion to Islam. At all events, some of its leaders treated with Muḥammad. Sajāḥ, who was originally a Christian, was also, it seems, the recipient of revelations in rhymed prose and must have had a certain number of supporters even before the death of Muḥammad, since she was able to sway a substantial portion of the tribe after it. Traditional accounts have attempted to discredit these two prophets of central Arabia and have taken pleasure in creating an obscene picture of the relations between them.

To the north-east, on the borders of the Persian Empire, lived the two tribes of Bakr ibn Wā'il and Taghlib, both of whom were largely Monophysite Christian. Their relations with Persia were sometimes friendly, when the Sassanid Empire was strong or paid them well, and sometimes hostile. We have seen that the Banū Bakr defeated a Persian force at the engagement of Dhū Qār. These tribes appear to have concluded a political agreement with Muḥammad, without many of their members becoming converted to Islam. After Muḥammad's death the Bakr and the Taghlib were the first to attack Persia in the name of Islam. It is not beyond the bounds of possibility that they may have embarked on various pillaging and harrying operations even earlier, encouraged by the collapse of Persia, and, in so far as they really had any close contact with him, by Muḥammad.

But Muḥammad's chief concern was with the region extending northwards from Medina, as far as the frontier of the Byzantine Empire – in other words with the north-west corner of Arabia. His military and diplomatic activities in this direction have already been noted. After the capture of Mecca, however, his interest in this region seems to have increased still more. In effect, the tribes which were converted or which had even concluded a political agreement with him pledged themselves at the very least not to fight amongst themselves. As more and more of Arabia began to conform in one way or another to this peaceable system, the traditional resources derived from raiding enemy tribes started to disappear. Men for whom continual petty skirmishes between rival groups constituted the only manly way of life became idle and felt somehow emasculated. Arabia had too many men and too little cultivable land to feed its population. Moreover, agriculture as a way of life was looked down on. There was only one answer: to direct the warlike energies of the Arabs against the civilized agricultural lands on the edges of the desert – against the Fertile Crescent, which belonged partly to the Byzantine and partly to the Persian Sassanid Empire. There, rich spoils were to be won, and warriors could find glory and profit without risk to the peace and internal security of Arabia. Now Persia was a long way from Medina and divided from it by tribes which, as we have seen, were not always well in hand.

Byzantine Syria and Palestine, on the other hand, were, so to speak, within easy reach. It is unlikely that Muḥammad ever considered actually conquering them, especially at a time when the victorious Heraclius seemed to be restoring Byzantine power to its earlier heights. But there was nothing against sounding out the ground and gaining a little plunder at the expense of frontier regions none too well defended by the Byzantines' Arab auxiliaries, the Ghassānids. Moreover, as we have seen, the Ghassānids had grievances of their own against the empire, and its Monophysite population was virtually in a state of rebellion against the orthodoxy which Byzantium was endeavouring to impose.

With the tribes living along the road to Syria, Muḥammad followed his usual tactics – a mixture of political negotiation and religious proselytizing. Very quickly he got the thing he wanted most: security for his troops travelling that way. Pro-Muslim parties grew up in a number of partly Christian tribes; these were all for strengthening their ties with the 'king' in Medina, and relaxing those which bound them to Byzantium. This policy must have met with some success, especially during the period of Persian ascendancy over Byzantium. At one point Muḥammad even appears to have succeeded in convincing a Ghassānid prince – a vassal of the empire. There were probably some who tried to play a double game. But on the whole the tribes on the edges of the Byzantine *limes* remained Christian and loyal to the empire. Muḥammad only succeeded in making some limited conversions, persuading some Christian communities to pay his protection tax and making alliances with others.

About ten months after the fall of Mecca, he embarked on a great expedition to the north. What was the motive for this campaign? Did he really mean to challenge Heraclius, who was at that time gathering his forces at Emesa (Ḥomṣ)? And if so, was he intending to embark on the vast series of Muslim conquests which would fall to the lot of his successors? Notwithstanding Caetani's views on the subject, this is highly doubtful.[29] His intentions may rather have been to avenge the defeat at Mu'ta on the frontier amīrs and to earn his men some rich pickings. At all events he must have foreseen that he was going to meet strong opposition, because he gathered together an unusually impressive number of men – some twenty or thirty thousand according to our sources, although this is probably an exaggeration. He also borrowed and raised a great deal of money. Contrary to his usual habit he published the object of the expedition. The effect of this was somewhat chilling. A great many Beduin and also some Muslims who were settled in Medina were tired of being so often at war; they wanted to enjoy their new-found wealth in peace at last, and refused to go with the Prophet. The enemy was known to be strong and the objective distant. (There will be more to be said about this opposition, which showed itself even in the armies on the march.) The expedition was ill-prepared and the time hardly propitious. It was gruellingly hot, there was little food, fodder or water to be found, and they could only march at night. Travelling by easy stages, they reached Tabūk, a place some two hundred and fifty miles from Medina, on the borders of the Byzantine Empire. The army stayed there for ten days, some say twenty. Its presence in this place in such strength was something of an achievement, a sign of the power of the Lord of Medina. The petty local princes realized this and came to treat with Muḥammad. In this way he concluded an agreement with Yuḥannā (John), the king of Ayla, ancient Elath – the small town at the end of the Gulf of 'Aqaba, on the northernmost shore of the Red Sea, where Solomon assembled his fleet and where also today Israel has a window on the southern sea. Yuḥannā, who was a Christian and wore a gold cross round his neck, pledged himself to pay three hundred dinars a year. Three Jewish settlements in the region made similar agreements. They were Jarbā and Adhruḥ in Transjordan and Maqnā, a fishing village on the Red Sea. During this same stay at Tabūk, Muḥammad also sent Khālid with a few hundred men to the oasis of Dūmat al-Jandal. Khālid forced the Christian king there to go to Tabūk to treat with Muḥammad and agree to pay the tribute. After these successes in the north, Muḥammad took his heat-oppressed army back to Medina without seeking a battle.

In spite of this curiously partial success at Tabūk, Muḥammad was triumphant. It would certainly be an exaggeration to claim, as tradition has suggested, that Arabia was unified under his dominion; but he had supporters, agents and allies in all the tribes and regions of Arabia, from the Persian and Byzantine frontiers to the distant Yemen, and from the Red Sea to the Persian Gulf. His direct authority extended over a wide area. The ideas and the ritual observances which he had instituted had spread throughout the settled lands and among the Beduin. He was rich and powerful. Nothing could happen in the peninsula without reference to him. The letters said by tradition to have been sent by him to foreign potentates are unlikely to be authentic; but it is quite probable that he made some attempt to enter into diplomatic relations with the neighbouring powers. He may even have been sufficiently naïve to call on them to convert to Islam.

Even so opposition was not dead. It was even gaining a new impetus. The share-out of the spoils at Ji'rāna had been the cause of a great deal of discontent. The gifts made to yesterday's enemies to conciliate them were not at all to the liking of Muḥammad's old supporters. In every party the earliest supporters tend to become a problem; they feel they have earned some rights by their long loyalty and keep fresh the memory of the movement's original principles – so often violated by opportunism, which the leadership is more or less forced to adopt. They fall naturally into opposition and are a favourite target for purges, violent or otherwise. After the capture of Mecca the Qurayshites, who had shown such hatred for Islam and the sincerity of whose conversion might reasonably be open to doubt, had become part of the ruling class of the new state. Plenty of loyalists from the early days found themselves cast in the shade by the wealth and prestige of these new powers. Abū Sufyān, the onetime arch-enemy and husband of the fanatical Hind, was now one of Muḥammad's most trusted advisers. He was pushing his family, the Banū Umayya (the Umayyads), into prominent positions. His son Yazīd became governor of Taymā, and his other son Mu'āwiya, who was later to become supreme head of all the Muslims, was appointed the Prophet's secretary.

At the time of the expedition to Tabūk, the opposition precipitated a real crisis. Many, as we have seen, refused to take part – some, apparently, in defiance of the Prophet's express commands. Secret conclaves were held in the house of a Jewish resident of Medina and Muḥammad had it burned down. 'Alī remained in Medina. Was it really on the Prophet's orders to watch over his family? One source goes so far as to say that those who assembled at the time of departure and then refused to leave were as numerous as the members of the expedition itself. Even some who did go were against it. One of these is said to have railed against those who were learned in the Koran: 'They have the most voracious stomachs of us all, the newest in nobility, and are the most cowardly in battle.' Another added, 'And these are the men who are now put over us to lead us! Muḥammad is right, we are worse than donkeys!'[30] Even on the way, when they were returning, an opposition party planned an attempt on the Prophet's life and wanted him thrown over a cliff. Their plan failed – thanks, it goes without saying, to the intervention of Allah. But who they were – these men, glimpsed only furtively in the dark, with veiled faces – was never known. They may have died in all the odour of sanctity.

It is understandable that on his return from Tabūk the Prophet made up his mind to deal firmly with the opposition. Before his departure he had been petitioned to authorize the building of a place of prayer, a covered mosque for use on rainy days and in winter, at Qubā' on the outskirts of Medina. (An open-air mosque seems to have existed there already.) He had been invited to come and consecrate it by his presence. Busy with his preparations for the expedition, he had answered that he would think about it on his return. On the way, he must have received some information which made him suspect the builders of the new mosque of ulterior motives. If they were unwilling to pray in the existing mosque this might be because they wanted to avoid mixing with the people of a hostile tribe. This was improper in itself, because Islam aimed at abolishing all tribal feuds. But it also meant that they would be on their own and free to hold discussions, and perhaps to conspire away from flapping ears. Muḥammad must have had some reason to suspect these men. Had he been warned of some connection between them and those who had wished to kill him? Was the place a centre of ill-disposed folk, of the kind who had refused to go with him to Tabūk? There seems to have been some suspicion that they were acting on the instigation of Abū 'Āmir (the monk), the Medinan who inclined towards Christianity and was an inveterate opponent of Muḥammad, and who had emigrated to Mecca and tried to suborn the Muslim forces at Uḥud. Had he departed into Syria or was he still in the vicinity?[31] At all events a revelation came.

Those who have made a mosque [for themselves] – out of opposition and unbelief and to divide the Faithful – as a place of ambush for those who formerly made war on Allah and his Messenger, swear: 'Our only object was the most beautiful [the reward of heaven]'; but Allah bears witness that they are lying. You shall not stand in it in any circumstances.

(Koran ix, 108 f.)

From his last halt before reaching Medina, Muḥammad sent two men to set fire to the building. An inquiry was also conducted regarding those who had not taken part in the expedition. A good many came to apologize. Three were sent to coventry. No one was allowed to speak to them. At the end of fifty days the Prophet told them that Allah had finally forgiven them.

Not long afterwards 'Abdallāh ibn Ubayy, the man who had been Muḥammad's chief opponent, died. In a conciliatory spirit Muḥammad attended his funeral and prayed at his tomb. There were protests among the Faithful, and a fight broke out in the cemetery itself. Later a revelation came, forbidding the Prophet to pray in future at the tombs of unyielding 'Doubters' (ix, 85). There was no longer any need for circumspection. The opposition was liquidated. The Prophet's success had rallied the masses to his side. His opponents found themselves isolated, humiliated and powerless. Everyone, whether or not they were sincere, joined Islam. The latent causes of tension remained – they were even to grow; but from now on whenever opposition appeared, whenever a body of opinion developed, it was under the banner of Islam, with argument taken from the Koran or from the Prophet's own example. In future new ideologies, whether based on submission to the state or protest and revolt, would all be Muslim.

The Prophet was growing old. At the time of the expedition to Tabūk he must have been in his sixties. Even so, he had not lost his fondness for women. In the year 8 (629–630), the year of the capture of Mecca, he apparently made two new marriages but both broke up almost at once. The two women in question refused to let him touch them, one because of a hysterical condition, the other because her father had been killed in a skirmish with the Muslims. Muḥammad had no alternative but to divorce them. By this time he seems to have had ten wives, not counting his concubines. At one time he contemplated getting rid of the oldest, Sawda, who was now well into her forties, a ripe old age for Arab women of the time. He did divorce her, but she came back and said to him: 'I am not asking you to sleep with me. I yield my turn to 'Ā'isha. But I want to be there, on the day of Resurrection, among your wives.'[32] He agreed to take her back.

One of his dearest wishes was satisfied at last, although only for a little while. His wives may have given him only daughters but a Coptic concubine who had been presented to him, Māriya, a pretty girl with a white skin and curly hair, finally gave birth to a son. The Prophet called him Ibrāhīm – the Arab version of Abraham, whom he regarded as his precursor.

He probably intended the child to succeed him in his religious and political work. But infant mortality in Arabia was very high. The boy died at the age of seventeen or eighteen months, before he was weaned. His eldest sister Zaynab, one of Khadīja's daughters, had died also (it is not known when), possibly as the result of a miscarriage brought on by a kick from a Meccan. Her sister Umm Kulthūm, another of Khadīja's daughters, who had been married to ʿUthmān, also died during the expedition to Tabūk.

There were problems in the harem. In order to avoid jealousy, Muḥammad spent his nights with each of his wives in turn. Each one, as we have seen, had her own little hut. Following the Prophet, this habit became the Islamic rule; grave lawyers of medieval Islam devoted endless screeds to the proper order to be observed in this regular rotation of marital obligations, laying down conditions and exceptions. One day when Ḥafsa, the daughter of ʿUmar, had gone on a visit to her father, it happened that the Prophet felt in an amorous mood. He made advances to Māriya and they slept together in Ḥafsa's hut. She returned unexpectedly and burst into angry tears. 'In my hut, on my own day and in my own bed!' Tiring of this, Muḥammad promised to have nothing more to do with Māriya and only asked her not to tell the others. But Ḥafṣa could not contain herself. She confided in her fellow wife ʿĀʾisha, who was her particular friend – a friendship cemented by that of their two fathers, ʿUmar and Abū Bakr. ʿĀʾisha was jubilant. She, like the rest of the harem, detested Māriya, the little nobody who had managed to give the Prophet a son. The two women could not conceal their triumph. Muḥammad was furious. He had done his best to pacify his wives, even going so far as to sacrifice the sweet, pretty and fecund Māriya; perhaps his comparatively illicit relations with her had made her all the more attractive. Surely he had done his best? But none of them was in the least grateful. Very well, they would see! He made up his mind to spend a whole month with Māriya and Māriya alone.

The repercussions of this were immense. His marriages were

not simply love matches; they were political alliances. Was all to be ruined because of Ḥafṣa's hysterical behaviour and 'Ā'isha's chattering tongue? According to later reports, 'Umar, Ḥafṣa's father, had this to say about the affair:

'There was [at that time] a rumour abroad amongst us that the Ghassān [the Arab auxiliaries of Byzantium] were shoeing their horses for an attack on us. My friend [this was a man who visited Muḥammad on alternate days to himself] went to the Prophet in his turn. He came back in the evening and knocked urgently on my door, calling out "Is he asleep?" I was afraid; and I went out to him. "Something terrible has happened," he said. I said: "What is it? Have the Ghassān come?" He said: "It is worse than that, and of greater significance; the Messenger of Allah has put away his wives." So Ḥafṣa had been disappointed and had lost. This, I had thought, might very easily happen. I straightened my garments and went to perform the dawn prayer with the Prophet. Afterwards he went into a high room (on the roof) all by himself. I hurried to Ḥafṣa, who was in tears. I said to her, "Why are you weeping? Didn't I warn you? So the Messenger of Allah has repudiated you?" She said: "I do not know. He is in the upper room now." I left her and went to the pulpit [of the mosque]. There were a number of men around it, some of them weeping. I sat down among them for a while. Then I could bear it no longer and went to the upper room where he was. I said to his young black slave: "Ask permission for 'Umar to enter." He went in and spoke to the Prophet; then he came out and said to me, "I announced you, and he said nothing." I went away and sat down with the people who were near the pulpit. Then I could bear it no longer and went [to the upper room]. He announced me [and this was] as the first time. I sat down [again] with the people who were near the pulpit. Then I could bear it no longer. I went to the slave again and I told him: "Ask permission for 'Umar to enter." He announced me as before. I was going away when the slave called me. He told me, "The Messenger of Allah will see you." I went in to him. He was lying on his side, on a mat which was not even covered with a blanket. The weave had left a pattern on his side. He was leaning on his elbow, on a leather cushion stuffed with palm fibre. I greeted him, then, still standing, I said to him,

"You have put away your wives?" He looked up at me and said, "No." Still standing, I went on, trying to soothe him, "Messenger of Allah, if only you had seen me! We others of Quraysh, we know how to control our women. But we have come among people [the Medinans] where it is the women who are in control." '

He described [his difficulties with his own wife who had been led astray by the Medinan example] and the Prophet smiled. 'I said, "If only you had seen me. I have been to Ḥafṣa and told her: 'You must not be led astray if your neighbour is neater and more beloved in the eyes of the Prophet than yourself.' " ' (He meant 'Ā'isha.) 'He smiled again. When I saw him smile, I sat down. Then I looked up and glanced round the room and, by Allah, I saw nothing there worth looking at except three untanned hides. I said, "Call upon Allah and let him give some comfort to your community! He has given affluence to the Persians and the Byzantines, and the world has been given to them when they do not worship Allah!" He was still leaning on his elbow. He said, "Do you doubt, Ibn al-Khaṭṭāb? They are people who have had the good things first, in this world [and they shall have nothing in the next]." I said, "Messenger of Allah, ask Allah to forgive me." '

The Prophet kept himself apart on account of this business, after Ḥafṣa had betrayed him to 'Ā'isha. He had said, 'I shall not go near them for a month,' because he was so extremely angry with them, but Allah admonished him. After twenty-nine days had passed he went first to 'Ā'isha. 'Ā'isha said to him, 'You swore that you would not come near us for a month and tonight makes twenty-nine nights. I have counted them.' The Prophet said, 'But there are twenty-nine days in the month!' And in fact that month there were twenty-nine days.[33]

Allah had intervened in this domestic crisis. It certainly seemed as though nothing which concerned his Messenger was unimportant to him. As on other occasions he reproached him for thinking that he ought not to yield to his inclinations, for having made the concession of promising to leave Māriya, and for having sworn to it:

Prophet, why do you make prohibited that which Allah has

made lawful for you, just to please your wives? Allah is forgiving and merciful. Allah has given you absolution from such oaths. He is your master. He is all-knowing and wise. The Prophet made a story secret to one of his wives and she repeated it, but Allah revealed it to him. . . . If he divorces you, perhaps his Lord will give him instead better wives than yourselves, devout Muslims, believers, prayerful and penitent, pious and given to fasting; women who may be either widows or virgins.

(Koran lxvi, 1–5)

The threat of a general divorce together with this month's example did the trick. His womenfolk became less enthusiastic about arguing with a prophet who was gallantly supported by his God. They let him do as he liked.

All the same it was wiser to keep Māriya apart from all those jealous wives. Muḥammad had found her lodging in the upper quarter of Medina, a long way from his house, with a male Coptic servant to bring her the wood and water she needed for her daily cooking. The wives could do no immediate harm to the lovely concubine, but they spread rumours about the relations between the two Egyptians when no one was there to watch them. In the end Muḥammad became uneasy and sent 'Alī to find out. He appeared sword in hand, scowling, just as the slave was in the act of climbing a palm tree. He slithered to the ground in terror, losing his clothes in the process so that 'Alī was able to see for himself that he was a eunuch and incapable of any threat to his countrywoman's virtue. Everything was for the best.

And so life in Medina went on, divided between the political problems which now involved all Arabia and were even beginning to spread beyond the peninsula, and the tragi-comic dilemmas of everyday life. But Muḥammad was still the Messenger of Allah and his chief duty, as he saw it, was still to teach men the truth about Allah and the proper way to worship him. Ideological unity was to be strengthened, bit by bit, in the interests both of the spread of the true faith and of the solidarity of the Muslim state. We have seen that, after the fall of Mecca, Muḥammad performed (for the second time since his Emigration) the rite of the *'umra*, the ritual processions around the Ka'ba and the journeys between Ṣafā and Marwa, close by the holy place. But he had not participated in the *ḥajj*, the great pilgrimage which took place every year in the month of Dhū l-Ḥijja to the shrines, close to Mecca, on the hills of 'Arafa and Muzdalifa and in the valley of Minā. No doubt the Prophet had long regarded this collection of curious ritual acts as typically pagan, which indeed they were. (At Minā, for example, stones, picked up at Muzdalifa, were thrown at sacred pillars.) Then, after the Jews had rejected him, he turned back to the national shrines and may from the outset have had some idea of depaganizing the *ḥajj*. The matter did not become urgent until after the capture of Mecca. In the following Dhū l-Ḥijja, 'Attāb, the governor whom Muḥammad had installed in Mecca, conducted the ceremony; both Muslims and pagans took part. Their objects in doing so were no doubt different. An earlier revelation was quite explicit. 'Perform the *ḥajj* and the *'umra* for Allah' (Koran ii, 192). For Allah and not for the other divinities. The following year, Dhū l-Ḥijja of the year 9 (March–April 631), Muḥammad still hung back from joining the *ḥajj*. He had not yet finalized his teaching on every detail of the pilgrimage and was unwilling to perform the rites in company with pagans. He sent Abū Bakr to preside over the ceremonies. He was overtaken on the way by 'Alī, who was the bearer of a brand new revelation from on high which it was his business to see implemented. Pagans generally were to take no further part in the pilgrimage. On the expiry of the sacred truce of four months, all who had not been converted or made a special agreement with Muḥammad would be dealt with as enemies. This was the last year that pagans were permitted to join the *ḥajj*.

One year later, in Dhū l-Ḥijja of the year 10 (March 632), the Prophet announced that he would personally conduct the ceremony, now that the temple and shrines were purified of all pagan presence. The news spread, and everyone wanted to take part in this historic event. Muḥammad was accompanied by all his wives and the most eminent of his Companions. He reached Mecca on 5 Dhū l-Ḥijja (3 March). With a great crowd around him, he performed the ceremonies of the *'umra*, the processions around the Ḳa'ba and the seven journeys between Ṣafā and Marwa, without dismounting from his camel. At Ṣafā and Marwa he dismounted and uttered seven times the sacred words: '*Allahu akbar!*' (Allah is greatest). As on his previous visit he would not enter any house, but rested in a tent outside the city. He made it clear that he intended only a brief stay in Mecca. On 8 Dhū l-Ḥijja, the ceremonies of the *ḥajj* began. All eyes were fixed on the Prophet, because his behaviour during the rites would become law. At Minā, 'Arafa and Muzdalifa he performed the accepted rites, the pauses, the prayers, the casting of stones and the sacrifices; but he took care to extend the sacred precincts around the original sanctuaries so as to make it clear that these acts were dedicated to Allah and to the worship of Allah and not to the divinities of those sanctuaries. He took every opportunity to free the rites from all their pagan associations. On the tenth, he had his head shaved according to custom and performed the ritual depurification. In the course of the ceremonies he spoke several times to the crowd. He entered into a dialogue with his assembled followers, and they responded fervently.

'What day is this?' 'The day of sacrifice!' 'What place is this?' 'The holy place!' 'What month is this?' 'The holy month!' 'This is the day of the great pilgrimage. Your lifeblood, property and honour are sacred, as is this place on this day of this month. Have I made [my message] clear?' 'Yes!' 'O God, be my witness!'[34]

Later on, all that could be recalled of these assertions, advice and instructions was collected into one great speech. In it Muḥammad forbade usury and vendettas on account of murders committed during the days of paganism. He repeated the specifications concerning the calendar, the four sacred months and the return to lunar computation. He also pronounced on the mutual duties of husbands and wives. An adulterous wife might be beaten, though not cruelly, and confined to her quarters; but she must be forgiven if she mended her ways. He also uttered a warning against Satan, commended the proper treatment of slaves and preached brotherhood amongst all Muslims. According to one version, he maintained that all men were equal before Allah, without distinction of social class or racial origin.

O people, your Lord is one and your ancestor is [also] one. You are all descended from Adam and Adam was [born] of the earth. *The noblest of you all in the sight of Allah is the most devout. Allah is knowing and all-wise* [Koran xlix, 13]. An Arab is superior to a non-Arab in nothing but devotion.[35]

This version may be suspected of reflecting the preoccupations of a later date; but the Koranic text it cites, while admittedly less explicit, is authentic, and this denunciation of racism placed in the Prophet's own mouth has provided a principle which has been more or less largely adhered to in Islamic practice.

Hardly were the ceremonies completed when the Prophet returned to Medina. He was never to set eyes on his native city again. His life was almost over. This pilgrimage was to remain in Muslim memory as the 'pilgrimage of farewell'.

Barely two months later the Prophet became ill. He had just planned a fresh military enterprise. Another expedition was to be sent northwards, towards the frontiers of the Byzantine Empire. This was to be another raid on a few small towns in Transjordan. So that the death of Zayd, the faithful freedman and adopted son, at Mu'ta in the same region might be properly avenged, the command was entrusted to Usāma, a flat-nosed Negro who was his son by an Abyssinian freedwoman, even though he was only a youth.

The Prophet had been suffering for some time from fever and severe headaches, possibly brought on by the fatigue of the pilgrimage, possibly as a result of a nocturnal visit to the graves of his Companions. He was in such pain that he cried out with it; but all the same he continued spending the night with each of his wives in turn. On Tuesday, 29 Ṣafar in the year 11 (26 May 632) he sent for Usāma and told him that he was putting him in command of the expedition. On the Thursday he presented him with the standard he was to carry and gave him his final instructions. Very soon after this (possibly on the Friday), he was forced to take to his bed. He asked his wives to agree to let him remain in ʻĀʼisha's hut. His legs were shaking so that he had great difficulty in making his way there; a bandage was round his head, and he leaned on ʻAlī and Faḍl ibn ʻAbbās. At first he continued to attend to business, make decisions and send letters. The murmurs aroused by young Usāma's appointment reached him, and he apparently dragged himself out once or twice more, the bandage still round his head, to speak to his followers from the pulpit in the courtyard of his house. The things he said, it was related later, filled the faithful with alarm. Allah had given him a choice between this world and the next. He had chosen the next. Abū Bakr wept and cried out: 'We will ransom you, we and our children.' Muḥammad said to him: 'Gently, gently, Abū Bakr.' He prayed for the dead of Uḥud and publicly confirmed Usāma's appointment, notwithstanding all advice to the contrary. Usāma himself was encamped at the gates of Medina, anxiously awaiting news.

The Prophet's illness grew worse. He began to suffer from fainting fits. Those close to him feared pleurisy. But he insisted that Allah could not subject him to any mortal disease; it was Satan attacking him. Sometimes, also, it is said, he remembered the piece of poisoned meat he had had in his mouth for a moment at Khaybar four years before. While he was unconscious, his wives and his uncle ʻAbbās slipped an Abyssinian remedy into his mouth. When he came to himself, he was very angry at what they had done and forced them, some said, to swallow the medicine themselves. Usāma came from the camp nearby to see him, but he was past speech. He raised his hand towards heaven and then laid it on the young man, who believed that the Prophet was praying for him. He was no longer capable of leading the prayers; for some days Abū Bakr had taken his place, acting on his instructions.

On the morning of Monday, the thirteenth of the month of Rabīʿ I, or 8 June 632, the invalid felt better. At the time for the morning prayer he even managed to get up and, lifting the curtain which served as a door to ʿĀʾisha's hut, appeared on the threshold, while the Faithful were kneeling in the great courtyard. They were awed and delighted. He signed to them to go on with their prayers and smiled to see their zeal, so that to one witness his face appeared more beautiful than ever before. The word went round that the Prophet was better. His wives began to comb their hair. Abū Bakr went off to the outlying district of Sunḥ to visit one of his wives who lived there and who had been somewhat neglected. Usāma expected to be able to announce the departure of his army at any time.

But after returning to his bed Muḥammad grew rapidly worse. He lay with his head in ʿĀʾisha's lap. One of her cousins came in to visit the sick man. He was carrying a sliver of green wood for use as a tooth pick. Picking the teeth was a perfectly natural custom in Arabia, even recommendable in society. ʿĀʾisha noticed her husband's eyes on the toothpick and asked him if he wanted it. He managed to say yes. She took it and, after first chewing it well to make it softer, she gave it to him. He picked his teeth intently.

After a time he became delirious. He apparently asked for materials to write a document which should keep the Faithful from error. Those present were much perplexed at this, wondering whether they ought to trust the abstractedness of a sick man. Supposing that the new text happened to contradict the Koran, surely it would sow the seeds of dissension and dismay? Ought they to obey him when he was not in his right mind? They argued so noisily that he gave up the idea and signed to them to go away.

He was growing steadily weaker; he talked disjointedly with his head on ʿĀʾisha's breast. In a little while she felt his head get heavier and looked at him. He raised his eyes and, staring fixedly at the roof, uttered a few words. She thought she heard him say: 'The highest Companion . . .' and knew that Gabriel had appeared to him. Then she saw that he was dead. She lifted his head and laid it on the pillow; then she began to wail and beat her breast and head. The other wives heard her and joined in. This took place early in the afternoon.

It came as a terrible shock. While neither his disciples nor he himself had ever regarded the Prophet as actually immortal, no one had expected him to die so soon or with so little warning. Everyone, himself included, had thought this nothing more than a passing ailment. No arrangements had been made for the future. This was disturbing enough in itself. How could Allah have failed to warn his Messenger, how could he have failed to pass on to him some instructions for the Faithful, to prepare them for such an unprecedented situation? He had built up a wholly new structure, like nothing which had gone before, with no traditions and no models. With him gone, everything was due to collapse.

'Umar refused to accept the stunning news. He stood squarely in the courtyard of the Prophet's house and harangued the crowds who came running from all directions, among them Usāma's men, who were disbanding and coming in search of news. Muḥammad, he declared, was not dead. He had gone to Allah for a little while, like Moses on Mount Sinai. He would return and cut off the hands and feet of those who had spread the rumour of his death. Abū Bakr had been sent for and came hurriedly from Sunḥ. He went straight into 'Ā'isha's hut and, lifting the cloak which covered the corpse, kissed the dead face of his master and friend. Then he came out and tried in vain to calm 'Umar. After this he spoke authoritatively to the crowd. 'Men,' he said, 'those who worshipped Muḥammad must know that Muḥammad is dead. But for those who worship Allah, Allah lives and will not die.' Then he quoted a verse from the Koran as proof: 'Muḥammad is only a Messenger. The other Messengers have passed away before him. Yet, if he dies or is slain, will you turn back upon your heels?' (iii, 138). The odd thing – which might even look a little suspicious – was that no one had any recollection of this text; but they were impressed by it. There could be no further doubt. ʿUmar collapsed. It was true. The Prophet was dead.

Utter confusion followed. The groups which Muḥammad's strong personality had bound together found themselves suddenly isolated, cut off from one another; each responded in his own way to the events. The Muslim community, based on the close union between an ideology and the structure of an embryonic state, seemed scarcely able to survive. This was the immediate problem facing those with any head for politics and especially the dead man's advisers – the men who had inherited his ideas of government and his faith, which had been formulated from the start as a political doctrine. It was not hard to foresee that the master's death would release the powerful anarchic tendencies of Arab society. The Beduin would renounce Islam and shake the authority of Medina, the Jews would raise their heads again, and the prophets of Yamāma and elsewhere would try to repeat Muḥammad's successes on their own account. What was needed was a firm central kernel to get matters in hand again and carry on the work. Without this, all was lost.

And yet this kernel seemed to be falling apart. The Medinans, especially those belonging to the tribe of Khazraj, sensed that the Qurayshite Emigrants who had come from Mecca with Muḥammad, of whom they had always been jealous, would now attempt to claim the leadership for themselves. The Prophet was dead. There was no longer any reason why they should submit to these foreigners. They called a meeting in the out-house of one of their clans, the Banū Sāʿida, to talk over the best way of safeguarding their interests. What they proposed to do was to elect one of their own leading men, Saʿd ibn ʿUbāda, as chief of Medina. Abū Bakr, who was in Muḥammad's house, was warned of this and hurried to the place along with his fellow politicians, ʿUmar and Abū ʿUbayda. They were joined on the way by the chief of another Medinan tribe, the Aws, rivals of the Khazraj. The last thing they wanted was to see power in the hands of the Khazraj. In the streets the excitement was spreading to the members of other tribes in Medina, who had no desire to play the part of pawns in any power game that was about to begin. As night fell, everyone had forgotten the body still lying in ʻĀʼisha's little hut.

The discussions that went on by the light of torches and oil lamps were lengthy, heated and confused. One Medinan proposed that two chiefs should be elected, one Qurayshite and one Medinan. Most people realized that that would be the way to court dissension and disaster for the community. Everyone was shouting at once; they may even have come to blows. Something had to be done. All these men were dimly aware that the collapse of the system would spell disaster for them. No Medinan would be capable of commanding unquestioning obedience, even in his own city. The tribes not from Medina would refuse to follow anyone who might be suspected of putting the interests of his own tribe first. The ideal candidate was one of those Qurayshites who had been detached from their own tribe by having emigrated long ago and having struggled against it for a long time, one of those who had inherited the dead man's ideas. Abū Bakr proposed ʻUmar or Abū ʻUbayda. The way he spoke, like a thoughtful and intelligent man who did not lose his head in a crisis such as their present one, impressed his hearers. ʻUmar had the reputation of being somewhat hotheaded and his name was received with some reservations. He stood down in favour of Abū Bakr. Late that night it was finally agreed that Abū Bakr should be the 'successor' (*khalīfa*, from which comes our 'Caliph') of the Messenger of Allah. Islam would go on.

Meanwhile the members of Muḥammad's family had assembled in his house. There were ʻAlī his son-in-law, his uncle ʻAbbās, Usāma, the son of his adopted son, and Shuqrān, one of his dependants. They were planning to obtain the dead man's inheritance for the benefit of their own clan, the ʻAbd Manāf of Quraysh. But they had few supporters, apart from a few Qurayshites of good standing such as Ṭalḥa, Zubayr and possibly the compromising Abū Sufyān. Well-intentioned informants brought them word of what was happening at the meeting in the out-house of the Banū Sā'ida. They were furious but powerless. They may have hoped that the time for their revenge would come. For months they refused to recognize Abū Bakr. That night, they did something both unusual and surprising. It might have been expected that the body would be solemnly interred in the cemetery of Baqī', alongside the Prophet's son Ibrāhīm, his daughter Ruqayya and so many of his Companions, as had been done so often before with less distinguished corpses. 'Alī, 'Abbās and their friends seem to have been anxious to avoid such a ceremony in which Abū Bakr, leading the funeral procession, would appear as the Prophet's appointed successor. One thinks of Antony at Caesar's funeral, or Stalin taking advantage in much the same way of the obsequies of Lenin. For whatever reason, they decided to bury the Prophet that same night in the hut in which he had died. They did not even tell 'Ā'isha (who was, after all, Abū Bakr's daughter), who must have been sleeping with one of her fellow-wives when she suddenly heard the sound of the grave-diggers' picks. The body was hastily washed, wrapped in three cloaks and placed in the bottom of the hole, and earth was shovelled over it. That was the end for ever of Muḥammad ibn 'Abdallāh, the Qurayshite.

7

Triumph over Death

IT WAS by no means the end of the Prophet of Islam. In that preposterous and pathetic quest for immortality which moves so large a part of mankind, the founders of ideologies or of states are at a distinct advantage. Their actions and their ideas, over the centuries, are the things that mould history. Muḥammad was both at once, combining Jesus Christ and Charlemagne in a single person.

His life was over; but his greatness was scarcely beginning. He had created an embryonic Arab state inspired by an Arab religion. That this creation fulfilled Arabia's deepest needs is clear, since it survived the terrible crisis which followed his death. Powerful factors, the nature of which I have tried to define, ensured the continuance of an edifice which answered to so many needs. But this pressure of the nature of things could only become a fact if there were men who understood it and translated it into a series of day-to-day political decisions. Muḥammad was lucky enough to find men fitted for the task. He had trained them. Now Abū Bakr, 'Umar and Abu 'Ubayda were there as a bulwark against the forces of disintegration, to maintain political and ideological unity, to drive off enemies and conquer fresh territories for the state and for the faith.

A fortnight after Muḥammad's death, Usāma set out for the Syrian border to accomplish the task the Prophet had assigned to him. Abū Bakr had firmly refused to cancel the expedition or to appoint a new commander. The Messenger of Allah must be obeyed beyond death. In September of the same year Khālid went to put down a revolt of Arabs in opposition. The following year he attacked the Persian Empire while Yazīd, Abū Sufyān's son, whom Abū Bakr had very diplomatically made a general, invaded Byzantine Palestine. The Arab peace, as we have seen, necessitated some external outlet both for the war-like energies of the tribes and to provide booty for them to live on. The Arabs had attacked the peoples of the Fertile Crescent many times before. At best, they had set up small states which were rapidly assimilated by the indigenous civilization, and were rapidly reduced to vassalage and final subject status by the powerful world-wide empires. At worst, they had been driven off or cut to pieces. But this time they had a unified state behind them and an ideology which resisted assimilation. In front of them there were only the crumbling empire of the Sassanids and the Byzantine Empire, which, in spite of its recent successes, was profoundly weakened and divided. As they advanced, armies collapsed before them out of apathy or with the more or less passive abetment of the rebellious and oppressed masses. They remained strong, united, mighty and resolute.

United? Not altogether. The clans, groups and associations of those with similar interests which had existed before Islam and those which had developed with it were breaking up. But the spectre of schism was fearful to all, and the greater part of the Arab masses found themselves united, whether in enthusiasm or resignation, behind the leader of the community. In 37 of the hegira (657), in the first great battle between Muslims, between 'Alī and Mu'āwiya at Ṣiffīn, the horror of the situation came home to them and some of the combatants fastened copies of the Koran to the points of their spears to call a halt to the fratricidal struggle. This was a political manoeuvre; but the appeal for Muslim unity made an impression on everyone and carried the day. They were obliged to stop fighting and resort to arbitration. With the exception of a few diehards, such as those known as the separatists (Khārijites), both sides rallied more or less willingly to the leader whom the current of history, political manoeuvring and the chances of war had placed at their head.

Initially the external successes of the Muslim armies were essentially Arab successes. It was the Arabs who were setting out to conquer the world, pushing further and further forwards as they found nothing capable of resisting them. They overran the weak opposing armies, captured cities, many of which were left open to them, and took in hand the administration of vast areas, the populations of which submitted without a murmur. No change of masters could surprise them. They had seen too many. The old masters had not been loved. A century after an obscure camel-driver named Muḥammad had begun collecting a few poor Meccans round him in his house, his successors were ruling from the banks of the Loire to beyond the Indus, from Poitiers to Samarkand.

It was an Arab empire. 'We Arabs were humiliated, other men trampled us beneath their feet while we trampled no one. Then Allah sent a prophet from amongst us . . . and one of his promises was that we should conquer and overcome these lands.'[1] The Arabs, now wholly Muslim, benefited collectively from the revenues of these vast, fertile lands. They levied a relatively light tax, in return for which the inhabitants were left to cultivate their lands, go about their business and conduct their private affairs as they liked. They were free to speak their own language, worship their own God and follow their own priests. The conquerors shared out the proceeds of this immense enterprise with reasonable fairness. At the head of this empire was the family of Quraysh, which had been the most determined in its opposition to the Prophet – the family of Abū Sufyān, the Umayyads. Its finest administrator was Mu'āwiya, the son of Abū Sufyān and also of Hind, the woman whose hysterical hatred of Islam was such that on the night after Uḥud she had torn out and eaten the liver of the Prophet's uncle Ḥamza, the lion of Allah. It was as if Muḥammad had worked and preached all for the greater glory and profit of his enemies. He had conquered an empire for those who had rejected him, the Quraysh. A not uncommon outcome of revolutions.

But ideas have a life of their own and that life, too, is

revolutionary. Once fixed in men's minds, set down in writing on papyrus, on parchment or even, as was the case with the Koran, on the blade-bones of camels, they continue to work, much to the discomfiture of the statesmen and churchmen who have made use of and canalized them and evolved a sophistry to eliminate those repercussions which could prove a threat to an ordered and well-regulated society. Jesus confronted the Scribes and the Pharisees with the words of the Law and the prophets. Heretics of all descriptions, through the centuries, have used the dynamic text of the Gospels against the rigid establishment of the Church. In decadent republics, protesters of all kinds oppose their governments with the Declaration of the Rights of Man. Lenin waved the ardent, revolutionary prose of Marx in the faces of the pundits of social democracy. The opponents of Stalinist oppression recalled the declarations of Lenin. And so history is made – by a torrent of live, boiling forces, which the hierarchies are constantly, yet vainly in the long run, striving to suppress.

So it was with Islam. The Koran, the incontrovertible word of Allah, passed down to generation after generation the message of an oppressed man who, at a given moment, had turned against injustice and oppression. It carried in the chaotic mixture of its text much invective and defiance of the mighty, and many appeals for justice and the equality of men. The day came when men were found to take up these words and make them into weapons. Arab rulers did not, as it has been believed in Europe, impose conversion by force. On the contrary, they strongly disapproved of it. It was a way by which men avoided taxation, and united with the Arabs on the receiving end, and thereby doubly reduced the share of the cake available to each Muslim. But how was it to be prevented? In Umayyad times some Christians, Jews or Mazdaeans who wanted to be converted to Islam were flogged; but this kind of scandal could not go on indefinitely. There was nothing in the Koran, or in the example of Muḥammad, to confine the knowledge of the truth of Allah to Arabs alone. Admittedly the last argument was illogical; but lack of logic has never been regarded as a political impediment. What was more important was that exclusion of non-Arabs undermined the fundamental ideology on which the empire was built. Moreover, Arab customs accepted and encouraged the adoption, by every clan, of people of all kinds and every nationality, who then became wholly Arab. The tide of conversions swelled slowly and then became an irresistible torrent. Persians, Syrians, Egyptians, Berbers, Goths, Greeks and a host of others joined the Arabs, considered themselves as Arabs and really became Arabs. But still greater numbers became Muslims.

Of thc new Muslims, those who were only arabized in a partial sense or not at all did not submit readily to Arab rule. They became the best students of the sacred text, of the story of the Prophet and of old Arabia. They created Arab philology and Muslim theology. Making use of the cultural heritage of all the nations from which they sprang, mingling ideas, techniques and examples, they laid the basis of Muslim art, Muslim science, Muslim philosophy, Muslim civilization. The original Arabs, now polished and refined, also had a share in this collective creation; but they had been obliged to accept equality with the men they had conquered – many of whom were now wholly indistinguishable from them. The revolutionary movement which enforced this equality triumphed in the name of the very values which had allowed the Arabs to conquer. It took as its banner the Koran, the Prophet as its pledge and example. Many another movement which rocked Islam through the centuries was to do the same.

At the bottom of all this – transformed, certainly, and redesigned to fit in with new ways of thought – were the ideas which had obsessed Muḥammad ibn ʿAbdallāh. Somewhere, at the root of these varyingly successful movements, these more or less justifiable, more or less inadequate concepts, there was the man who had been an obscure camel-driver from a humble family of Quraysh. How precisely are we to estimate his contribution, the legacy he left, the way in which human history was altered because he lived and because his life was as it has been described? For faithful Muslims, his coming marks a reversal, a revolution, a major turning-point. Before was ignorance and darkness, tempered only by faint lightning flashes diffused by the imperfect teaching of the Jewish and Christian revelations. Afterwards was the reign of truth, normality and divine Law – just, wise, reasonable, not always adhered to, to be sure, but always held up as a standard, a norm, something to fall back on, and in this way making its mark on men's actions, influencing events and bending human history for the good.

Inevitably the historian regards things in a much more complex way. He cannot extricate himself by assuming some kind of primitive determinism or an elementary form of Marxism: if Muḥammad had never been born, the situation would have called forth another Muḥammad in his place. No, things would certainly have been very different. We can speculate indefinitely on what would have become of the two great empires and of Arabia. A different Muḥammad, coming twenty years later, might perhaps have found the Byzantine Empire consolidated, ready to fight off the attacks of the desert tribes successfully. Arabia might have been converted to Christianity. The situation called for solutions to a number of crucial problems, as we have seen; but these solutions might easily have been quite different ones from those that actually occurred. A different throw of the dice and chance takes another turning.

We do not know what might have been; but we do know what was. And Muḥammad's legacy was considerable. Certainly he did not foresee, especially at the beginning, what was to come of his slightest decisions. The chain of events was such that each choice of his, however trivial and commonplace for anyone else, had enormous repercussions for millions of men and women yet unborn. There were days when everything depended on which way he walked down some back alley in Mecca, while if he had been killed at Badr, though the technological development of humanity in general and its advance towards more productive forms of economy would probably not have been noticeably affected, how much else would have been different, from western Europe to the Philippines!

But for him it is unlikely that an Arab empire, which he probably never foresaw, would ever have come into being. This vast political unit, which was later confined to an ideological and cultural unity, made possible a strong interplay of men and methods, ideas and ways of life from China to Spain, the birth of a new civilization with its own moral, artistic and ideological values. Each element of this civilization was drawn from its own complex origins, an origin in which Muḥammad and ancient Arabia often figured only in a small way, if at all; but their development, association and expansion would not have come about without the previous activities of the Prophet of Quraysh.

In some way, then, and in some degree, all this history starts with him. From him sprang the Arab influence on twenty different lands, from the banks of the Tigris and Euphrates to the Atlantic; the severance of the links between the Latin west, cut off from North Africa, and the newly Arab east; all the Muslim empires and kingdoms down to the Ottoman Empire, which threatened Vienna. From him came the knights and seamen, the merchants and the pirates, the artists in bronze engraving and the inspired architects, the Mosque of Cordoba and the Taj Mahal.

Next we come, more immediately and with greater certainty, to the Prophet's spiritual and ideological legacy. It is not true, as the Faithful believe, that the entire mental landscape of Islam is derived from the ideas he expressed. As we shall see in a moment, there are many other sources for this body of thought. Over the centuries, thousands of ideas have been consecrated by being attributed to the Prophet: although actually inspired by the spirit of the times and by the widest cultural influences, they have nevertheless been blanketed with his authority. And yet, in spite of everything, these alien ideas have been made to fit in more or less with a pre-existing system, and this system was the one which he had evolved, gradually, by taking and transforming the ideas he found in his surroundings according to the pattern of his own mind. In this way, his ideas have permeated all later Muslim ideology. But, more than all this, there is still the Koran, the product, as I have said, of his unconscious mind; the Koran, read, re-read, recited, intoned and learned by heart from childhood by all his followers. For educated Muslims, with access to other books and open to other influences, the part played by the Koran is a considerable one. For how many millions of simple souls has it represented the one source of any kind of higher ideas, the sole point of reference, whether ideological, moral or spiritual? In this way, Muḥammad's mental world exerts a direct effect on the mind of the peasant, just as it does on the philosopher or statesman, and in the most immediate and straightforward manner. This effect can be felt with great intensity. Hence a direct, crushing, terrified apprehension of what seems to be divine reality, a feeling of helplessness in the hands of an implacable master, and a surrender to his incomprehensible will. But hence, also, an active and positive orientation towards the realities of human existence, an earnest endeavour to shape them to one's liking, a refusal to be filled with anguish or despair, a rejection of suffering and a hedonistic eagerness to enjoy life and its pleasures to the full extent permitted by God's will; hence too an intense but fairly brief moral consciousness, which is, to our way of thinking, a little too readily accessible to reason, a little too resigned to human imperfection, a little lacking in that desperate concern in face of the impossible demands of perfection – that tragic and heroic tension which Jesus has accustomed us to regard as necessary for a deeply moral life.

Man does not live by bread alone. In order to live he needs at least a few guiding principles concerning his place and role in the world, a few rules by which to direct his brief existence. Before modern ideologists, it was the prophets and religious reformers who offered to the mass of the people a satisfactory system compounded of certain of these principles and rules. Religious people today, Muslims as well as others, have a tendency to retain only the moral precepts of their faith and to regard the ideas as of less importance, even as symbolic or wholly negligible. Hence their indignation when such as ourselves, who concentrate first and foremost on studying the origin of ideas and their connection with the conditions of the period which gave them birth, have a tendency to treat as banal and uninteresting that aspect of the moral teaching which is universal and seize only on what is specific and consequently depends to the greatest extent on conditions of time, place and social background. For them Muḥammad is, above all else, the one who required them to be just and upright and good. It is necessary to understand this point of view too. We could certainly show that preaching of this kind has frequently also acted as a cover for submission to an established order and, as a result, for resignation to injustice. Nowadays we may prefer a more overt morality, one less bound up with irrational taboos. Above all, we may condemn ideas which look to us like myths. But for many centuries this broader morality and our more accurate concept of the world were unattainable by the millions hungry for justice, for peace, for elementary guidance to enable them to lead a decent life, and for simple ideas to give a meaning to their life on earth. We have seen with our own eyes the birth and development of ideologies, some of which have been based on broad principles and accurate information scientifically worked out. Yet even so they have engendered their own myths, their own narrowness and iniquities. Let us not, therefore, deal too arrogantly or severely with past ideologies, which have given so many men something to live for and, if one may be permitted a guess at the future, will continue to do so in some form or other for a long time to come. And let us, without undue naïvety or too many illusions, acknowledge the greatness of the creators of the systems which have played so large a part in the world; and among them, Muḥammad.

For those under attack by his followers, and for the Christians in particular, he became the arch-enemy, an object of execration, an epileptic fraud. The accounts given of him by his disciples were taken and twisted to make a hideous portrait of a cruel and lascivious individual, steeped in every kind of viciousness and crime, who borrowed his few ideas shamelessly from erring Christians and drew his credulous followers to him by means of conjuring tricks. Popular legend went still further. He was said to have once been a good Christian and to have converted many souls to the Christian faith. Some even had it that he was a cardinal. But the Church failed to award him what he regarded as due recognition for his services. Another man was elected Pope. And so, driven by pride which made him determined to be first, he founded a schismatic religion and led many astray. It is the way of successful ideologies to explain away all dissidence by pride; it is a good way of praising the humble conformity of the obscure disciple. Some went on to say that he got drunk and was devoured by pigs, thus explaining his followers' dislike of this animal. Some – we find an example of this in the *Chanson de Roland* – saw him as a pagan god, an idol who was the object of the disgusting worship of the 'mahomeries'.

Adherents, on the other hand, grew in numbers from one century to the next. The ideology which provided millions of Muslims with their purposes in life was, after all, wholly dependent on this one man who was the last mouthpiece of the word of Allah. As he had been the source of the Muslim community, so he remained the symbol of its ideological unity. As it found fewer leaders to absorb its devotion, fewer 'charismatic' personalities endowed with divine graces to receive its respect and reverence, the more it tended to fill the gap with the idealized figure of its departed founder. The smallest details of his behaviour served as a model for all to follow. All courses, standards or ideas could be defended by attributing their origin to his words or actions. He had laid down the rules for divorce and for government, just as he had shown how one should behave oneself at table, blow one's nose or make love. As a man, he had been perfect and beyond criticism. In spite of his own express denials, he was credited with an increasing number of miracles. 'No prophet has ever performed miracles that our Prophet has not performed the like of,' wrote the Moroccan *qāḍī*, 'Iyāḍ, at the beginning of the twelfth century. Arab folklore, Jewish, Christian, Mazdaean and even Buddhist legend were all pressed into service to provide him with a miraculous life story that should be worthy of him and of Islam.

When he was born, the palace of the Persian emperor trembled, fourteen of its towers fell, the Mazdaean sacred fire went out, a lake was dried up, a marvellous light shone from his mother's breast and its brightness spread as far as Syria, and the stars came so close that one witness was afraid they would fall on him. It was said of him that his body threw no shadow, that the flies would not settle on his garments, and that when his hair fell in the fire it did not burn. A fantastic tale grew up from one verse of the Koran according to which Allah had made the moon serve him. To convince the Meccans, the moon, at the Prophet's summons, travelled seven times around the Ka'ba and then split in two. She paid homage to Muḥammad 'in a voice which could be heard by all, from the farthest to the nearest'. One half of the moon went up his right sleeve and emerged from his left, the other did the same thing in reverse. Gabriel brought him five apples from the celestial gardens, one for himself and one for each of the first four Caliphs. His apple spoke to him, singing of his glory and enumerating the marvels which attested his mission.

Poets and prose writers sang his praises. Here, for instance, is what Būṣīrī, a devout Egyptian Berber poet, said of him in the thirteenth century:

Muḥammad is lord of two worlds, and two species having
weight [men and genii],
Of two [human] groups, the Arabs and the Foreigners.
It is he, our prophet, who commands and forbids: none
Is more truthful than he, in his yea and his nay.
He is the beloved [of God] whose intercession is to be hoped
for,
Against all sudden terrors . . .
He has surpassed all prophets in his powers of body and mind,

And they cannot equal him in knowledge or in greatness of soul . . .
There is no one whose virtues are like his:
He possesses the undivided essence of all goodness . . .
If the greatness of his miracles were equal to his lofty status,
The invocation of his name would make dry bones live . . .
He is as a flower for sweetness, the full moon for splendour,
The sea for generosity and time for the magnitude of his plan . . .[2]

To take another random example, an Egyptian mystic of the same period named Dīrīnī records some traditions that were current about him.

Muḥammad said: 'The first light which Allah created was my light.' They say that when Allah created his divine Throne he wrote on it in letters of light: There is no God but Allah and Muḥammad is the Messenger of Allah. When Adam went out of Paradise he saw the name of Muḥammad coupled with the name of Allah written on the leg of the Throne and everywhere in Paradise. He said: 'Lord, who then is this Muḥammad?' Allah, the Most High, answered him: 'He is thy descendant and, but for him, I should not have created thee.' Then Adam said: 'By the holy nature of this child, have mercy on the father.' Then a voice cried out: 'O Adam! Had you but called on Muḥammad to intercede with Us, from all the inhabitants of heaven and earth, then We should have granted it. . . .' Among the signs of his mission are that he made water spring from between his fingers and made it into many times more by his *baraka*, on many occasions which are set down in authentic traditions. One of these tells how they were at Zawrā', in the bazaar of Medina. When the time came for the afternoon prayer, he put his hand in a jar and about three hundred men performed the rite of ablution with the water. Anas said: 'I have seen water spout from between his fingers. . . .' Also among these signs was the *baraka* for multiplying food so that it would feed a host of people and keep for a long time. He had gone into the house of Abū Ṭalḥa where there was some barley bread. He asked for the loaves and crumbled them, after which melted fat was poured over them. Then he pronounced the words that Allah willed and then said: 'Invite ten men to come in.' They were invited and they ate their fill. Then they went out and ten more were asked and so on until all had eaten and they were about eighty . . .

The animals sang his praises and reproached those who did not follow him.

The words of the wolf to Uhbān ibn Aws are well known. He was pasturing his flock. The wolf stopped before him and said to him: 'What is so astonishing about you is that you sit there pasturing your flocks and neglect a prophet, more mighty than whom Allah has never sent, a prophet to whom the gates of Paradise have been opened, whence its inhabitants look down from on high at the battle of his Companions. There is nothing between you and him but this flock and, but for that, you would be among the armies of Allah.' Uhbān went and was converted.

His virtues and merits were endless.

He bears witness for those who believe in him and are guided by him and against those who deny him and are hostile to him, he brings the good news of the divine reward to whoever obeys his Master, he announces the punishment of whoever prefers to follow his own desires. He has called on Allah with his permission, giving proofs of his power; he is the torch to light the way for the man who believes in him and searches for his light; and such a man shall see the broad way. His light has continued from the days of Adam. . . . Adam knew him and made him his intermediary to intercede with Allah. . . . He surpasses the other prophets as the sun surpasses the moon and as the sea surpasses the drop of water. . . . He is the pole of their authority, the essence of their decree, the finest pearl in the necklace they form, the impress of their setting, the most perfect verse of their poem, the centre of their circle, the sun of their morning, the crescent moon of their night. . . . Rise, *imām* of the earth, and lift yourself up to the supreme royalty, become *imām* of the people of heaven. . . . The archangels have come to greet the supreme head, his light is brighter, his evidence more dazzling, the secret he holds more manifest, his power and his merit more lofty, his fame more lovely, his aspect more pleasing, his religion more perfect, his speech more eloquent, his prayer more effective, his knowledge higher, his voice better heard, his requests better satisfied, his intercession more efficacious; his help is strong, his name is 'praised' [*muḥammad*], his body is most pious. . . . He is the beloved of the Master, he is the most endowed with virtues, with all the Faithful . . .[3]

There is a highly detailed description of a journey he made to heaven one night while his body lay on his bed, guided by Gabriel mounted on the woman-headed mare Burāq. Books were written about it. One was translated into Latin in medieval times and may have inspired Dante. It was certainly known to Tuscan poets in his time. In each of the seven heavens he met the prophets who had gone before him, and angels of immense stature appeared before him. Gabriel expounded the secrets of heaven and hell. He came before Allah himself, who placed his hand on his head so that he should be permeated with divine wisdom.[4]

Mystics, theologians and philosophers have speculated and refined upon his role, his qualities and the meaning of his coming. For the great Spanish mystic Muḥyī ad-Dīn ibn al-'Arabī, his well-known fondness for women was a symbol of the fondness of the whole for the parts, of the love of God for his creatures and his desire for them to be united with him. For the mystics, 'everything – heavens, earth, angels, men, jinns – was created from the spirit, soul, heart and flesh of Muḥammad' (L. Gardet).[5]

The ordinary people honour and respect him. His name is never spoken or written without being followed by some words of praise: 'May God's blessing and peace be upon him.' Men swear by his name. Many refrain from eating any food that he did not eat. The orientalist Edward W. Lane was admiring some very pretty *nargileh* pots in a Cairo bazaar one day. He asked the potter who had made them why he had not put his own mark on them. 'God forbid,' the man replied. 'My name is Aḥmad [one of the names attributed to the Prophet]. Would you have me put it in the fire?'[6]

There was a widespread belief that to have the same name as the Prophet entitled the bearer to a special indulgence on the part of Allah.[7] But 'Umar tried to have it forbidden, because it might result in people abusing, insulting or mocking the name 'Muḥammad'. Indeed, there have been occasions on which non-believers who have said, for instance, that a particular 'Muḥammad' lied have found themselves in serious trouble; as for insults to the Prophet himself, these, according to religious law, are punishable by death. At a conference in Beirut not so very many years ago, a European professor caused a great furore merely by quoting, purely as historical evidence and with no personal intent, some medieval Christian abuse of Muḥammad. The matter became a diplomatic incident.

For a long time the belief was held that it was generally irreligious to smoke or drink coffee, because both these habits were unknown in the Prophet's time. People used to wear plaques, medallions or stones inscribed with descriptions of his physical and spiritual perfections and anticipate miraculous effects. It was recorded that he had said:

> If any man shall see the description of my qualities after me, it shall be as if he had seen me; and he who shall look at it with love for me shall be kept by Allah from hell fire – he shall be spared the ordeal of the grave and shall not be naked on the Day of Resurrection.[8]

His names were piously enumerated and found to number ninety-nine, like the names of Allah. People carry them as amulets and pendants. Everywhere popular poets, orators and street singers bawl his praises to awed and attentive audiences.

The Prophet's descendants, the members of his own family, have special privileges. They make up the class of *sharīf* (noblemen) and *sayyid* (lords). They are entitled to respect, reverence and love. Their injustice and their excesses must be borne with. None shall endure the pains of hell because the Prophet had said: 'All ties of kinship by blood or marriage shall be undone on the Day of Resurrection, except for mine.' They marry among themselves in order to preserve the purity of the sacred blood. In certain countries they have exploited their descent to acquire power and wealth. The Shī'ite confession, the official religion of Iran since the sixteenth century, credits the *imāms*, who are the successive first-born descendants of the Prophet in each generation, with infallibility and supernatural graces. In the tenth century, when the Negro Kāfūr, the omnipotent ruler of Egypt, was riding through the streets and let his whip fall to the ground, a *sharīf* picked it up and handed it to him. At this he exclaimed: 'Now I can die. What more is there to hope for in life when a descendant of the Messenger of God has handed me my whip?' And, the story goes on to say, so he did die, not long afterwards.

Stones he sat on or leaned against are venerated. One of these, at Maḥajja in the Ḥawrān,[9] was supposed to bring ease in childbirth. Not far off, at Mālikiyya, there used to be a sacred wooden bowl from which he had eaten. At Qubā' one was shown a well into which he spat, whereupon its brackish water grew sweet. In Jerusalem, in Damascus, at Dībīn in the Ḥawrān and in numerous other places one could see and may still see the print of his foot in stones, since, it was said, whenever he stepped on a rock his foot sank into it, leaving an indelible mark. In about 1200 one of his descendants carried a relic of this kind about with him and made money from it. Many of the same kind can still be seen in India to the present day.[10] His birthplace in Mecca was turned into a mosque and was especially honoured. In 1184 the Spanish pilgrim Ibn Jubayr came to marvel at the green marble slab ringed with silver, which marked the exact spot. 'We rubbed our cheeks', he wrote, 'on that holy place where the most illustrious of new-born babes dropped to the ground and which was touched by the purest and noblest of all infants.'[11] A multitude of relics of him are preserved everywhere: hairs, teeth, sandals, his cloak, his prayer rug, a sword hilt, an arrow used by him. Constantinople, when it had become the capital of the Muslim world, boasted of the number of these relics to be found there. Two hairs from his beard were kept there in forty bags sewn one inside the other, and were solemnly shown to worshippers once a year.

Popular piety went so far sometimes as to constitute a threat to monotheism similar to that of which the Koran accused the Christians and the Jews. One commentator had actually explained a verse of the Koran by claiming that Allah had seated the Prophet by him on his Throne! The venerable theologian Ṭabarī (*c.* 900) protested, and the Faithful of Baghdad stoned the door of his house.[12] In a number of places an invocation in honour of the Prophet was early inserted into and alongside the ritual prayers. This invocation was credited with miraculous virtues. It came to be said that eighty 'blessings' of this sort equalled the remission of eighty sins, or even of the sins of eighty years. A mystic saw a being of light step between himself and the avenging angel in the next world; it was a being formed of the countless 'blessings' he had recited during his life in the Prophet's honour. Moreover, Muḥammad himself interceded with God in person from Paradise, where his soul dwelt, while his body remained miraculously uncorrupted in the grave.

In Medina, the humble grave where his body had been laid to rest so furtively had become the spiritual centre of a mosque adorned with gold, silver, marble, mosaics and diamonds. The rulers of Islam have heaped rich gifts upon it and vied with one another in embellishing it. Beside the Prophet lie his companions Abū Bakr and ʿUmar. There is a popular legend that a place is still reserved there for Jesus, when he returns at the end of time.[13] After pilgrimage to Mecca, the majority of pilgrims go on to Medina to visit this tomb. Did the Prophet not say: 'If any man visits me after my death, it shall be as if he had visited me in my life'? The following advice is given by a modern Muslim.

You go into the Mosque . . . and walk towards the tomb. [ʿĀʾisha's hut] is now a room with only one door, which is not opened except on important occasions. The exterior walls are hung with long green curtains. A dark narrow passage surrounds it, into which no light can reach. On one side, the only one you will see, there rise magnificent screens of delicate workmanship, divided by pillars the bases of which, unlike the rest, are of white marble decorated with gold fluting. These white pillars, which are seen again in the breadth of the gallery, mark the boundary of the 'noble garden' (*rawḍa ash-sharīfa*) – the mystic, spiritual garden. To say one's prayers there, according to tradition, is like praying in paradise. And so you will not behold the Prophet's tomb.

The present-day reformist, fearful of idolatry, goes on to add: 'You stand upright before the screen and do not pray. Prayer is reserved for God. . . . But you will not lack pious thoughts (which you will utter softly), that will pay great honour to the Messenger of God' (J. Roman).[14]

The same fear – inspired, it must be admitted, by a faithful adherence to the truth of Muḥammad's message in the face of the cult dedicated to the Prophet by the ignorant masses – has driven some reformists to more radical measures. When the puritan Wahhābi armies captured Medina in 1804, they demolished as many as they could of the domes which had been raised over the sacred tomb and carried off all the valuables. But nothing has been able to root out the pious veneration of the masses for the man to whom they owe their faith; and this piety will find an outlet. How can it do so except in forms which appear vulgar to the élite?

Not all the Faithful can go to Medina; yet all want to display their reverence for the Prophet at frequent, regular intervals. Some centuries after the hegira – the exact date is not known – a festival of the birthday of the Prophet was initiated and spread rapidly. It was fixed arbitrarily for a Monday, the twelfth of the month of Rabīʿ I. It was on a Monday that he died and on a Monday also that he set out on his Emigration to Medina. The festival differs in detail from one place to another, but in most places there are torchlight processions, free meals for the poor; sweets are distributed to all and sundry and traders put up tents and stalls, which are lit by lanterns after dark, for the sale of coffee and sweetmeats. There are rope dancers, snake charmers, story-tellers and entertainers of every description. Children are dressed up in new clothes and people exchange visits, let off fireworks, drench themselves in scent and show themselves off on richly caparisoned horses.

It is all fantastically gay. The members of mystic brotherhoods pass by in procession, calling on the names of Allah and of Muḥammad over and over again, waving their arms with an abandon which soon turns to delirium, then falling into trances and uttering religious cries. In Cairo a shaikh on horseback used to ride over the backs of several dozen prostrate dervishes. Everywhere men recite a constant stream of prayers, litanies, songs and poems to the glory of the Prophet. Speakers demonstrate how the world was plunged in darkness and ignorance before the coming of Muḥammad, and how he brought the light of truth to shine in the hearts of men.[15] In Turkey they recite the celebrated poem by the dervish Sulaymān Chelebi, composed at the beginning of the fifteenth century (with additions by other poets of the same period). They sing, also, of the birth of the Prophet.

All things created joyfully acclaimed him,
Sorrow was done, new life the world was flooding.
The very atoms joined in mighty chorus,
Crying with sweetest voices: Welcome, welcome!
Welcome, O matchless sultan, thou art welcome!
Welcome, O source of knowledge, thou art welcome! . . .
Welcome, thou, Nightingale of Beauty's garden!
Welcome, to him, who knows the Lord of Pardon,
Welcome, thou, moon and sun of God's salvation,
Welcome, who knowst from Truth no deviation.
Welcome, the rebel's only place of hiding,
Welcome, the poor man's only sure confiding . . .[16]

While Christianity regarded him as the arch-enemy, evil and lascivious, and while Islam was extolling him as 'the best of all created things', other men appeared who, with little understanding of religious faith and of Islam less than any, tried to find in him a man who thought and moved on the same level as themselves. The Comte de Boulainvilliers, early in the eighteenth century, hailed him as a free-thinker, the creator of a religion of reason. Voltaire used him as a weapon against Christianity by making him a cynical impostor who yet managed to lead his people to the conquest of glory with the help of fairy stories. The eighteenth century as a whole saw him as the preacher of natural, rational religion, far removed from the madness of the Cross. The Academies praised him. Goethe devoted a magnificent poem to him, in which, as the very epitome of the man of genius, he is compared to a mighty river. The rivers and streams, his brothers, call on him to help them reach the sea which is waiting for them. Majestic, triumphant, irresistible, he draws them onwards.

> Und so trägt er seine Brüder,
> Seine Schätze, seine Kinder
> Dem erwartenden Erzeuger
> Freudebrausend an das Herz.

('And thus he carries his brothers, his treasures, his children, all tumultuous with joy, to their waiting Parent's bosom.' [Trans., Dr David Luke])

Carlyle puts this great soul among the heroes of mankind in whom some spark of divinity is to be seen. After him the scholars came to reconstruct the story of his life from the early sources, from a closer and closer study of the Arab historians. The Arabist Hubert Grimme, at the end of the nineteenth century, saw him as a socialist who was able to impose fiscal and social reform with the help of a (strictly minimal) 'mythology', invented deliberately to terrify the rich and enlist their support. Whereas the majority of orientalists endeavour to temper their judgements and to highlight his religious fervour, the Belgian Jesuit Henri Lammens, with his extensive knowledge of the sources (but with deadly hatred, too), still expresses bitter doubts as to his sincerity. Russian scholars argue whether he was a reactionary or a progressive. Nationalists, socialists and even communists in Muslim countries claim him for their own.

Everyone, in fact, has sought in him a reflection of their own doubts and anxieties and those of their time. Everyone has ignored what they have not understood. Everyone has shaped him after their own passions, ideas or fantasies. I do not claim to be immune from this general rule. But even if pure objectivity is unattainable, it would be a sophism to suggest that it was necessary instead to be deliberately partial. We know very little for certain about this man whose ideas and actions have shaken the world, but, as with Jesus, we may get, through the unreliable tales and one-sided traditions, a glimpse of something that is the echo of a remarkable personality which astonished the ordinary men who gathered around it. It is this echo, as I believe I have glimpsed it, that I have tried to capture in this book. The picture is not a simple one. It is neither the satanic monster of some or the 'best of all created things' of others, neither the cold-blooded impostor nor the political theorist, nor the mystic wholly in love with God. If we have understood him rightly, Muḥammad was a complex man, full of contradictions. He was fond of his pleasures, yet indulged in bouts of asceticism. He was often compassionate, yet sometimes cruel. He was a believer, consumed with the love and fear of his God, and a politician ready for any expedient. Without any great gift of eloquence in ordinary life, he was able for a short period to produce, from his unconscious, phrases of disturbing poetic quality. He was cool and nervous, brave and timid, a mixture of cunning and frankness, forgiving and at the same time capable of terrible vindictiveness, proud and humble, chaste and sensual, intelligent and, in certain things, oddly stupid. But there was a power in him which, with the help of circumstances, was to make him one of the rare men who have turned the world upside down.

Ought we to be surprised at these complexities and contradictions, this mixture of strength and weakness? He was, after all, a man like other men, subject to the same weaknesses and sharing the same powers, Muḥammad ibn 'Abdallāh of the tribe of Quraysh, our brother.

Notes and References

CHAPTER 1: *Introducing a World*

1. J. W. McCrindle, trans., *The Christian Topography of Cosmas, an Egyptian Monk*, London, Hakluyt Society, 1897, p. 71 (113B–C).
2. ibid., pp. 119–21 (169B–D).
3. Ethérie, *Journal de voyage*, ed. and French trans. Hélène Pétré, Paris, Éditions du Cerf, 1948, pp. 268 f.
4. C. Diehl, *Les grandes problèmes de l'histoire byzantine*, Paris, A. Colin, 1943, pp. 15 f.
5. Ethérie, op. cit., p. 269.
6. cf. F.-M. Abel, *Revue biblique*, 1931, pp. 1–31; Procopius, *De Aedificiis*, V, ix, ed. and trans. H. B. Dewing and Glanville Downey, London, Heinemann (Loeb Classical Library), 1940.
7. Ethérie, op. cit., XX, 12.
8. A. Christensen, *L'Iran sous les Sassanides*, Paris, Geuthner, 1944, p. 397.
9. Tha'ālibī, *Histoire des rois des Perses*, ed. and French trans. H. Zotenberg, Paris, Imprimerie nationale, 1900, pp. 698 f.
10. McCrindle, op. cit., p. 72 (113D).
11. Theophylact Simocatta, *Historiae*, IV, 11, ed. C. de Boor, Leipzig, Teubner, 1887, p. 169; cf. G. E. von Grunebaum, *Medieval Islam*, Chicago, University Press, 1953.
12. Ethérie, op. cit., I, 1.
13. ibid., III, 1–2.
14. ibid., III, 8.
15. Procopius, *De Aedificiis*, V, viii, 7–9, ed. cit., pp. 356–7; translation of this passage from P. N. Ure, *Justinian and His Age*, Harmondsworth, Pelican Books, 1951, pp. 239–40.

CHAPTER 2: *Introducing a Land*

1. Ammianus Marcellinus, *Historiae*, XIV, iv, 4, ed. and trans. J. C. Rolfe, London, Heinemann, and Cambridge, University Press (Loeb Classical Library), 1935, vol. I, pp. 27–30.
2. Ammianus Marcellinus, *Historiae*, XXXI, xvi, 6, ed. cit., vol. III, pp. 500–503.
3. Ammianus Marcellinus, *Historiae*, XXIII, vi, 45–7, ed. cit., vol. II, pp. 374–7, slightly modified.
4. cf. Jacques Ryckmans, 'Le Christianisme en Arabie du Sud préislamique', in *L'Oriente cristiano nella storia della Civiltà*, Rome, Accademia nazionale dei Lincei, 1964, pp. 413–53.
5. McCrindle, op. cit., p. 73 (113D–116A).

CHAPTER 3: *Birth of a Prophet*

1. R. Blanchard, in *Géographie Universelle*, ed. P. Vidal de la Blache and L. Gallois, vol. VIII, Paris, A. Colin, 1929, p. 172.
2. Ibn Hishām, *Sīra, Das Leben Muhammeds*, ed. F. Wüstenfeld, Göttingen, 1859–60, p. 101.
3. Ibn Sa'd, I, ii, *Ṭabaqat*: *Biographien Muhammeds, seiner Gefahrten . . .*, ed. Sachau, Leiden, 1904–21, vol. I, 2, pp. 58 f.
4. ibid., vol. I, 1, p. 71.
5. ibid., vol. I, 1, pp. 69 f.; cf. Ibn Hishām, ed. cit., p. 106, etc.
6. Ṭabarī, *Annales*, ed. M. J. de Goeje et al., Leiden, 1897–1901, vol. I, 3, p. 1124.
7. Ibn Sa'd, I, ed. cit., vol. I, 1, p. 80.
8. Ibn Is'ḥāq, in A. Guillaume, *New Light on the Life of Muhammad*, Manchester, University Press, 1960, pp. 7, 27, 59.
9. Bukhārī, *ṣaḥīḥ*, kitāb LXIII, bāb 20, last ḥadīth.
10. S. Krauss, 'Geschichte: Griechen und Römer', *Monumenta Talmudica*, V, 1, Vienna and Leipzig, Orion, 1914, p. 57.
11. Ibn Hishām, ed. cit., p. 105.
12. 'La Compilation dite de Frédégaire', iv, 64–5, ed. in G. Monod, *Études critiques sur les sources de l'histoire mérovingienne*, vol. II, Paris, A. Franck, 1885, p. 147.

13. 'Shāhpurakān', quoted by Bīrūnī, *Chronologie orientalischer Vōlker*, ed. E. Sachau, Leipzig, 1923, p. 207; cf. A. Adam, *Texte zum Manichäismus*, Berlin, 1954, pp. 5–6.
14. cf. 'The Acts of Thomas', translated in M. R. James, *The Apocryphal New Testament*, Oxford, Clarendon Press, 1924, p. 365.
15. cf. A. Cohen, *The Talmud*, French translation, Paris, Payot, 1950, pp. 417–18.
16. 'Targum Threni' in *Monumenta Talmudica*, V, 1, ed. cit., p. 52.

CHAPTER 4: *Birth of a Sect*

1. 'Castillo interior', primeras moradas, chapter I, 1, and chapter II, 8, in P. Silverio de Santa Teresa, ed., *Obras de Santa Teresa de Jesus*, Burgos, 1939, pp. 488, 495.
2. C. Huber, *Journal d'un Voyage en Arabie (1883–1884)*, Paris, Imprimerie nationale, 1891, p. 748.
3. 'La Montagne de contemplation', chapter XXIV, in J. Gerson, *Initiation à la Vie mystique*, Paris, Gallimard, 1943, p. 72.
4. cf. Tor Andrae, *Les Origines de l'Islam et le Christianisme*, French trans., Paris, Adrien-Maisonneuve, 1955, pp. 45, 191.
5. Silverio de Santa Teresa, op. cit., 'Castillo interior', moradas quintas, chapter I, 9, p. 540.
6. ibid., 'Castillo interior', moradas sextas, chapter IX, 10, p. 611.
7. ibid., 'Castillo interior', moradas sextas, chapter III, 7, p. 573.
8. Bukhārī, op. cit., kitāb 1, ḥadīth 3; kitāb 91, ḥadīth 1; Muslim, *ṣaḥīḥ*, kitāb 1, bāb 71, ḥadīth 252–3 and parallel passages.
9. Jalāl al-Dīn Suyūṭī, *al-itqān fī 'ulūm al-qur'ān*, Cairo, 1318 H., vol. I, p. 46, top.
10. Silverio de Santa Teresa, op. cit., 'Castillo interior', moradas sextas, chapter VIII, 3, p. 604.
11. Ste Thérèse de Jésus, *Relations spirituelles*, French trans. of *Las relaciones* . . . (relacion vi) by the R. P. Grégoire de St Joseph, Paris, 1928, pp. 66–7.

12. L. Gardet, *Expériences mystiques en terres non-chrétiennes*, Paris, Alsatia, 1953, p. 15.
13. See the commentary, references and French translation of this poem in Hoceïn Mansûr Hallâj, *Dîwân*, ed. and trans. Louis Massignon, Paris, Cahiers du Sud, 1955, pp. 108–9.
14. R. Blachère, *Histoire de la Littérature arabe des origines à la fin du XVᵉ siècle de J.-C.*, Paris, Adrien-Maisonneuve, 1964, vol. I, fasc. 2, p. 197.
15. cf. Max Eastman, *The Literary Mind: Its Place in an Age of Science*, New York, Scribner, 1931.
16. D. S. Margoliouth, *Mohammed and the Rise of Islam*, New York, Putnam, 3rd edn, 1905, pp. 83 f.
17. Ibn Sa'd, ed. cit., vol. I, 1, p. 133, etc.
18. F. Buhl, *Das Leben Muhammeds*, German trans. H. H. Schaeder, Leipzig, Quelle und Meyer, 1930, p. 153, n. 72.
19. Ibn Hishām, ed. cit., p. 782.
20. ibid., p. 260.
21. ibid., pp. 185–7.
22. Ṭabarī, ed. cit., vol. I, 3, pp. 1192 f.
23. Ṭabarī, *tafsīr*, Cairo, 1321 H., vol. XVII, p. 120.
24. Ṭabarī, *Annales*, ed. cit., vol. I, 3, pp. 1180 f.
25. Ibn Hishām, ed. cit., pp. 206 f.
26. ibid., p. 207.
27. ibid.
28. Ṭabarī, *Annales*, I, 3, pp. 1180 f.
29. Ibn Hishām, ed. cit., p. 225.
30. ibid., pp. 225 ff.
31. ''Omar ibn al-Khaṭṭāb', *Encyclopaedia of Islam*, London, Luzac, 1936, vol. III, p. 982.
32. T. Izutsu, *The Structure of the Ethical Terms in the Koran: a Study in Semantics*, Tokyo, Keio Institute of Philological Studies, 1959.
33. Ibn Hishām, ed. cit., p. 227.
34. The Anonymous of Jerusalem (probably the Patriarch Modestus who died in 634) in Migne, *Patrologia Graeca*, LXXXVI, cols. 1351 ff.; cf. Ch.-J. Ledit, *Mahomet, Israël et le Christ*, Paris, La Colombe, pp. 25, 92.
35. Ibn Hishām, ed. cit., p. 178.
36. Ibn Sa'd, ed. cit., vol. I, 1, p. 145.

37. Ibn Hishām, ed. cit., p. 283; Ṭabarī, *Annales*, vol. I, 3, pp. 1205 f.
38. F. Stark, *The Southern Gates of Arabia*, 2nd edn, Harmondsworth, Penguin Books, 1945, p. 123.
39. Ibn Sa'd, ed. cit., vol. I, 1, p. 146.
40. Ibn Hishām, ed. cit., pp. 286 f.
41. ibid., p. 334.

CHAPTER 5: *The Prophet in Arms*

1. Ibn Hishām, ed. cit., p. 337.
2. ibid.
3. ibid., pp. 341 ff.; cf. W. Montgomery Watt, *Muhammad at Medina*, Oxford, Clarendon Press, 1956, pp. 221–8.
4. Ibn Hishām, ed. cit., 292 f. Guillaume's translation seems to me erroneous.
5. ibid., p. 995.
6. ibid.; Wāqidī, *The kitāb al-maghāzī*, ed. Marsden Jones, London, O.U.P., 1966, p. 172.
7. Ṭabarī, *Annales*, ed. cit., vol. I, 3, p. 1265 top.
8. ibid., vol. I, 3, p. 1285.
9. ibid., vol. I, 3, p. 1305.
10. Ibn Hishām, ed. cit., p. 445.
11. ibid.
12. ibid., p. 458.
13. ibid.
14. 'Di qui nacque che tutt' i profeti armati vinsono, e li disarmati ruinorono' (Macchiavelli, *Principe*, VI).
15. Ibn Sa'd, ed. cit., vol. I, 2, 134; Abū Da'ud, xxxii, 10, etc.; cf. Margoliouth, op. cit., p. 250.
16. Ibn Hishām, ed. cit., p. 996; cf. Wāqidī, ed. cit., pp. 172–4.
17. Ibn Hishām, ed. cit., p. 546.
18. ibid., pp. 548 f.
19. ibid., pp. 547 f.
20. ibid., p. 558.
21. ibid., p. 559.
22. ibid., p. 562.
23. C. G. Montefiore and H. Loewe, eds., *A Rabbinic Anthology* London, Macmillan, 1938, p. 574.

24. cf. D. Sidersky, *Les Origines des légendes musulmanes dans le Coran et dans les vies des prophètes*, Paris, Geuthner, 1933, pp. 51–3.
25. Wāqidī, ed. cit., p. 533.
26. ibid.; Ibn Hishām, ed. cit., pp. 981 f.
27. Ibn Hishām, ed. cit., p. 641; Wāqidī, I, ed. cit., p. 359.
28. Balādhurī, *futūḥ al-buldān*, ed. M. J. de Goeje, Leiden, 1866, p. 17; ed. Cairo, 1932, p. 31.
29. Ṭabarī, *Annales*, ed. cit., I, 3, p. 1450; Ibn Sa'd, ed. cit., vol. II, 1, 41.
30. According to a variant reading in the Cairo edition, A.D. 1937, III, p. 203, n. 2.
31. Ibn Hishām, ed. cit., pp. 657 ff.
32. Wāqidī, ed. cit., vol. I, p. 411.
33. Wāqidī, ed. cit., vol. I, p. 413. In the French edition of this book, published before Jones' edition of Wāqidī, I was misled by Wellhausen's translation (*Muhammed in Medina*, Berlin, G. Reimer, 1882, p. 179).
34. Ibn Hishām, ed. cit., pp. 726 f.
35. ibid., pp. 727 f.
36. ibid., p. 732.
37. Carlo Levi, *Cristo si e fermato a Eboli*, French trans. Jeanne Modigliani, Paris, Gallimard, 1948, p. 93.
38. Ibn Hishām, ed. cit., p. 733.
39. Ibid., p. 734.
40. E.g. Tirmidhī, *ṣaḥīḥ*, kitāb 44 ('tafsīr al-qur'ān'), on sūrat al-aḥzāb (Koran xxxiii), ḥadīth 9a to 11 (ed. Cairo, 1292 H., vol. II, p. 209 f.).
41. Ṭabarī, *Annales*, ed. cit., vol. I, 3, p. 1475, 11. 8–9.
42. Ibn Hishām, ed. cit., p. 701.
43. ibid., 690 f.
44. ibid., 679.

CHAPTER 6: *Birth of a State*

1. Caetani, *Annali dell'Islam*, Milan, Hoepli, vol. I, 1905, p. 661; cf. Margoliouth, op. cit., p. 217.
2. F. Buhl, op. cit., pp. 141 f.
3. cf. F. Buhl, 'Muhammad', *Encyclopaedia of Islam*, London, Luzac, 1936, p. 641.
4. cf. G. Levi della Vida, ' 'Omar ibn al-Khaṭṭāb', *Encyclo-*

paedia of Islam, London, Luzac, 1936, p. 982; T. Nöldeke, *Orientalische Skizzen*, Berlin, n. d., p. 31.

5. Wāqidī, ed. cit., II, 855 (Wellhausen's translation, p. 345); cf. R. Bell, *Introduction to the Qur'an*, Edinburgh, University Press, 1953, p. 18, etc.
6. 'L'an IX de l'hégire' in *Légende des siècles*, Paris, Gallimard (Pléiade series), 1950, p. 129.
7. 'Le "triumvirat" Abou Bakr, Omar et Abou 'Obaida' in *Mélanges de la Faculté orientale de Beyrouth*, t. 4, 1910, pp. 113–44.
8. Lucy Mair, *Primitive Government*, Harmondsworth, Penguin Books, 1962, p. 53.
9. *The Origins of Muhammadan Jurisprudence*, Oxford, Clarendon Press, 1950; *An Introduction to Islamic Law*, Oxford, Clarendon Press, 1964.
10. *Muhammedanische Studien*, Halle, 1890, vol. II.
11. G. A. Wilcken, *Het Matriarchat bij de oude Araberen*, Amsterdam, 1884 (German translation, *Das Matriarchat . . . bei den alten Arabern*, Leipzig, 1884); W. Robertson Smith, *Kinship and Marriage in Early Arabia*, Cambridge, University Press, 1885; new edition, London, 1907 (reprinted: Oosterhout, Netherlands, Anthropological Publications, 1966).
12. 'La Société bédouine ancienne', in *L'antica società beduina*, Rome, Centro di studi semitici, 1959, pp. 69–93.
13. *Muhammad at Medina*, Oxford, Clarendon Press, 1956, p. 281; cf. pp. 273 ff.
14. Muhammad Hamidullah, *Le Prophète de l'Islam*, Paris, Vrin, 1959, pp. 462 ff.
15. 2 Esdras of the Geneva Bible (1560), and of subsequent English versions; also known as the Ezra Apocalypse. This translation is from R. H. Charles, *The Apocrypha and Pseudepigrapha of the Old Testament in English*, Oxford, Clarendon Press, 1913, vol. II, p. 621.
16. Hubert Grimme, *Mohammed*, Münster, i. W., Aschendorff, 1892–5, vol. II, p. 160, n. 9.
17. cf. Tor Andrae, *Der Ursprung des Islams und das Christentum*, Uppsala-Stockholm, Almqvist and Wiksell, 1926, pp. 146 ff.; French translation, *Les Origines de l'Islam et le Christianisme*, Paris, Adrien-Maisonneuve, 1955, pp. 151 ff.

18. 'Eine christliche Parallele zu den Paradiesjungfrauen des Korans?' in *Orientalia Christiana Periodica*, 14, 1948, pp. 198–405; 'Les Houris du Coran et Ephrem le Syrien' in *Mélanges*, Institut Dominicain d'Études Orientales du Caire, 6, 1959–61, pp. 405–8.
19. M. R. James, *The Apocryphal New Testament*, Oxford, Clarendon Press, 1924, pp. 36 f.; cf. Irenaeus, *Adversus haereses*, V, 33, 3 (in Migne, *Patrologia Graeca*, vii, col. 1213); E. Preuschen, *Antilegomena . . .*, Giessen, Ricker, 1901, p. 60, etc.
20. *Ecclesiastical History*, III, xxxix, 12 f.; also Harmondsworth, Penguin Classics (*The History of the Church*), 1965, p. 152.
21. Muhammad Hamidullah, op. cit., p. 491.
22. Ibn Sa'd, ed. cit., vol. II, 1, p. 67, l. 14.
23. Ibn Hishām, ed. cit., p. 815.
24. Ṭabarī, *Annales*, ed. cit., vol. I, 3, p. 1640; Wāqidī, ed. cit., vol. II, p. 856.
25. ibid., vol. III, p. 949.
26. ibid., vol. II, p. 816.
27. H. Pirenne, *Mahomet et Charlemagne*, Paris, Alcan and Brussels, Nouvelle Société d'Éditions, 2nd edn, 1937, p. 129.
28. Ibn Hishām, ed. cit., p. 938 = *dīwān*, XXV, 12; cf. O. A. Farrukh, *Das Bild des Frühislam in der arabische Dichtung . . .*, Leipzig, A. Pries, 1937, p. 130.
29. See the review by T. Nöldeke of Caetani's *Annali dell'Islam*, vols. I and II, 1 in *Wiener Zeitschrift für die Kunde des Morgenlandes*, 21, 1907, pp. 307 f.
30. Wāqidī, ed. cit., vol. III, pp. 1066 f.; Wellhausen's translation, p. 396; Wāqidī, ed. A. von Kremer, Calcutta, 1856 (Bibliotheca Indica, nos. 110 etc.), p. 426.
31. cf. Balādhurī, op. cit., pp. 2 f.; cf. Caetani, *Annali dell'Islam*, vol. II, 1, Milan, Hoepli, 1907, p. lxxi.
32. Ibn Sa'd, ed. cit., vol. VIII, pp. 36 f.
33. Bukhārī, op. cit., XLVI, 25; ed. Cairo, 1332 H., vol. II, pp. 47 f.
34. Ibn Sa'd, ed. cit., vol. II, 1, p. 132, ll. 4 ff.
35. Jāḥiẓ, *kitāb al-bayān wa-t-tabyīn*, ed. Hārūn, Cairo, 1367/1948, II, pp. 31 ff.; ed. Sandūbī, Cairo, 1351/1932, II, pp. 24 ff.; ed. Aṭawī, Beirut, 1968, pp. 228 ff.; cf. Blachère, op. cit., p. 246.

CHAPTER 7: *Triumph over Death*

1. Abū Yūsuf Ya‘qūb, *kitāb al-kharāj*, Cairo, 1346 H., p. 39, ll. 8 ff.
2. Būṣīrī, *burda*, ll. 34–6, 38, 42, 46, 58; cf. the full English translation by Arthur Jeffery in *A Reader on Islam*, The Hague, Mouton, 1962, pp. 607–20. I have also followed, in part, the interpretations of the French translation by René Basset, *La Bordah du Cheikh-el-Bousiri*, Paris, Leroux, 1894.
3. Dīrīnī, *ṭahārat al-qulūb* . . . , Cairo, 1296 H., pp. 26–8, 30–32.
4. cf. E. Cerulli, *Il ‘Libro della Scala’ e la questione delle fonti arabo-spagnole della Divina Commedia*, Vatican City, 1949.
5. L. Gardet, *La Pensée religieuse d'Avicenne* (*Ibn Sīnā*), Paris, Vrin, 1951, p. 113.
6. E. W. Lane, *An Account of the Manners and Customs of the Modern Egyptians*, London, C. Knight, 1836–7, vol. I, ch. xiii, p. 384; London, Dent (Everyman's Library), p. 288.
7. cf. J. Reinaud, *Monumens arabes, persans et turcs du Cabinet de M. le duc de Blacas* . . . , Paris, Imprimerie royale, 1828, vol. II, p. 97.
8. ibid., vol. II, pp. 80–82.
9. Harawī, *kitāb al-ishārāt ilā ma‘rifat az-ziyārāt*, ed. J. Sourdel-Thomine, Damascus, Institut français, 1953, p. 16; French translation, *Guide des Lieux de pèlerinage*, Damascus, Institut français, 1957, p. 42.
10. ibid.: Arabic, pp. 14, 17, 95; French, pp. 36, 43 f., 216; T. W. Arnold, ‘Qadam sharīf’, *Encyclopaedia of Islam*, 1st edn, vol. II.
11. Ibn Jubayr, *Travels* . . . , ed. W. Wright, Leiden, 1852; 2nd edn, ed. M. J. de Goeje, Leiden, 1907, pp. 162 ff.
12. cf. I. Goldziher, *Muhammedanische Studien*, Halle, 1890 (reprint: Hildesheim, G. Olm, 1961), p. 168; Tor Andrae, *Die Person Muhammeds in Lehre und Glauben seiner Gemeinde*, Stockholm, 1918, p. 271.
13. cf. R. F. Burton, *Personal Narrative of a Pilgrimage to Al Madinah and Meccah*, London, G. Bell, 1913 (Bohn's Popular Library), vol. I, pp. 315 ff.
14. Jean Roman, *Le Pèlerinage aux lieux saints de l'Islam*, Algiers, Baconnier, 1954, pp. 34 f.

15. cf., e.g., M. Ḥadj-Ṣadok, 'Le *mawlid* d'après le *mufti*-poète d'Alger Ibn 'Ammār' in *Mélanges Louis Massignon*, Damascus, Institut français, 1957, vol. II, pp. 269–91; H. Fuchs 'Mawlid', *Encyclopaedia of Islam*, 1st edn, vol. III.
16. According to the verse translation of F. Lyman MacCallum (Süleyman Chelebi, *The Mevlidi Sherif*, London, John Murray [Wisdom of the East series], 1943, pp. 23 f.). In the French text of this book I chose some slightly different readings of the Turkish text; cf. Süleyman Çelebi, *Vesîletü 'n-necât Mevlid*, ed. Ahmed Atesh, Ankara, Türk Tarih Kurumu Basïmevi, 1954, p. 67.

THE LINEAGE OF MUHAMMAD AND OF SEVERAL RELATED FAMILIES

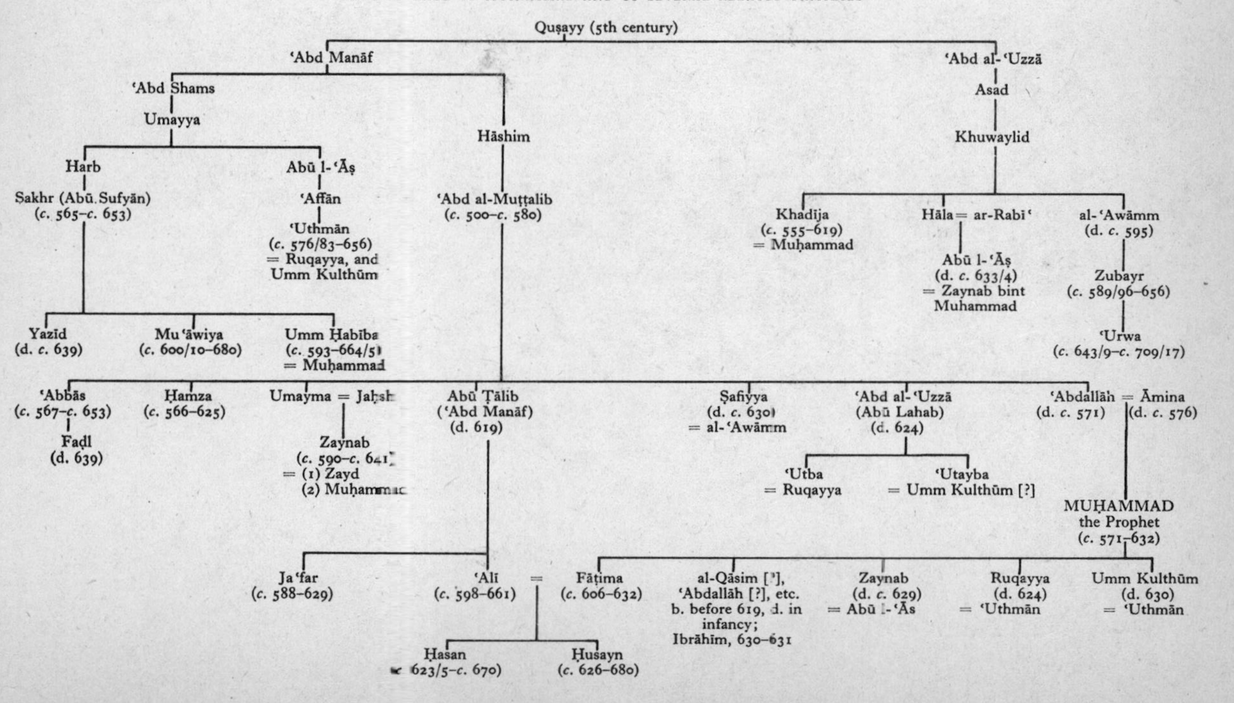

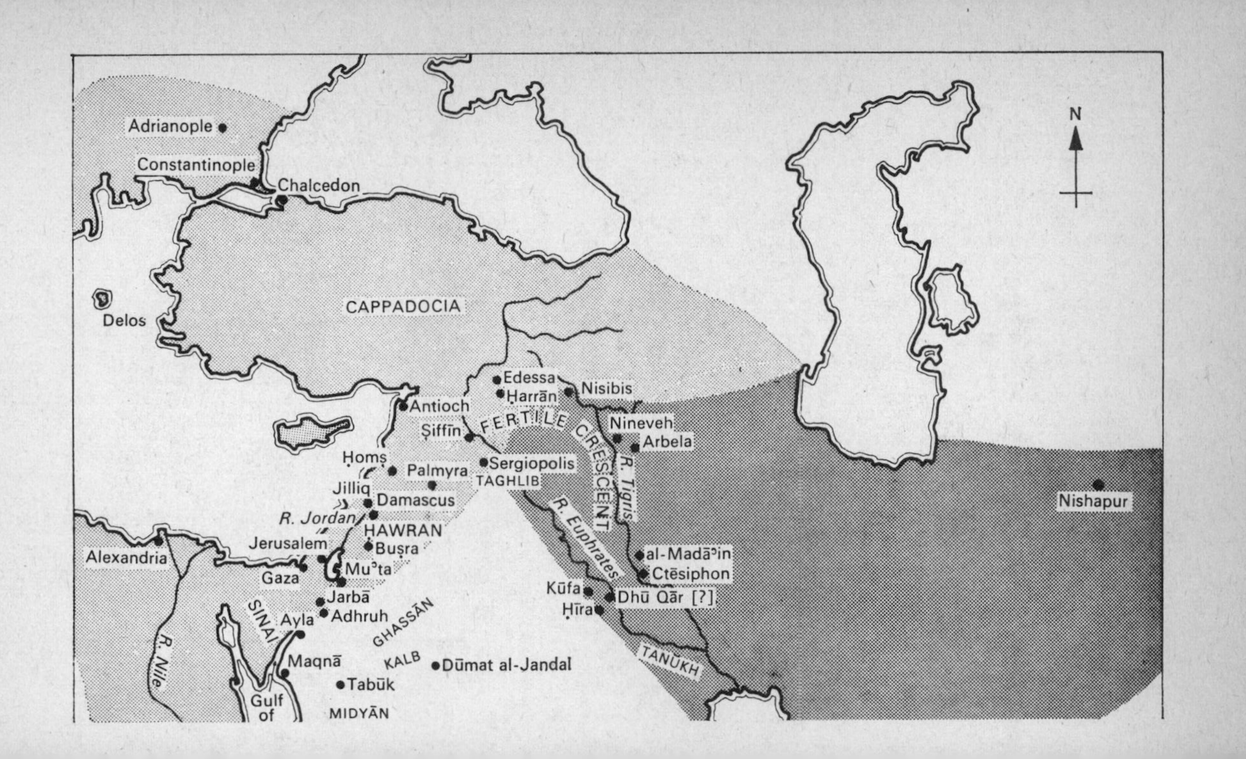
N
Adrianople
Constantinople
Chalcedon
Delos
CAPPADOCIA
Edessa
Ḥarrān
Nisibis
Antioch
FERTILE CRESCENT
Ṣiffīn
Nineveh
Arbela
R. Tigris
Ḥomṣ
Palmyra
Sergiopolis
TAGHLIB
Jilliq
Damascus
R. Jordan
ḤAWRAN
Nishapur
Jerusalem
Buṣra
Alexandria
Muʾta
Gaza
R. Euphrates
al-Madāʾin
Ctēsiphon
Kūfa
Dhū Qār [?]
Ḥīra
Jarbā
Adhruh
SINAI
Ayla
GHASSĀN
R. Nile
Maqnā
KALB
Dūmat al-Jandal
Tabūk
TANŪKH
Gulf of
MIDYĀN

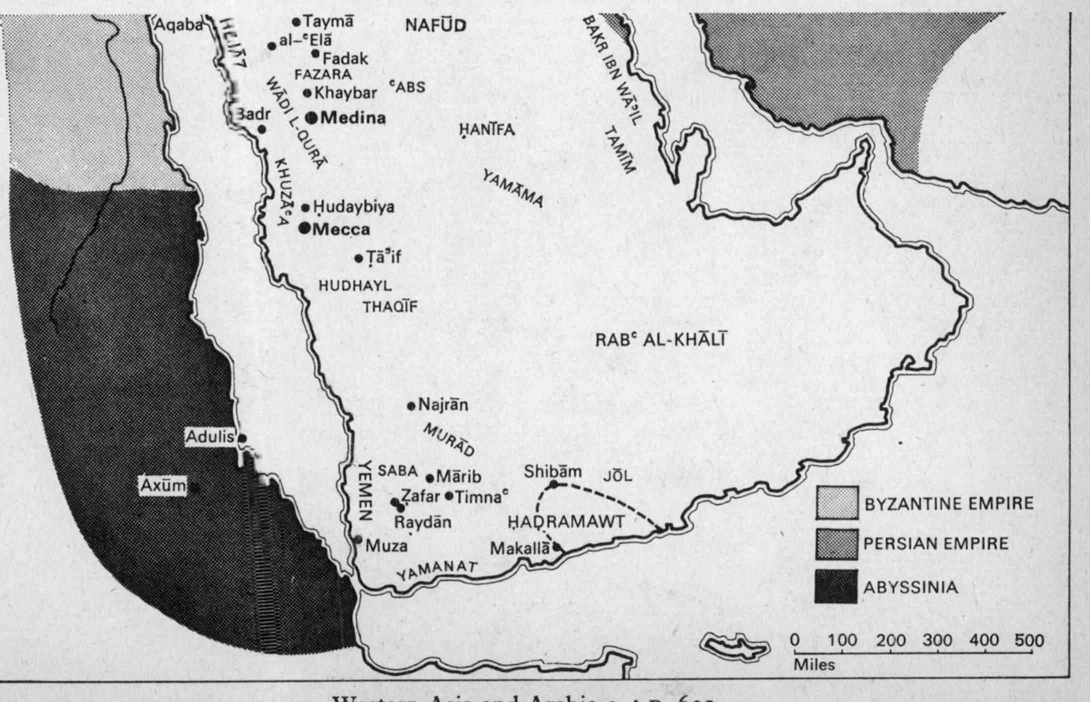

Western Asia and Arabia *c.* A.D. 630

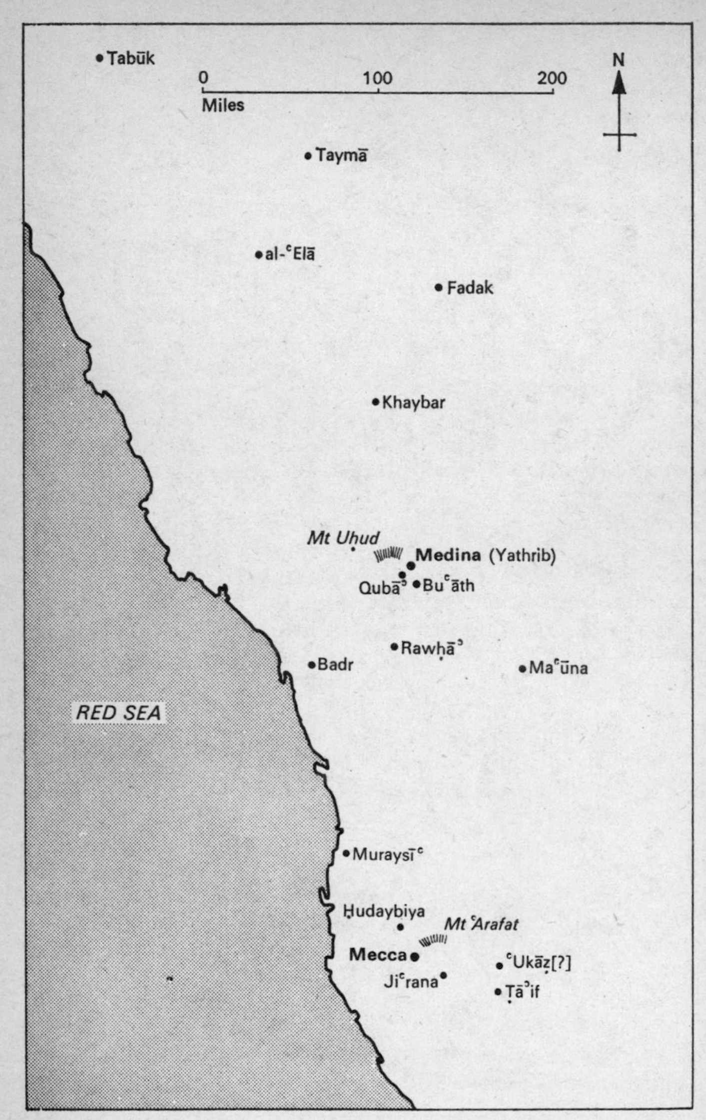

The Environs of Mecca and Medina

Explanatory Table of Arabic Words and Names of Individuals and Ethnic Groups

This is not an index. Its object is to enable the reader to recall the meanings of Arabic words, or the facts about individuals or groups which he may have forgotten as he read further. I have therefore only put into this list words and names that recur several times with intervals between. I have also added those names which are so similar as to give rise to possible confusion, and other names which require further clarification. I do not give references to every page on which they occur (see the index below), but only to those where substantial passages of explanation or identification are to be found.

Before studying this list, readers may find it useful to re-read the section of the Foreword that deals with Arabic pronunciations.

'Abbās ibn 'Abd al-Muṭṭalib, a banker in Mecca and uncle of Muḥammad; pp. 255, 259.

'Abd . . . , the word itself means 'servant', or 'slave'. Names with 'Abd mean 'servant of x', x referring to a pagan divinity in pagan times, or one of the names of Allah since the coming of Islam.

'Abd Manāf, the common ancestor of several major Quraysh clans; as a whole they compose the ethnic group of the Banū 'Abd Manāf. This is also the real name of Abū Ṭālib, and possibly that of one of Muḥammad's sons who died very young; p. 51.

'Abd al-Muṭṭalib ibn Hāshim, the grandson of 'Abd Manāf, and grandfather of Muḥammad, p. 41; his descendants are sometimes considered as a special ethnic group, the Banū 'Abd al-Muṭṭalib.

'Abd ar-Raḥmān ibn 'Awf, of the Zuhra clan, known before his conversion as 'Abd al-Ka'ba, a Qurayshite, one of Muḥammad's first Companions, and very skilled in business; pp. 151, 248.

'Abd Shams ibn 'Abd Manāf, the eponymous ancestor of a major Quraysh clan including, most importantly, the Banū Umayya (q.v.); p. 41.

'Abdallāh ibn 'Abd al-Muṭṭalib, the father of Muḥammad; pp. 38 ff.

'Abdallāh ibn Muḥammad, a son of Muḥammad, who died very young; p. 51.

'Abdallāh ibn Sa'd, the secretary of Muḥammad, foster-brother of 'Uthmān ibn 'Affān, a Qurayshite; pp. 219, 261.

'Abdallāh ibn Ubayy, a Medinan chief of the Khazrajite clan of 'Awf; p. 156.

'Abdallāh ibn Unays, a Medinan Muslim, assassinated Sufyān ibn Khālid, p. 189.

Abraha, a Christian sovereign of South Arabia; pp. 32, 33.

Abū, an Arabic word meaning 'father'; in the following composites: 'father of x' (it is then the *kunya*, see p. 336 of this list), but it can sometimes mean 'the man of . . . ' or 'the man with . . . ' – e.g. Abū Ḥimār, literally 'the father of the donkey', but meaning 'the man with the donkey' – in which case it is a nickname. When it is used as a genitive Abū becomes Abī, hence such forms as 'Alī ibn Abī Ṭālib, i.e. 'Alī son of Abū Ṭālib.

Abū 'Afak, a Medinan elder and anti-Muslim poet; pp. 157, 171–2.

Abū 'Āmir, known as ar-Rāhib, 'the monk', a monotheist from Medina, fanatically anti-Muslim; p. 158.

Abū l-'Āṣ ibn ar-Rabī', a nephew of Khadīja (that is, the son of Hāla bint Khuwaylid), he married his cousin on his mother's side, Zaynab bint Muḥammad, and was thus the Prophet's son-in-law; pp. 52, 248.

Abū Bakr ibn Abī Quḥāfa, of the Taym clan, one of Muḥammad's first Companions, his adviser, his father-in-law (the father of 'Ā'isha), and his successor; p. 99.

Abū Jahl, of the Makhzūm clan, an influential Qurayshite strongly opposed to Muḥammad; p. 109.

Abū Lahab, this was the nickname (meaning 'man of flame' which may at first have meant 'handsome', but was later interpreted as 'destined for hell') of 'Abd al-'Uzzā ibn 'Abd al-Muṭṭalib, Muḥammad's uncle, at one point father-in-law to two of his daughters, and one of his fiercest opponents; p. 52.

Abū l-Qāsim, a *kunya* for Muḥammad; p. 51.

Abū Sufyān Ṣakhr ibn Ḥarb, of the Qurayshite clan of 'Abd Shams, a grandson of Umayya, husband of Hind, father of Mu'āwiya, Yazīd and Umm Ḥabība (who married Muḥammad), an adversary of Muḥammad; he became chief of the Qurayshites; pp. 164–5, 174–5.

Abū Ṭālib 'Abd Manāf ibn 'Abd al-Muṭṭalib, uncle and tutor of Muḥammad, father of 'Alī and Ja'far; p. 46.

Abū 'Ubayda, a Qurayshite, an influential adviser of Muḥammad; p. 222.

Abū l-Walīd, a *kunya* for 'Utba ibn Rabī'a (q.v.).

'Ād, a more or less mythical tribe or people of ancient Arabia, said to have been giants, and to have left monuments; p. 121.

'Ā'isha bint Abī Bakr, daughter of Abū Bakr, Muḥammad's beloved child-bride; p. 151.

al-, Arabic article (sometimes becomes ar- az-, etc , or may be shortened to -l-); names beginning with it will be found under the word it goes with.

'Alī ibn Abī Ṭālib, son of Abū Ṭālib, and a cousin of Muḥammad. He married his daughter Fāṭima, was the father of Ḥasan and Ḥusayn, and was to be the fourth Caliph from 656 to 661; p. 51.

Allāt, a pre-Islamic Arab goddess; p. 16.

Āmina bint Wahb, a Qurayshite of the Zuhra clan, wife of 'Abdallāh ibn 'Abd al-Muṭṭalib; Muḥammad's mother; p. 38.

'Ammār ibn Yāsir, a confederate of the Banu Makhzūm, one of the first converts to Islam; p. 101.

Ammianus Marcellinus, a fourth-century Latin historian.

Anṣār, 'the Helpers', the name given to Muḥammad's Medinan followers as opposed to the *muhājirūn* (q.v.); p. 151.

arāk, thorny tree fed upon by camels and other animals.

Arethas, Greek transcription of the Arab name Ḥārith.

al-Arqam ibn 'Abd Manāf, a Qurayshite of the Makhzūm clan; he offered the Muslims his house as a meeting-place; p. 112.

'ashūrā, literally 'the tenth', the (arabized) Aramaic name for the Jewish fast of *yōm kippūr*, the Day of Atonement.

'Aṣmā' bint Marwān, a poetess from Medina; p. 157, 171.
'Attāb ibn Asīd, a governor established by Muḥammad in Mecca; p. 214.
'Awf, a Medinan clan of the Khazraj tribe.
Aws, one of the two great non-Jewish Medinan tribes; p. 139.
Aws Manāt, group of Medinan clans of the tribe of Aws; p. 141.

Bakr ibn 'Abd Manāt (Banū); a section of the Kināna tribe whose territory bordered upon Mecca; p. 257.
Bakr ibn Wā'il (Banū), a large tribe from north-eastern Arabia; pp. 65, 272.
Banū . . . , 'sons of': can be put in front of the names of tribes (see under individual names); they may be referred to either as Quraysh, or Banū Quraysh, or, with a Greek or Latin suffix, as Qurayshites, Umayyads, Ghassānids; what is meant in each case is the tribe, clan or family which considers itself as consisting of the children or descendants of Quraysh, Umayya or Ghassān.
baraka, literally 'blessing', often thought of in terms of some kind of fluid, a beneficent magic effluent available from people, places or objects that are especially holy.
Bilāl, a Negro slave, one of the first converts to Islam; his stentorian voice enabled him to become Muḥammad's herald, the first muezzin (the man who gives the call to prayer); p. 101.

Cosmas, known as *Indicopleustes* (traveller to India), a sixth-century Egyptian merchant; pp. 1, 8.

Dhū Nuwās (the man with the hanging locks), a nickname for Yūsuf As'ar, also known as Yath'ar (the avenger?), a judaizing king of South Arabia in the early sixth century; pp. 30, 32.
dīnār, a gold coin (from the Latin *denarius*; hence English d. for 'penny, pence').
dirham, a silver coin (from the Greek *drakhmé*, or *drachma*).

Faḍl ibn 'Abbās, son of 'Abbās (*see above*), and consequently a cousin of the Prophet; p. 287.
Fāṭima bint 'Amr, of the Qurayshite clan of the Makhzūm, wife of 'Abd al-Muṭṭalib, mother of Abū Ṭālib and also of 'Abdallāh, the Prophet's father; p. 41.

Fāṭima bint al-Khaṭṭāb, a sister of ʿUmar; p. 116.
Fāṭima bint Muḥammad, a daughter of Muḥammad the Prophet and of Khadīja; the wife of his cousin ʿAlī ibn Abī Ṭālib, and mother of Ḥasan and Ḥusayn.
Fazāra, a tribe from north-west Arabia; p. 211.

Ghassān, the Ghassānids, an Arab dynasty from Syria; Monophysite Christians, subjects of the Byzantine Empire; p. 27.
Ghaṭafān, nomad tribe from north-west Arabia; p. 192.

ḥadīth, 'prophetic tradition', a short account of some act or word of Muḥammad's; in its classic form it is passed on by one authority who has received it from another, and so on back to an actual eye-witness; for a typical example see pp. 44 ff.
Ḥafṣa bint ʿUmar, daughter of ʿUmar ibn al-Khaṭṭāb, and wife of Muḥammad; p. 176.
ḥajj, the Pilgrimage, first pagan, then Muslim, to the Kaʿba and surrounding holy places; pp. 237, 284–5.
Hāla bint Khuwaylid of the Asad clan, sister of Khadīja, and mother of Abu l-ʿĀṣ ibn ar-Rabīʿ; p. 51.
Hāla bint Wuhayb, of the Zuhra clan, wife of ʿAbd al-Muṭṭalib and cousin of Āmina, the Prophet's mother; p. 41.
Ḥalīma bint ʿAbdallāh, of the Saʿd clan (of the Hawāzin tribe), Muḥammad's nurse; p. 44.
Ḥamza ibn ʿAbd al-Muṭṭalib, Muḥammad's uncle; p. 112.
ḥanīf (pl. *ḥunafāʾ*), a name given to the Arabs who, in pre-Islamic times, tended to monotheism, but without actually belonging to either of the two great monotheist religions, Judaism or Christianity; pp. 64–5.
Ḥanīfa, a large tribe of the Yamāma in central Arabia; p. 67.
al-Ḥārith ibn Jabala (Arethas in Greek), Ghassānid chief (phylarch), and vassal of Byzantium from about 539 to 570; pp. 27, 33.
ḥarra, fields of deeply embedded volcanic rocks, of which there are many in Arabia.
Hāshim, a clan of the Quraysh tribe to which Muḥammad belonged; its eponymous ancestor, Hāshim, was said to have been the son of ʿAbd Manāf and father of ʿAbd al-Muṭṭalib; p. 41.

Ḥasan ibn ʿAlī, son of ʿAlī ibn Abī Ṭālib and Fāṭima bint Muḥammad, and thus grandson of the Prophet; brother of Ḥusayn.

Ḥassān ibn Thābit, from Medina, Muḥammad's official poet; pp. 175, 201–2.

Hawāzin, large tribe from northern and western Arabia; pp. 40, 263 ff.

hegira, *see hijra.*

Heraclius, Byzantine emperor from 610 to 641; p. 59.

hijra, 'emigration', a word we often transcribe as 'hegira'; applied above all to the Emigration of Muḥammad and his first followers from Mecca to Medina; the beginning of the year in which this emigration took place is the starting point of the Muslim era.

Hind bint ʿUtba, daughter of ʿUtba ibn Rabīʿa, wife of Abū Sufyān, mother of Muʿāwiya, and long a fierce enemy of Muḥammad's; pp. 177, 180–81.

Homerites, the Greek transcription of the name of the Ḥimyarites, the dominant tribe in South Arabia from about the beginnings of the Christian era onwards; p. 2.

Hubal, a god of Mecca, represented by a red cornelian idol.

Hūd, a mythical prophet sent to the people of ʿĀd; pp. 121, 123.

Hudhayl, a confederation of western Arabian tribes; p. 188.

Ḥusayn ibn ʿAlī, son of ʿAlī ibn Abī Ṭālib and Fāṭima bint Muḥammad, and thus grandson of the Prophet; brother of Ḥasan.

Ibn Abī Kabsha (the son of the man on the hill?), a title given to Muḥammad whose meaning was forgotten very early on.

Ibn Is'ḥāq (Muḥammad), a Muslim historian, who died about 768, who left a classic biography of the Prophet, published by his disciple Ibn Hishām.

Ibn al-Khaṭṭāb, *see* ʿUmar.

Ibn Saʿd, a Muslim historian, who died in 845, having put together a compilation of biographies of the Prophet and his Companions.

Ibn Ubayy, *see* ʿAbdallāh ibn Ubayy.

Ibn Unays, *see* ʿAbdallāh ibn Unays.

Ibrāhīm, the Arabic name for Abraham; pp. 64, 123, 185–7.

Ibrāhīm ibn Muḥammad, son of the Prophet and of Māriya; p. 279.

Imru' l-Qays ibn 'Amr, of the tribe of Lakhm, who died in 328, had 'king of all Arabs' inscribed on his tomb, the oldest Arabic inscription we know of; p. 27.

Imru' l-Qays ibn Ḥujr, king of Kinda, and a major Arab poet who lived in the first half of the sixth century; pp. 29–30.

'Īsā, Arabic name for Jesus in the Koran; p. 239.

Islām, literally 'submission', 'total self-abandonment [to God]', became the name of the religion founded by Muḥammad rather late in his lifetime; it is the infinitive of the verb of which *muslim* (q.v.) is the active participle.

Ismā'īl, Arabic form of Ishmael, son of Abraham, who was looked upon as their ancestor; pp. 64, 185–7.

Ja'far ibn Abī Ṭālib, son of Abū Ṭālib, brother of 'Alī, cousin of Muḥammad; pp. 115, 256.

Jibrīl, Arabic version of the name of the Archangel Gabriel; p. 72.

jinns, lesser spirits, genii.

Justin II, Byzantine emperor (565–578), nephew and successor to Justinian.

Justinian, Byzantine emperor (527–565).

Juwayriyya bint al-Ḥārith, daughter of the chief of the Banū l-Muṣṭaliq, wife of Muḥammad; p. 196.

Ka'b ibn al-Ashraf, a half-Jew from Medina; pp. 174, 176.

Ka'ba, literally 'cube'; a building of approximately cubic form, an ancient sanctuary in Mecca; cf. pp. 39, 186–7.

kāhin (pl. *kuhhān* or *kahana*), a kind of 'soothsayer' among pre-Islamic Arabs; etymologically, the word is the same as the Hebrew *kōhen*, 'priest'; p. 57.

Kalb, an Arab tribe, largely Christian, living on the border of Byzantine Syria.

Kawādh, Sassanid Persian emperor (448–531), father and predecessor of Khusrō Anōsharwān; he put into effect the 'communist' notions of the social reformer Mazdak.

Kawādh II, called Shērōē, son of Khusrō II Abharwēz whom he dethroned and had killed, a Sassanid Persian emperor who ruled for about six months in 628.

Khabbāb ibn al-Aratt, a blacksmith, confederate of the Banū Zuhra, one of the first converts to Islam; pp. 101, 117.

Khadīja bint Khuwaylid, of the clan of Asad, a rich widow, engaged and later married to Muḥammad, the mother of Fāṭima and several of his other children, sister of Hāla bint Khuwaylid; p. 49.

Khālid ibn Sa'īd ibn al-'Āṣ, of the clan of 'Abd Shams, a young Qurayshite, who joined Islam as the result of a dream; p. 100.

Khālid ibn al-Walīd, of the clan of Makhzūm, a Qurayshite general and very considerable strategist, a late convert to Islam, known as Sayf Allāh, the Sword of God; p. 180.

Khaṭma, a Medinan clan of the Aws Manāt group.

Khazraj, one of the two chief non-Jewish Medinan tribes; p. 139.

Khusrō I, called Anōsharwān (the immortal-souled), son and successor to Kawādh I, Sassanid Persian emperor, who ruled from 531 to 579; pp. 6, 26.

Khusrō II, called Abharwēz (the Victorious), a Sassanid Persian Emperor, who ruled from 591 to 628; pp. 58, 266.

Khuzā'a, an Arab tribe from the Mecca area; pp. 39, 257.

kunya, a name many Arabs had, meaning 'father of x' (Abū x) or 'mother of x' (Umm x) – x generally being the eldest son; for instance, Muḥammad was called Abū l-Qāsim after his son al-Qāsim who died quite young; similarly Umm Misṭaḥ was the mother of Misṭaḥ; usually it was used only as a name among intimates, but could become the person's normal title; *see also* Abū, *above*.

Lakhm (Banū), Lakhmids, an Arab family of the tribe of Tanūkh, which founded the kingdom of Ḥīra, and was subject to the Sassanid Persians; pp. 27–9, 65.

Makhzūm, a Qurayshite clan; p. 101.

mala', 'Senate', 'Council of Elders', a name given to the groups of the important members of a clan, tribe or town who held, in theory at least, the power to make decisions in ancient Arabia.

Manāt, the goddess of fate worshipped in Arabia, and thought to be the daughter of Allah; p. 16.

Māriya, an Egyptian slave, a concubine of Muḥammad and the mother of his son Ibrāhīm; p. 279.

Maryam, the Arabic name for the Virgin Mary, confused in the Koran with the sister of Moses; p. 239.

Maslama, the prophet of the Banū Ḥanīfa in the Yamāma in central Arabia; Muslim writers refer to him as Musaylima, a diminutive form which orientalists have generally seen as pejorative – but this is a view contested by some who consider Musaylima to have been his true name; pp. 119, 272.

Maymūna, the sister-in-law of ʿAbbās, a widow, wife of Muḥammad; p. 255.

Mazdaeans, the followers of the religion founded by Zarathustra (Zoroaster), the official religion of the Sassanid Persian Empire.

Muʿāwiya ibn Abī Sufyān, son of Abū Sufyān and of Hind; brother of Yazīd; he became Muḥammad's secretary, and was later to become Caliph (from 661 to 680); the founder of the Umayyad dynasty and enemy of ʿAlī; pp. 190, 264, 294.

muhājirūn, literally 'the Emigrants', the name given to the supporters of Muḥammad among the Qurayshites of Mecca who went with him to Medina; p. 151.

Muḥammad ibn ʿAbdallāh, the Prophet, of the clan of Hāshim, of the tribe of Quraysh.

mu'min, 'believer', one of the first names given to Muḥammad's disciples (pl. *mu'minūn*).

munāfiqūn, 'the Doubters', a word borrowed from the Ethiopic, used to describe the reluctant, sceptical, reticent, etc.; in Arabic, the word comes from a root which also suggests the behaviour of the jerboa which hurries to hide in its hole at the approach of any danger; the Koran uses it of the lukewarm people of Medina, whose faith is suspect, and it is traditionally rendered as 'Hypocrites'; p. 184.

al-Mundhir ibn al-Ḥārith, in Greek Alamundaros, a Ghassānid chief (phylarch), about 570–581; p. 28.

al-Mundhir I ibn an-Nuʿmān, a Lakhmid king of Ḥīra, about 418–462; p. 27.

al-Mundhir III, his descendant, a Lakhmid king of Ḥīra, about 505–554; pp. 28, 31.

Muṣʿab ibn ʿUmayr, a Qurayshite Muslim, and lieutenant of Muḥammad in Medina before the hegira; pp. 144, 159.

Musaylima, *see* Maslama.

muslim (pl. *muslimūn*), literally 'subject (to the will of Allah)' (*see* Islam, *above*), a name which came, apparently quite late in Muḥammad's life, to be applied to those who followed his religion; this word has given us 'moslem' and 'mussulman'; pp. 129, 188.

Naḍīr (Banū) or Banū n-Naḍīr, one of the three great Jewish tribes of Medina; pp. 139, 191–3.

nagāshī (or, as a common Arabic pronunciation has it, *najāshi*), title of the king of Ethiopia or Abyssinia (a variant of the present title *negūs*, which we have turned into 'negus').

Nu'mān ibn al-Mundhir, a Ghassānid prince, around 581–584; p. 28.

Nu'mān III ibn al-Mundhir, a Lakhmid king of Ḥīra, about 580–602; p. 65.

Procopius, a sixth-century Byzantine historian.

al-Qāsim, son of Muḥammad and Khadīja, who died very young; p. 51.

Qaynuqā', one of the Jewish tribes of Medina; pp. 139, 172–4.

qur'ān, 'recitation', a word derived from its Syriac counterpart, used first of the particular revelations transmitted by the Archangel Gabriel (Jibrīl) from Allah to Muḥammad, which he then recited and invited his followers to recite; the name was later given to the book containing those revelations which we call the Koran; pp. 83 ff., 130, 241.

Quraysh, the eponymous ancestor of the tribe who lived in Mecca, and also the name of the tribe; p. 39.

Qurayẓa, a Jewish tribe from Medina; pp. 139, 209–14.

Quṣayy, the ancestor of the major Quraysh tribes, pp. 39–40.

ar-Raḥmān, in Arabic 'the merciful one' (in South Arabian 'Raḥmānān'); a name given by the South Arabians (according to the Aramaic and Hebrew model) to the god of the Jews, and to God the Father in the Christian Trinity; it was taken over by Maslama and Muḥammad as one of the names of Allah; pp. 67, 119, 252.

Rayḥāna bint Zayd, a Jewess of the Naḍīr tribe, taken by Muḥammad as a concubine after the execution of her husband who belonged to the Banū Qurayẓa; p. 213.

Ruqayya bint Muḥammad, a daughter of Muḥammad and Khadīja, who married first a son of Abū Lahab, and then 'Uthmān ibn 'Affān; pp. 51, 100, 292.

Sabaeans, the inhabitants of the kingdom of Sabā; p. 21; not to be confused with the Ṣābians (q.v.); p. 116.

Ṣābians, members of a Baptist sect in Mesopotamia whom some people apparently confused with the first Muslims; p. 116. (Not to be confused with the Sabaeans, q.v.).

Sa'd, a name of several clans and tribes; the Banū Sa'd, a clan of the Hawāzin tribe to which Muḥammad's nurse belonged (pp. 44–5) are not the same as the clan mentioned on p. 219 who lived near Fadak.

Sa'd ibn Mu'ādh, a Medinan chief of the 'Abd al-Ash'hal clan of the tribe of Aws; pp. 156, 212.

Ṣafiyya, a Jewess from Khaybar who married Muḥammad; p. 254.

Ṣafwān ibn al-Mu'aṭṭal as-Sulamī, a young Muslim of the Beduin tribe of the Sulaym who found 'Ā'isha when she was lost, the incident causing immense scandal; p. 200.

Sā'ida, a clan of the Medina tribe of Khazraj; pp. 290–92.

Ṣakhr ibn 'Āmir, common grandfather through the female line of Umm Misṭaḥ and Abū Bakr; p. 201.

Ṣakhr ibn Ḥarb, *see* Abū Sufyān.

ṣalāt, ritual prayer composed of a fixed pattern of genuflexions, prostrations and recitals of sacred texts; p. 127.

Sassanids, the dynasty who ruled the Persian Empire from 224 up to the Arab conquest (636–651).

Sawda bint Zam'a, a Qurayshite who married Muḥammad as her second husband; pp. 134, 279.

sayyid, a title given to chiefs of Arab tribes, which has come to us (following a dialect pronunciation) as 'the (Spanish) Cid' and 'sidi' (meaning 'my lord', or 'sir'); p. 14.

Ṣuhayb ibn Sinān, the Rūmī, a freedman, one of the first converts to Islam; p. 101.

sūq, the sector of an Arab town where merchants and artisans congregated.

sūra, 'chapter', collections of fragments of Koranic revelation often looked upon later as a real unity; thus the text of the Koran is divided into 114 *sūras* (to which the Roman numbers given in the quotations refer), which are in turn subdivided into verses; pp. 83, 131.

Ṭabarī, an Arab historian (839–923); p. 309.

Ṭalḥa ibn 'Ubaydallāh, a Qurayshite of the Taym clan, one of the very earliest converts to Islam; p. 101.

Tamīm, Arab tribe from the east of the peninsula; p. 272.

Targūm, the name given to the Aramaic translations of the various books of the Old Testament which have come down from the Jews of the high Middle Ages. They are more or less periphrastic, and here and there introduce additions; p. 66.

Tha'ālibī, an eleventh-century Arab historian.

Thamūd, a tribe or people of ancient Arabia to whom various ancient monuments were attributed; p. 121.

Thaqīf, tribe to which the inhabitants of the town of Ṭā'if belonged; p. 137.

Torah, the Hebrew name (the Arabic form being *tawrāt*) for the Pentateuch – the first five books of the Old Testament attributed to Moses.

tubba', collective name given by the Arabs to the ancient kings of South Arabia, like Pharaoh in Egypt, or Caesar in Rome.

'Umar ibn al-Khaṭṭāb, a Qurayshite of the 'Adī clan, a convert to Islam, adviser and father-in-law to Muḥammad, father of Ḥafṣa, and the second Caliph from 634 to 644; pp. 116–17.

Umayya ibn 'Abd Shams, a Qurayshite, grandfather of Abū Sufyān and ancestor of the Umayyad family; pp. 41, 174.

Umayya (Banū), *see* Umayyads.

Umayyads, family of the descendants of Umayya, of the Qurayshite clan of 'Abd Shams, who were, under Mu'āwiya ibn Abī Sufyān, to become the ruling dynasty of the Muslim world from 661 to 750, and later in Spain; p. 174.

umma, 'community', and especially the Muslim community; pp. 152–4, 228.

Umm Ḥabība bint Abī Sufyān, the daughter of Abū Sufyān, who became a Muslim, and having been widowed once, married Muḥammad; p. 258–9.

Umm Kulthūm, daughter of Muḥammad and Khadīja, wife (possibly as a second marriage) of 'Uthmān ibn 'Affān; pp. 51–2, 280.

Umm Misṭaḥ bint Abī Ruhm, mother of Misṭaḥ; her mother was a sister of Salmā bint Ṣakhr, the mother of Abū Bakr; p. 201.

'umra, the complex of ritual ceremonies in the Ka'ba and its immediate vicinity, later integrated into the *ḥajj* (q.v.); pp. 249, 258.

'Urwa ibn az-Zubayr, an authority on the traditions of the beginnings of Islam, born between 643 and 649, died between 709 and 717; son of a nephew of Khadīja, Zubayr (q.v.); he wrote, at the request of the Umayyad Caliph 'Abd al-Malik (685–705), a series of reports on the historical events of the time of the Prophet.

Usāma ibn Zayd, the son of Zayd ibn Ḥāritha and an Abyssinian freedwoman, inheriting his mother's dark skin, was much loved by Muḥammad who chose him to lead an expedition; born about 614; pp. 202, 286–93.

Usayd ibn al-Ḥuḍayr, chief of the 'Abd al-Ash'hal clan of the Medina tribe of Aws; p. 156.

'Utba ibn Rabī'a, a Qurayshite elder of the 'Abd Shams clan, father of Hind, the wife of Abū Sufyān, killed at Badr; his *kunya* was Abū l-Walīd; pp. 105–6.

'Uthmān ibn 'Affān, of the Umayya family, one of the first converts to Islam; he married Ruqayya, Muḥammad's daughter, and after her death, her sister Umm Kulthūm; was the third Caliph, from 644 to 656; pp. 100 ff.

'Uthman ibn Maẓ'ūn, a Qurayshite of the Jumaḥ clan, one of the earliest converts to Islam; pp. 114–15.

'Uyays, another name for al-Walīd ibn al-Walīd; p. 110.

'Uzayr, apparently the Arabic transcription of the name of Esdras (Ezra) in the Koran; p. 238.

'Uzzā, 'she who is most powerful', an Arab goddess identified with the star Venus, held to be the daughter of Allah; p. 16.

Wahhābis, a Puritan Muslim sect to which the present kings of Sa'udi Arabia belong.

al-Walīd ibn al-Walīd, also known as 'Uyays, a Qurayshite of the Makhzūm clan, one of the first converts to Islam; p. 109.

Waraqa ibn Nawfal, cousin of Khadīja, a Qurayshite of the Asad clan, a *ḥanīf*; pp. 42, 73.

Yazīd ibn Abī Sufyān, son of Abū Sufyān, and brother of Mu'āwiya; became governor of Taymā' and a general; pp. 264, 277, 294.

zakāt, ritual tax imposed by the Muslim religion as one of the believer's fundamental obligations; in theory all revenue from it is devoted to helping the poor of the community; p. 246.

Zayd ibn Ḥāritha, of the Kalb tribe, a slave of Khadīja, freed by Muḥammad who adopted him as a son (as a result of which he became known as Zayd ibn Muḥammad); he married Zaynab bint Jaḥsh and was father of Usāma; pp. 51, 205–7, 256.

Zaynab, a Jewess from Khaybar who tried to poison Muḥammad; p. 254.

Zaynab bint Jaḥsh, a cousin of Muḥammad on his mother's side, daughter of ʻAbd al-Muṭṭalib; married first Zayd ibn Ḥāritha, then Muḥammad; pp. 205–7.

Zaynab bint Khuzayma, of the tribe of ʻĀmir ibn Ṣaʻṣaʻa, the wife of a Qurayshite, then of his brother, a Muslim killed at Badr, then of Muḥammad; p. 194.

Zaynab bint Muḥammad, daughter of Muḥammad and Khadīja, who married Abū l-ʻĀṣ ibn ar-Rabīʻ; pp. 51, 248, 280.

az-Zubayr ibn al-ʻAwāmm, one of the first converts to Islam, a nephew of Khadīja (his father's sister), and Muḥammad's cousin on his mother's side – she being the daughter of ʻAbd al-Muṭṭalib; father of ʻUrwa; p. 291.

Zuhra, a Qurayshite clan; pp. 41, 101, 257.

Zuhrī, authority on traditions, a Qurayshite of the Zuhra clan, pupil of ʻUrwa ibn az-Zubayr; born around 670, died in 742; p. 99.

Select Bibliography

The bibliography is vast. I would refer the reader to my 'Bilan des Études mohammadiennes' in *Revue historique*, vol. 229, fasc. 465, January/March 1963, pp. 169–220. Excellent short bibliographies are to be found in J. Sauvaget, *Introduction to the History of the Muslim East*, Berkeley and Los Angeles, University of California Press, 1966, and in B. Spuler, *Der Vordere Orient in islamischer Zeit*, Berne, A. Francke, 1954.

On the subjects of pre-Islamic Arabia, Muḥammad's life, and the Koran, the following books are suggested. For pre-Islamic Arabia there are the vivid, though not entirely reliable, books of Henri Lammens: *L'Arabie occidentale avant l'hégire*, Beirut, Imprimerie catholique, 1928; *Le Berceau de l'Islam, l'Arabie occidentale à la veille de l'hégire*, vol. I, the only one to have appeared; *Le Climat, les Bédouins*, Rome, Pontificium Institutum Biblicum, 1914. Edouard (Bishr) Farès' book, *L'Honneur chez les arabes avant l'Islam*, Paris, Adrien-Maisonneuve, 1932, is particularly helpful on Beduin society. Also extremely valuable is a small book by G. Ryckmans, *Les Religions arabes préislamiques*, Louvain, Publications universitaires et Bureaux du Muséon, 1951. I myself tried to collect all the known facts in a brief account ('L'Arabie avant l'Islam' in *Histoire universelle*, vol. II of the *Encyclopédie de la Pléiade*, Paris, Gallimard, 1957), but the text now needs considerable revision. It does however give further bibliographical suggestions. In English, there are a very sensible and competent sketch by G. Levi della Vida, 'Pre-Islamic Arabia', in N. A. Faris (ed.), *The Arab Heritage*, New York, Russell, 1944, here and there outdated, of course; and a sufficiently reliable chapter in P. K. Hitti's *History of the Arabs*, 3rd edn, London, Macmillan, 1943.

On Muḥammad's own life I shall simply give the most recent

biographies where the reader will find further bibliographical help:

Tor Andrae, *Mohammed, the Man and his Faith*, London, George Allen & Unwin, 1936: a fine biography, the translation of a work which first appeared in 1930; its viewpoint is mainly psychological and religious.

Régis Blachère, *Le Problème de Mahomet*, Paris, P.U.F., 1952: a piece of sound scholarship, unfortunately abridged before publication, which has the advantage of basing itself on the proved text of the Koran.

W. Montgomery Watt, *Muhammad at Mecca*, Oxford, Clarendon Press, 1953; *Muhammad at Medina*, Oxford, Clarendon Press, 1956; and their abridgement, *Muhammad, Prophet and Statesman*, Oxford, Clarendon Press, 1961. These are excellent books whose methodological importance I have spoken warmly of elsewhere (in *Diogenes*, 20, October 1957); they are possibly a trifle over-confident in their attempted reconstructions.

Charles-J. Ledit, *Mahomet, Israël et le Christ*, Paris, La Colombe, 1956: a most readable book, but chiefly concerned with Christian theological ideas.

M. Gaudefroy-Demombynes, *Mahomet*, Paris, Albin-Michel, 1957 (reprinted 1969): a massive collection of information, gathered scientifically and analysed with great subtlety; however it suffers from having been in process of being written for more than twenty years before it was published, by which time the author was 94 and not fully in touch with recent work.

Rudi Paret, *Mohammed und der Koran*, Stuttgart, Kohlhammer, 1957: an excellent and thoughtful little study by one of the greatest living specialists.

Muhammad Hamidullah, *Le Prophète de l'Islam*, 2 vols., Paris, Vrin, 1959: by a Muslim with vast knowledge but no critical sense at all.

Apart from these more or less recent works, I should like to mention two other biographies from different points of view:

Frants Buhl, *Das Leben Muhammeds* (translated into German by H. H. Schaeder, Leipzig, 1930, and reprinted Heidelberg, Quelle u. Meyer, 1955): this is the most compact of all the biographies, with a mass of scholarly notes, each of great value; a work to which one must constantly refer. (Abridgement in

English: 'Muhammad' in *The Encyclopaedia of Islam*, vol. III, Leiden, Brill, 1936.)

E. Dermenghem, *La Vie de Mahomet*, 2nd edn, Paris, Charlot, 1950: extremely well written and readable, though without any apparatus of scholarship.

As a universal basis, we have the vast volumes of the *Annali dell'Islam* by L. Caetani, prince of Teano, especially vol. I (Milan, Hoepli, 1905) and vol. II, 1 (Milan, Hoepli, 1907), in which all the sources can be found, year by year, quoted, analysed and compared.

Very original studies, based on the methods of structural semantic analysis, have been written by the Japanese scholar Toshihiko Izutsu: *The Structure of the Ethical Terms in the Koran*, Tokyo, Keio Institute of Philological Studies, 1959; *God and Man in the Koran, Semantics of the Koranic Weltanschauung*, Tokyo, Keio Institute of Philological Studies, 1964.

I should like to warn the reader against the wide-ranging lucubrations produced in several recent works by the late Hanna Zacharias, which met with some success among non-specialists. (The name was a pseudonym used by the Dominican G. Théry, who was disowned with regard to his writing by the Order; see the balanced judgement given by Père Jomier in *Études*, January 1961, pp. 82–92.)

Anyone who wants to get an idea of the texts upon which all these books are based must first of all read the Koran. The English translation by Richard Bell, *The Qur'ān*, 2 vols., Edinburgh, T. & T. Clark, 1937, goes further than any in its analysis and dissection of the text. Unfortunately, on publication, a large part of the notes were excised, but they are substantially to be found in the same author's *Introduction to the Qur'ān*, Edinburgh, University Press, 1953 – the most advanced critical study yet published. A. J. Arberry has given a splendid poetical translation: *The Koran Interpreted*, London, George Allen & Unwin, 1955; see the explanations of his method of translating chiefly in his previous *The Holy Koran, an Introduction with Selections*, London, George Allen & Unwin, 1953. Of the French translations, that most in touch with the latest critical work is Blachère's *Le Coran*, Paris, G. P. Maisonneuve, 1947–51, 3 vols., one of which is an introduction: and there is an attractive one-volume edition without a number of the scholarly notes, Paris, G. P. Maisonneuve–Max Besson, 1957. Blachère has also published his *Introduction au Coran* by itself, Paris, Besson et Chantemerle, 1959, and more recently a most useful little summary, *Le Coran*, Paris, P.U.F., 1967. The translation by Muhammad Hamidullah and M. Leturmy, Paris, Club français du Livre, 1959, is nicely presented and very readable, with the advantage (or otherwise) of having been done by a Muslim (the pious and scholarly apologete whose life of the Prophet I mentioned above).

One of the three chief Arabic biographies of the Prophet has been translated into English: *The Life of Muhammad, a Translation of Is'hāq's 'sīrat rasūl allāh'*, by A. Guillaume, London, Oxford University Press, 1955. (It also exists in German, as does the abridged translation of Wāqidī's biography.)

Finally, some more general studies: Bernard Lewis's *The Arabs in History*, London, Hutchinson, 1950 (3rd edn, 1964) is a short study which combines great knowledge with remarkable understanding; Carleton S. Coon's *Caravan: the Story of the Middle East*, New York, Holt, Rinehart & Winston, 1951, is a very clever introduction to the general conditions of life and historical dynamics in the Middle East; Xavier de Planhol's *Les Fondements géographiques de l'histoire de l'Islam*, Paris, 1968 (English translation to be published by the University of California Press) is more specialized, but intelligent and readable. (It contains some points open to dispute.)

Index

Please see also the Explanatory Table of Arabic Words and Names of Individuals and Ethnic Groups, pp. 329–42.

INDEX

INDEX

INDEX

INDEX

MAXIME RODINSON is Professor of Old Ethiopic and Old South Arabian Languages at the École Pratique des Hautes Études at the Sorbonne. He served in Syria during World War II, and stayed for seven years in Lebanon working as a professor in a Moslem high school and as an official in the French Department of Antiquities for Syria and Lebanon; during this time he traveled frequently in the Middle East. He returned to Paris in 1947 to take charge of Oriental printed books in the National Library, and from 1950 to 1951 he published *Moyen-Orient,* a political monthly on the Middle East.